ANTHROPOLOGIES OF EDUCATION

ANTHROPOLOGIES OF EDUCATION

A Global Guide to Ethnographic Studies
of Learning and Schooling

Edited by

Kathryn M. Anderson-Levitt

berghahn
NEW YORK · OXFORD
www.berghahnbooks.com

Published in 2012 by

Berghahn Books

www.berghahnbooks.com

Published with the support of the
Swiss National Science Foundation
Stiftung Irene Bollag-Herzheimer
Adolf und Mary Mil-Stiftung

Library of Congress Cataloging-in-Publication Data

Anthropologies of education : a global guide to ethnographic studies of
    learning and schooling / edited by Kathryn M. Anderson-Levitt.
      p. cm.
    Includes bibliographical references and index.
    ISBN 978-0-85745-273-3 (hardback) — ISBN 978-1-78238-057-3
    (paperback) — ISBN 978-1-78238-058-0 (retail ebook)
    1. Educational anthropology. I. Anderson-Levitt, Kathryn M.

    LB45.A823 2012
    306.43--dc22

                                                                    2011014588

British Library Cataloguing in Publication Data
A catalogue record for this book is available from the British Library

Printed in the United States on acid-free paper.

ISBN: 978-1-78238-057-3 (paperback) ISBN: 978-1-78238-058-0 (retail ebook)

❧ Contents

ACKNOWLEDGMENTS   vii

INTRODUCTION. ANTHROPOLOGIES AND ETHNOGRAPHIES
OF EDUCATION WORLDWIDE   1
     Kathryn M. Anderson-Levitt

1. TOWARDS A HISTORICAL CULTURAL ANTHROPOLOGY OF
EDUCATION: THE BERLIN RITUAL STUDY   29
     Christoph Wulf

2. THE PAROCHIAL PARADOX: ANTHROPOLOGY OF EDUCATION
IN THE ANGLOPHONE WORLD   49
     Sara Delamont

3. ANTHROPOLOGICAL RESEARCH ON EDUCATIONAL PROCESSES
IN MEXICO   71
     Elsie Rockwell and Erika González Apodaca

4. ANTHROPOLOGY AND EDUCATION IN THE ARGENTINE
CONTEXT: RESEARCH EXPERIENCES IN BUENOS AIRES   93
     María Rosa Neufeld

5. ANTHROPOLOGY AND EDUCATION IN BRAZIL: POSSIBLE
PATHWAYS   111
     Ana Maria Rabelo Gomes and Nilma Lino Gomes

6. ETHNOGRAPHIES OF EDUCATION IN THE FRENCH-SPEAKING
WORLD   131
     Maroussia Raveaud and Hugues Draelants

7. ANTHROPOLOGY OF EDUCATION IN ITALY   151
     Francesca Gobbo

8. CENTRAL EUROPE (BULGARIA, THE CZECH REPUBLIC,
HUNGARY, POLAND, ROMANIA, SLOVAKIA)   167
     Gábor Eröss

9. EDUCATIONAL ANTHROPOLOGY IN A WELFARE STATE
PERSPECTIVE: THE CASE OF SCANDINAVIA   193
     Sally Anderson, Eva Gulløv, and Karen Valentin

10. THE DEVELOPMENT OF ETHNOGRAPHIC STUDIES OF
SCHOOLING IN JAPAN 213
Yasuko Minoura

11. BAMBOO SHOOTS AFTER RAIN: EDUCATIONAL
ANTHROPOLOGY AND ETHNOGRAPHY IN MAINLAND CHINA 235
Huhua Ouyang

12. ETHNOGRAPHY OF EDUCATION IN ISRAEL 257
Simha Shlasky, Bracha Alpert, and Naama Sabar Ben-Yehoshua

13. SOCIOLOGICAL AND ETHNOGRAPHIC RESEARCH IN
FRENCH-SPEAKING SUB-SAHARAN AFRICA 279
Boubacar Bayero Diallo

CONCLUSION. ETHNOGRAPHY OF EDUCATION AROUND
THE WORLD: A THOUSAND VARIETIES, A SHARED PARADIGM 303
Agnès van Zanten

NOTES ON CONTRIBUTORS 319

NAME INDEX 325

SUBJECT INDEX 337

❦ ACKNOWLEDGMENTS

This project originated with an invitation from Jean-Louis Derouet to edit a theme issue on anthropologies around the world for the journal *Éducation et Sociétés* (no. 17, 2006). Since then, conversations and e-mail correspondence with many colleagues have helped me identify anthropologists and ethnographers of education around the world, and have shaped this book and its introductory essay in important ways. Errors of interpretation and of fact are my own, and I apologize in advance for the many important areas of work that this book, which is still an early effort, leaves out. Particular thanks go to Elsie Rockwell, Bradley Levinson, Yuko Okubo, Géraldine André, Ouyang Huhua, Neriko Musha Doerr, Judith Green, Greg Poole, Deborah Reed-Danahay, Francesca Gobbo, Margaret Gibson, Audra Skukauskite, and new friends at the Danish School of Education. Thanks, too, to my family, Leon, Noah, and Anna Levitt, for their interest, support, and readiness to travel in order to discover new realms of educational anthropology.

 INTRODUCTION

ANTHROPOLOGIES AND ETHNOGRAPHIES OF EDUCATION WORLDWIDE

Kathryn M. Anderson-Levitt

Toward a World Tour

In the 1950s, a branch of educational research known as the anthropology of education first appeared in the United States, and by the 1970s its practitioners were publishing the *Anthropology and Education Quarterly.* Also in the 1950s, pedagogical anthropology emerged in Germany, and more than a dozen books have now appeared with the title *Pëdagogische Anthropologie.* In the United Kingdom, the ethnography of education has blossomed since the late 1960s, although few of its practitioners identify themselves as anthropologists. Anthropology of education or ethnography of education has also emerged in other European countries, Latin America, Israel, Japan, India, and China.

What is going on here? Do anthropology of education, pedagogical anthropology, and related terms mean the same thing in different parts of the world? What counts as ethnography of education from one nation to another? This book addresses those questions by surveying anthropologies and ethnographies of education around the world. It asks how practices of the disciplines vary, what accounts for their differences or similarities, and why research beyond our own national and linguistic boundaries merits our attention.[1]

Why a World Tour?

Globalization does not mean that international academia is melting into a single, homogenous whole. For example, although the majority of academic journals on the subject of education—about five thousand of them—publish articles or at least abstracts in English,[2] there are another three thousand academic journals on education that do not publish a word in English. There is, then, much to explore, and this is the moment to do it. UNESCO is launching an annual report on the state of the social sciences around the world (UNESCO & ISSC 2010).[3] Translations of "other people's anthropologies" into English have burgeoned (Boškovic 2008; see also Barth et al. 2005; Dracklé, Edgar, and Schippers 2003; Ribeiro and Escobar 2005; Vermuelen and Alvarez Roldán 1995; Yamashita, Bosco and Eades 2004), and both anthropology and the educational sciences are seeking to expand and institutionalize a multilingual global dialogue. In 2005, anthropologists from Brazil, Japan, and other countries founded the World Council of Anthropological Associations,[4] while 2009 saw formation of the World Educational Research Association, another association of associations (AERA 2009).

As this volume will demonstrate, exploration is worth the effort. A world tour of anthropologies and ethnographies of education enables us to discover realms of scholarship outside our normal ken and helps us recognize their significance. Without such a broader comparative perspective, we tend to focus too narrowly on a few nationally relevant questions (Anderson-Levitt 2011); we fail to recognize that "the analytic categories used to construct ethnographic texts are not autonomous; they are rooted in the societies in which they are first used, and they reflect actual ways of constructing difference in those societies" (Rockwell 2002: 3). The pragmatic purpose of this overview, then, is to seek new angles on old questions and hence, perhaps, to glimpse new solutions. A related purpose is to raise our awareness of inequities and distortions caused by ethnocentrism in academic publishing.

Meanwhile, a global review of our disciplines raises questions about social, cultural, and historical influences on social science in general. This book proposes a modest anthropology of the anthropology of education; it offers anthropologies and ethnographies of education as a case study in the sociology of social science (compare Larsson 2006). It provides an opportunity to ask how a discipline—or a cluster of disciplines with family resemblances—is organized at the global level. For example, what are the channels in which scholarly ideas flow (Heilbron, Guilhot, and Jeanpierre 2008)? Who borrows freely from whom, and where are there barriers (Hannerz 1992)? Is there convergence or divergence of thinking over time? In fact, given the context-bound nature of our subject matter, is a global social science even possible?

The Approach and Its Limitations

The approach here is simple. First, in this introductory essay, I attempt an overview of scholarship across the globe by drawing on published reviews of the literature and collected volumes—cross-national work (such as Candela, Rockwell, and Coll 2004; Derouet, Henriot-van Zanten, and Sirota 1990; Gibson 1997; and Souza Lima 1995) as well as the more geographically focused reviews cited in sections below. This essay also draws on personal e-mail communications from scholars in different parts of the world, on public web sites, and on my experience as a former editor of a journal that received international submissions.

Second, in each of the chapters, I invited colleagues to introduce a sample of the anthropologies and ethnographies of education from their part of the world. Many of the resulting thirteen chapters are written by senior scholars and others by newer scholars, all of whom have taken on a difficult and delicate task. I specifically asked the chapter authors *not* to attempt comprehensive reviews of the literature, but rather to develop introductory guides addressed to the naïve newcomer, written as if to a visiting scholar or a brand-new student, and designed to orient the novice and encourage further independent exploration. The chapter authors addressed questions such as:

- How do you and your colleagues define the "anthropology" or "ethnography" of education? What kinds of scholarship do you include?
- What have been the major themes or the major debates within the literature as you define it?
- To what scholars or schools of thought do you point as sources of inspiration?

I also invited chapter authors to include their own personal experiences where doing so would help outsiders understand the historical or social context.

The chapters represent a fairly wide sample, covering several parts of Europe, parts of the Americas, one region in Africa, and two important countries from East Asia. I deliberately restricted the space allocated to the "hegemonic" English-language and French-language literatures to leave more room for scholarship in other languages. The particular sampling is limited by space but also by my own access to academic networks; unfortunately, it leaves out important parts of international academia, including Russia, India, Spain, and Portugal, and work in Flemish and Dutch, meaning that much exploration remains for the future.

Of course, it would be foolhardy to think that a small group of scholars could accurately summarize the research traditions across the globe. This book will necessarily exhibit gaps and misunderstandings, and this introductory overview in particular may appear hopelessly superficial. Nonetheless, taking the broadest possible comparative view, in spite of the superficiality of such an approach, can provide certain insights. Patterns may emerge that are visible only when the whole world or at least a very large sample is examined, as has been illustrated by world culture theorists' survey of curricula around the world (Meyer, Kamens, and Benavot 1992), and by the controversial but productive "mass comparison" of world languages (e.g., Greenberg 1966).

Another problem with this volume is the lack of a coherent unit of analysis. Rather than organize strictly by nation, strictly by multinational regions, or strictly by language zones, I could not escape a messy, eclectic approach. The significance of language barriers quickly emerged, and language zone became the first of multiple criteria used to order these bodies of scholarship. For example, France is clustered with French-speaking Belgium, Switzerland, and Canada in a single chapter because they share a common professional organization and publish in some common journals (although multilingual West Africa is treated separately because it is not as well integrated into the French-language network). However, national identity also proved to be important. Thus, although I cluster Spanish- and Portuguese-speaking countries in this essay, the book devotes separate chapters to Mexico, Argentina, and Brazil in order to recognize the distinct effects of their national and political histories. Finally, I use regional groupings, here simply for pragmatic reasons, to cluster smaller and diverse countries, although one could also have identified multinational and multilingual regions on principled grounds, for example, by tracing the area influenced by German anthropology (Eröss, this volume) or by continental European pedagogical philosophy (Alexander 2001a).

A third challenge is how to determine which scholars "belong" to each language zone, country, or region. Clearly place of birth is not the appropriate criterion; both students and senior scholars move across borders, sometimes returning home and sometimes taking a job in a new part of the world, and in both cases serving as conduits of ideas from one location to the other (Heilbron, Guilhot, and Jeanpierre 2008). In this volume, the chapter authors and I have generally excluded the work of ethnographers who visited from elsewhere to do research, but we have generally counted expatriate scholars who permanently settle at a university or research institute inside an adopted country as belonging to that country.

The English language also limits this volume. Some of the chapters were originally written in other languages, and we will make those versions available on the web. I encouraged chapter authors to emphasize in their brief reference lists works that do *not* appear in English so as to point readers toward that voluminous but less visible work.

Finally, this volume creates the danger that readers will mistakenly ascribe one and only one kind of anthropology or ethnography of education to each nation or each linguistic zone. In fact, scholarship is never so homogeneous; the brief sketches in this book mean to identify some prominent themes but certainly not all the topics or debates within a given country or region. By the same token, the chapter authors do not necessarily claim to represent the only or even the most typical trends within their own countries.

Anthropologies, Ethnographies, and Other Affiliations

Some readers will object that anthropology of education should not be conflated with ethnography of education. After all, anthropology is the holistic study of human beings, whereas ethnography is a philosophy of research practiced in several disciplines. Nonetheless, this volume includes ethnographers who identify with disciplines other than anthropology. It does so partly because the definitions of disciplines vary across nations, as we shall see; partly because nonanthropologists like Paul Willis, Hugh Mehan, and Michelle Fine have helped to shape anthropology of education; but especially because many nonanthropological ethnographers define ethnography more or less as anthropologists would. For example, the editors of the journal *Ethnography and Education* describe ethnography as "long-term engagement with those studied in order to understand their cultures" (Troman 2010), echoing anthropologist Harry Wolcott's formulation that "the purpose of ethnographic research is to describe and interpret cultural behavior" (1987: 42–43).

In any case, "anthropology" does not mean the same thing everywhere, nor is it a global term for the discipline as practiced by anthropologists of education in the United States. There are actually several versions of anthropology and related disciplines. For example, the discipline called "philosophical anthropology" pursues the question of what it means to be human by seeking generalizations about the human condition. It is concerned with general human Culture—Culture with a capital C and in the singular. A philosophical anthropology of education, then, is concerned with the human capacity for learning as an important part of the species' toolkit for survival.

Meanwhile, the discipline called "cultural anthropology" (or sometimes "ethnology") in the United States examines human beings living in cultural worlds, that is, in worlds of meanings constructed by people rather than given in nature. It examines cultures in the lower case and the plural—and turns attention to learning when it asks how children and other newcomers come to construct understandings held in common with other people. Within the realm of education, then, cultural anthropology leads to an anthropology of learning.

The discipline called "social anthropology" in the English-speaking world focuses on the social, that is, on relationships among persons and groups. Its questions about relationships, such as how social hierarchy is maintained or how children move into adult roles, direct attention to schooling as a central institution in complex societies and thus lead to an anthropology of schooling. However, the distinction between cultural and social anthropology has always been tenuous (Spencer 2000), and an anthropology of schooling can also direct attention to the construction of cultural worlds of meaning within classrooms, schools, and other academic settings.

This book will also make reference to disciplines, variously called "ethnology" or "ethnography" in parts of Europe, Asia, and Africa, that have often developed from folklore studies or museum studies and that examine local cultures in the researcher's home country. It will also note the practice of ethnographic methods by sociologists and by psychologists, and will cite the influence of history, cultural historical activity theory, critical race theory, feminist theory, and other disciplines. In addition, chapter authors will point out that fields within the educational sciences themselves, including curriculum and instruction, didactics, teacher education, and intercultural education, are important locations for practicing anthropology or ethnography of education.

Organization

There is no single, logical itinerary through the different literatures, particularly since the unit of analysis in this book is not consistent. This essay and the chapters are organized, therefore, simply to serve the flow of the argument. I begin with the German-language zone to "make the familiar strange," for its extensive literature and its versions of anthropology of education will be less familiar if not surprising to many English-speaking readers. Next I turn to the hegemonic English-language literatures as a more familiar baseline, and then to two broad language zones, first Spanish- and Portuguese-speaking countries, and then the French-speaking world. Next, I address the vibrant traditions in "smaller" European languages. A section on Asia includes both the large, long-established body of work in Japan and a new, burgeoning literature in China. Finally, I turn to newer and emergent work in the

Middle East and Africa. The volume concludes with important comments from a leading sociologist of education, Agnès van Zanten, who points out key lessons from the chapters.

Philosophical and Historical Anthropology of Education in Germany

We begin our world tour, then, in the German-language zone. More accurately, although scholars from Austria, Switzerland, and Luxemburg participate in German-language conferences on anthropology and education, this section focuses on Germany.

In his chapter in this volume, Christoph Wulf locates the original source of German educational anthropology within philosophical anthropology. Since the work of Wilhelm von Humboldt, philosophical anthropology asks what distinguishes "man in general" from animals on the one hand and from machines on the other. Any discussion of education concerns learning in the broadest terms as a generic human experience (e.g., Bollnow 1987).

Wulf and his colleagues have reacted against philosophical anthropology's abstract and unwittingly Eurocentric and masculine picture of human beings to create a more complex historical cultural anthropology of education. Even though the German work reacts against excess abstraction, some readers from a US or UK tradition may nonetheless perceive some of it, such as Wulf (2003), as surprisingly philosophical and still Eurocentric. Nonetheless, its philosophy is deeply grounded in ethnography. The Commission on Anthropology of Education of the German Educational Research Association has conducted a twelve-year ethnographic study on learning and everyday life in school and family, as Wulf reports here, and the result is a fascinating meditation on ritual and performance in education and socialization. Meanwhile, other recent German anthropology and ethnography of education explores cultures of home and school in ways that may be more familiar to US readers (e.g., Breidenstein 2007; Hünersdorf, Maeder, and Müller 2008; Qvarsell and Wulf 2003).

The English-Speaking World

I cluster the English-speaking countries of the global North here because scholars can easily read one another across boundaries within it, although Delamont in this volume argues that the flow of readership is unidirectional. Moreover, there is a tendency of scholars outside this language zone to treat it as a single unit. Some, including authors in this volume, refer collectively to the English-language literature of the United Kingdom, North America, Australia, and New Zealand as the "Anglo-Saxon" world—a label that can shock authors from inside that zone who identify themselves as "African-American," "Irish-Australian," or anything but Anglo-Saxon. There are also reviews of the literature that treat ethnography of education within the entire English-language zone without making regional distinctions (Derouet, Henriot-van Zanten and Sirota 1990; Gordon, Holland, and Lahelma 2001; Goodman 2001; Osborne 1996). The English-language research literature of India does not appear in such reviews, and I therefore treat India separately in the section on Asia.

The United States and English-Speaking Canada

Anthropology of education in the United States is rooted, first, in cultural anthropology and specifically in the study of cultural transmission; it has thus been an anthropology of learning since Margaret Mead published *Coming of Age in Samoa* in 1928. However, beginning in mid-century, US pioneers like George and Louise Spindler and Murray and Rosalie Wax (see Delamont, this volume) expressed interest not only in the transmission of culture, but also in inequalities in the schooling of different ethnic populations within the United States. Soon young researchers who were attracted by this approach, some of them former schoolteachers, established a new subdiscipline, an anthropology of schooling. In Canada as well, English-language anthropology of education focused heavily in early years on schooling, particularly of indigenous peoples (Fisher 1998) and now frequently of immigrants and minoritized ethnic groups.

Today in both Canada and the United States, ethnography is popular as a research method not only among the anthropologically trained, but also among sociologists, linguists, and other educational researchers, who publish in journals like *Ethnography and Education, Journal of Contemporary Ethnography, Linguistics and Education, Educational Researcher,* and occasionally in *Sociology of Education.* However, in this volume, British scholar Sara Delamont focuses her assessment of the vast English-language literature on anthropology, not ethnography more broadly, and limits her chapter to the United States and Canada. She describes US anthropologists of education as obsessed by school failure among ethnic and racial minorities to the point of being blinded to other important topics. North American scholars will probably object that she underplays smaller yet still sizeable bodies of US work on a wide array of topics, from gender to social class to higher education to school success. However, Delamont's analysis of citation patterns is compelling, and other reviews support her argument. Thus, as reported in Anderson-Levitt (2011), a Swiss study found that 63 percent of the articles published by the *Anthropology and Education Quarterly* from 1995 to 2005 concerned schooling and, within that set, 52 percent, or thirty-nine articles, addressed success and failure; the articles that were not about schooling tended to address culture and ethnicity, language, and identity (Jacquin 2006; see also Henriot-van Zanten and Anderson-Levitt 1992).

The United Kingdom

In Great Britain and Northern Ireland, even though classic anthropology tended to focus less on the concept of culture than did US anthropology, a few midcentury anthropologists like Raymond Firth and Audrey Richards showed interest in cultural transmission and the education of the child (Mayer 1967; Middleton 1970; see also Goodman 2001). Today, however, scholarship in the United Kingdom generally does not focus on learning.

Instead, ethnographic studies of schooling abound. Max Gluckman of the Department of Sociology and Social Anthropology at the University of Manchester encouraged ethnography at home, and under his influence D. H. Hargreaves and Colin Lacey studied schools in Britain in the late 1970s and early 1980s (Goodman 2001). At about the same time, scholars variously educated as anthropologists and as sociologists were inspired by symbolic interactionism and by feminist scholarship as well as by social anthropology to conduct qualitative studies of classroom interaction and the social construction of meaning by teachers and students (Atkinson, Delamont, and Hammersley 1988). Those originally educated as anthropologists did not find a disciplinary home in anthropology (Delamont, this volume) and their work is referred to as ethnography rather than anthropology of education.

Most ethnographers of schooling in the United Kingdom conduct research at home, although there have been a few forays abroad, particularly to compare Britain with France (e.g., Sharpe 1992; van Zanten and Ball 2000). Some anthropologically trained scholars in the field of comparative education range further afield, such as Goodman (1990) and Alexander (2001b).

Ethnography of schooling in the United Kingdom, unlike US anthropology of education, consistently attends to social class and very often to gender (Gordon, Holland, and Lahelma 2001). However, since the rise of cultural studies, UK ethnographers are paying more explicit attention to cultural processes, and some UK scholars have turned their attention to race and ethnicity (Gillborn 1997). UK scholars took the lead in creating the international journal *Ethnography and Education*, which, as mentioned above, embraces the concept of culture (Troman 2010).

Other English-Speaking Areas

Australia has a rich ethnographic tradition. Delamont notes that Forsey (2007) is an anthropologist, but other ethnographers such as Connell (1989), Walker and Hunt (1988), and Kipnis (2001) write in the same vein as UK qualitative sociologists, and on the same subjects—social class and gender. Others, like Osborne (1996), resemble US ethnographers of education and focus on cultural differences and culturally relevant pedagogy. Australians also conduct ethnography abroad; for example, Dolby conducted research in South African schools (2002) and Okano studied Korean-origin students in Japan (1997).

Spanish- and Portuguese-Speaking Countries

I group Spanish- and Portuguese-speaking nations together because both scholars and publications seem to flow across the two languages zones and between Latin America and the Iberian peninsula (see Candela, Rockwell and Coll 2004). For example, Portuguese-speaking Brazilian scholars assume that clearly written Spanish is a "normal" language to read.[5]

Spain and Portugal

At least three distinct strands of anthropology of education can be found in Spain. First, works in the philosophical anthropology of education are widely disseminated (e.g., Barrio Maestre 2004). Secondly, the neo-Vygotskian and cultural psychological current is vividly present (e.g., del Río and Álvarez 1995), as evidenced in the journal *Cultura y educación*, which has been published since 1990.[6] Finally, the anthropology of schooling seems to be flourishing at several centers across Spain. An important volume of English-language works, translated and interpreted, appeared in 1993 (Velasco Maillo, García Castaño, and Díaz de Rada 1993), and a recent overview of anthropologically oriented work appeared in the *Revista de Antropología Social* (Franzé Mudanó 2007). In the latter volume, Jociles (2007) argues that a majority of anthropologists of education in Spain focus on studies of ethnic minorities and of diversity. For example, Silvia Carrasco Pons studies the children of immigrants and minorities (2003), while ethnographer David Poveda (2001), himself educated in psychology, works with colleagues to study classroom interactions and ethnicity. Poveda also edits an electronic journal, *Working Papers on Culture, Education and Human Development*.[7] Portuguese scholars likewise show strong interest in ethnography of education, to judge by articles in the journal *Educação, Sociedade e Culturas*[8] and publications by scholars like sociologist of education Telmo Caria (2003).

Latin America

Reviews of ethnographic studies conducted in Latin America include Anderson and Montero-Sieburth (1998), Levinson et al. (2002), Rockwell (1998), and Rockwell and Gomes (2009). This volume includes chapters on three of the largest Latin American centers—Mexico, Argentina, and Brazil.

In Mexico, Elsie Rockwell and her colleagues in the DIE (Departamento de Investigaciones Educativas) have built up a rich collection of studies of classrooms and schools and of the education of rural and indigenous students. Their team uses ethnographic methods similar to approaches used in the United States, but adds a sensitivity to social history influenced by French scholars and an attention to discourse shaped by sociolinguistics. From this blend, they have developed new concepts such as the idea of *el trabajo docente*, teaching work. Rockwell and González in this volume review themes of the research conducted by the DIE and by ethnographers across Mexico.

With support from the Canadian government and in conversation with Mexican ethnographers, Latin America has developed a network of researchers clustered in several teams in Argentina and Chile. In this volume, María Rosa Neufeld shows how anthropology of education developed in Argentina—specifically, in the Department of Anthropology and Education within the Institute of Anthropology of the University of Buenos Aires—as part of a postmilitary regime renaissance of the social sciences. The department hosted the eleventh Simposio Interamericano de Investigación Ethnográfica en Educación, the first such symposium held in South America. Neufeld shows that, as in Mexico, anthropology of education in Argentina is firmly rooted in the discipline of anthropology and has strong links to history.

In Brazil, according to Ana Gomes and Nilma Gomes in this volume, there has been an interest in anthropology of education since the 1950s;

however, the influence of the "precursor studies" faded under the "myth of racial democracy" and the military regime, until new scholars returned to questions of ethnicity, race, and schooling in the 1980s. Meanwhile, in Brazil there is also a neo-Vygotskian current (Souza Lima 1995) as well as a bubbling up of research inspired by Freire and pedagogical action projects (Oliviera Gonçalves and Gonçalves e Silva 1998).

The French-Speaking World

In this volume, Raveaud and Draelants present a concise survey of ethnographies of education in French-speaking Europe and Canada. They show that this language zone functions as a single domain not only because of shared language but also because of collegial ties within the international association of French-speaking sociologists (AISLF). They demonstrate that ethnographic studies have usually been conducted by sociologists of education in a reaction against the primarily quantitative approach that had dominated France for so long, although they point to a few developments among anthropologists as well. French ethnographers have gradually expanded their focus on social class to recognize and analyze ethnicity among the children of immigrants, while Belgian, Swiss, and Québequois ethnographers have demonstrated greater interest in linguistic diversity—not surprisingly, given the linguistic diversity of their respective nations.

In France, sociology of education focuses almost exclusively on schooling (Duru-Bellat and van Zanten 2006), as does the chapter in this volume. Although anthropologists of the French-speaking world have paid little attention to either schooling or learning, ethnologists of France, practitioners of the discipline that evolved from earlier folklore studies, occasionally turn their attention to the acquisition of culture (e.g., Delbos and Jorion 1984). Recently, the journal *Ethnologie française* has also published anthropological studies of schooling (Filliod 2007; Garcion-Vautour 2003), and has noted the establishment of the European Society of Ethnographers of Education (Boumard and Bouvet 2007).

Other Language Zones in Europe

Interest in ethnography also flourishes in European countries outside of the English-, German-, and French-language zones.

In Italy, as Francesca Gobbo explains in this volume, traditional anthropologists have attended to the question of how schooling "creates illiteracy" and have written broad treatises on anthropology of education that border on philosophical anthropology. Meanwhile, as ethnographers working in a faculty of education, Gobbo and her students focus on fieldwork, which calls into question the cultures of the school as well as the cultures of ethnic minority children.

In Central Europe, as Gábor Eröss details in this volume, the disciplines of "ethnography" (in the sense of folklore studies) and of Roma studies have been the main inspirations for ethnographic research on education, and the Roma and other minority ethnic groups have been the principal topic, with the exception of Poland, where a German-style philosophical anthropology of education has prevailed. Eröss notes new trends, however, including a political anthropology of education inspired by developments in French sociology.

Scandinavia, where Danish, Norwegian, and Swedish scholars find one another's languages mutually intelligible, is particularly rich in anthropologists of education. Anderson, Gulløv, and Valentin in this volume describe a long tradition of ethnographic studies and a more recent stream of specifically anthropological work in Scandinavia, much of it focusing on childhood and youth (see also Larsson 2006). Like the Flemish-speaking scholars of Belgium and the Netherlands (e.g., Eldering 1996; Timmerman 2000), Scandinavian ethnographers publish regularly in English as well as in their own languages.

At this writing, except for a reference to some discussion of qualitative research and action research drawing on hermeneutics or phenomenology in Lithuania,[9] I have not encountered ethnography of education in the Baltic states, in Greece, in Turkey, or in Russia. However, it is important to note that in Russia, the ideas of Lev Vygotsky have experienced a renaissance since the 1960s (Shepel 1995). Known in the United States as "cultural psychology" or "cultural historical activity theory," Vygotsky's ideas have been an important inspiration for the anthropology of learning in the United States and other countries including, as noted, Brazil and Spain (e.g., Rogoff 2003; Souza Lima 1995).

Asia

Japan has had a long history of anthropology of education, which began in conjunction with studies by ethnographers of education visiting from the United States (Minoura, this volume). Some Japanese ethnographers publish in English and, in my experience, Japan has been the country with the second largest representation in the Council on Anthropology and Education of the American Anthropological Association. However, by detailing the rich body of literature published in the last two decades, Minoura in this volume opens a vista on the extensive literature available only in Japanese. Although some of this literature focuses on ethnic minority students, a large part of it analyzes ordinary educational practices and life in mainstream schools, presenting an interesting contrast to the US focus on failure. Dr. Minoura also notes the interest in ethnography of education among educational psychologists in Japan.

In China, programmatic statements on the anthropology of education have been published for some time, but ethnography of education is burgeoning just now (Ouyang, this volume). Elsewhere in Asia, a few anthropologists in Malaysia, Vietnam, the Philippines, India, and Pakistan express interest in educational problems, according to the Worldwide Email Directory of Anthropologists (Jarvis n.d.; see also http://www.academia.edu). India in particular, which has a strong tradition of applied anthropology and also of sociology of education, as manifested in the work of Krishna Kumar, has published ethnographies of education (contrary to my earlier mistaken impression in Anderson-Levitt 2006a). Anthropologist and sociologist Meenakshi Thapan conducted an ethnographic case study of an innovative private school in 1991, and more recently Indian scholars have published ethnographic studies on teacher and school culture in public schools (Clarke 2001; Sarangapani 2003).

The Middle East and Africa

Ethnographers of education are active in Israel (Shalsky, Alpert, and Sabar-Ben Yehoshua, this volume) and although many publish in English, the chapter in this volume notes the literature available in Hebrew. The chapter demonstrates a strong interest in immigrants and Sephardic Jews, and more restrained interest in politically difficult topics such as Arab students and Orthodox Jewish schools.

In the Arabic-speaking world, ethnographic studies appear to be rarer. Most typical is work by insider-outsiders like Christina (2006). However, Herrera and Torres (2006) bring together critical ethnographies by Egyptian researchers, which were published simultaneously in an Arabic version. There is also interest in action research and ethnography among Palestinian scholars; Nakhlen and Wahbeh (2005) report on 432 master's theses granted by three Palestinian universities, from 1997 to 2004, and note occasional instances of fieldwork and of collaboration with teachers as researchers (see also Khaldi and Wahbeh 2000), while qualitative research is conducted by faculty of the Academic Institute for Arab Teachers of Beit Berl College in Israel.[10]

In sub-Saharan Africa, conducting research is not easy, nor do researchers necessarily control the topics of research, as Diallo reports in this volume. He shares here an analysis of 654 African studies by Maclure (1997) alongside his own recent survey of scholars, showing that qualitative and quantitative methods are often combined. As in Palestine, there is an interest in applied, practitioner, and action research. Many anthropologists in Africa find education a high priority and urgent topic of study. For example, in Cameroon, the Association of Research Students in Anthropology at the University of Yaoundé I reported that one of its members, Nkongho Manchang, recently completed a study of educational reforms and their effects on the community; another member, Abamboh Robert, was writing a thesis on illiteracy and its long-term socioeconomic effects on communities).[11]

African researchers in doctoral, postdoctoral, and professorial positions in Europe, Canada, and the United States are also publishing important ethnographic research. See, for example, Egbo's study of women's literacy in Nigeria (2000) and Diallo's study of girls' successes in middle school in Guinea (2004).

Conclusion

The world is vast. In every country visited here, there are dozens if not hundreds or thousands of educational researchers who practice ethnography or who use anthropological ideas. Although this rapid tour has surely missed or misinterpreted important scholarship, we can nonetheless draw tentative lessons from it to address the three questions posed at the beginning: How do practices of the anthropology or ethnography of education vary, if they do? Why do they vary, or not vary? And why it is important to attend to research beyond one's own national and linguistic boundaries?

Commonalities and Variation

The literatures visited here manifest certain similarities. By definition their research methods are similar; everywhere ethnographers of education use participant observation and open-ended interviewing to get at insiders' understandings of the situation, as I note elsewhere: "The participant-observation is usually of long duration, although lack of time and resources can require 'condensed fieldwork,' particularly in the Global South (Crossley and Vulliamy 1997)" (Anderson-Levitt 2011: 16). More specific supplementary research techniques vary. For example, scholars in West Africa are open to combining ethnographic methods with quantitative methods (Diallo, this volume), while in Israel and in China one finds strong interest in narrative inquiry (Shlasky et al. this volume; Ouyang this volume). Practitioner research, action research, and research to shape policy emerge as particular themes among Palestinian, West African, and Chinese ethnographers (Nakhlen and Wabeh 2005; Diallo this volume; and Ouyang this volume, respectively).

Another commonality is that the concept of culture is used by scholars in all the nations surveyed here, even if French researchers treat it with "suspicion" (Raveaud and Draelants this volume). Indeed, the concept of cultural difference has been borrowed by teachers and the general public to the point that US and Argentine anthropologists, among others, worry about its misuse to reify differences and explain away differential school performance (González 1999; Neufeld this volume).

More surprisingly, the anthropology or ethnography of education is defined largely as the study of schooling in most places, even though early anthropologies of education originated from an interest in learning in all kinds of settings. Scandinavia seems to be an exception with its focus on children and youth, but even there most of the research examines children and youth in institutional contexts. Another exception is the German research, which focuses consistently on learning, but it too begins from a school setting.

Another commonality is that ethnographers of education are more likely to study schooling or learning "at home" rather than "abroad," even in countries where most anthropology is conducted away from home. Research abroad is more common in countries of the global North with a history of colonialism (and now of international aid) — particularly in the United States, Scandinavia, and Japan, but also, as noted, in the United Kingdom and Australia as well as in France (in Filiod 2007) and Germany (in Qvarsell and Wulf 2003). In every nation where it exists, however, anthropology of education conducted away from home appears to be a minority tradition.

In spite of the common interest in schooling as an institution in society, particularly in one's own society, however, this survey has revealed considerable variation. There are really several different anthropologies of education and ethnographies of education around the world.

First, there are older and newer traditions. Anthropologies of education can be traced back to the 1950s or earlier in Germany, the United

States, Japan, Brazil, and Mexico, whereas ethnographic studies of learning or schooling have emerged only since the 1970s or later in countries like France, Israel, Hungary, China, and Guinea.

Secondly, as anticipated, anthropologists and ethnographers of education publish in many languages besides English. There are hefty literatures in Japanese, French, Spanish, Portuguese, and Chinese, and even where scholars publish frequently in English—as in the Netherlands, Scandinavian countries, Israel, and perhaps Germany—many of their works do not appear in English.

Moreover, anthropologies and ethnographies of education have grown from distinct disciplinary roots that show different geographical distributions. Philosophical anthropology of education is an important tradition in Germany and Poland, and can be found in Spain and Italy. An anthropology of learning flourishes in Mexico, Spain, and anywhere that scholars make use of cultural historical activity theory. An anthropology of schooling is well institutionalized in the United States, while an ethnography of schooling with roots in sociology and social anthropology structures the field in the United Kingdom and France. Meanwhile, locally focused ethnology turns out to be the source discipline for ethnography of education in China and in Central European countries, and also contributes in countries like France.

Perhaps as a result, ethnography of education as a research philosophy also tends to be affiliated with different disciplines in different countries. It is practiced largely by sociologists in France, while in Japan it appeals to educational psychologists as well as sociologists. In Central Europe, ethnography of education serves Roma studies, while researchers in Italy and the Netherlands use it in the service of intercultural education. In Mexico and Argentina, there is a strong reliance on the broader discipline of anthropology and in those two countries as well as in Germany, anthropologists of education are also attracted to a historical approach.

Finally, the most common research themes vary from region to region. For example, as noted, Scandinavian ethnographers of education pay a great deal of attention to the anthropology of children and youth, perhaps because Scandinavian welfare policies emphasize "good childhoods" (Anderson et al. this volume). The rituals of schooling draw particular attention in Germany and in Israel—in Germany perhaps because of the intellectual interest in mimesis, but in Israel because of the deliberate use of rituals by the state to create a new national identity. In the United States, central themes are racial and ethnic minorities, the cultural gap between home and school and, as Delamont argues in this volume, school failure.

Global Flow and Local Inventions and Reinventions

First, why the similarities? One explanation of commonalities across these cases is the global flow of academic knowledge. "Books and articles do get distributed beyond their home countries, the web and email make texts much more widely available, and some scholars are privileged to attend international conferences" (Anderson-Levitt 2011: 13). There is also an international flow of students and postdoctoral fellows going to study in the United Kingdom, France, Germany, Quebec, and elsewhere; for example, Gobbo, Minoura, and van Zanten, authors in this volume, studied in the United States. There is another flow of scholars employed outside their birth countries. Visiting scholars sometimes transmit ideas, as in the influence on Japan of the US scholars who conducted early ethnography of education there. Finally, participation on joint projects, such as the European projects mentioned in this volume by Eröss, provide opportunities for mutual intellectual influence.

Chapter authors make explicit reference to the borrowing of ideas as a result of these flows. The Chicago school of sociology seems to have had particularly wide impact, as have US anthropology of education, UK ethnography of education, and Vygotskian ideas, but the chapters also reveal many further instances of borrowing.

While ideas have been borrowed, there have also been occasional cases of independent invention. Sometimes this led to differences, as where distinct disciplinary traditions, such as philosophical anthropology in Germany and cultural anthropology in the United States, seem to have independently inspired different kinds of anthropology of education. At the same time, a common situation—the spread of Western-style schooling, which now touches at least 90 percent of the world's children (EFA 2011)—may have independently inspired a similarity, the common focus on schooling, among anthropologists and ethnographers in different parts of the world.[12] On a more mundane level, the apparent fact that most ethnographers of education work in faculties of education and educational research institutes would likewise tend to direct their attention toward schools. Like the focus on schooling, the tendency to study problems at home rather than abroad underscores that anthropologies and ethnographies of education are commonly organized as applied disciplines. Social scientists and policy makers around the globe agree on the common goal of equal access to quality education (Meyer 2001), and ethnographers who work closely with families, students, and educators feel the urgency of that goal.

In spite of a transnational traffic in ideas and the common framework of worldwide schooling, however, there are also barriers to intellectual exchange. Distinct disciplines develop in different zones or regions or countries because scholars may be politically or economically isolated, because they cannot read one another, or because when they can read they do not understand and appreciate what they read.

Political isolation has happened when political regimes have discouraged ethnography of education. "Batallán (1998) observes that ethnography of education could not have developed under the former authoritarian regimes of Chile and Argentina" (Anderson-Levitt 2011: 16), as does Neufeld in this volume, and Ouyang in this volume comments on the threat that ethnography may seem to pose to people in power. Meanwhile, economic isolation happens because not everyone enjoys the resources to participate in international conferences or to access international journals.

More generally and in more complex ways, ideas do not flow freely because anthropologies and ethnographies of education appear in multiple languages. Language barriers constrict the flow even between adjoining territories; thus, to judge by reference lists in articles and books, Francophone authors read English-language work much more often than German-language work, and Anglophone authors rarely read anything published in languages other than English. There are two Canadas, one more strongly linked to the literature of the United States and Britain, the other to the literature of France and French-speaking Belgium. Belgium and Switzerland likewise have two different faces, while the copious literature in Japanese is not read outside of Japan (Anderson-Levitt 2011). Of course, some work gets translated, but the flow of translations is remarkably uneven. In the last seventy-five years, over a million books have been translated from English into other languages, but only a little more than 100,000 books have moved in the opposite direction, from other languages into English (UNESCO 2010). As a result, scholars who are monolingual in English suffer from a huge "blind spot" by missing most of the literatures originating outside their language zone.

However, translation alone does not guarantee that ideas flow, for readers can fail to understand and appreciate what they read. One reason is that conventions of writing unfamiliar to an audience can obscure the significance of the work. Thus, to European and Latin American readers, US anthropology of education seems to lack sufficient theoretical grounding, while European and Latin American work may seem to lack empirical findings and discussion of research methods to US readers (compare the introductory comments in Levinson et al. 2002). Each set of scholars may fail to take the other seriously.

In addition, readers of a translated or imported work can mistakenly dismiss it as unimportant when they lack familiarity with the implicit assumptions, terminology, local canons, and ongoing conversations to which it refers. Thus the disciplinary differences noted above, compounded by linguistic barriers, can make it difficult to appreciate the intellectual significance of a work. If readers have not been "keeping up with" the literature in German philosophical anthropology or Hungarian ethnology, not only because these are not their disciplines but also because they do not read German or Hungarian, can they properly interpret a new work in these fields? If readers do not know the significance of, say, Max Scheler or Marianne Gullestad or Kazuhiro Ebuchi, all influential scholars cited in this volume, will they miss the importance of arguments that take the work of such scholars as implicit background?

Readers can also fail to grasp the significance of "foreign" research when they do not recognize the relevance of the topic. Yet, as pointed out above, common research themes vary by location. One reason is that the favorite themes of anthropologists or ethnographers derive from their nation's particular history. As argued in Anderson-Levitt (2011), it is hardly surprising, for example, that in countries formed by recent conquest like Canada and the United States or Mexico and Chile, a focus on indigenous education has emerged. Similarly, given their peculiar histories of slavery, it is not surprising that race and racism preoccupy researchers in the United States and in Brazil.[13] Not by chance, the ethnography of education in France, the Netherlands, Italy, and Central Europe shows increased interest in immigrants as the number of immigrants to Europe rises. The place of a country in the world economy can also shape how researchers choose topics. As Diallo notes in this volume, international donors tend to control research topics in poorer countries since they fund almost all scholarship except for master's theses, and it is thus the influence of Western donors that explains, for example, why West African research focuses so heavily on gender equity. Place in the world economy also affects attitudes toward schooling, for where schooling cannot be taken for granted, it can serve to undo stratification rather than to stratify; thus, as pointed out in Anderson-Levitt (2011: 18), "whereas in the United States and Europe, educational literature sometimes compares schools to factories or prisons," in Mexico "public schools can sometimes be seen as a liberating force that offers a relatively equalizing experience" to the nation's children, which Rockwell (1998) demonstrated.

There are many reasons, then, that good and significant research conducted in your country may remain unexplored and unknown in mine: people in my country may not read your language, and no one has bothered to translate your work; we may not understand the arguments your scholars are making because we do not know your canon of key works; or we may not care about the issues you analyze because our country's history and social structure directs our attention to other issues. Even if you publish in English in an "international" journal, you may have reshaped your argument to align with the reviewers' canon or to address the relevance of North American or British problems, so that readers do not encounter the most typical or most central ideas from your nation or language zone in your English-language article.

Some Lessons and Next Steps

This survey suggests that anthropologies and ethnographies of education, in the plural, have emerged in different places at different times, sometimes from different roots. Some traditions appear to have been independently invented as expressions of different disciplinary interests or different historical and social concerns. Some were borrowed from visiting researchers or imported by scholars who studied abroad. Wherever borrowing occurred, however, the literature on borrowing suggests that it was probably selective, designed to suit local interests and needs (Steiner-Khamsi 2004; Anderson-Levitt and Alimasi 2001). Moreover, even where anthropologies of education flow from a common source or share common literatures, one can expect them to diverge over time because when researchers import an idea, they "creolize" what they borrow, transforming it to make it their own (Hannerz 1987, 1992). For example, as I note in Anderson-Levitt (2011), Ouyang has reported elsewhere how he has combined his US-inspired sociolinguistics and anthropology of education with Chinese-inspired sociology of societal transformation, psychology, politics, and educational reform history (Ouyang 2006). "In the same manner, scholars in Mexico, Brazil, and the Netherlands borrow from the United States and the United Kingdom and creolize what they borrow to create new approaches and novel analyses. UK and US scholars creolize imported concepts as well, such as Bourdieu's ideas from France, Freire's from Brazil, and Vygotsky and his colleague's from Russia" (Anderson-Levitt 2011: 21). Creolization is a process rich in creativity. It means that when an idea is borrowed it never remains the same; hence, one must always expect national or regional or linguistic variations.

Because research traditions develop in response to local concerns (as is appropriate for an applied field, or even inevitable as Eröss demonstrates in this volume), it is worth the effort to break the language barrier and decode unfamiliar canons. On a purely pragmatic note, deciphering other peoples' literatures is a skill that facilitates publishing in "international" journals, a task increasingly demanded of scholars around the world. More importantly for development of the social sciences, travel into unfamiliar literatures challenges habitual ways of thinking. For example, I have learned from interactions with Mexican scholars, as just noted, that schooling is not necessarily oppressive. Would it be useful in France or the United States or China to reflect more on school as liberating? Would it meanwhile behoove educators in West Africa to beware the oppressive side of schooling? I have learned from Delamont's chapter in this volume that the United States may focus so closely on school failure, albeit out of passionate commitment to rescue failing children, that US scholars miss opportunities to analyze the deeper problems or to recognize what successful learning requires. Would more emphasis on what local participants take to be normal, unproblematic schooling as conducted in Japan or the United Kingdom provide US educators with fresh models for improving education for all? Meanwhile, would more attention to ethnicity or "race" be salutary in Germany, and might US scholars gain from deeper reading of work on gender from the United Kingdom, Australia, and West Africa? Finally, what could all of us who focus too narrowly on schooling learn from a close look at the study of learning in other settings as practiced, for example, in Germany or Denmark?

As anticipated, anthropologies and ethnographies of education also offer rich ground for practicing the sociology of social science, as Larsson (2006) has pointed out. The chapters here help us understand why the social sciences have been strongly marked by national traditions in recent centuries (Heilbron, Guilhot, and Jeanpierre 2008), but also may point to prospects for a global discipline (as van Zanten concludes in this volume). I hope the volume will inspire some readers to further explore whether good analyses of social problems are necessarily place-bound and time-bound or a global anthropology of education is possible.

In the meantime, authors of this book and many others who have contributed to our initial conversations will work to continue the discussion. We are establishing a web site to share some of the chapters in their original languages or in more detailed versions, and to share longer bibliographies of recommended work. We hope to see the cases expanded to many other countries, and to entertain rebuttals and additions to the current volume. This book is simply the beginning of the journey.

Notes

1. An earlier analysis appeared in Anderson-Levitt (2006a) and a related discussion appears in Anderson-Levitt (2011).

2. Analysis based on Ulrich's Periodicals Directory 2009.

3. Thanks to Bayero Diallo for pointing out this important report.

4. World Council of Anthropological Associations (WCAA). http://www .wcaanet.org/. Retrieved 2 September 2010. Note that the International Union of Anthropological and Ethnological Sciences, IAUES, active since the 1930s, brings together individual scholars rather than national and regional associations.

5. Ana Gomes, e-mail communication, 16 June 2009.

6. See http://www.ingentaconnect.com/content/fias/cye, accessed 22 September 2010.

7. Working Papers on Culture, Education and Human Development, http:// www.uam.es/otros/ptcedh/default.htm, accessed 8 September 2010.

8. http://www.fpce.up.pt/ciie/revistaesc/, accessed 22 September 2010.

9. Audra Skukauskite, e-mail communication, 18 August 2010.

10. Personal communication, Dr. Abdel Mana, Director, February 13, 2011.

11. Nkongho Manchang, e-mail communication, 25 May 2005.

12. Thanks to Francesca Gobbo for this point.

13. History could explain lack of research as well. Beach and Lunneblad (2011) offer historical and political reasons for avoidance of the topics of "race" or "color" in Scandinavian ethnography.

Bibliography

AERA (American Educational Research Association). 2009. "Singapore Meeting of Education Research Associations Sets the Stage for Establishing a World Education Research Association." *Educational Researcher* 38: 70–72.

Alexander, R. J. 2001a. "Border Crossings: Towards a Comparative Pedagogy." *Comparative Education* 37: 507–23.

Alexander, R. J. 2001b. *Culture and Pedagogy: International Comparisons in Primary Education.* Malden, MA: Blackwell.

Anderson, Gary L., and Martha Montero-Sieburth. 1998. *Educational Qualitative Research in Latin America: The Struggle for a New Paradigm.* New York: Garland.

Anderson-Levitt, Kathryn M., 2006a. "Les divers courants en anthropologie de l'éducation." *Éducation et Sociétés* 17: 7–27.

———. 2006b. "Ethnography." In *Handbook of Complementary Methods in Educational Research*, 3rd ed., eds. Gregory Camilli, Patricia B. Elmore, and Judith Green. Washington, DC: American Educational Research Association.

———. 2011. "World Anthropologies of Education." In *A Companion to the Anthropology of Education*, ed. Bradley A. U. Levinson and Mica Pollack. New York: Wiley-Blackwell.

Anderson-Levitt, Kathryn M., and Ntal-I'Mbirwa Alimasi. 2001. "Are Pedagogical Ideals Embraced or Imposed? The Case of Reading Instruction in the Republic of Guinea." In *Policy as Practice: Toward a Comparative Sociocultural Analysis of Educational Policy*, ed. Margaret Sutton and Bradley A. U. Levinson. Norwood, NJ: Ablex Publishing.

Atkinson, Paul, Sara Delamont, and Martyn Hammersley. 1988. "Qualitative Research Traditions: A British Response to Jacob." *Review of Educational Research* 58, no. 2: 231–50.

Barrio Maestre, José María. 2004. *Elementos de Antropología Pedagógica.* Madrid: Ediciones Rialp.

Barth, Fredrik, Andre Gingrich, Robert Parkin, and Sydel Silverman. 2005. *One Discipline, Four Ways: British, German, French and American Anthropology.* Chicago: University of Chicago Press.

Batallán, Graciela. 1998. "Appropriating Ethnography for Research in Education: Reflections on Recent Efforts in Argentina and Chile." In *Educational Qualitative Research in Latin America: The Struggle for A New Paradigm,* ed. Gary Anderson and Martha Montero-Sieburth. New York: Garland.

Beach, Dennis, and Johannes Lunneblad. 2011. "Ethnographic Investigations of Issues of Race in Scandinavian Education Research." *Ethnography and Education* 6, no. 1: 29-43.

Bollnow, Otto Friedrich. 1987. *Crisis and New Beginning: Contributions to Pedagogical Anthropology.* Pittsburgh: Duquesne University Press.

Boškovic, Aleksandar. 2008. *Other People's Anthropologies: Ethnographic Practice on the Margins.* New York: Berghahn Books.

Boumard, Patrick, and Rose-Marie Bouvet. 2007. "La Société européenne d'ethnographie de l'éducation." *Ethnologie française* 4: 689–97.

Breidenstein, Georg. 2007. "The Meaning of Boredom in School Lessons. Participant Observation in the Seventh and Eighth Form." *Ethnography and Education* 2: 93–108.

Candela, Antonia, Elsie Rockwell, and César Coll. 2004. "What in the World Happens in Classrooms? Qualitative Classroom Research." *European Educational Research Journal* 3, no. 3: 692–713.

Caria, Telmo H. 2003. *Experiência etnográfica e teoria social.* Porto, Portugal: Afrontamento.

Carrasco Pons, Sílvia. 2003. "La escolarización de los hijos e hijas de inmigrantes y de minorías étnico-culturales." *Revista de educación,* no. 330: 99–136.

Christina, Rachel. 2006. *Tend the Olive, Water the Vine: Globalization and the Negotiation of Early Childhood in Palestine.* Greenwich, CT: Information Age.

Clarke, Prema. 2001. *Teaching and Learning: The Culture of Pedagogy.* New Delhi: Sage.

Connell, R. W. 1989. "Cool Guys, Swots and Wimps: The Interplay of Masculinity and Education." *Oxford Review of Education* 15, no. 3: 291–303.

Crossley, Michael, and Graham Vulliamy. 1997. "Qualitative Research in Developing Countries: Issues and Experience." In *Qualitative Educational Research in Developing Countries,* ed. Michael Crossley and Graham Vulliamy. New York: Garland.

del Río, Pablo, and Amelia Álvarez. 1995. "Directivity: The Cultural and Educational Construction of Morality and Agency. Some Questions Arising from the Legacy of Vygotsky." *Anthropology and Education Quarterly* 26: 384–409.

Delbos, Geneviève, and Paul Jorion. 1984. *La transmission des savoirs.* Paris: Maison des Sciences de l'Homme.

Derouet, Jean-Louis, Agnès Henriot-van Zanten, and Régine Sirota. 1990. "Approches ethnographiques en sociologie de l'éducation: L'école et la communauté, l'établissement scolaire, la classe." In *Sociologie de l'Éducation: Dix ans de recherche. Recueil de notes de synthèse publiées par la Revue Française de Pédagogie*, ed. Jean Hassenforder. Paris: Institut National de Recherche Pédagogique and l'Harmattan.

Diallo, Boubacar Bayero. 2004. *Parcours scolaires des filles en Afrique: le cas de la Guinée*. Unpublished doctoral dissertation, Université de Québec à Montréal, Montréal, Canada.

Dolby, Nadine. 2002. "Making White: Constructing Race in a South African High School." *Curriculum Inquiry* 32, no. 1: 7–29.

Dracklé, Dorle, Iain R. Edgar, and Thomas K. Schippers. 2003. *Educational Histories of European Social Anthropology*. New York: Berghahn Books.

Duru-Bellat, Marie, and Agnès van Zanten. 2006. *Sociologie de l'école*, 3rd ed. Paris: Armand Colin.

EFA Global Monitoring Report Team. 2011. Education for All 2011. The Hidden Crisis: Armed Conflict and Education *EFA Global Monitoring Report*. Paris: UNESCO.

Egbo, Benedicta. 2000. *Gender, Literacy and Life Chances in Sub-Saharan Africa*. Clevedon, UK/Buffalo, NY: Multilingual Matters.

Eldering, Lotty. 1996. "Multiculturalism and Multicultural Education in an International Perspective." *Anthropology and Education Quarterly* 27, no. 3: 315–30.

Filiod, Jean-Paul. 2007. "Anthropologie de l'école. Perspectives." *Ethnologie française* no. 37: 581–95.

Fisher, A. D. 1988. "Anthropology and Education in Canada, the Early Years 1850–1970." *Anthropology and Education Quarterly* 29, no. 1: 89–102.

Forsey, Martin. 2007. *Challenging the System?: A Dramatic Tale of Neoliberal Reform in an Australian High School*. Greenwich, CT: IAP.

Franzé Mudanó, Adela, ed. 2007. "Antropología de la educación y la escuela" (theme issue). *Revista de Antropología Social*, no. 16. Available at http://dialnet.unirioja.es/servlet/revista?codigo=1517.

Garcion-Vautour, Laurence. 2003. "L'entrée dans l'étude à l'école maternelle. Le rôle des rituels du matin." *Ethnologie Française*, no. 33: 141–47.

Gibson, Margaret A. 1997. "Complicating the Immigrant/Involuntary Minority Typology." *Anthropology and Education Quarterly* 28, no. 3: 431–454.

Gillborn, David. 1997. "Ethnicity and Educational Performance in the United Kingdom: Racism, Ethnicity, and Variability in Achievement." *Anthropology and Education Quarterly* 28, no. 3: 375–393.

González, Norma. 1999. "What Will We Do When Culture Does Not Exist Anymore?" *Anthropology and Education Quarterly* 30: 431–35.

Goodman, Roger. 1990. *Japan's International Youth: The Emergence of a New Class of Schoolchildren*. Oxford: Clarendon Press.

———. "Education: Anthropological Aspects." In *International Encyclopedia of Social and Behavioral Sciences*. Oxford: Elsevier Science Ltd.

Gordon, Tuula, Janet Holland, and Elina Lahelma. 2001. "Ethnographic Research in Educational Settings." In *Handbook of Ethnography*, ed. Paul A. Atkinson, Amanda Coffey, Sara Delamont, John Lofland, and Lyn H. Lofland. London: Sage.

Greenberg, Joseph. 1966. *Languages of Africa.* The Hague: Mouton.

Hannerz, Ulf. 1987. "The World in Creolisation." *Africa* 57: 546–59.

———. 1992. *Cultural Complexity: Studies in the Social Organization of Meaning.* New York: Columbia.

Heilbron, Johan L., Nicolas Guilhot, and Laurent Jeanpierre. 2008. "Toward a Transnational History of the Social Sciences." *Journal of the History of the Behavioral Sciences* 44: 146–60.

Henriot-van Zanten, Agnès, and Kathryn M. Anderson-Levitt. 1992. "L'Anthropologie de l'éducation aux États-Unis: méthodes, théories et applications d'une discipline en évolution." *Revue Française de Pédagogie*, no. 101: 79–104.

Herrera, Linda, and Carlos Alberto Torres, eds. 2006. *Cultures of Arab Schooling: Critical Ethnographies from Egypt.* Albany: SUNY Press.

Hünersdorf, Bettina, Christoph Maeder, and Burkhard Müller, eds. 2008. *Ethnographie und Erziehungswissenschaft: Methodologische Reflexionen und empirische Annäherungen.* Weinheim/München: Juventa Verlag.

Ingold, Tim. 1994. "General Introduction." In *Companion Encyclopedia of Anthropology: Humanity, Culture, and Social Life*, ed. Tim Ingold. London: Routledge.

Jacquin, Marianne. 2006. "La revue *Anthropology and Education Quarterly.* Analyse des dix dernières années." *Éducation et Sociétés*, no. 17: 89–104.

Jarvis, Hugh W. *Worldwide Email Directory of Anthropologists.* http://anthropology.buffalo.edu/WEDA/.Retrieved 2 September 2010.

Jociles, María Isabel. 2007. Panorámica de la antropología de la educación en España: estado de la cuestión y recursos bibliográficos. *Revista de Antropología Social*, no. 16: 67–116.

Khaldi, M., and Nader Wahbeh. 2000. "Teacher Education in Palestine: Understanding Teachers' Realities and Development through Action Research." In *Teacher Education in the Euro-Mediterranean Region*, ed. R. G. Sultana. New York: Peter Lang.

Kipnis, Andrew. 2001. "Articulating School Countercultures." *Anthropology and Education Quarterly* 32: 472–92.

Larsson, Staffan. 2006. "Ethnography in Action. How Ethnography Was Established in Swedish Educational Research." *Ethnography and Education* 1: 177–95.

Levinson, Bradley A. U., Sandra L. Cade, Ana Padawer, and Ana Patricia Elvir, eds. 2002. *Ethnography and Educational Policy across the Americas.* Westport, CT: Praeger/Greenwood.

Maclure, Richard, Ed. 1997. *Overlooked and Undervalued: A Synthesis of ERNWACA Reviews on the State of Education Research in West and Central Africa.* Washington, DC: USAID Bureau for Africa/Office of Sustainable Development.

Mayer, Phillip, ed. 1967. *Socialization: The Approach from Social Anthropology.* London: Association of Social Anthropologists of the Commonwealth.

Meyer, John W. 2001. "Reflections: The Worldwide Commitment to Educational Equality." *Sociology of Education* 74: 154–58.

Meyer, John W., David Kamens, and Aaron Benavot. 1992. *School Knowledge for the Masses: World Models and National Primary Curricular Categories in the Twentieth Century.* Washington, DC: Falmer.

Middleton, John. 1970. *From Child to Adult: Studies in the Anthropology of Education.* Garden City, NY: Natural History Press for the American Museum of Natural History.

Nakhlen, Khalil, and Nader Wahbeh. 2005. "Doing Research on Improving the Quality of Basic Education in Palestine." Paper presented at the Global Conference on Education Research in Developing Countries sponsored by Global Development Network. Prague, Czech Republic.

Ogbu, John U., ed. 2008. *Minority Status, Oppositional Culture and Schooling.* New York: Routledge.

Okano, Kaori. 1997. "Third-generation Koreans' Entry into the Workforce in Japan." *Anthropology and Education Quarterly* 28: 524–49.

Oliviera Gonçalves, Luis Alberto, and Petronilha Beatriz Gonçalves e Silva. 1998. *Jogo das Diferenças: o Multiculturalismo e Seus Contexto.* Belo Horizonte: Autêntica.

Osborne, A. Barry. 1996. "Practice into Theory into Practice: Culturally Relevant Pedagogy for Students We Have Marginalized and Normalized." *Anthropology and Education Quarterly* 27, no. 3: 285–314.

Ouyang, Huhua. 2006. Author's note preceding "Un aller simple. Parcours d'une enseignante novatrice en Chine continentale." *Éducation et Sociétés,* no. 17: 49–72.

Poveda, David. 2001. "La Ronda in a Spanish Kindergarten Classroom with a Cross-Cultural Comparison to Sharing Time in the U.S.A." *Anthropology and Education Quarterly* 32, no. 3: 301–25.

Qvarsell, Birgitta, and Christoph Wulf, eds. 2003. *Culture and Education.* Munich: Waxmann Münster.

Ribeiro, Gustavo Lins, and Arturo Escobar. 2006. *World Anthropologies: Disciplinary Transformations within Systems of Power.* New York: Berg.

Rockwell, Elsie. 1998. "Ethnography and the Commitment to Public Schooling: A Review of Research at the DIE." In *Educational Qualitative Research in Latin America,* ed. Gary Anderson and Martha Montero-Sieburth. New York: Garland.

———. 2002. "Constructing Diversity and Civility in the United States and Latin America." In *Ethnography and Educational Policy Across the Americas,* ed. Bradley A. U. Levinson, Sandra L. Cade, Ana Padawer, and Ana Patricia Elvir. Westport, CT: Praeger/Greenwood.

Rockwell, Elsie, and Ana Maria R. Gomes. 2009. "Introduction to the Special Issue: Rethinking Indigenous Education from a Latin American Perspective." *Anthropology and Education Quarterly* 40, no. 2: 97–109.

Rogoff, Barbara. 2003. *The Cultural Nature of Human Development.* Oxford: Oxford University Press.

Sarangapani, Padma. 2003. *Constructing School Knowledge: An Ethnography of Learning in an Indian Village.* New Delhi: Sage.

Sharpe, Keith. 1992. "Educational Homogeneity in French Primary Education: A Double Case Study." *British Journal of Sociology of Education* 13: 216–37.

Shepel, Elina N. Lempert. 1995. "Teacher Self-Identification in Culture from Vygotsky's Developmental Perspective." *Anthropology and Education Quarterly* 26, no. 4: 425–42.

Souza Lima, Elvira. 1995. "Vygotsky in the International Scene: A Brief Overview." *Anthropology and Education Quarterly* 26: 490–99.

Spencer, Jonathan. 2000. "British Social Anthropology: A Retrospective." *Annual Review of Anthropology* 29: 1–23.

Steiner-Khamsi, Gita, ed. 2004. *The Global Politics of Educational Borrowing and Lending.* New York: Teachers College Press.

Thapan, Meenakshi. 1991. *Life at School: An Ethnographic Study.* Oxford: Oxford University Press.

Timmerman, Christiane. 2000. "Secular and Religious Nationalism among Young Turkish Women in Belgium: Education May Make the Difference." *Anthropology and Education Quarterly* 31, no. 3: 333–54.

Troman, Geoff. 2010. "Ethnography and Education. Aims and Scope." Retrieved August 30, 2010, from http://www.tandf.co.uk/journals/titles/17457823.asp

UNESCO. 2010. Index Translationum—World Bibliography of Translation. http://portal.unesco.org/culture/en/ev.php-URL_ID=7810andURL_DO=DO _TOPICandURL_SECTION=201.html. Retrieved 16 May 2010.

UNESCO & ISSC (International Social Science Council). 2010. *World Social Science Report: Knowledge Divides.* Paris: UNESCO Publishing & ISSC.

van Zanten, Agnès, and Stephen Ball. 2000. "Comparer pour comprendre: Globalisation, réinterprétations nationales et recontextualisations locales des politiques éducatives néolibérales." *Revue de l'Institut de Sociologie* 14: 113–31.

Velasco Maillo, Honorio M., F. Javier García Castaño, and Ángel Díaz de Rada. 1993. "Lecturas de antropología para educadores. El ámbito de la antropología de la educación y de la etnografía escolar." In *Colección Estructuras y Poresos. Serie Ciencias Sociales.* Madrid: Trotta Editorial.

Vermuelen, Hans F., and Arturo Alvarez Roldán. 1995. *Fieldwork and Footnotes: Studies in the History of European Anthropology.* London: Routledge.

Walker, James C., and Christine Hunt. 1988. *Louts and Legends: Male Youth Culture in an Inner-City School.* Sydney: Allen and Unwin.

Wolcott, Harry F. 1987. On Ethnographic Intent. In *Interpretive Ethnography of Education: At Home and Abroad,* ed. George Dearborn Spindler and Louise Spindler. Hillsdale, NJ: Lawrence Erlbaum Associates.

Wulf, Christoph. 2003. *Anthropology of Education,* Lit Verlag. (*Anthropologie de l'éducation.* Paris: L'Harmattan, 1999; *Anthropologie der Erziehung.* Weinheim: Beltz. 2001).

Yamashita, Shinji, Joseph Bosco, and J. S. Eades. 2004. *The Making of Anthropology in East and Southeast Asia.* New York: Berghahn Books.

§ 1

Towards a Historical Cultural Anthropology of Education
The Berlin Ritual Study

Christoph Wulf

Introduction

Since the very beginnings of Western thought, anthropology and pedagogy have been linked. Even though the term *anthropology* was coined only in the sixteenth century, the resonance between pedagogy and anthropology is manifest in Plato's *Republic* and in the writings of St. Augustine and St. Thomas of Aquinas. It cannot be denied in the seventeenth century in the works of Comenius, nor in the eighteenth century in the writings of Rousseau and Pestalozzi nor yet in the nineteenth century in Kant's, Herbart's, Humboldt's and Schleiermacher's oeuvre. In the course of the twentieth century, anthropology grew steadily in influence, particularly within philosophy. Max Scheler explains that, in about ten thousand years of history, our era is the first in which man has become "problematical" through and through, but also the first in which he does not know what he actually is, and at the same time knows he does not know (Scheler 2009). That situation constitutes the starting point of pedagogical anthropology, which has, in the second half of the twentieth century, developed into a very important field of educational knowledge.

According to Kant the human situation is as follows: What human beings are depends on what they must be and on what they may be. Human beings are nothing by and of themselves and must make themselves into who they are and turn themselves into who they must become, while in so doing they frequently hurl themselves against their very own limits. The study of these interconnections constitutes, for Kant, the duty of pragmatic anthropology (cf. Kant 1982: 699), which examines the field of human action and human freedom.

If we wish to discharge this duty properly, it is first of all necessary to resolve what we understand, today, by *anthropology*. What meaning does this term have for the humanities? As I will argue, anthropology today can be developed only within the framework of the historical, ethnological, and philosophical study of human beings, that is to say as historical cultural anthropology.

Anthropological Paradigms

If we wish to put the epistemology of anthropology of education on a more profoundly reflected footing, then a confrontation, at once critical and constructive, with the anthropological paradigms that are internationally significant is indispensable. I am referring to:

- evolution and hominization
- philosophical anthropology developed in Germany
- historical anthropology and the history of mentalities, initiated by historians in France and taking its cue from the *Annales*-School
- the American tradition of cultural anthropology and
- historical cultural anthropology.

In order to provide a framework for educational anthropology, I suggest that we use the paradigm of historical cultural anthropology as a basis for further research (Wulf 2002, 2004). This paradigm integrates perspectives from the other four major anthropological paradigms and provides a basis for an adequate understanding of educational phenomena, processes, and institutions in a globalized world. In this brief chapter, I shall focus on diachronic and synchronic perspectives and historical and cultural research within educational anthropology. To provide an example of ethnographic research in education, I have selected just one of the major research projects in the field of historical cultural anthropology in Germany to present to you. Together with historical and philosophical methods, the ethnographic approach is one of the main methods of educational anthropology, conceived as historical and cultural anthropology.

Evolution and Hominization

The branch of anthropology that studies hominization stems from an attempt to fit the natural history of human beings into the horizon of anthropology in order to understand the "lost paradigm," the human (Morin 1973). Yet the natural history of human evolution can be understood only when considered as part of (social and cultural) history. Its irreversibility, as well as that of the history of life itself, is grasped today as a consequence of material self-organization (Eigen and Winkler-Oswatitsch 1992).

Hominization, the long process of evolution from *Australopithecus* to primitive human beings, can be understood as a multidimensional morphogenesis arising from the interplay between ecological, genetic, cerebral, social, and cultural factors. This process necessitated three types of change. The first were ecological changes, which led to the expansion of the savannah and thus to an "open" biotope. Second, a genetic change took place in the highly developed primates, which were already walking upright. Third, there was a change in social self-reproduction due to the splitting off of young groups and the use of new territories. It was the new ecosystem—the savannah—which triggered the dialectic between the feet, hands, and brain that became the source of technology and all other human developments. The process of hominization was intensified by a prolonged infancy or neoteny, incomplete development of the brain at birth and prolonged childhood with longer affective ties between the generations, with the associated potentials for comprehensive cultural learning. The cerebralization, prolonged youth, and increased social and cultural complexity were mutually dependent. The complexity of the brain requires a corresponding sociocultural complexity. The creative potential of the brain can be expressed and develop only in a sociocultural environment that grows in parallel. This dialectic relationship means that humans have been cultural beings from the very beginning, i.e., their "natural" development is cultural.

The final stage of this process of hominization is, in fact, also a beginning. The human species, which has reached its completion in *Homo sapiens*, is a youthful and childlike species: our brilliant brains would be feeble organs without the apparatus of culture; all our capabilities need to be bottle-fed. Hominization was completed with the irreversible and fundamental creative incompleteness of human beings. The course of hominization also clearly illustrates that *Homo sapiens* and *Homo demens* are inseparably linked and the great achievements of humankind have their downside: the horrors and atrocities perpetrated by the human race (Wulf 2004).

Philosophical Anthropology

While taking evolution into account in anthropology serves to highlight the shared lineage and mutual parentage of all forms of life and the long time-span of hominization as well as the general laws of evolution, philosophical anthropology turns its attention to the particularity of "man's" character.

The centerpieces of philosophical anthropology are the anthropological works of Max Scheler, Helmuth Plessner, and Arnold Gehlen. In 1927, Max Scheler gave a lecture in Darmstadt entitled "Die Sonderstellung des Menschen," which was published in 1928 under the title *Die Stellung des Menschen im Kosmos* (The Human Place in the Cosmos) and is regarded as the beginning of philosophical anthropology. When Scheler died in the same year, he left no concrete preparatory material for the anthropological work he had intended to publish in 1929. The philosopher and biologist Helmuth Plessner, however, published his main anthropological work *Die Stufen des Organischen und der Mensch* (Levels of Organic Being and Man) in 1928. Despite their differences, Scheler's seminal article (2009) and Plessner's book (1928) share the assumption that organic life is structured in levels. Arnold Gehlen's work (1988) took a different approach and focuses on humans as acting beings.

The preoccupation of this strand of anthropological thought was to understand the essence, the nature of human beings in general. Within this framework, anthropology concentrated upon a comparison between "man" and animal (Gehlen 1988; Plessner 1970), with a view to distinguishing shared features and differences. To grasp the *conditio humana,* philosophical reflections were brought to bear upon biological insights. It was thought that the conditions for the formation of the human species could be glimpsed in biological and above all morphological characteristics. This perspective has had two consequences: a focus of anthropological reflection and research on the human body, and a generalizing discourse relating to *one* unique and unitary model of man.

Due to its focus on *the* human being as such, philosophical anthropology fails to address the historical and cultural diversity of human beings in the plural. To investigate the diversity of human life is the aim of a branch of historical science that is oriented towards anthropological issues.

The Annales School and the History of Mentalities

Anthropology underwent an additional development and refinement in a historical turn, which can be discerned in the historical treatments of anthropological topics of the *Annales* school and the history of mentalities that flowed from it (Burke 1991; Ariès and Duby 1987–1991). Quite opposed to those who insist that social structures as well as the social actor's subjective experiences be rooted in a character common to all human beings, the practitioners of historical studies with an anthropological orientation inquire into the specifically historical and cultural character of each of these phenomena. Fernand Braudel's study of the Mediterranean (Braudel 1949), Emmanuel Leroy Ladurie's on the village of Montaillou (Leroy Ladurie 1978), and Carlo Ginzburg's on the world of a miller around 1600 (Ginzburg 1980) may be cited as successful examples for this endeavor.

Historical anthropology investigates elementary situations and basic experiences of being human. It studies a basic stock of patterns of thought, feeling, and behavior that is anthropologically constant (Dinzelbacher 1993); basic human phenomena; and elementary human behavior, experiences, and basic situations (Medick 1989), not to make statements about humans in general but to gain an understanding of the multidimensional conditions of life and experiences of real people in their respective historical contexts. This diversity of phenomena is paralleled by the multidimensionality and open-endedness of anthropological definitions and research paradigms. From the point of view of the historical sciences, the feelings, actions, and events under investigation can be understood only in terms of their historic uniqueness. It is this that lends them their dynamic nature and makes them subject to historical change.

Cultural Anthropology or Ethnology

Even though anthropology is the result of a process of philosophical and scientific evolution, it can no longer pretend, these days, that at the end of the day Europeans are the only human beings and act as though European human beings are the only possible yardstick. It is obvious, even in an era of globalization deeply marked in its content and form by Western culture, that different forms of human life exist today, influenced by various local, regional, and national cultures. The Anglo-Saxon tradition of cultural and social anthropology has turned its attention to this situation. Its accent lies on the social and cultural diversity of human life. Its research explains both to what extent cultural evolutions are heterogeneous and to what extent the profound diversity of human life remains unnoticed. It is precisely the analysis of foreign cultures that makes it plain to us how limited and problematic our understanding is. Thanks to the analysis of cultural manifestations drawn from heterogeneous cultures, anthropological inquiries make an important contribution to the elaboration and development of anthropology while its ethnographical methods oblige practitioners to draw upon historical sources. Besides creating a sensitivity for the strange and foreign character of other cultures, it creates a sensitivity for that which is strange and foreign in its own culture. The (self-)reflexive point of view adopted by cultural anthropology towards European cultures has contributed to a considerable evolution and advance of anthropological knowledge (see Geertz 1973, 1993; Sahlins 1976; Harris 2001; Evans-Pritchard 1965; Malinowski 1922; Mead 1950; Lévi-Strauss 1992).

Historical Cultural Anthropology

Confrontation with philosophical reflection has given rise to a critique of anthropology. The specific situation of human beings in the world, the comparison with animals or machines, is no longer anthropology's center of interest. Instead, historical and cultural inquiries focus on understanding the cultural diversity of social life. A particular and very pronounced interest in the study of current phenomena is noticeable. Expanding on historical anthropology, historical cultural anthropology touches upon the historical and cultural determination of culture and its manifestations, and demands that their study and reflection take into account ethnological and philosophical perspectives and questions. Committed to this task, historical cultural anthropology makes an important contribution to the self-comprehension and self-interpretation of cultures and societies today. In this process of cultural understanding, research efforts rapidly run the risk of being unable to move beyond the level of their own initial insights. To safeguard against this risk, historical cultural anthropology needs to reflect upon its relation to power and knowledge, as well as to make efforts specifically aimed at bringing to light the involuntary and often unacknowledged normative implications of its own research.

Within this frame of reference, "reflexive historical cultural anthropology" designates multiform transdisciplinary and transnational efforts to pursue the universal idea of an abstract anthropological norm and to continue analyzing diverse human phenomena. Historical cultural anthropology is the common denominator of history and the humanities. Nevertheless, it is not limited to a history of anthropology as a discipline nor to making a contribution to history from the perspective of an anthropological subdiscipline. It attempts, rather, to bring into an accord the historical and cultural determination of its perspectives and methods with the historical and cultural determination of its object of study. It can harness insights gleaned in the humanities to those yielded by a critique of anthropology based on the history of philosophy, and bring both to fruition in order to create new perspectives and lines of inquiry out of a new consciousness of methodological problems. Historical anthropology is limited neither to certain spatial frames nor to particular epochs. Reflecting on its own historicity and its own cultural condition, it succeeds both in leaving behind the Eurocentrism of the humanities and moves from the interest in history to concern with current and future problems (Wulf 1997, 2002, 2004; Wulf and Kamper 2002).

Building on the four prior paradigms, a historical cultural educational anthropology has been developed over the last twenty years and has now become an institutionalized branch within the German Educational Research Association. The range of research in this field includes a variety of theoretical, historical, and empirical studies, the most prominent of which is the Berlin Study on Rituals. This study combines ethnographic research in an inner-city school with conceptual work on the dynamics and performativity of rituals and their potential for engendering social relationships in education and community life. In what follows, I shall demonstrate how ethnographic research on rituals contributes to a historical cultural anthropology of education.

The Berlin Study on Rituals

What role do rituals play in the genesis of the social dimension in people's lives in contemporary society? Answering this question is what the Berlin Study on Rituals (*Berliner Ritualstudie*), conducted over the past twelve years aims to do (Wulf et al. 2001, 2004, 2007, 2010a, 2010b). The research focuses upon the importance and meaning of rituals for the learning and educational processes of children and adolescents, drawing on rituals from four areas of socialization, namely, family, school, children's and youth culture, and media. Empirically, the study's main focus is on the children of an inner-city elementary school and their families, where the research is confronted with the usual conditions prevalent at such inner-city schools: about three hundred pupils from twenty different ethnic communities. The school in question is an innovative UNESCO model school with an excellent principal and a very active and competent teaching body.

The results of this ethnographic project are extensive and can be covered only cursorily in the framework of this article. I will begin with an overview of five broad lessons from the project.

First, rituals and ritualizations play a central role in the pedagogy, education, and socialization of primary-school children. They structure the children's lives and help them to become integrated in a social order and also to work with it. Rituals shape transitions between fields of socialization as well as between institutions, and they also facilitate social learning, which is vital in the classroom.

Second, pedagogic rituals and ritualizations are performed in all fields of socialization. The performativity of actions becomes apparent in the way that children carry out their behavior and actions either by themselves or together with adults. The performative character of pedagogic and social practices points to their corporality.

Third, important parts of cultural life among children take place by way of mimetic processes, that is, the incorporation of the images, schemata, and imaginations of other people, social situations, events, and actions and their integration into a mental world of images. Through mimetic processes, children acquire a practical knowledge that enables them to learn, act, live, and be together.

Fourth, in the face of globalization and Europeanization, pedagogy and education in Europe have taken on an intercultural task, for which rituals and ritualizations, pedagogic and social gestures, the performativity of social practices as well as mimetic forms of learning all play an important role.

Fifth, ethnography and qualitative methods are useful for the investigation of rituals and ritualizations, of the performativity of pedagogic practices as well as of mimetic and intercultural processes of education. Participant observation, video-based observation, video performance, and photo analysis as well as interviews and group discussions are among the most important research methods; they can be combined to complement each other. This diversity of methods is particularly suited to provide complex and methodically transparent research findings.

The following sections will sketch particular facets of the Berlin Study, and discussion of broader findings on the functions of rituals will follow.

Families

Families from the school were persuaded to participate in the research, and we studied their rituals as well as those of the school. Family rituals include the family breakfast, through which the family members each morning reaffirm their mutual devotion and their overall togetherness. Another ritual, children's birthday celebrations, focuses attention on the offspring, i.e., the distinctive feature of the family as opposed to the relationship of a couple. At the same time, a child's birthday party is an important opportunity to celebrate for members of an age cohort, important for the community, which they stage and perform on such occasions. The most important of the cyclically recurring family rituals, however, is Christmas, in which the family puts itself on stage and performs itself in relation to the birth of Christ and the unity of the "holy family." Family holidays, too, in which the dross of everyday is left behind and communal experiences reminiscent of paradise are made — again, a yearly occurrence — number among these rituals replenishing and renewing the family.

School

It is obvious that school is a ritual activity, the study of which permits fundamental insights into the relationship of institutions and rituals as well as into relationships of hierarchy and power. From the very beginning to the end, during the festivities marking enrollment and graduation, in which transitions are ritually staged and performed, these insights emerge with great clarity. In the enrollment celebration, this school with its innovative pedagogy styles and stages itself as a "school family" with the intent to ease the new pupils' passage from the world of family life and kindergarten into the world of school education. Manifold and multiform are the rituals that produce both the class as a group (which accounts for the greater part of the children's everyday world while they are at school) and the school as a community. Ritual summer, Advent, and Carnival celebrations are part of normal routine for the classes and the school as a whole. They include discussion, work, play, and special events, which are all part and parcel of learning activities and school life. Alongside the rituals enumerated above, we can identify a host of microrituals in the everyday routine of teaching and learning at school, in which the interaction among the children as well as that between children and teachers is staged and performed. Each Monday morning, for example, all classes hold a "morning circle," in which the children give one another accounts of what they have experienced and undertaken during the weekend. Through this ritual, the passage from the children's familial world on the weekends to the social and academic demands that the school places on its pupils is made tangible. Another ritual (the opening of which many teachers mark with a gong) consists of having the children practice meditative silence, a task which many children relish but which they find far from easy. Teachers and pupils, during teaching and more generally while at school, stage processes of learning and formation in rituals and ritualization and in so doing negotiate and deal with differences between the intentions of the pupils and those of the school as an institution.

Children's and Youth Culture

The social dimensions of children's and youth culture, too, develop in and are abetted by rituals, as evidenced by games the children play during recess in the schoolyard, when various groups are formed through inclusion and exclusion. Important determining criteria are the kind of game played, gender, and ethnicity. The games played during the breaks produce social groups that remain stable over longer periods and that are more or less open towards new arrivals. Among adolescents, break dance and street dance groups and their rituals staged on the sites of open-access community work with youths are particularly popular. The LAN-parties (Local Area Network) that we investigated, in the context of which many young people gather in large gyms or halls in order to play one another in a certain electronic game, also exhibited a fixed, ritualized game and group structure.

Media

In the case of media-oriented rituals, we started out by investigating ritualized media formats and mises-en-scène; we attempted, in other words, to work out how ritualized media representation such as advertising, newscasts, talk shows, and crime films influence the children's world of imagination. In order to find out what influence such ritualized televised sequences have upon the behavior and the actions of children, we invited them to produce movies themselves, with the aid of a camera and in volunteer work groups where some were actors, others directors and camera operators. It was fascinating to observe during these "shoots" the degree to which the ritual structures of German TV had imprinted themselves upon the collective imagination, the collective world of fancy of these children, traversing all ethnic boundaries. At the present time, we are investigating how the use of another medium, personal computers in both the official and the unofficial school curriculum, informs processes of learning.

Methods

In the field of research thus constructed we are working with qualitative methods, allowing us to address the kinds of question the study asks while sticking closely to the objects of inquiry. At the same time, we aim to adapt and develop these tools in the very process of reconstructing and analyzing the empirical data. Part of our inspiration stems from *Grounded Theory* (Glaser and Strauss 1969; Strauss and Corbin 1994) with its plea to understand theory as a process and the recommendations on collecting, coding, and analyzing data that ensue. Since the performative character of ritual-based processes of learning and education is our central focus, we have chosen methods of inquiry that on the one hand shed light on the mise-en-scène and the staging of ritual actions while on the other yielding information about the meanings that the participants ascribe to the rituals and about the way they grasp and interpret the learning and education processes embodied within them. In order to attain the first goal, we undertake participatory observation as well as *video-based observation.* In order to do justice to our second aim, large-scale *group discussions* and *interviews* are conducted. Each method yields different kinds of information, which is accordingly coded and interpreted differently. Given the fundamental limitations of all methods of inquiry and the known advantages and drawbacks of each one, we attempt in many instances to investigate the same ritual actions with the aid of overlapping methodological tools (Flick, von Kardorff, and Teinke 2004; Flick 2007; Bohnsack 2003). In the various constituent parts of our study, the methods are combined and weighted differently according to the structure of the specific field of research and the nature of the questions posed within it.

Central Functions of Rituals

The following section will examine the most important findings of the performative approach to ritual research in education, where the focus is on the performative arrangement and the practical and bodily side of rituals and ritualized educational practices. It touches on many forms of theoretical and empirical research and demonstrates the complexity of ritual structures and activities and their important role in historical cultural anthropology of education.

First, rituals create social relationships in education. Without rituals, social relationships and communities would be unthinkable. The symbolic and performative content of ritual practices creates and stabilizes the identity of communities. Rituals create structures of order where all members of the educational or the social community—albeit with differing levels of influence—help to decide which form these structures should take. The structures are both real and rooted in the imaginary of the participants. They give participants a feeling of security, as the actions of other ritual participants are predictable. This ritual framework creates the familiarity of the practices of everyday life (van Gennep 1960; Tambiah 1979; Grimes 1995). Practices outside of this framework seldom occur. When they do occur, their consequences are analyzed or the framework is changed. The framework relates the practices of the ritual participants to each other in such a way that they respond to each other and thereby create new practices. Communities are formed in ritual activities as performative communities (Wulf et al. 2001, 2004, 2007, 2010a, 2010b).

Second, during the performative arrangement of rituals, a new social and educational reality is created. This reality is not completely new—previous models of it have existed before; however, it has not been present in this particular form at this particular location before this particular time. Taking earlier rituals as a basis, every performative arrangement in education creates a new ritual reality and a new ritual community. This ritual community can develop among the children or people who carry out the ritual practices for the first time, but it can also involve a repetition, whereby the community confirms its status as such. The actual performance of rituals or ritual practices is essential for the forming of social and educational communities. The community expresses itself in the performative style of the performance. The ritual presentation enables the expression of something that cannot be expressed otherwise. Therefore the ritual staging should be seen as a "window" that allows a glimpse into the foundations of the community and the culture that creates it, something previously not visible.

The staging of rituals in education is always conducted in the context of previous ritual performances. However, these can vary enormously. In some cases the relationship between old and new ritual performances is very close and in other cases very loose. In any case, the performance of rituals and ritualized practices constitutes a form of continuity that is vital for the effectiveness of the ritual. Continuity gives rise to the impression that the social or educational situation created in the ritual has always been thus and is therefore "natural." This is frequently used to ensure the continuation of the current distribution of power in societies and to maintain social hierarchies—a matter that requires ideological critical analysis.

Third, the performative character yields its full effect in the staging and performative arrangement of rituals in education; in other words, staging and performative arrangement matter (Goffman 1959, 1986; Schechner 1977; Turner 1982, 1969; Bell 1992; Wulf, Göhlich and Zirfas 2001; Wulf and Zirfas 2007). The term *staging* in this case refers to the way in which the ritual scene is set. There is room for maneuver in every ritual performance; forced practices that allow for no deviations are highly infrequent and occur only in pathological cases. The staging of rituals can take many forms. As in the case of the inauguration of American presidents, it may involve a staging that has remained constant for a long period where the scenes have been planned in detail and have even been rehearsed. In other cases, the staging is more spontaneous and can be barely distinguished from the performance itself. A ritual template is used in the latter cases, but it is decided only during the actual performance of the ritual how this template is to be used. Spontaneous demonstrations are examples of rituals in education in which staging and performance largely coincide. Especially in such cases, the question arises as to who is staging the educational ritual—who is the agent and who is the agency of its performance? Is it a tradition, a group, a person, or a collective imaginary and practical knowledge that emerges from the ritual?

Fourth, the bodies of the participants are implicitly involved in the staging and performance of rituals in education. How do the bodies appear in a ritual? How do they take their place in the scene? What does their arrangement in the ritual tell us about the community, the individuals, and their culture? The movements and practices of bodies require our attention. How is the ritual space measured in terms of bodies, and what rhythm do they follow? The distance between bodies and the manner in which they approach each other and keep their distance is significant. What positions do they take? Are they standing or sitting? Which movements do they make when dancing in a school performance or peer group activity? The figurations of bodies are symbolically coded and are used to communicate messages. The "logic" of the body, its presentation and expression play an important role in the performance of rituals in education. This is especially true for the preconscious perception of bodily expressions, which forms the basis on which the atmosphere of ritual arrangements is sensed. The bodies of other people look at us before we become consciously aware of them, and they determine our perception of them in this way. In order for the performance of rituals to result in community-forming processes, the children need to experience the flow of energies and force between people—a physical and psychological process that takes place at the outer reaches of our consciousness (Wulf and Zirfas 2004, 2005, 2007).

Fifth, social hierarchies and power structures are staged and placed in context in the ritual performances. This can be illustrated by the example of the inauguration of American presidents. This staged ritual shows that there is only one president; the arrangement clearly shows who is the power-bearer. Ritual power structures are not always so easy to recognize. Judith Butler (1997) has illustrated in several works that ritual repetition is one of the most effective social strategies for establishing and securing power structures in education. Even belonging to a gender is tied to ritual repetitions, which are required to create our initial identities in this respect. Power issues between the genders and generations are also dealt with in everyday rituals at the family breakfast table; this occurs in a seemingly casual manner that is all the more effective for its relaxed appearance. Ritual staging and performance allow several matters to be handled simultaneously in education. The coherence of educational settings and communities depends on the distribution of power, and therefore the control of this distribution is one of the central tasks of rituals. A stable balance of power is maintained, regardless of whether issues of authority are addressed directly, dealt with in passing, or analyzed in detail.

Sixth, rituals in education and socialization are tied to space; their cultural and historical conditions are experienced under these conditions. Different spaces have differing effects on the structure, quality, and style of the rituals taking place within them. Ritual spaces differ from physical spaces. On the one hand, ritual spaces create ritual staging and performance; on the other hand, rituals create ritual spaces using body movements, scenarios, and symbolic and indexical frames of reference. Educational rituals and spaces have an interactive relationship. In education and socialization both rituals and space are performative. A decorated gymnasium provides the room for a school ball just as a church can stage a confirmation ceremony. However, the school ball also turns the gymnasium into a room of celebration, and the confirmation ceremony changes the church into a room of sacred activity. The meshing of real, virtual, symbolic, and imaginary space with the bodily movements of those taking part plays an important role in the development of ritual activities.

This interconnection of real, virtual, symbolic, and imaginary space to bodily movements takes place in an environment shaped by historical and cultural factors; this produces an atmosphere that affects the mood of the participants of the ritual. Actions are repeated as part of an attempt to absorb the nature of the atmosphere, structure, and function of the space. These actions have taken place here before, and the space is suited to their performance. The participants of the ritual change by mimetically re-creating the conditions of the space around them. The performative effects of ritual spaces such as the church, the family living room, and the virtual space of electronic media are very different and have differing socialization effects.

Seventh, in addition to space, time is the other constituent condition of ritual activity in education and socialization. There are two complementary views that are important for the manner in which humans deal with time. First, rituals play a vital part in introducing children to the way time is ordered in society. Parents attempt to adapt the rhythms of childhood to the time rhythms of adult life, and therefore even infants grow accustomed to the socially normed manner of handling time. The corresponding rituals ensure that time becomes *the* power of order in childhood. Second, ritual activity involving time allows us to glean practical knowledge that is essential for the staging and performance of rituals. Their repetitive character inscribes the order of time into the body, which then becomes structured, by time.

Cyclical rituals serve to secure the presence of the community and to reassert its order and potential for transformation through this repetition. Rituals stage continuity, timelessness and unchanging nature of communities and individuals as well as their process and projective character. The ritual treatment of time results in time skills as social skills; ritual ordering of time structures every aspect of social living today.

Eighth, between the beginning and the end of a ritual in education, there are different sequences of ritual activity where different practices are expected and conducted. Adherence to rules of ritual activity is closely connected to its sequential character. The ritual practices follow an order that is also a chronological order. The process of rituals creates periods of time that differ from the uniformity of everyday life and become important moments of life. This intensification is achieved by the density of events, their exceptional character, and their fast sequence. In many rituals, time is sacred time. Remembrance and ties to the past are constitutive elements of all religions, which, with the aid of rituals, transfer canonized content from communicative memory to cultural memory and thereby make it available to its members in a way that it can be used to shape the future.

Ninth, rituals play an important role in the treatment and handling of difference and alterity in education (Wulf 2002, 2006a; Dieckmann, Wulf, and Wimmer 1997). In the multicultural context of inner-city schools, they are important for interaction between children of different ethnicities. They provide support for children to approach others with different cultural backgrounds, overcome differences, and live together in harmony. School communities offer examples of both success and failures in this area; the imaginary, symbolic, and performative elements are equally important here (Hüppauf and Wulf 2009).

Tenth, the synchronous and diachronic aspects of mimetic processes are vital for the success of ritual practices in education. During the performance of rituals and ritual practices, the participants relate immediately and directly to the actions of other participants. This takes place in a largely mimetic manner, using the senses, the movements of the body, and the common understanding of words, sounds, language, and music. A complete arrangement and complete occurrence of a ritual only takes place when all ritual actions are successfully coordinated and precisely orchestrated. Prerequisite for this is the staging, but the performance itself is the decisive factor, as the ritual actions must be in exact relation to each other. Otherwise the results are farcical, and the ritual is deemed as having failed. Harmonious interaction in education requires that the ritual practices relate to each other mimetically (Gebauer and Wulf 1995). If this happens, energies can "flow" between the ritual participants and they can be experienced as intensive, pleasant, and bonding. Just as in dance or wooing, the rational control of actions also has its limits in rituals. The feeling that a ritual has succeeded only occurs if a mimetically created harmony that is beyond rational control occurs in bodies, movements, and gestures. This mimetic occurrence is the basis for the feeling of belonging and community as well as the experience of the sacred.

Where the synchronic dimension of mimetic processes relates to the importance of mimetic processes in the actual execution of rituals in education, the diachronic dimension relates to the historical aspects of rituals. Rituals in education always relate to others that have taken place—either rituals in which one has participated or rituals of which one has heard an account. This makes the historical dimension a basic condition of rituals. Ritual actions involve mimetic references to earlier rituals. Mimetic reference does not mean that the ritual is recreated in exactly the same manner every time. Mimetic referencing is "taking on similarities," i.e., the repetition of a similar action that would not be possible if the previous ritual activity had not taken place. In some cases the result of this mimetic referencing also leads to critical distancing from the reference point of the ritual, which has been updated by mimetic processes and integrates the old ritual with a new purpose and a new appearance (Wulf 2004, 2005).

Eleventh, mimetic processes are also essential because they enable the learning of the practical knowledge necessary for the ritual practices (Wulf 2006b; Wulf et al. 2007; Gebauer and Wulf 1995, 1998, 2003; Boëtsch and Wulf 2005). Ritual knowledge, which allows children to develop the skills required for rituals, evolves from real or imaginary participation in ritual activities. Children take part in ritual practices by means of mimetic processes; these processes are corporal and are independent actions as well as actions that relate to other ritual ceremonies or arrangements. These processes incorporate ritual figurations, scenes, consequences, images, and behavior patterns that are all composite parts of the correct execution of a ritual practice.

Rituals connect the past, present, and future. They create continuity and enable historical and cultural change. They are not only guardians of society and culture; they also cause change. Reform and innovation are not possible unless rituals change. Rituals in education are not static; they are dynamic. The practical knowledge required for their performance, which is acquired in mimetic processes, means that they are social dramas, and the performative character of these dramas changes social orders. Rituals help to channel the potential for violence present in every society. This is an issue of power and its potential for implementing or preventing social and cultural change.

Twelfth, the more monolithic rituals, which bestride different areas of life, seem to be becoming less important for children. They are being replaced by smaller rituals that relate to specific areas of life and that change according to institution and context. As rituals are becoming more specific, they bring fewer people together than previously. As most children and adults live in several segments of society, they participate in different rituals and rites. These partial rituals include many leisure-time rituals that one has to complete with a certain degree of skill in order to be accepted into the corresponding group. However, the diversification of ritual activity does not necessarily mean a fundamental loss of significance of rituals. Children and adults need rituals and ritual activities more than ever for the performative creation of partial communities; many rituals evolve that are valid only in a limited context but that are nevertheless indispensable.

Perspectives

Historical cultural educational anthropology is an anthropology whose rich potential is about to come into its own. It takes into account both the historicity and the culturality of its subject matter and of its own research methods and perspectives, and thus it has a fundamental significance in education and in education studies research. As to its content, there are no limits. The Berlin Study on Rituals that I have outlined here is a prime example, among (many) others, of research in historical cultural anthropology. Rituals produce the social; they form educational fields and communities in the framework of which human beings develop. They are indispensable in the family, at school, in children's and youth culture as well as in the media. For institutions and organizations, there are of constitutive importance. Rituals have safeguarding, but also evolutionary, even innovative functions in education. For too long, this social dynamic of rituals has been obscured, and it is only now that new perspectives on them are beginning to emerge.

Bibliography

Ariès, Philippe, and Georges Duby, eds. 1987–1991. *A History of Private Life*, 5 vols. Cambridge, MA: Belknap Press of Harvard University Press.

Bell, Catherine. 1992. *Ritual Theory, Ritual Practice*. New York: Oxford University Press.

Boëtsch, Gilles, and Christoph Wulf, eds. 2005. "Rituels" (theme issue), *Hermès* 43.

Bohnsack, Ralf. 2003. *Rekonstruktive Sozialforschung. Einführung in qualitative Methoden*. Opladen: Leske und Budrich.

Braudel, Fernand. 1949. *La Méditerranée et le monde méditerranéen à l'époque de Philippe II*. Paris: A. Colin.

Burke, Peter. 1991. *The French Historical Revolution: The Annales School, 1929–89*. Stanford: Stanford University Press.

Butler, Judith. 1997. *The Psychic Life of Power. Theories in Subjection*. Stanford: Stanford University Press.

Dieckmann, Bernhard, Christoph Wulf, and Michael Wimmer, eds. 1997. *Violence. Nationalism, Racism, Xenophobia*. Munich: Waxmann.

Dinzelbacher, Peter, ed. 1993. *Europäische Mentalitätsgeschichte. Hauptthemen in Einzeldarstellungen*. Stuttgart: Kroener.

Eigen, Manfred, and Ruthild Winkler-Oswatitsch. 1992. *Steps towards Life. A Perspective on Evolution*. New York: Oxford University Press.

Evans-Pritchard, Edward Evan. 1965. *Theories of Primitive Religion*. Oxford: Oxford University Press.

Flick, Uwe. 2007. *Designing Qualitative Research*. Thousand Oaks, CA: Sage Publications.

Flick, Uwe, Ernst von Kardorff, and Ines Teinke, eds. 2004. *A Companion to Qualitative Research*. Thousand Oaks, CA: Sage Publications.

Gebauer, Gunter, and Christoph Wulf.1995. *Mimesis: Culture, Art, Society*. Berkeley: California University Press.

———. 1998. *Spiel, Ritual, Geste. Mimetisches Handeln in der sozialen Welt*. Reinbek: Rowohlt. (Danish edition 2001; French edition 2004)

———. 2003. *Mimetische Weltzugänge. Soziales Handeln, Rituale und Spiele — ästhetische Produktionen*. Stuttgart: Kohlhammer. (Brazilian edition 2005)

Geertz, Clifford. 1973. *The Interpretation of Cultures*. New York: Basic Books.

———. 1993. *Local Knowledge. Further Essays in Interpretative Anthropology*. London: Fontana.

Gehlen, Arnold. 1988. *Man: His Nature and Place in the World*. New York: Columbia University Press.

Gennep, Arnold van. 1960. *The Rites of Passage*. Chicago: The University of Chicago Press.

Ginzburg, Carlo. 1980. *The Cheese and the Worms: The Cosmos of a Sixteenth-Century Miller.* Baltimore: Johns Hopkins University Press.

Glaser, Barney, and Anselm Strauss. 1969. *The Discovery of Grounded Theory.* Chicago: Chicago University Press.

Goffman, Erving. 1959. *The Presentation of Self in Every Day Life.* New York: Doubleday Anchor.

———. 1986. *Frame Analysis: An Essay of the Organization of Experience.* Boston: Northeastern University Press.

Grimes, Ronald. 1995. *Beginnings in Ritual Studies*. Columbia: University of South Carolina Press.

Harris, Marvin. 2001. *The Rise of Anthropological Theory: A History of Theories of Cultures.* Walnut Creek, CA: Altamira Press.

Hüppauf, Bernd, and Christoph Wulf, eds. 2009. *Dynamics and Performativity of Imagination: The Image between the Visible and the Invisible.* New York: Routledge.

Kant, Immanuel. 1982. *Schriften zur Anthropologie, Geschichtsphilosophie, Politik und Pädagogik 2.* Frankfurt/M.: Suhrkamp.

LeRoy Ladurie, Emmanuel.1978. *Montaillou: Cathars and Catholics in a French Village, 1294–1324.* London: Scholar Press.

Lévi-Strauss, Claude. 1992. *Tristes tropiques.* New York: Atheneum.

Malinowski, Bronislaw. 1922. *Argonauts of the Western Pacific.* London: G. Routledge & Sons.

Mead, Margaret. 1950. *Sex and Temperament in Three Primitive Societies.* New York: New American Library.

Medick, Hans. 1989. "'Missionare im Ruderboot.' Ethnologische Erkenntnisweisen als Herausforderung an die Sozialgeschichte." In *Alltagsgeschichte. Zur Rekonstruktion historischer Erfahrungen und Lebensweisen,* ed. Alf Luedtke. Frankfurt/M. and New York: Lang.

Morin, Edgar. 1973. *Le paradigme perdu.* Paris: Seuil.

Plessner, Helmuth. 1928. *Die Stufen des Organischen und der Mensch* [Levels of Organic Being and Man]. Berlin: W. de Gruyter.

———. 1970. *Laughing and Crying: A Study of the Limits of Human Behavior.* Evanston, IL: Northwestern University Press.

Sahlins, Marshall. 1976. *Culture and Practical Reason.* Chicago: Chicago University Press, 1976.

Schechner, Richard. 1977. *Essays on Performance Theory 1970–1976.* New York: Drama Book Specialists.

Scheler, Max. 2009. *The Human Place in the Cosmos.* Evanston, IL: Northwestern University Press.

Strauss, Anselm, and Juliet Corbin. 1994. "Grounded Theory: An Overview." In *Handbook of Qualitative Research,* ed. Norman K. Denzin and Yvonne S. Lincoln. Thousand Oaks, CA: Sage.

Tambiah, Stanley. 1979. "A Performative Approach to Ritual." *Proceedings of the British Academy* 65: 113–63.

Turner, Victor. 1969. *The Ritual Process: Structure and Anti-Structure.* Chicago: Aldine.

————. 1982. *From Ritual to Theatre: The Human Seriousness of Play.* New York: PAJ Publications.

Wulf, Christoph, ed. 1997. *Vom Menschen. Handbuch Historische Anthropologie.* Weinheim and Basel: Beltz. (French and Italian edition 2002; Japanese edition 2008; Chinese edition in preparation)

————. 2002. *Anthropology of Education.* Münster and New York: Lit. (French edition 1999; German edition 2001; Spanish edition 2002; Brazilian edition 2005; Romanian edition 2007)

————. 2004. *Anthropologie. Geschichte, Kultur, Philosophie.* Reinbek: Rowohlt. (second edition Köln 2009; Russian, Spanish and Hungarian edition 2008; Arabic and Turkish edition 2009; American, French, Japanese and Chinese editions in preparation)

————. 2005. *Zur Genese des Sozialen: Mimesis, Performativität, Ritual.* Bielefeld: transcript. (French edition 2007; Russian edition 2009; Chinese edition forthcoming)

————. 2006a. *Anthropologie kultureller Vielfalt. Interkulturelle Bildung in Zeiten der Globalisierung.* Bielefeld: transcript.

————. 2006b. "Praxis." In *Theorizing Rituals. Issues, Topics, Approaches, Concepts,* ed. Jens Kreinath, Jan Snoek, and Michael Stausberg. Leiden and Boston: Brill.

Wulf, Christoph, Birgit Althans, Kathrin Audehm, Constanze Bausch, Michael Göhlich, Stephan Sting, Anja Tervooren, Monika Wagner-Willi, and Jörg Zirfas. 2001. *Das Soziale als Ritual. Zur performativen Bildung von Gemeinschaften.* Opladen: Leske und Budrich. (French edition 2004)

————. 2010a. *Ritual and Identity. The Staging and Performing of Rituals in the Lives of Young People.* London: The Tufnell Press.

Wulf, Christoph, Birgit Althans, Kathrin Audehm, Constanze Bausch, Benjamin Jörissen, Michael Göhlich, Ruprecht Mattig, Anja Tervooren, Monika Wagner-Willi, and Jörg Zirfas. 2004. *Bildung im Ritual. Schule, Familie, Jugend, Medien.* Wiesbaden: VS Verlag für Sozialwissenschaften.

Wulf, Christoph, Birgit Althans, Kathrin Audehm, Gerald Blaschke, Nino Ferrin, Michael Göhlich, Benjamin Jörissen, Ruprecht Mattig, Iris Nentwig-Gesemann, Sebastian Schinkel, and Jörg Zirfas. 2007. *Lernkulturen im Umbruch.* Wiesbaden: VS Verlag für Sozialwissenschaften.

Wulf, Christoph, Birgit Althans, Kathrin Audehm, Gerald Blaschke, Nino Ferrin, Ingrid Kellermann, Ruprecht Mattig, and Sebastian Schinkel. 2010b. *Die Geste in Erziehung, Bildung und Sozialisation. Ethnografische Fallstudien.* Wiesbaden: VS Verlag für Sozialwissenschaften.

Wulf, Christoph, Michael Göhlich, and Jörg Zirfas, eds. 2001. *Grundlagen des Performativen. Eine Einführung in die Zusammenhänge von Sprache, Macht und Handeln.* Weinheim and Munich: Juventa.

Wulf, Christoph, and Dietmar Kamper, eds. 2002. *Logik und Leidenschaft.* Berlin: Reimer.

Wulf, Christoph, and Jörg Zirfas, eds. 2004. *Die Kultur des Rituals.* Munich: Wilhelm Fink.

————, eds. 2005. *Ikonologie des Performativen.* Munich: Wilhelm Fink.

————, eds. 2007. *Die Pädagogik des Performativen.* Weinheim and Basel: Beltz.

2

THE PAROCHIAL PARADOX
Anthropology of Education in the Anglophone World

Sara Delamont

Preface

I studied anthropology at Cambridge, but I did not become an anthropologist by doing foreign fieldwork and then teaching in an anthropology department. I did fieldwork in girls' schools and became an educational ethnographer. Writing this chapter was hard, because (1) I am not an "insider," and (2) because the editor deliberately decided to decenter American anthropology of education in this volume by commissioning an outsider, and by treating the American research as only one segment of the Anglophone literature. Arguing that American authors are frequently ignorant of, or choose to ignore, fellow scholars from other Anglophone countries has been a recurrent feature of my publishing career, and it has not made me popular. That is not a problem. However, boundary disputes—whether a particular author or monograph is or is not "in anthropology"—are. Am I an anthropologist? Or am I "only" an ethnographer? Do I have the right to speak about the anthropology of education? I think of myself as at least 50 percent anthropologist, and the editor chose me to speak. In making space for non-American work, in criticizing American work and in—by necessity—reducing the space allocated to American authors to make room for the non-Americans and for the criticism, I know I have written an "unpopular" chapter.

Introduction

This chapter explores anthropology of education in the Anglophone world. It separates the anthropology of education from the much wider field of educational ethnography, outlines the sources used, highlights the parochial paradox of the title, and then makes seven points about the dominant North American scholarship.

The "Field" Defined

This essay focuses upon anthropology of education in the Anglophone world. It only covers the wider field of educational ethnography to contrast with, and therefore to define, the anthropology of education. Any distinction drawn between the anthropology and the ethnography of education is made in a contested border country, in which categories and processes of incorporation and exclusion are complex and are, themselves disputed. Because of all the ethnographic work done by sociologists, geographers, psychologists, and educational researchers, the field of "ethnography and education" is wide and disparate. In contrast, the anthropology of education remains a small, strongly bounded, and generally inward-facing intellectual community *within* ethnography of education. Fifty years ago anthropologists were the only ethnographers of education (Spindler 1955) and they have remained distinct as a much more diverse field has grown up around them. Ethnographies of educational settings have been produced in abundance throughout the Anglophone world, not only from the United States, Canada, the United Kingdom, Australia, and New Zealand, but also from Malta (Darmanin 1990, 2003; Sultana 1991) and Cyprus (Phitiaka 1997).

In countries other than the United States and Canada, the learned societies for anthropologists do not have educational sections, there are no journals for anthropology of education, educational research does not figure in the anthropological journals, and it is hard for a researcher to study education and sustain a credible, peer-validated identity as an anthropologist, either in anthropology or in education. Involvement in the Council on Anthropology and Education (CAE) and even "knowledge" of work published in *AEQ* is not career enhancing for non-Americans, for example. Wright (2004) is the United Kingdom's leading anthropologist writing about education. However, when she explained "why education matters to anthropology" to the members of the UK Royal Anthropological Institute, she did not make any connections to the North American tradition, but rather argued as if no anthropology of education had ever been done. Mills (2004), Sinclair (1997), and Street (1995) are the only authors writing explicitly about anthropology and education, and are unusual in maintaining an anthropological identity. An earlier generation of British graduates in anthropology who do ethnographies of education (including the author) did not "become" anthropologists, because no UK anthropology department would hire anyone with an educational specialization. In Australia Forsey (2007a, 2007b, 2010) is the exception who proves the rule that "real" anthropologists do not study education.

As a rough-and-ready categorization device, I have treated as an anthropologist of education any scholar who publishes regularly in *Anthropology and Education Quarterly* and/or who is treated as an "insider" by authors who have served on the editorial board of *AEQ*. The much wider and more disparate range of people who are educational ethnographers or who do "qualitative research" in education write for *AEQ* rarely and are not cited or included in the discourse of the CAE "core set" (a useful concept from the sociology of science—see Collins 1985). Needless to say there is a degree of arbitrariness about such classifications, or at least a degree of fuzziness to the categories. Other commentators might use different criteria and might come up with marginally different classifications. The overall picture, however, is likely to be fairly stable, as membership of the core set of anthropologists and the patterns of mutual citation remain constant. Drawing these boundaries, the anthropology of education written in English is overwhelmingly American, whereas the Anglophone ethnography of education is spread across all those nations where scholars publish in English.

The next section outlines the sources consulted on the anthropology of education, before the main analysis is presented.

Disciplinary Sources

Anthropology of education in North America has been well served by *AEQ*, a journal of the American Anthropological Association, and a regular output of books and review articles. *AEQ* has reached volume 40, and remains the main journal in which anthropological research on education appears. There have been special issues of other journals on anthropology of education such as *Human Organization* (vol. 27, no. 1) in 1968, *Teachers College Record* (vol. 109, no. 1) in 2007, and *Teaching and Teacher Education* (vol. 26, no. 1) in 2010. Occasional textbooks have appeared since Spindler (1955) and Kneller (1965) and regular collections of papers including Gruber (1961), Holmes (1967), Chilcott, Greenberg, and Wilson (1968), Fischer (1970), Lindquist (1971), Wax, Diamond and Gearing (1971), Weaver (1973), Ianni and Storey (1973), Spindler (1974), Middleton (1976), Roberts and Akinsanya (1976), Gearing and Sangrea (1979), Spindler (1982), Spindler and Spindler (1987), Jacob and Jordan (1996), Levinson, Foley and Holland (1996), Spindler (2000), Zou and Trueba (2002), and Levinson and Pollack (2011) are produced.

This essay draws on those books and on a series of reviews of the field starting from Brameld and Sullivan (1961), Shunk and Goldstein (1964), Sindell (1969), LaBelle (1972), Masemann (1976), Foley (1977), and Vierra, Boehm and Neely (1982). Two reviews contained major bibliographies. Burnett (1974) has a 157-page annotated bibliography and is dwarfed by Rosentiel's (1977) 646 pages containing 3,425 items. Later came Wilcox (1982), Foley (1991), and Levinson and Holland (1996) leading on to Spindler (2000), Yon (2003) and Strong (2005). A content analysis of all articles published in *AEQ* since its inception, by this author, also underlies the, apparently sweeping, generalizations.

Analysis of the Discipline

This essay explores the main characteristics of the discipline analytically in seven sections. The first includes some discussion of the wider ethnographic literature; the other six contain material only about the North American anthropology of education more narrowly defined:

1. The Parochial Paradox
2. Populations studied
3. Level of focus
4. Analytic concepts
5. Theoretical frameworks
6. Methods and methodology
7. Rhetorical strategies

The Parochial Paradox

The paradoxical feature of the Anglophone anthropology of education is that the majority of it, which is done by North Americans, is ethnocentrically and parochially American. While the fieldwork done is conducted all over the world and the general stance is antiracist and pluralist, the published product is written about, and for, a narrowly focused community. These are strong claims, and the evidence to substantiate them is largely elsewhere (Delamont and Atkinson 1995; Delamont 2002; Delamont, Atkinson, and Pugsley 2010) and is not recapitulated here for reasons of space. American and Canadian schooling are taken for granted, and scholars outside North American are ignored. The former judgment is substantiated in the third section of the paper, while the latter is briefly substantiated here.

The failure to recognize relevant ethnographies done by non Americans is readily apparent if the Gordon, Holland and Lahelma (2001) re-

view essay is compared with Yon's (2003). The former, based in Finland
and the United Kingdom, cover publications from many countries. Yon's
paper appeared in the *Annual Review of Anthropology,* where editors and
peer reviewers generally ensure that the papers are consensual representations of the state of the field. There he claims a larger territory *"the*
history of educational ethnography" (emphasis mine) than he, in fact,
discusses. He also displays the parochial ethnocentrism that has been a
feature of his subdiscipline for forty years, despite repeated criticism. A
similar comment can be made about Heath and Street's (2008) textbook,
although Street is British. The ethnocentric bias of North American anthropology of education reflects that of the wider communities of educational ethnographers and of qualitative researchers of all kinds, but it
is particularly striking that *anthropologists* should display it.

This ethnocentric bias is a defining characteristic not only of the anthropology of education but also of educational ethnographers based
in North America. The new *Handbook of Critical and Indigenous Methodologies* (Denzin, Lincoln, and Smith 2008) is actually a handbook of
North American, Maori, and Pasifika indigenous methods. There are
no chapters on European indigenous people's methods (Sami, Basque,
Irish, Breton, Sard, or Vlach, for example); none on the Indian subcon-
tinent or the rest of Asia or on Central and Latin America. This is not
a limitation of the more recent publications alone. When ethnographic
research in education first became fashionable, edited collections began
to appear. The decade following the publication of the Spindler (1982)
and the Popkewitz and Tabachnick (1981) volumes saw a continuing
stream of qualitative research on *American* education being produced.
Unusually Spindler and Spindler (1987) contains two chapters (of nineteen) by a British researcher, Paul Yates (1987a, 1987b).

Much more typically, in the AERA journal of record, Jacob (1987)
published a review essay on "qualitative research traditions." It was,
in fact, only about American traditions, prompting a response from
the United Kingdom (Atkinson, Delamont, and Hammersley 1988).
Despite that strong corrective essay appearing in a flagship AERA
journal, pointing out that there was educational ethnography beyond
the United States and Canada, American anthropologists of education
other than Levinson and Holland (1996) continue to ignore the work
discussed in it when writing historical accounts, do not cite any of the
authors listed in it, and have not corrected their ethnocentric stance.
Lareau and Shultz (1990) include a four-page "selective guide to the
literature" (237–40) with a bibliography of 208 items. There are citations
to five novelists, and sixteen scholars not based in North America, but
the *only* non-American ethnographic monograph cited is the ubiqui-

tous Willis (1977). Collections such as Eisner and Peshkin (1990) and Zou and Trueba (2002) on qualitative research are all American as is deMarrais (1998a). Graduate students and new recruits to the anthropology of education would not be exposed to the traditions of research in other countries via these collections.

Populations Studied

The pioneers of educational anthropology, Murray and Rosalie Wax, and George and Louise Spindler, set the pattern of the discipline when they focused upon Native or First Americans. The Spindlers studied the Blood Indians and the Menominee, and then schooling in West Germany during its postwar, American-funded "reconstruction." Murray and Rosalie Wax began with ethnography among the Cherokee. Wolcott (1967) lived in a Kwakiutl village in British Columbia teaching in the school for his first project. In Burnett's (1974) bibliography, 89 of the entries are studies of Native North Americans, 38 of African Americans, 23 of Mexicans in the United States or Mexico, 14 of Puerto Ricans in Puerto Rico or America, 8 of Inuit in the United States or Canada, 6 of deprived rural populations, and 5 of Asian Americans. These were all what Hechter (1975) called "internal colonies," and, noticeably, all populations "failing" in the state education system. That is, all were groups with low rates of high school graduation and even lower rates of college entry.

Since Burnett, an analysis of the populations studied in the papers published in *AEQ* showed that the same pattern persisted, but attention was also paid to the schooling of young people from successive waves of immigration: Vietnamese, Hmong, Cambodians, and Laotians after the end of the Vietnam War and the arrival of boat people; Haitians, Cubans, and Central Americans; and then those freed to emigrate by the end of the Soviet empire after 1989 such as Russians, Latvians, and Ukrainians. There have been shifts in the particular groups focused on over the forty years. While African Americans (Fordham 1996, 2008), Latinos and Latinas (Pugach 1998) and First Americans and First Canadians (deMarrais 1998b; Strong 2005) are studied throughout the period, other groups appear and then vanish. Whatever the particular ethnic group, they are studied when failing, and then vanish from the discipline if the school achievement "improves" to the norm: No one is currently publishing on the schooling of Laotian Americans or Laotian Canadians. The persistence of papers on Native Americans and Canadians, on African Americans and Canadians, and on Hispanic Americans and Canadians is an indicator that those populations continue to "underachieve," "fail," "drop out," or be "at risk" in the school system.

The research outside mainland North America does focus on all continents, but there are concentrations in areas where American political influence is strong. Burnett (1974) listed twenty-eight projects done in Australasia and the Pacific Islands, but closer inspection showed them to be on Hawaii, Guam, and the Philippines not Tahiti, New Zealand, or Vanuatu. To find more projects done on Guam than on Brazil and Argentina combined reinforces the point about political sphere. There is relatively little attention paid to *either* the education of linguistic or ethnically distinct indigenous groups in other industrialized countries (e.g., Sami in Finland, Welsh in the United Kingdom, Ainu in Japan) *or* the education of immigrant minorities in such countries (e.g., Greeks in Australia, African Caribbeans in the Netherlands, Croatians in Denmark, Turks in Germany). Anderson-Levitt (1987, 1989) on France is an exception.

Level of Institutional Focus

The anthropology of education, like educational ethnography, is limited to a focus on *schools*, and limited in scholarly depth *by* its focus on schools. Of course *AEQ* does carry some papers about school students learning outside school (e.g., Finders 1996; Fisherkeller 1997; Guberman, Rahm, and Menk 1998) and some papers on education outside formal schools and colleges (e.g., Jacobs-Huey 2003; Prince and Geissler 2001; Rose 1999; Wolcott 1990). However, when researchers study learning, teaching, and enculturation in settings other than schools and universities, the ethnographies do not get incorporated into the "educational" research canon. This point was made by Wax and Wax (1971), Wolcott (1977, 1981), Hess (1999), and Singleton (1999) who commented, "The central confusion of education with schooling continues to bedevil us" (457). Varenne (2007a: 1539) reiterated: "The great paradox of work on education by social scientists is that it is mostly about schools." Anderson-Levitt (2007) made a similar point about the overemphasis on formal schooling. The continued emphasis on schools is surprising given the popularity of Lave and Wenger's (1991) calls for scholars to think about learning away from "the school." They argued that "issues of learning and schooling" had "become too deeply interrelated in our culture" (39–40) for any useful analysis of either learning or teaching to be done.

While no one can dispute the importance of schools as a field site for anthropology, the richness of the projects on learning elsewhere, such as the study of apprentices in Japan (Singleton 1998) could have inspired researchers to seek out more nonschool settings. Research on higher education is sparse, and that on learning and teaching in other contexts, such as *capoeira* academies (Lewis 1992), apprenticeship to a Bektasi Sage (Trix 1993), or a catering college (Fine 1985) is not drawn upon by anthropologists of education. Despite the exemplary anthropologies of higher education, such as those by Moffatt (1989), Holland and Eisenhart (1990), Sinclair (1997), and Shumar (1997) these projects have not been mainstreamed into the anthropology of education.

Not only is the focus on schools, it is overwhelmingly concentrated on pupils and teachers, not other people in the setting, such as secretaries, school nurses, counselors, lab technicians, or janitors. Rich understandings of educational settings as the workplaces of many adults who are not teachers could be gained if they were observed. The anthropological research on schools is generally focused on a comparison between the school as an institution and the (usually uneasy) relationships with the neighborhood or community surrounding it. Frequently parents and community members appear, usually contrasted with "teachers." There are evocative portraits of the landscape and the core values of the adults in the community (King 1967; Kleinfeld 1979; Grobsmith 1981; Phillips 1983). This is exemplified by the recurrent articles on Navajo schooling in general and the history of the Rough Rock School in particular, culminating in McCarty's (2002) book. From the 1968 evaluation (Erickson and Schwartz 1969) through the dispute about it (Collier 1988) including the special issue of *School Review* [see Szasz (1999)] and on to McCarty (1987, 1989) and Deyhle (1986, 1998), especially McCarty et al. (1991) and Lomawaima and McCarty (2006): the reader learns little about interaction in the classrooms, but a great deal about the culture clashes between various non-Navajo teachers, bureaucrats, politicians, and educational evaluators and the core values of the *Dine* themselves. A scholar wishing to know about different pupil styles, about talk in science versus talk in motor mechanics, or about bodily self-presentation in the cafeteria or in the gym, or about teachers' interactions in the faculty lounge would not be able to discover anything about them despite forty years of research at Rough Rock (and other Navajo schools).

That generalization may seem strange given the large body of research on classroom talk, and the multiple ways in which the "normal" patterns of teacher-student interaction in North American schools do not "work" with African-American children (Labov 1969; Heath 1982, 1983) or with First Americans and Canadians from Hawaii to Alaska (Wax, Wax, and Dumont 1964; Au and Jordan 1981; Erickson and Mohatt 1982; Philips 1972, 1983; Wolcott 1967). The detailed studies of classroom language, and the projects intended to (re)train teachers to interact differently so that they engage pupils in culturally acceptable patterns of talk that advance their engagement and learning are a major research achievement. Foley (1996) argues that this area has been "too" successful, so that a new stereotype, the "silent Indian," has become a cliché; a barrier to deeper and more rounded insights relevant to the dropout and failure of First Americans. My point is that this research also focuses on a culture clash: around talk and interaction at the expense of exploring other wider aspects of school processes and interactions, especially those that "disaggregate" the minority culture and its interface with education.

Analytic Concepts

There are two points to be made here. First, the anthropology of education is not, generally, deploying the analytic concepts at the frontiers of social and cultural anthropology; and second, it is not using anthropology to make education unfamiliar (Delamont, Atkinson, and Pugsley 2010) because of the emphasis on student failure. These are both serious criticisms.

The first point can be illustrated by three of the many possible works from mainstream anthropology that produced clear analytic advance, relevant to ethnographies in educational settings, that have not been seized upon and deployed in the anthropology of education. Herzfeld (1985), for example, used the analytic concept of poetics to advance the anthropological understanding of manhood and masculinities. Subsequent mainstream anthropology builds on that concept, but educational anthropology does not cite Herzfeld or utilize his analytic insights. Consequently all the work on manhood and masculinities in the anthropology of education is analytically impoverished and increasingly detached from the heart of the discipline.

The second example from mainstream anthropology centers on memory and its opposite, neglect. Connerton's (1989) discussions of memory and forgetting triggered a vibrant research strand in mainstream anthropology (e.g., Littlewood 2009) that has not produced analytic work on memory in educational settings. Peshkin (1997) gives Connerton one footnote in his epilogue: one citation more than most of those in the subdiscipline. Yet all areas of education are rich in memory and replete with its opposite. Following Connerton could produce insights into educational phenomena superior to those of other disciplines, especially an anthropological "take" on school "reform." Similarly it is twenty years since Lutz (1988) drew attention to the analytic power of a focus on emotion and sentiment, leading to a rich vein of anthropological work. This is an approach of enormous potential for anthropology of education both to illuminate social processes and to connect the subfield with the mainstream, yet is largely unexploited.

These are just three examples of twenty-year-old analytic perspectives in mainstream anthropology that are not readily apparent in the anthropology of education, which routinely fails to engage with the same conceptual repertoire as the wider discipline. Rather, the literature in the anthropology of education routinely deploys the concept of culture clash. An outsider reading anthropology of education could become seriously pessimistic about schooling. Study after study focuses on culture clashes between state schooling and ethnic or linguistic minorities, which produce drop out, low achievement, alienation, and resistance in the pupils.

Ogbu (1974, 1978, 1981, 1982, 1987, 1988) was the major exception to that discourse, regularly pointing out that big historical factors (such as slavery and colonialism) and contemporary structural features of North American societies needed to be central to analyses of schooling. His contrasts between the "fate" of populations of voluntary migrants compared to those conquered or enslaved are particularly important for understanding educational outcomes.

The anthropology of education is overwhelmingly a close observation of failure, which may partially explain the strange fascination with Willis's (1977) twelve "lads" and their "resistance." Repeatedly the only non-American work cited, lauded without reference to the many criticisms it has received for its sexism, lack of integration between theory and data, and naïve treatment of respondents' accounts, *Learning to Labour* apparently meets some need in North American authors and fits into their prevailing discourse. Levinson and Holland (1996) are rare anthropologists who criticize Willis; generally the American response is uncritical. Outside America Walford (2007) provides the latest in a long line of devastating critiques of Willis, but the celebrations of the book (e.g., Dolby and Dimitriadis 2004) continue unabated.

The fascination with the particular culture clashes focused upon by Willis, social class and gender, is perhaps because these culture clashes are rarely found in the anthropology of education. Willis's "lads" rejected their school as middle class, effete, and effeminate, in contrast to the world of work (hard physical labor among men in factories or construction) they planned to escape to. In the anthropology of education clashes of social class, and Anglo male pupils with their male teachers, are almost entirely absent. They appear in some American sociology of schooling (Weis 1990; Fine and Weis 1998) but not in anthropology with the exception of the historical, interview-based study done by an anthropologist (Ortner 2003). Some of the studies on African-American or Latino men rejecting education do focus on gender, but are about masculinity in an ethnic context rather than a class context. Ethnicity is routinely prioritized over class.

If the aim of the discipline is to learn about education, it would be more productive to abandon case studies of failure and focus upon highly successful pupils in other cultures. Understanding how and why educational success occurs, especially among groups who are *not* upper-middle-class Anglo Americans, is a more productive research strategy. The familiarity of schooling is made anthropologically strange when the criteria of, and strategies to achieve, success are explored. It is "achievement" that needs scholarly scrutiny, to make it problematic. Singleton's (1971) material on *Nichū,* a Japanese school, raises many important questions. Two ethnographies, from thirty years ago, still raise important intellectual issues about "culture clash" that did *not* result in school failure, one from the United States, the other Austra-lian. Neither has been followed up to see why *those* culture clashes did not impede school achievement. In Hostetler and Huntington's (1971) *Children in Amish Society,* the children were very successful in school, and so unlike the Native American groups, but the schooling was dia-metrically opposed to standard American education. Similarly, the Or-thodox Lubavitcher (Chassidic) Jews in Australia studied by Bullivant (1978) were highly successful in their school. Yet they rejected much of the "Australian" knowledge in the syllabuses and adhere to Chas-sidic beliefs and practices. These books showed two contrasting "mi-nority" schools, each judged "successful" by its community, in which knowledge, teacher-pupil interaction, and pupil behavior are all quite startlingly different from the majority culture with which they are sur-rounded. Read alongside each other they contrast Protestant and Jew, rural and urban, agricultural and industrial, American and Australian, mixed and single-sex schooling. Neither book is about deviant or rebel-lious pupils, only those who are dancing to a different drummer from any that most ethnographers know.

A rare study of academically achieving ethnic-minority pupils is Gibson's (1987a, 1987b, 1988) on Punjabi pupils in a Californian high school, which focused on adolescents who were regarded as peculiar by the staff because they worked too hard and did not "party" like WASP teenagers. To non-Americans, the teachers' rejection of this ethnic group because they were committed only to the school's academic mission and avoided its social programming provides a fascinating insight into American education that the book's author is apparently unaware of. Only in the United States do teachers believe that a core purpose of secondary education is to play games, edit yearbooks, learn cheerleading, have picnics, and organize the prom rather than translate Homer, write Latin prose, read a tenth or twelfth Shakespeare play, do more advanced calculus, or study catalysis.

The focus of anthropology of education on the "failure" of ethnic minority groups leaves core features of American education taken for granted. Some serious attention to the school systems of Germany, France, or the Scandinavian countries, where schools are about advanced academic work, might help American anthropologists of education focus upon the microprocesses of schooling to explore in more depth exactly what is being rejected and where the "failures" occur. Doing such ethnography, with a clear intention of learning more about mainstream American schooling contrasted with parallel systems in equivalent countries, means therefore all our taken-for-granted assumptions about what school is for are challenged. The work of Maryon McDonald (1989) on Breton and Deborah Reed-Danahay (1987, 1996) on rural French schooling could begin to serve that purpose.

Theoretical Frameworks

Anthropology of education papers do not normally embed the research in anthropological theory. If one takes papers from each decade since 1970 and compares *AEQ* papers with those in other anthropological journals, such as the *Journal of the Royal Anthropological Institute* or *Current Anthropology*, the theoretical disputes in mainstream anthropology are not apparent. The rise and fall of big theoretical concepts in the parent discipline is not mirrored in *AEQ* or the chapters in the edited collections. Structuralism, Marxism, semiotics, poststructuralism, postmodernism, feminist theory, and the rhetorical turn are very rarely apparent. Reed-Danahay's (1996) use of Bourdieu is a striking exception in an undertheorized field. Spindler (2000) does not list Bourdieu, Douglas, Geertz, Herzfeld, Lévi-Strauss, or Sperber in the author index, nor are there any index entries on structuralism, semiotics, poststructuralism, postmodernism, rhetoric, Marxism or feminist theory in the subject index. Anthropologists of the next generation are no more likely to embed their work in anthropological theory, so, for example, Peshkin's series of insightful ethnographies on Nigerians, rural Americans, school amalgamations, separatist born-again Christians, Native

Americans, and elite WASPS are all entirely devoid of anthropological theory (Peshkin 1972, 1982, 1986, 1991, 1994, 1997, 2001).

Methods and Methodology

Although the past thirty years has seen an enormous increase in the number of methods books, especially handbooks, the anthropology of education remains characterized by very brief, unreferenced, factual accounts of the data collection methods; little or no discussion of methodology; and noticeably very little reflection on methods of data collection, analysis, writing, and representation, or reading, of the types that have become widespread since 1986 and are common in sociology or education (e.g., Coffey 1999). The papers in *AEQ* do not cite the methods texts that exist, even those by anthropologists, such as Sanjek (1990) on field notes or Wolcott (1981) on what to observe and record. Noticeable too is the lack of attention paid by most educational ethnographers to the work of sociologists who do highly relevant ethnographies that do analyze their methods, that reflect on methodology. So, for example, Fine's (2003) important position paper on "peopled ethnography" is not cited in *AEQ* articles. This work is neither utilized, cited, *nor criticized.* There are collections of papers by anthropologists that contain some reflections on methods, and autobiographical accounts of projects such as those anthologized by Lareau and Shultz (1990), deMarrais (1998a), Generett and Jeffries (2003), and McLean and Leibing (2007). However, these focus much more on the personal, confessional narratives and autobiographies of the authors rather than raising methodological issues. Methods and methodology are presented as tacit, unexamined, and taken-for-granted features of a shared culture, rather than explicit, scrutinized, and problematized topics set out for the benefit of readers who are not in the core set.

Rhetorical Strategies

It is twenty-five years since Clifford and Marcus (1986) refocused anthropological reflexivity upon writing, reading, and analysis, but *AEQ* and the monographs by anthropologists show little sign of their influence. Although there were scholarly analyses of the rhetoric of social science long before Clifford and Marcus, as Atkinson and Delamont (2008) demonstrate, the publication of *Writing Culture* was the paradigm-changing volume in anthropology. Three new research areas opened up. Papers were published in anthropological journals and edited collections that analyzed the rhetoric of the canonical texts, reflected on the writing of both field notes and publications, and attempted to change the rhetorical canon. This last trend involved putting the authorial voice into texts in much less detached and authoritative styles, experimenting with new textual forms, and trying to preserve the voices of the informants. Brown's (1991) study of a voudou priestess, for example, has traditional ethnographic text, fictional episodes, autoethnography, and autobiography blended in one text. While these trends are seen in many anthropological journals and collections, they are not noticeable in *AEQ*. It does not contain the new textual forms (poems, plays, messy texts), the agonized reflections on polyvocality, the toe-curling autoethnographies, and the self-indulgent musings on 9/11 or Hurricane Katrina that fill *Qualitative Studies in Education* and *Qualitative Inquiry*. The Special Issue of *AEQ* on 9/11 is not self-indulgent in the ways that the equivalent issue of *Qualitative Inquiry* was. The failure to engage with the debates that followed Clifford and Marcus—see Behar and Gordon (1995)—is another sign that Anglophone anthropology of education is detached from its parent discipline.

Conclusions

This paper has argued that anthropology of education is unsurpassed in its richly detailed evocations of school failure, based on thick description and observer engagement. However, there are longstanding and serious shortcomings. These have been pointed out by leading scholars in the anthropology of education repeatedly for over forty years. It has focused on a narrow range of populations, is dominated by studies of schools, is not reflexive about its methods or methodology more generally, ignores theoretical frameworks and debates about theory in anthropology, and has been untouched by the "rhetorical turn." These are serious charges, which can be made by a scholar anywhere in the Anglophone world. What dwarfs all those criticisms for a non-American, however, is the parochial ethnocentricity of the field.

The Anthropology of Education is as all-American as Yellowstone Park. Studying back issues of *AEQ* is salutary for non-Americans. The lack of challenge to the American authors' and readers' sense of familiarity does not alter; nor does their ethnocentric citation pattern. We and our countries do not exist. The anthropology of education is, in this respect, thoroughly American. American authors and editors practice routine, casual, unthinking ethnocentrism, which makes all of "us" second-class citizens of "their" global colonialism.

Bibliography

Anderson-Levitt, Kathryn M. 1987. "Cultural Knowledge for Teaching First Grade." In *Interpretive Ethnography of Education at Home and Abroad,* ed. George D. Spindler and Louise Spindler. Hillsdale, NJ: Laurence Erlbaum.

———. 1989. "Degrees of Distance between Teachers and Parents in Urban France." *Anthropology and Education Quarterly* 20, no. 2: 97–117.

———. 2007. Editorial. *Anthropology and Education Quarterly* 38, no. 4: 317–22.

Atkinson, Paul A., and Sara Delamont. 2008. "Ethnographic Representation and Rhetoric." In *Representing Ethnography,* ed. P. Atkinson and Sara Delamont. London: Sage.

Atkinson, Paul A., Sara Delamont, and Martyn Hammersley. 1988. "Qualitative Research Traditions: A British Response." *Review of Educational Research* 58, no. 2: 231–50.

Au, Kathryn H., and Jordan, Cathie. 1981. "Teaching Reading to Hawaiian Children." In *Culture in the Bilingual Classroom,* ed. Enrique. T. Trueba, Grace Pung Guthrie, and Kathryn H. Au. Rowley, MA: Newbury House.

Behar, Ruth, and Deborah A. Gordon, eds. 1995. *Women Writing Culture.* Berkeley: University of California Press.

Brameld, Theodore, and Edward B. Sullivan. 1961. "Anthropology and Education." *Review of Educational Research* 31, no. 1: 70–79.

Brown, Karen M. 1991. *Mama Lola.* Berkeley: University of California Press.

Bullivant, Brian M. 1978. *The Way of Tradition.* Victoria: ACER.

Burnett, Jacquetta Hill. 1974. *Anthropology and Education.* The Hague: Mouton.

Chilcott, John H., Norman C. Greenberg, and Herbert B. Wilson, eds. 1968. *Readings in the Socio-Cultural Foundations of Education.* Belmont, CA: Wadsworth.

Clifford, James, and George E. Marcus, eds. 1986. *Writing Culture.* Berkeley: University of California Press.

Coffey, Amanda. 1999. *The Ethnographic Self.* London: Sage.

Collier, John, Jr. 1988. "Survival at Rough Rock: A Historical Overview of Rough Rock Demonstration School." *Anthropology and Education Quarterly* 19, no. 3: 253–69.

Collins, Harry M. 1985. *Changing Order.* London: Sage.

Connerton, Paul. 1989. *How Societies Remember.* Cambridge: Cambridge University Press.

Darmanin, Mary. 1990. "Sociological Perspectives on Schooling in Malta." PhD thesis, University of Wales College of Cardiff.

———. 2003. "When Students Are Failed." *International Studies in Sociology of Education* 13, no. 2: 141–70.

Delamont, Sara. 2002. *Fieldwork in Educational Settings.* London: Routledge.

Delamont, Sara, and Paul A. Atkinson. 1990. "Writing about Teachers." *Teaching and Teacher Education* 6, no. 2: 111–25.

Delamont, Sara, and Paul A. Atkinson. 1995. *Fighting Familiarity.* Cresskill, NJ: Hampton Press.

Delamont, Sara, Paul A. Atkinson, and Lesley Pugsley. 2010. "The Concept Smacks of Magic." *Teacher and Teacher Education* 26, no. 1: 3–10.

deMarrais, Kathleen Bennett, ed. 1998a. *Inside Stories*. Mahwah, NJ: Erlbaum.

———. 1998b. "Mucking around in the Mud: Doing Ethnography with Yup'ik Eskimo Girls." In *Inside Stories*, ed. Kathleen Bennett deMarrais, 87–96. Mahwah, NJ: Erlbaum.

Denzin, Norman K., Yvonna S. Lincoln, and Linda T. Smith, eds. 2008. *Handbook of Critical and Indigenous Methodologies*. London: Sage.

Deyhle, Donna. 1986. "Success and Failure." *Curriculum Inquiry* 16, no. 4: 365–89.

———. 1998. "The Role of the Applied Anthropologist: Between Schools and the Navajo Nation." In *Inside Schools*, ed. Kathleen Bennett deMarrais, 35–48. Mahwah, NJ: Erlbaum.

Dolby, Nadine, and Greg Dimitriadis, eds. 2004. *Learning to Labor in New Times*. New York: Routledge Falmer.

Eisner, Elliot, and Alan Peshkin, eds. 1990. *Qualitative Inquiry in Education*. New York: Teachers College Press.

Erickson, Donald, and Henrietta Schwartz. 1969. *Community School at Rough Rock: A Report Submitted to the Office of Economic Opportunity*. Washington, DC.

Erickson, Frederick, and Gerald Mohatt. 1982. "Cultural Organization of Participation Structures in Two Classrooms of Indian Students." In *Doing the Ethnography of Schooling*, ed. George D. Spindler, 132–75. New York: Holt, Rinehart and Winston.

Finders, Margaret. 1996. "Queens and Teen Zines: Early Adolescent Females Reading Their Way Toward Adulthood." *Anthropology and Education Quarterly* 27, no. 1: 71–89.

Fine, Gary Alan. 1985. "Occupational Aesthetics." *Urban Life* 14 (1): 3–32.

———. 2003. "Towards a Peopled Ethnography." *Ethnography* 4, no. 1: 41–60.

Fine, Michelle, and Lois Weis. 1998. *The Unknown City*. Boston: Beacon Press.

Fischer, Joseph, ed. 1970. *The Social Sciences and the Comparative Study of Educational Systems*. Scranton, NJ: International Textbook Company.

Fisherkeller, Joellen. 1997. "Everyday Learning about Identities among Young Adolescents in Television Culture." *Anthropology and Education Quarterly* 28, no. 4: 467–92.

Foley, Douglas E. 1977. "Anthropological Studies of Schooling in Developing Countries." *Comparative Education Review* 21, no. 3: 311–28.

———. 1991. "Rethinking School Ethnographies of Colonial Settings." *Comparative Education Review* 35, no. 3: 532–51.

———. 1996. "The Silent Indian as a Cultural Production." In *The Cultural Production of the Educated Person*, ed. Bradley A. Levinson, Douglas E. Foley, and Dorothy C. Holland. Albany: SUNY Press.

Fordham, Signithia. 1996. *Blacked Out*. Chicago: The University of Chicago Press.

———. 2008. "Beyond Capitol High." *Anthropology and Education Quarterly* 39, no. 3: 227–46.

Forsey, Martin G. 2007a. "The Strange Case of the Disappearing Teachers." In *Methodological Developments in Ethnography*, ed. Geoffrey Walford. Oxford: JAI, Elsevier.

————. 2007b. "Challenging the System." In *Policy as Practice*, eds. Margaret Sutton and Bradley A. Levinson. Westport, CT: Ablex Publishing.

————. 2010. "Publicly Minded, Privately Focused." *Teaching and Teacher Education* 26, no. 1: 53–60.

Gearing, Frederick O., and Lucinda Sangrea, eds. 1979. *Towards a General Cultural Theory of Education*. The Hague: Mouton.

Generett, Gretchen Givens, and Rhonda Baynes Jeffries, eds. 2003. *Black Women in the Field*. Cresskill, NJ: Hampton Press.

Gibson, Margaret. 1987a. "Punjabi Immigrants in an American High School." In *Interpretive Ethnography of Education*, ed. George D. Spindler and Louise Spindler. Hillsdale, NJ: Laurence Erlbaum.

————. 1987b. "The School Performance of Immigrant Minorities." *Anthropology and Education Quarterly* 18, no. 4: 262–75.

————. 1988. *Accommodation without Assimilation*. Ithaca, NY: Cornell University Press.

Gordon, Tuula, Janet Holland, and Elina Lahelma. 2001. "Ethnographic Research in Educational Settings." In *Handbook of Ethnography*, ed. Paul A. Atkinson, Amanda Coffey, Sara Delamont, John Lofland, and Lyn Lofland, 188–203. London: Sage.

Grobsmith, Elizabeth S. 1981. *Lakota of the Rosebud*. Philadelphia: University of Pennsylvania Press.

Gruber, Frederick C., ed. 1961. *Anthropology and Education*. Philadelphia: University of Pennsylvania Press.

Guberman, Steven R., Irene Rahm, and Debra W. Menk. 1998. "Transforming Cultural Practices: Illustrations from Children's Game Play." *Anthropology and Education Quarterly*. 29, no. 4: 419–45.

Heath, Shirley Brice. 1982. "Questioning at Home and at School." In *Doing the Ethnography of Schooling*, ed. George D. Spindler, 96–101. New York: Holt, Rinehart and Winston.

————. 1983. *Ways with Words*. Cambridge. Cambridge University Press.

Heath, Shirley Brice, and Brian Street. 2008. *Ethnography*. New York: Teachers College Press.

Hechter, Michael. 1975. *Internal Colonialism*. London: Routledge and Kegan Paul.

Herzfeld, Michael. 1985. *The Poetics of Manhood*. Princeton, NJ: Princeton University Press

Hess, G. Alfred, Jr. 1999. "Keeping Educational Anthropology Relevant." *Anthropology and Education Quarterly* 30, no. 4: 404–12.

Holland, Dorothy C., and Margaret A. Eisenhart. 1990. *Educated in Romance*. Chicago: University of Chicago Press.

Holmes, Brian, ed. 1967. *Education Policy and Mission Schools*. New York: Humanities Press.

Hostetler, John A., and Gertrude Enders Huntingdon. 1971. *Children in Amish Society*. New York: Holt, Rinehart and Winston.

Ianni, Francis A. J., and Edward Storey, eds. 1973. *Cultural Relevance and Educational Issues*. Boston: Little, Brown.

Jacob, Evelyn. 1987. "Qualitative Research Traditions." *Review of Educational Research* 57, no. 1: 1–50.

Jacob, Evelyn, and Cathie Jordan, eds. 1996. *Minority Education.* Norwood, NJ: Ablex.

Jacobs-Huey, Lanita. 2003. "Ladies Are Seen, Not Heard: Language Socialization in a Southern, African American Cosmetology School." *Anthropology and Education Quarterly* 34, no. 3: 277–99.

King, A. Richard. 1967. *The School at Mopass.* New York: Holt, Rinehart and Winston.

Kleinfeld, J. S. 1979. *Eskimo School on the Adreafsky.* New York: Praeger.

Kneller, George F. 1965. *Educational Anthropology.* Malabar, FL: Krieger

LaBelle, Thomas J. 1972. "An Anthropological Framework for Studying Education." *Teachers College Record* 73, no. 4: 519–38.

Labov, William. 1969. "The Logic of Non-Standard English." In *Linguistics and the Teaching of English,* ed. J. E. Alatis. Washington, DC: Georgetown University Press.

Lareau, Annette, and Jeffrey Shultz, eds. 1990. *Journeys through Ethnography.* Boulder, CO: Westview.

Lave, Jean, and Etienne Wenger. 1991. *Situated Learning.* Cambridge: Cambridge University Press

Levinson, Bradley A., Douglas E. Foley, and Dorothy C. Holland, eds. 1996. *The Cultural Production of the Educated Person.* Albany: SUNY Press

Levinson, Bradley A., and Dorothy C. Holland. 1996. "The Cultural Production of the Educated Person." In *The Cultural Production of the Educated Person,* ed. Bradley A. Levinson, Douglas E. Foley, and Dorothy C. Holland, 1–54. Albany: SUNY Press.

Levinson, Bradley A., and Mica Pollack, eds. 2011. *A Companion to the Anthropology of Education.* New York: Wiley-Blackwell.

Lewis, J. Lowell. 1992. *Ring of Liberation.* Princeton, NJ: Princeton University Press.

Lindquist, Harry M. 1971. "A World Bibliography of Anthropology and Education." In *Anthropological Perspectives on Education,* ed. Murray Wax, Stanley Diamond, and Frederick O. Gearing. New York: Basic Books.

Littlewood, Roland. 2009. "Neglect as Project." *Journal of the Royal Anthropological Institute* 15, no. 1: 113–30.

Lomawaima, K. Tsianina, and Teresa L. McCarty. 2006. *To Remain an Indian.* New York: Teachers College Press.

Lutz, Catherine A. 1988. *Unnatural Emotions.* Chicago: University of Chicago Press.

Masemann, Vandra. 1976. "Anthropological Approaches to Comparative Education." *Comparative Education Review* 20, no. 4: 368–80.

McCarty, Teresa L. 1987. "The Rough Rock Demonstration School." *Human Organization* 46: 103–12.

———. 1989. "School as Community." *Harvard Education Review* 59: 484–503.

———. 2002. *A Place to be Navajo.* Mahwah, NJ: Erlbaum.

McCarty, Teresa L., Stephen Wallace, Regina Hadley Lynch, and Ancita Benally. 1991. "Classroom Inquiry and Navajo Learning Styles." *Anthropology and Education Quarterly* 22, no. 1: 42–59.

McDonald, Maryon. 1989. *We Are Not French!* London: Routledge.

McLean, Athena, and Annette Leibing, eds. 2007. *The Shadow Side of Fieldwork.* Oxford: Blackwell.

Middleton, John, ed. 1976. *From Child to Adult.* Austin: University of Texas Press.

Mills, David. 2004. "Disciplinarity and the Teaching Vocation." In *Teaching Rites and Wrongs,* ed. David Mills and Mark Harris, 20–39. Birmingham, UK: C-SAP.

Moffatt, Michael. 1989. *Coming of Age in New Jersey.* New Brunswick, NJ: Rutgers University Press

Ogbu, John U. 1974. *The Next Generation.* New York: Academic Press.

———. 1978. *Minority Education and Caste.* New York: Academic Press.

———. 1981. "School Ethnography." *Anthropology and Education Quarterly* 12, no. 1: 3–29.

———. 1982. "Cultural Discontinuities and Schooling." *Anthropology and Education Quarterly* 13, no. 4: 290–307.

———. 1987. "Variability in Minority Responses to Schooling: Nonimmigrants vs. Immigrants." In *Interpretive Ethnography of Schooling,* ed. George D. Spindler and Louise Spindler, 255–280. Hillsdale, NJ: Erlbaum.

———. 1988. "Understanding Cultural Diversity and Learning." *Educational Researcher* 21, no. 8: 5–14.

Ortner, Sherry B. 2003. *New Jersey Dreaming.* Durham, NC: Duke University Press.

Peshkin, Alan. 1972. *Kanuri Schoolchildren.* New York: Holt, Rinehart and Winston.

———. 1982. *The Imperfect Union.* Chicago: University of Chicago Press.

———. 1986. *God's Choice.* Chicago: University of Chicago Press.

———. 1991. *The Color of Strangers, the Color of Friends.* Chicago: University of Chicago Press.

———. 1994. *Growing up American: Schooling and the Survival of Community.* Prospect Heights, IL: Waveland Press.

———. 1997. *Places of Memory.* Mahwah, NJ: Erlbaum.

———. 2001. *Permissible Advantage?* New York: Routledge.

Philips, Susan U. 1972. "Participant Structure and Communicative Competence." In *Functions of Language in the Classroom,* ed. Courtney Cazden, Vera John, and Dell Hymes. New York: Teachers College Press.

———. 1982. *The Invisible Culture.* New York: Longman.

Phitiaka, Helen. 1997. *Special Kids for Special Schools.* London: Falmer.

Popkewitz, Thomas S., and B. Robert Tabachnick, eds. 1981. *The Study of Schooling.* New York: Praeger.

Prince, Ruth, and P. Wenzel Geissler. 2001. "Becoming 'One Who Treats': A Case Study of a Luo Healer and Her Grandson in Western Kenya." *Anthropology and Education Quarterly* 32, no. 4: 447–71.

Pugach, Marlene C. 1998. *On the Border of Opportunity.* Mahwah, NJ: Erlbaum.

Reed-Danahay, Deborah. 1987. "Farm Children at School." *Anthropological Quarterly* 60, no. 2: 83–89.

———. 1996. *Education and Identity in Rural France.* Cambridge: Cambridge University Press.

Roberts, Joan I., and Sherrie K. Akinsanya, eds. 1976. *Educational Patterns and Cultural Configurations.* New York: McKay.

Rose, Mike. 1999. "'Our Hands Will Know': The Development of Tactile Diagnostic Skill—Teaching, Learning, and Situated Cognition in a Physical Therapy Program." *Anthropology and Education Quarterly* 32, no. 2: 133–60.

Rosentiel, Annette. 1977. *Education and Anthropology.* New York: Garland.

Sanjek, Roger, ed. 1990. *Fieldnotes: The Making of Anthropology.* Ithaca, NY: Cornell University Press.

Shumar, Wes. 1997. *College for Sale.* London: Falmer.

Shunk, William R., and Bernice Z. Goldstein. 1964. "Anthropology and Education." *Review of Educational Research* 34, no. 1: 71–84.

Sinclair, Simon. 1997. *Making Doctors.* Oxford: Berg

Sindell, Peter S. 1969. "Anthropological Approaches to the Study of Education." *Review of Educational Research* 39, no. 4: 593–605.

Singleton, John C. 1971. *Nichū: A Japanese School.* New York: Holt, Rinehart and Winston.

———, ed. 1998. *Learning in Likely Places.* Cambridge: Cambridge University Press.

———. 1999. "Reflecting on the Reflections." *Anthropology and Education Quarterly* 30, no. 4: 455–59.

Spindler, George D., ed. 1955. *Education and Anthropology.* Stanford, CA: Stanford University Press.

———, ed. 1974. *Education and Cultural Process.* New York: Holt, Rinehart and Winston.

———, ed. 1982. *Doing the Ethnography of Education.* New York: Holt, Rinehart and Winston.

Spindler, George D. ed. 2000. *Fifty Years of Anthropology and Education: A Spindler Anthology/ George and Louise Spindler.* Mahwah, NJ: Erlbaum.

Spindler, George D., and Louise Spindler, eds. 1987. *Interpretive Ethnography of Education.* Hillside, NJ: Erlbaum.

Street, Brian. 1995. *Social Literacies.* London: Longman.

Strong, Pauline Turner. 2005. "Recent Ethnographic Research on North American Indigenous People." *Annual Review of Anthropology* 34: 253–68.

Sultana, Ronald. 1991. *Themes in Education.* Msida, Malta: Mireva Publications.

Szasz, Margaret C. 1999. *Education and the American Indian,* 3rd ed. (Albuquerque: University of New Mexico Press).

Trix, Frances. 1993. *Spiritual Discourse.* Philadelphia: University of Pennsylvania Press

Varenne, Hervé. 2007a. "Alternative Anthropological Perspectives on Education." *Teachers College Record.* 109, no. 7: 1539–1544.

Varenne, Hervé. 2007b. "Difficult Collective Deliberations." *Teachers College Record* 109, no. 7: 1559–88.

Vierra, Andrea, Christopher Boehm, and Sharlotte Neely. 1982. "Anthropology and Educational Studies." In *The Social Sciences in Educational Studies,* ed. Anthony Hartnett. London: Heinemann.

Walford, Geoffrey. 2007. "Everyone Generalizes." In *Methodological Developments in Ethnography,* ed. Geoffrey Walford, 155–68. Oxford: JAI Elsevier.

Wax, Murray, and Rosalie Wax. 1971. "Great Tradition, Little Tradition and Formal Education." In *Anthropological Perspectives on Education*, ed. Murray Wax, Stanley Diamond, and Frederick O. Gearing. New York: Basic Books.

Wax, Murray, Rosalie H. Wax, and R. V. Dumont. 1964. "Formal Education in an American Indian Community." *Social Problems* 11, no. 4: 1–25.

Wax, Murray, Stanley Diamond, and Frederick O. Gearing, eds. 1971. *Anthropological Perspectives on Education*. New York: Basic Books.

Weaver, Thomas. 1973. *To See Ourselves*. Glenview, IL: Scott, Foresman.

Weis, Lois. 1990. *Working Class without Work*. New York: Routledge

Wilcox, Kathleen. 1982. "Ethnography as a Methodology and Its Applications to the Study of Schooling." In *Doing the Ethnography of Schooling*, ed. George D. Spindler. New York: Holt, Rinehart and Winston.

Willis, Paul. 1977. *Learning to Labour*. Farnborough, UK: Saxon House.

Wolcott, Harry F. 1967. *A Kwakuitl Village and School*. New York: Holt, Rinehart and Winston.

———. 1977. *Teachers versus Technocrats*. Eugene, OR: Center for Educational Policy and Management, University of Oregon (Reprinted in 2005 by Alta Mira Press).

———. 1981. "Confessions of a 'Trained' Observer." In *The Study of Schooling*, ed. Thomas S. Popkewitz and B. Robert Tabachnick. New York: Praeger.

———. 1990. "Peripheral Participation and the Kwakiutl Potlatch." *Anthropology and Education Quarterly* 27, no. 4: 467–92.

Wright, Susan. 2004. "Why Education Matters to Anthropology." *Anthropology Today* 20, no. 6: 16–18.

Yates, Paul. 1987a. "A Case of Mistaken Identity." In *Interpretive Ethnography of Education*, ed. George D. Spindler and Louise Spindler. Hillsdale, NJ: Laurence Erlbaum.

———. 1987b. "Figure and Section." In *Interpretive Ethnography of Education*, ed. George D. Spindler and Louise Spindler. Hillsdale, NJ: Laurence Erlbaum.

Yon, Daniel A. 2003. "Highlights and Overview of the History of Educational Ethnography." *Annual Review of Anthropology* 32: 411–29.

Zou, Yali, and Enrique T. Trueba, eds. 2002. *Ethnography and Schools*. Lanham, MD: Rowman and Littlefield.

§ 3

ANTHROPOLOGICAL RESEARCH ON EDUCATIONAL PROCESSES IN MEXICO

Elsie Rockwell and Erika González Apodaca

The past two decades have seen considerable diversification and increase in anthropological studies on education in Mexico.[1] In this review, we privilege studies engaging concepts such as culture, language, ethnicity, and power from an anthropological perspective. However, we also include ethnographic research on education informed by other disciplines insofar as it has provided important references for anthropologists studying educational processes; in fact, disciplinary boundaries are quite arbitrary. We include only research based in Mexico, regrettably omitting studies done by Mexicans in other countries[2] and reference to scholars from other countries deeply involved in research in Mexico.

Anthropological engagement with education began in the 1930s in close contact with the Mexican government's *indigenista* policies and practices for integrating indigenous peoples. In the 1970s anthropologists challenged those policies, and in 1987 Guillermo Bonfil published his controversial book (*México Profundo*) arguing, against the ideology of *mestizaje*, that Mesoamerican heritage had strongly configured the nation. During these years, scholars initiated research projects on education, primarily at CISINAH/CIESAS and at the DIE/Cinvestav in Mexico City. Since then the field has expanded to other institutions, in dialogue with leading anthropological trends in the country. Nevertheless, within institutional anthropology in Mexico (associations, graduate programs, publications), the study of education is less consolidated than topics such as ethnicity, migration, medicine, or religion; rather, the field has developed in close relation with other educational sciences. In this context, a significant interdisciplinary venue has been the Inter-American Symposium on Ethnographic Research in Education inaugurated in 1989, which has been held five times in Mexico and led to significant publications (e.g., Calvo, Delgado, and Rueda 1998).

Changing Contexts of Anthropological Research on Education

Educational research in the 1980s was strongly influenced by the social movements of the 1960s and 1970s in Latin America, including student and teacher mobilizations claiming schools as spaces for democratic vindication and the provision of free, universal public education as a responsibility of the state. Ethnographic research revealed deep contradictions between official discourse and an educational reality characterized by high levels of exclusion and inequity, as well as disdain of indigenous and popular cultures. Reflection centered on the structural and cultural specificities of Latin America versus "first world" countries, and on the complexity of contested social processes, including reproduction and resistance, occurring through formal schooling.

The political context in Mexico has changed considerably since then. Both the traditional PRI regimes of the 1990s and the right-wing PAN favored by elections since 2000 guaranteed strict compliance with international neoliberal policies. With economic instability the country suffered increasing levels of poverty, migration, organized crime, and "low-intensity" warfare. However, new social movements also emerged. Particularly salient were indigenous movements, including the *Ejército Zapatista de Liberación Nacional,* but new political identities were also forged by other social actors claiming specific rights (youth groups, urban and feminist movements, migrant workers). An emerging sector of indigenous intellectuals became increasingly vocal, influencing political discourse and claiming recognition of cultural survival as a collective right. As the struggle opposed the traditional uniformity of educational policy, the government, following international trends, adopted diversified curricular models, including bilingual intercultural education, while maintaining strict political control and promoting economic models that have undermined the economy.

Extreme economic inequality, asymmetrical power relations, contested elections, and the dynamics of transnationality, globalization, and violence marked the emerging contexts. These conditions in turn have propelled new research questions, oriented towards understanding—and ethnographically describing—relations between schooling, the state, and diverse social actors, within rural and urban contexts of social, cultural, and ethnic diversity. By emphasizing the hegemonic and counterhegemonic processes that take place in this arena, including the power struggles of new political subjects, research has shown the constant negotiation, contestation, and manipulation of diverse meanings of education. Anthropologists in Mexico continue to engage in public debates surrounding educational policies that deepen the inequalities of the school system and social structure. In doing so, they have given new import to the concepts of *culture, power, identity,* and *indigenous rights,* and increasingly approach *education as a cultural process* that extends far beyond schooling.

Methodological Approaches

As in other countries, in Mexico, methodological and theoretical convergence marks the field, making any clear delimitation between anthropological studies and other qualitative research difficult. The fundamental approach in the studies reviewed has been ethnography, understood as research that involves extended fieldwork in one locale, engagement with local knowledge and meaning, and theoretically grounded descriptions of sociocultural processes. Books on the ethnographic perspective in education have been published by Maria Bertely (2000) and Elsie Rockwell (2009), and several articles by other scholars. Nevertheless, it is important to note that this approach has been complemented by others: discourse analysis, in-depth interviews, public policy studies, archival research, and oral history all figure importantly in the work reviewed below. Furthermore, an emerging trend stresses collaborative research and native authoring or coauthoring. In this line it is noteworthy that a growing number of dissertations are written by indigenous scholars, including Refugio Nava, Fernando García, Juan Julian, Lucas Ramírez, and Rafael Cardoso.

Thematic Lines

Our review of over 100 published books and 160 chapters and articles as well as approximately 50 doctoral dissertations and 70 master's theses[3] found in this field revealed nine thematic lines, which we now summarize.[4]

Structures and Cultures of Schooling

In this field, the conception of schooling as a social construction has widely transcended the normative view, leading to interest in the processes whereby school cultures and governing structures are reproduced, negotiated, resisted, or re-elaborated in everyday social relations. Analyses have explored how teachers, directors, parents, authorities, and students each propose and contest the meanings and representations of schooling, as well as how space, time, and material resources are used. Studies show how strategies for interpreting rules and policies produce multiple school realities, often distant from what official policy dictates or common sense assumes, although within existing constraints. Complementing work on social reproduction and cultural production, studies of appropriation stress the active transformation of social institutions and strategic use of cultural resources, as all those involved engage with everyday representations and practices in and around schools.

A common thread of school ethnographies in Mexico is their contextualization within the national school system. Viewed through anthropological lenses, schools appear marked by strong cultural traditions, such as the civic ceremonies studied by Eva Taboada (1998) and ritual practices described by Gloria Ornelas (2007). However, ethnographic approaches have also revealed the import of structural elements, related to national and local policies, on educational practice. For secondary schools, Rafael Quiroz (2000, 2003) and his students (Díaz 1998; Gutiérrez and Quiróz 2007) underscore the influence of curricula, schedules, resources, and evaluations on teaching practices and student strategies, while Etelvina Sandoval (2000) contrasted the consequences of different relationships among principals, teachers, and students in urban secondary schools. Rural and technical schools have been a fertile terrain for exploring this process, as seen in several qualitative studies (Ezpeleta and Weiss 2000; López and Weiss 2007; Díaz Tepepa 2001). Research by Beatriz Calvo and colleagues (2002), by Justa Ezpeleta (2004) and her students, and by Cecilia Fierro (2005) has uncovered the complex networks involved in school management and supervision, tied into administrative and union structures, in the new field of "policy in practice."

Elsie Rockwell's initial interest in everyday schooling has developed into a line of research on the dynamic and contradictory interplay of social processes and cultural meanings on the boundaries between schooling and other social contexts. Recent studies by her students describe facets of this interface in different settings: Gilberto Pérez (2005) detailed the co-construction of nonformal courses on child-rearing practices for mothers, while Florencia Ortega (2006) uncovered children's strategies in public libraries. Working with adolescents, Claudia Saucedo (2003) identified cultural models in school leavers' narratives, Leonel Pérez (2010) traced cultural influences on imagined future careers, and Octavio Falconi (2003) articulated writing practices and public spheres during a student strike. Alicia Vistrain (2009) explored children's elaborations of popular culture in primary school classes, while Valeria Rebolledo and Teresita Pérez centered their master's theses on the experiences of indigenous families and teachers with dominant language schooling. These studies have drawn on alternative concepts of culture, language, literacy, and learning in the anthropological and sociocultural traditions.

Studies on universities constitute a special category, where the lines between qualitative and ethnographic research tend to be diffuse. While early research by Larisa Adler-Lomnitz and her students drew on anthropological theory to characterize the transmission of the scientific ethos in peripheral countries, later qualitative studies on higher education, reviewed by Mario Rueda (2007), many focusing on instructional methods and personal trajectories, are informed rather by sociological and curricular theory. The work of Eduardo Remedi (2008) and his students has been particularly significant, although he inscribes it in social and analytic psychology and institutional analysis. An important exception to this sociological trend is the anthropological dissertation of Luis Arturo Ávila Meléndez (2011) which contrasted two private colleges as alternative projects based on cultural selections of regional values.

The Work of Teaching

The concept of *trabajo docente,* the work of teaching, unifies research in this field, displacing more neutral terms such as "instruction" or "practice." It stresses the collective, negotiated, historically constructed nature of this work, to be understood on its own terms, rather than with reference to prescriptive or evaluative models. In recent research, Ruth Mercado (2002) has deepened her analysis of reflexive, multivoiced *saberes docentes* (teaching knowledges) and the continuous transformative appropriations of educational resources, and with her students (Espinosa and Mercado 2007; Estrada and Mercado 2008) explores teachers' strategies in dealing with educational reforms. Teacher training has been another theme of recent research, with studies of normal schools and training programs undertaken by Mercado (1997) and Patricia Medina (2000).

Inquiry on the multidimensional identity processes and organizational cultures of teachers continues to occupy an important place. Susan Street (1996, 2000, 2001) and her students (Jiménez L 2003; Flor Bermúdez) have worked on three successive teacher union movements and their changing political positions and ideological frameworks, from trade-unionist identity to use of *trabajo docente* as a political and cultural category. Street (2008) has stressed a gender perspective in the study of teachers, as has Oresta López (1997), who has done extensive work on the feminization of the teacher corps. In Mexico, a particularly salient theme involves the contradiction, tension, and conflict within and around the teacher corps, which explains both the reproduction and transformations of the system.

Classroom Ethnography

Researchers studying classroom interaction in Mexico have understood the need to integrate discourse analysis with an anthropologically informed ethnographic approach. This has led to novel studies, in which both student and teacher agency are situated in particular cultural contexts and studied within classrooms characterized by historically constructed teaching traditions. In this approach, knowledge of formal curricular contents is distinguished from knowledge as represented in classrooms and co-constructed between teachers and students. Antonia Candela has led this trend, through studies of science classes in which she stresses the power of children to influence discourse (1999, 2005). She and her students (Naranjo and Candela 2006; de la Riva and Candela 2010) are currently using actor network theory and multimodal analyses to explore science classes in elementary and university settings (Candela 2010). Working from the related perspective of sociocultural psychology, Silvia Rojas (2000) and her colleagues have studied exploratory talk and other discourse strategies in classrooms. Drawing on Bakhtin, Rockwell has contributed studies on oral teaching genres (2000) and literacy practices (2006) in rural classrooms. Recent research in this line is questioning the notion of the classroom as a "closed space," showing the diversity of cultural, social, political, and historical references influencing everyday dialogic teaching processes.

Language and Literacy

Classroom ethnography overlaps with sociolinguistic studies reviewed by Podestá and Martínez (2003), yet given the importance of this field, we consider it separately. The long-term research of Muñoz and Lewin (1996) and Enrique Hamel (2008) advanced the understanding of language ideologies and diglossia in bilingual communities and schools. Studies of classroom uses of oral and written language by Hector Muñoz and Patricia Mena (Mena, Muñoz, and Ruiz 1999), Hamel (2002), Rossana Podestá (2000) and her student Alicia Guerrero, revealed tensions among indigenous students and teachers and the frequent loss of cultural referential contents of native language instruction, shedding light on the contradictions of bilingual education policies in Mexico.

Research on language and literacy in Mexico has gone far beyond the classroom, however. José Antonio Flores Farfán (2001, 2005) has been a foremost proponent of language revitalization processes in nonschool contexts. This position is strengthened through research on nonschool contexts. For example, Refugio Nava (2008), a student of Flores and later of Lourdes de León, studied language loss and maintenance in Nahuatl-Spanish bilingual communities, viewing language socialization as a syncretic system used for locating speakers in diverse social situations. Studies of the appropriation and use of written Spanish by adults in nonschool settings add to this perspective. Through the analysis of narratives and cultural practices beyond formal schooling, Rockwell (2001, 2010) shows how indigenous adults have appropriated dominant language literacy and used it for communal purposes. Judith Kalman (1999, 2004) has contributed innovative studies on social literacies of Spanish-speaking adults in several domains: interaction with commercial scribes, domestic tasks, literacy classes, and popular religion. She and some of her students are currently focusing on digital literacy in and out of the classroom (Guerrero and Kalman 2010).

Cultural Learning and Infant Socialization

This central anthropological line includes work—primarily done among indigenous groups—that approaches learning as a process mediated by social and cultural factors that are not a direct result of formal methods or modalities of teaching. It addresses sociocultural aspects of learning, in school, family, and community contexts, from the interpretative traditions of cultural anthropology and anthropological linguistics.

Ruth Paradise, initiator of this line in Mexico, has approached the sociocultural styles of learning of indigenous children using a concept of culture linked to nonverbal communication and the practices of everyday life. Her work has analyzed various facets, such as observation, autonomy, tacit collaboration (Paradise 1996), and reciprocity (Paradise and de Haan 2009; Paradise and Rogoff 2009). Her students have explored many aspects of indigenous education and school experience: Fernando García (2007) studied the notion of respect in his own Quechua community, and Rafael Cardoso studied the conception of learning in his Mixe community. Rosaura Galeana (1997) studied the experience of street children and then focused on intercultural learning among Mixtec migrant children, while Gabriela Czarny (2008) studied the resignification of schooling experiences with three urban Triqui leaders. Other students explored native uses of story-telling (Paloma Ramírez) and sense of time (Adriana Robles). Paradise's line of research recasts the issue of continuities and discontinuities between family, community and school contexts, by comparing and contrasting ways of learning in and out of school (Paradise 1998, 2002).

Recent research by Lourdes de León (2005), a noted linguist, is related to infant socialization and is located in the interdisciplinary dialogue between cultural anthropology, sociolinguistics, and developmental psychology. Her longitudinal study analyzes cultural dimensions present in language acquisition and their role in indigenous Tzotzil children's socialization. Starting from the analysis of babies' interaction with their parents, she describes visual, corporal, and emotional dimensions as indicators of the "arrival of understanding" or of the "soul" and then explores the first Tzotzil vocabularies and their semantic fields, documenting a linguistic structure that converges with the cultural texture of the Zinacantec socialization.

In general, research is marked by a significant absence of children's voices as subjects. Children's play activities are analyzed by Nancy Villanueva (2000) and by Ramos and Martínez and coauthors (2000). However, most worthy of note are the innovative collaborative and interpretative methodologies used by Paloma Escalante in her study of identity processes of Guatemalan refugee children (2006), and Rossana Podestá (2006) in a collaborative study with children as coauthors. This approach should appear more often in future research.

Youth Cultures

The salience of diverse youth cultures in the public domain has led to a number of anthropological studies. Rossana Reguillo (2000) has used a variety of approaches to analyze the construction of youth identities outside of school and their communicative and organizational practices, documenting their countercultural potential as well as the sociocultural and ideological dimension of the media's link between youth and violence. Diana Sagástegui (2006) explores the sociocultural aspects involved in the gap in access to digital technology, the cognitive mediation of the new technologies, and their use in structured social contexts, and Gladys Ortiz presented her thesis on the everyday appropriation of the internet by university youth. Maritza Urteaga (2000) has studied diverse aspects of youth cultures, including issues of gender and ethnicity. Other studies approach aspects of indigenous youth in rural and urban nonschool contexts and stress the dynamic and heterogeneous nature of the values constituting ethnicity in these groups (Urteaga

2008; Pérez Ruiz 2008a, 2008b). A recent surge of graduate research on youth cultures promises to enrich this field.

Studies conducted in this line by Eduardo Weiss and his students use hermeneutic sociology in dialogue with ethnography and sociocultural theory. While noting structural elements, such as the fragmented character of knowledge and everyday school experience, Weiss nevertheless sees high schools as a significant "youth space." *Students* constitute the central topic, but they are seen as *youths,* bearing special identities and giving meaning to their school experience, which is considered not only in academic terms, but rather as a process of subjectivization with peers and significant "others" (Weiss et al. 2008). Dissertations in this line by Irene Guerra and by Elsa Guerrero (2004) addressed meanings of young people's entry into the labor market, and ways in which youth resignify the structural conditions that characterize their school and their labor trajectories, including gender perspectives. The configuration of student identity is further developed by Weiss's students through attention to symbolic resources and the reflexive construction of moral discourses on maturity, responsibility, and freedom (Hernández G. 2006; Job Avalos), as well as to learning in the "figured world" of graffiti artists (Valle and Weiss 2010).

Sociologists doing interpretive research on secondary and university students provide an important addition to this line. These include Juan Manuel Piña (2003) and his colleagues at UNAM who have studied the implicit meanings present in student life, through the analysis of actor subjectivities, expressed in common-sense knowledge, imaginaries, and social representations, as well as in feelings, values, and judgments of schooling. In a similar tradition, Adrian de Garay (2004) studied social identities and student experience as a complex, dynamic, and internally diverse social construct, and Carlota Guzman (2007) used narratives to understand the working lives of university students. Important collections of this research were edited by Guzmán and Saucedo (2007) and Piña and Pontón (2002).

Ethnicity, Indigenous Educational Projects, and New Identities

In Mexican anthropology generally there is a growing interest in ethnicity as a political construct, which has provided theoretical force to research in this line. The work reported here considers the ethnogenetic processes through which the indigenous people have been able to negotiate, resist, and vindicate their claims to educational resources. Studies of ethnogenesis show how indigenous people too reinvent their traditions and reestablish their imagined communities, in order to reconstitute themselves and achieve common advantages in the face of the transformation of their ways of life produced by the global dynamics of modernity, nationalism, industrialization, and migration. Struggling within unequal terms of power, indigenous peoples use emblematic identities strategically to determine ethnic boundaries and to negotiate cultural policies and resources in their relationship with the state. In this sense, ethnicity makes of ethnolinguistic difference a reference for political action in struggles for the recognition of indigenous rights (de la Peña 2002, 2006).

Many Mexican anthropologists have given theoretical-methodological guidelines and inspired or advised several graduate dissertations on ethnicity, *indigenista* policy and Indian education. Maria Eugenia Vargas (1994) documented, in the Tarasco/P'urhépecha case, the contradictory results of training programs for bilingual teachers, their contribution to ethnic consciousness and to identification as bilingual intellectuals of their native communities. María Bertely (2005, 2006a), who studied with Guillermo de la Peña, analyzed ethnogenetic processes surrounding the social history of schooling among Zapotecs of Yalalag, Oaxaca, and their descendants in Mexico City, documenting the ethnic uses of Spanish and school knowledge from different social positions. Gunther Dietz (1999) conceptualized the P'urhépecha social movement as an emerging social actor that reconstitutes itself through mythological temporalizations and uses its symbolic resources to confront the modern liberal state and its educational policies.

Dissertations and recent publications in dialogue with this work approach various expressions of ethnicity in and around educational spaces and policies. Benjamín Maldonado (2002, 2011) focused on ethnic resistance and educational projects generated by ethnopolitical organization in Oaxaca. Erika González A. (2008) analyzed the landscape of intercultural education in the Mixe region of Oaxaca as a political arena and documented the roles of lobbying and political intermediation of the Mixe professionals in ethnic appropriations of intercultural postsecondary education. The practice and intermediation of bilingual teachers, professionals, and native intellectuals, situated between the state and indigenous schools, communities, and organizations, has been further documented in books on Mayo (P. Medina 2008), Mixtec (Ramos 1996), Tzotzil (Pérez P. 2003) and Zapotec communities (Jiménez N. 2009), and in master's theses in anthropology on Choles (Rosalba Pérez V.), Mazahuas (Sergio Pérez S.), Mixtec and Otomí peoples (Mutsuo Nakamura), Nahuas (Stefano Sartorello, Nelson Antequera), P'urhépechas (Elizabeth Martínez B., Jerny González, Jaime González), Tzotziles (Gloria Benavides), and Yaquis (Enriqueta Lerma).

Educational experiences designed "from below" as alternatives to official educational policies, with participation of indigenous intellectuals, have been studied among Huicholes by Angélica Rojas, Mixes by González A. (2004), as well as in the multiethnic Mountain region of Guerrero by Norma Angélica López. Masters' theses by Kathia Núñez (forthcoming), Raúl Gutiérrez (forthcoming), and Alicia Guerrero, and the doctoral dissertation by Bruno Baronnet (2008), all based on fieldwork in the autonomous Zapatista communities and schools in Chiapas, have addressed continuity between family and school socialization, the confluence of indigenous languages, and the alternative educational practices of native teachers.

Some researchers have used emergent perspectives based on the sociocultural application of communal learning, conceptualized as educational experiences structuring new identities. María Ana Portal (1997) has approached different nonschool contexts of socialization and education in relation to popular religiosity and urban identities in a barrio of Mexico City. Her student, Rossana Podestá (2007) used evocative methods to study Nahua children's social representations of territory and their construction of residential identity, communal affiliation, and ethnic consciousness, either inside communities, or—with Nahua descendants in the city—through close contact with their parent's places of origin. She found that although these groups do not express the same social representations of their territories, they do share similar topics and manifest aspects of the same ethnic identity. Communal ethnogenesis has also been studied in urban contexts by Bertely and her students: Claudia Gómez's dissertation on family histories as pedagogical resources, Liliana Amaro's study on children's play activities as an educational process, and Leonor Pastrana's dissertation (2007) on popular Catholicism and patron saint festivities in Mexico City barrios, practices consolidating identities of "urban peoples."

Finally, the multidisciplinary field of intercultural education and indigenous rights shows emergent anthropological influence. A political-academic debate emerges between positions that depart from essentialism and propose a transversal "interculturalization" of public schools (Dietz 2003) and those that defend a strategic essentialism in the face of power relations, and note the political and ethical relevance of using "distinctive cultural types" to inspire indigenous educational projects (Bertely 2008a). Under this approach, the systematization of educational experiences with Chiapas Maya teachers (Bertely 2007, 2008b) explored sociocultural knowledge implicit in communal practices, and articulated it with school knowledge and indigenous rights literacy (Bertely and UNEM 2007).

Indigenous Migration and Urban Schools

This emerging line addresses the deterritorialization of ethnic bound-aries at national and transnational levels and the reinvention of imag-ined communities and re-creation of links with territories of origin, in strongly asymmetric contexts. Dynamic concepts of "community" explain the cultural transformations, appropriations, negotiations, and resignifications that occur in educational spaces. This line has been sup-ported notably by Guillermo de la Peña and Regina Martínez Casas.

Using interpretative anthropology, semiotics, and sociolinguistics, Martínez Casas (2007) analyzed the strategies and mechanisms used by Otomí migrants in Guadalajara City to resignify their culture and negotiate cultural meanings, positing that their holistic model contrasts with the individualized model dominant in urban culture. Her students worked in the same context: Angélica Rojas (2010) studied the spatial and mathematical knowledge that migrant Otomí children use and ne-gotiate, at home, at school, and while selling and buying, and Ivette Flores found significant differences in literacy expectations in children of ethnic origin in comparison with nonindigenous children. The pres-ence of indigenous children in urban schools has been documented by Nicanor Rebolledo (2007a, 2007b) and by Gabriela Czarny, who noted the relative "invisibility" of indigenous children in Mexico City. Grow-ing interest in indigenous migration is also seen in several theses ad-dressing "migrant knowledge" and "migrant worker knowledge" in communities (M. Angel Escalante), interethnic relations in urban schools (Elizabeth Martínez B., Adriana Robles), and school-commu-nity relations in contexts of transnational migration (Alfonso Cruz).

The Historical Dimension of Educational Processes

Although not a thematic line, we highlight as an important aspect of Mexican anthropology of education the attention to the temporal di-mension, which reflects the close relationship between anthropology and history in academic institutions.[5] The search for explanations has led to significant calls to historicize anthropology of education (Rock-well 1999, 2009, 2011). In fact, analyses of the social construction of schooling and the fragmentary implementation of reforms in the past have yielded important insights that explain current confrontations be-tween educational policies and school realities.

Several important collections, for example, on indigenous educa-tion (Bertely 2006b) and on women teachers (Galván and López 2008) include both ethnographic and historical chapters. Additionally, many studies mentioned above include this historical dimension. For example, Bertely (2005, 2006a) traced a century of schooling (from 1885 to 1950) in Yalalag through documentary and epistolary files and family history, as an important antecedent to the cultural processes developed by native factions and their descendants in Mexico City. Street (2008) reconstructs transformations in the discourse and practice of teacher union leaders and movements that she has studied over the past thirty years, as the "educator" state becomes an "evaluator" state. Oresta López (2010) has integrated oral history and ethnographic approaches in the study of women and indigenous teachers and directed numerous theses in this direction.

The historical dimension is deemed crucial for understanding present-day configurations. Rockwell's research on Tlaxcala (1996) shows how indigenous populations have drawn on their own histories to transform or resist the government's educational policies. She shows how contemporary cultures of schooling reflect and refract successive educational reforms and practices (2000, 2007). As others, she reminds us that the phenomenon of formal schooling must be historicized, particularly in contrast with indigenous ways of learning (Rockwell and Gomes 2009). Finally, anthropological theory on power and ethnicity, particularly as developed at El Colegio de Michoacán by Andrew Roth (Roth, Martínez Buenabad, and Sosa Lázaro 2004) informs historical studies done by anthropologists, including his student Ávila Meléndez's (2011) ethnographic study of two private colleges, and the research of his colleague Marco Calderón (2002) on indigenous education in the postrevolutionary context. These studies, among others, help us understand the unfinished process of state formation and consequences of neoliberal policies and their relation to Mexican education.

Theoretical Debates and Tensions Present in the Research

We conclude by considering four interrelated concepts that reveal some of the tensions and concerns present in the field: culture, power, identity, and indigenous rights.

First, we suggest there is an emerging consensus around a processual and relational concept of culture, conceived as a complex social configuration situated within historical processes. This conception is present—at times only implicitly—in the analysis of the practices (or praxis) of both traditional and emergent educational actors. The social interaction, discourse, social representation, experience, and subjectivity of these actors become relevant heuristic categories in the effort to explain the diversity of cultural configurations present in classrooms and schools, but also in families, barrios, communities, and contexts of migration.

A second theoretical concern appears with making explicit the relationship between culture and power that frames social action. Often conceived as control of material and symbolic resources, the exercise of power is documented in interactions between local actors and educational authorities. Appropriation of cultural resources, as shown in several studies, occurs in both directions, and signals both the agency of collective social actors and the simultaneously enabling and constraining nature of culture (Rockwell 1996). By approaching culture as mediated by power, immersed in the construction of hegemony, educational realities are analyzed as conflictive processes of negotiation of the social order. This poses the problem of both describing social interactions in these terms and accounting for the structural and macrosocial dimensions that circumscribe them.

The anthropological study of local cultures—school, youth, written and oral, migrant, ethnic, communal—reveals a diverse, complex, and asymmetric landscape that is expressed at the local, regional, national, and supranational scales (Dietz 2003). Within this array, studies in Mexico have approached cultural diversity as a product of the permanent border crossing of cultural and identity boundaries, generally leaving behind essentialist categories of identity. Specific processes, however, can be differentiated through the analysis of asymmetrical relationships. In relation to ethnicity, for example, Bertely (2005) establishes a distinction between the ethnogenetic processes that characterize historically strategic relationships of indigenous populations with public education, linking it with long-term political struggles for indigenous rights, and other emergent political identities (youth cultures, urban, feminist, or migrant identities) constituted strategically through the appropriation of cultural resources within and beyond schooling.

The emphasis of much recent research on the analysis of culture, power, identity, and indigenous rights responds to the economic, political, and educational changes of the past two decades on the national scene, and to the challenge of international trends towards the diversification, fragmentation, and privatization of public education. In light of this reality, Mexican scholars express a renewed concern with the need to defend a public education of quality for all. The call is put forth to honor the historical debts of public education in Mexico, by responding equally and specifically to the needs that derive from diversified contexts, actors, and realities. We hope to have contributed to this task by offering an account of the current directions and issues of anthropological research on education.

Notes

1. A slightly different version of this text will be published in Spanish, in *Inventario Antropológico* 10, 2010. Previous reviews include Bertely and Corenstein 1998, Rockwell 1998, Bertely and González A. 2003, Podestá and Martínez B. 2003, Robles and Czarny 2003, and Rueda 2007.

2. Mexican scholars and students have done work, for example, on Mexican immigrants in the United States, indigenous schools in Brazil, and immigrants in schools in Spain and France. Latin Americans working or studying at Mexican institutions have done studies in their home countries (Peru, Guatemala, Argentina, Brazil, Colombia). Anthropologists from the United States and Europe, and Mexican students doing dissertations abroad, too numerous to name, have also studied educational processes in Mexico.

3. We include master's theses based on original field research.

4. References include only a selection of publications and unpublished doctoral dissertations of the past fifteen years, although in the text we also name graduate students who produced significant studies in each line but have not published. A full list will be available on the website for this volume. We thank María Elena Maruri and our graduate students for helping us locate and review the material.

5. In Mexico, anthropology as a discipline is strongly linked with the study of history, through the National Institute of Anthropology and History, and its higher education institution, the National School of Anthropology and History.

Bibliography

Ávila Meléndez, Luis Arturo. 2011. *Educación superior privada durante la reforma neoliberal en dos regiones de Michoacán.* Mexico City: Instituto Politécnico Nacional.

Baronnet, Bruno. 2008. "Rebel Youth and Zapatista Autonomous Education." In *Latin American Perspectives* 35, no. 4: 112–124.

Bertely, María. 2000. *Conociendo nuestras escuelas.* Mexico: Paidós.

———. 2005. "¿Apropiación escolar o etnogénesis?" In *Memoria, conocimiento y utopía,* ed. Oresta López. Mexico: Pomares.

———. 2006a. "Configuraciones y reconfiguraciones étnicas en Zapotecos migrantes." In *Historia, saberes indígenas y nuevas etnicidades en la escuela,* ed. María Bertely. Mexico City: Centro de Investigaciones y Estudios Superiores en Antropología Social (CIESAS).

———, ed. 2006b. *Historia, saberes indígenas y nuevas etnicidades en la escuela.* Mexico City: CIESAS.

————. 2007. *Conflicto intercultural, educación y democracia activa en México.* Mexico City: CIESAS.

————. 2008a. "Educación intercultural para la ciudadanía y la democracia activa y solidaria." In *Multiculturalismo, educación intercultural y derechos indígenas en las Américas,* ed. Gunther Dietz, Rosa Guadalupe Mendoza Zuany, and Sergio Téllez Galván. Quito: Abya-Yala.

————. 2008b. "Droits indigènes et citoyenneté interculturelle. Résultats d'un projet réalisé avec des éducateurs tsotsiles, tseltales y ch'oles du Chiapas, Mexique." In *Égalités/inégalité(s) dans les Amériques,* ed. Christine Zumello and Polymnia Zagefta. Paris: Institut des hautes études de l'Amérique latine.

Bertely, María, and Marta Corenstein. 1998. "An Overview of Ethnographic Research in Mexico." In *Educational Qualitative Research in Latin America,* ed. Gary L. Anderson and Martha Montero-Sieburth. New York: Garland.

Bertely, María, and Erika González. 2003. "Etnicidad y escuela." In *Educación, derechos sociales y equidad,* vol. 1, ed. María Bertely. Mexico City: Consejo Mexicano de Investigación Educativa (COMIE).

Bertely, María, and UNEM. 2007. *Los hombres y las mujeres del maíz.* Mexico City: CIESAS.

Calderón, Marco Antonio. 2002. "Ciudadanos e indígenas en el Estado populista." In *Ciudadanía, cultura política y reforma del Estado en América Latina,* eds. Marco Antonio Calderón Mólgora, Willem Assies, Ton Salman. Zamora: El Colegio de Michoacán.

Calvo, Beatriz, Margarita Zorrilla, Guillermo Tapia, and Silvia Conde. 2002. *La supervisión escolar de la educación primaria en México: prácticas, desafíos y reformas.* Paris: UNESCO.

Calvo, Beatriz, Gabriela Delgado, and Mario Rueda, eds. 1998. *Nuevos paradigmas, compromisos renovados.* Ciudad Juárez: Universidad Autónoma de Ciudad Juárez (UACJ).

Candela, Antonia. 1999. *La ciencia en el aula.* Mexico City: Paidós.

————. 2005. "Local Power Construction in a School of Socially Disadvantaged Students." In *Language, Literacy and Power in Schooling,* ed. Teresa McCarty. Mahwah, NJ: Lawrence Erlbaum.

————. 2010. "Time and Space: Undergraduate Mexican Physics in Motion." *Cultural Studies of Science Education* 5, no. 3: 701–27.

Czarny, Gabriela. 2008. *Pasar por la escuela.* Mexico City: Universidad Pedagógica Nacional (UPN).

de Garay, Adrian. 2004. *Integración de los jóvenes en el sistema universitario.* Mexico City: Pomares.

de la Peña, Guillermo. 2002. "Social Citizenship, Ethnic Minority Demands, Human Rights and Neoliberal Paradoxes: A Case Study in Western Mexico." In *Multiculturalism in Latin America,* ed. Rachel Sieder. New York: Palgrave.

————. 2006. "Contesting Citizenship in Latin America: The Rise of Indigenous Movements and the Postliberal Challenge." *Nations and Nationalism* 12, no. 3: 542–44.

de la Riva, María and Antonia Candela. 2010. "El tiempo en clases de ciencias: Tránsito de primaria a secundaria." *CPU-e. Revista de Investigación Educativa* 11.

de León Pasquel, Lourdes. 2005. *La llegada del alma. Lenguaje, infancia y socialización entre los Mayas de Zinacantán.* Mexico City: Instituto Nacional de Antropología e Historia (INAH), CIESAS.

Díaz Pontones, Mónica. 1998. "Estrategias de enseñanza en la escuela secundaria." In *Nuevos paradigmas, compromisos renovados,* ed. Beatriz Calvo P., Gabriela Delgado Ballesteros, and Mario Rueda Beltrán. Ciudad Juárez: UACJ.

Díaz Tepepa, María Guadalupe. 2001. *Técnica y tradición.* Mexico City: Plaza y Valdés.

Dietz, Gunther. 1999. *La comunidad P'urhépecha es nuestra fuerza.* Quito: Abya-Yala.

———. 2003. *Multiculturalismo, interculturalidad y educación.* Mexico City: CIESAS.

Escalante, Paloma. 2006. "Fantasía, realidad y color. Construcción de la identidad entre los niños del sur del Estado de Quintana Roo." In *Itinerarios: cultura, memoria e identidades,* ed. José Luis González and Franco Savarino. Mexico City: INAH.

Espinosa, Epifanio, and Ruth Mercado. 2007. "Mediación social y apropiación de nuevas propuestas pedagógicas." *Revista Latinoamericana de Estudios Educativos* 37, no. 3–4.

Estrada, Pedro, and Ruth Mercado. 2008. "Procesos de negociación de significado en una escuela normal mexicana." *Psicología & Sociedade* 20, no. 3: 391–401.

Ezpeleta, Justa. 2004. "Innovaciones educativas. Reflexiones sobre los contextos en su implementación." *Revista Mexicana de Investigación Educativa* 9, no. 21: 403–24.

Ezpeleta, Justa, and Eduardo Weiss. 2000. *Cambiar la Escuela Rural.* Mexico City: Departamento de Investigación Educativa (DIE-Cinvestav).

Falconi, Octavio. 2003. "La construcción de un espacio público entre estudiantes del CCH-Sur." *Nueva Antropología* 62: 55–75.

Fierro Evans, Cecilia. 2005. "El problema de la indisciplina desde la perspectiva de la gestión directiva en escuelas públicas del nivel básico." *Revista Mexicana de Investigación Educativa* 10, no. 27: 1133–48.

Flores Farfán, José Antonio. 2001. "Culture and Language Revitalization, Maintenance and Development in Mexico." *International Journal of the Sociology of Language* 152: 185–97.

———. 2005. "Towards an Intercultural Dialogue In and Around the School in Mexico." In *Dialogues In and Around Multicultural Schools,* ed. Wolfgang Herrlitz and Robert Maier. Tübingen: Max Niemeyer Verlag.

Galeana Cisneros, Rosaura. 1997. *La infancia desertora.* Mexico City: Fundación SNTE para la Cultura del Maestro Mexicano.

Galván, Luz Elena, and Oresta López, eds. 2008. *Entre imaginarios y utopías.* Mexico City: CIESAS.

García Rivera, Fernando. 2007. "Coexistencia de prácticas socio-culturales en una localidad andina del Perú." *Signos lingüísticos* 5: 119–37.

González Apodaca, Erica. 2004. *Significados escolares en un bachillerato Mixe.* Mexico City: Coordinación General de Educación Intercultural Bilingüe, Secretaría de Educación Pública (CGEIB, SEP).

————. 2008. *Los profesionistas indios en la educación intercultural. Etnicidad, intermediación y escuela en territorio Mixe.* Mexico City: Juan Pablos.

Guerra, Irene, and Elsa Guerrero. 2004. *¿Qué sentido tiene el bachillerato? Una visión desde los jóvenes.* Mexico City: UPN.

Guerrero, Irán, and Judith Kalman. 2010. "La inserción de la tecnología en el aula: estabilidad y procesos instituyentes en la práctica docente." *Revista Brasileira de Educação* 15, no. 44: 213–229.

Gutiérrez Narváez, Raúl. Forthcoming. "Dos proyectos de sociedad en Los Altos de Chiapas: escuelas secundarias oficial y autónoma entre los tsotsiles de San Andrés." In *Luchas 'muy otras', zapatismo y autonomía en la comunidades indígenas de Chiapas,* ed. Bruno Baronnet, Mariana Mora, and Richard Stahler-Sholk. México City: CIESAS.

Gutiérrez, Edgar, and Rafael Quiróz. 2007. "Usos y formas de apropiación del video en la secundaria." *Revista Mexicana de Investigación Educativa* 12, no. 32: 338–57.

Guzmán, Carlota. 2007. "Experiencia e identidad de los estudiantes de nivel superior que trabajan." In *La voz de los estudiantes,* ed. Carlos Guzmán Gómez and Claudia Saucedo Ramos. Mexico: Pomares.

Guzmán, Carlota, and Claudia Saucedo, eds. 2007. *La voz de los estudiantes.* Mexico City: Pomares.

Hamel, Enrique. 2002. "Indigenous Literacy Teaching in Public Primary Schools." In *One Voice, Many Voices: Recreating Indigenous Language Communities,* ed. Teresa L. McCarty, Ofelia Zepeda, and Victor H. Begay. Tucson: Arizona Press.

————. 2008. "Bilingual Education for Indigenous Communities in Mexico." In *Encyclopedia of Language and Education,* vol. 5, ed. James Cummins and Nancy Hornberger. New York: Springer.

Hernández González, Joaquín. 2006. "Construir una identidad: vida juvenil y estudio en el CCH Sur." *Revista Mexicana de Investigación Educativa* 11 no. 29: 459–481.

Jiménez Lozano, Luz. 2003. "La reestructuración de la escuela y las nuevas regulaciones del trabajo docente." *Revista Mexicana de Investigación Educativa.* 8. no. 19: 603–30.

Jiménez Naranjo, Yolanda. 2009. *Cultura comunitaria y escuela intercultural.* Mexico City: CGEIB-SEP.

Kalman, Judith. 1999. *Writing on the Plaza.* Cresskill, NJ: Hampton Press.

————. 2004. *Saber lo que es la letra.* Mexico City: UNESCO, Secretaría de Educación Pública (SEP).

López, Oresta. 1997. "Las mujeres y la conquista de espacios en el sistema educativo." *Revista Latinoamericana de Estudios Educativos* 27, no. 3: 73–93.

————. 2010. *Que nuestras vidas hablen: historias de vida de maestras y maestros indígenas tenek y nahuas de San Luis Potosí.* San Luis Potosí: El Colegio de San Luis.

López Espinoza, Susana, and Eduardo Weiss. 2007. "Una mirada diferente a las prácticas: un taller de electrónica en el Conalep." *Revista Mexicana de Investigación Educativa* 12, no. 35: 1329–56.

Maldonado, Benjamín. 2002. *Los indios en las aulas.* Mexico City: INAH.

————. 2011. *Comunidad, Comunalidad y Colonialismo en Oaxaca*. Oaxaca: Colegio Superior para la Educación Indígena Intercultural de Oaxaca.

Martínez Casas, Regina. 2007. *Vivir invisibles*. Mexico City: CIESAS.

Medina Melgarejo, Patricia. 2000. *¿Eres maestro normalista y/o profesor universitario?* Mexico City: Plaza y Valdés.

————. 2008. *Identidad y conocimiento*. Mexico City: Plaza y Valdés.

Mena, Patricia, Héctor Muñoz, and Arturo Ruiz. 1999. *Identidad, lenguaje y enseñanza en escuelas indígenas bilingües de Oaxaca*. Oaxaca: UPN Oaxaca.

Mercado, Ruth. 1997. *Formar para la docencia en la educación normal*. Mexico City: SEP.

————. 2002. *Los saberes docentes como construcción social*. Mexico City: Fondo de Cultura Económica.

Muñoz, Héctor, and Pedro Lewin, eds. 1996. *Significados de la diversidad lingüística y cultural*. Mexico City: Universidad Autónoma Metropolitana Iztapalapa (UAMI), INAH Oaxaca.

Naranjo, Gabriela, and Antonia Candela. 2006. "Ciencias naturales en un grupo con un alumno ciego: los saberes docentes en acción." *Revista Mexicana de Investigación Educativa* 11, no. 30: 821–45.

Nava, Refugio. 2008. "Amo polihuiz in totlahtol, No se perderá nuestra lengua: Ideologías, prácticas y retención del náhuatl en San Isidro Buensuceso, Tlaxcala." PhD diss., CIESAS.

Núñez Patiño, Kathia. Forthcoming. "De la casa a la escuela zapatista: prácticas de aprendizaje en la región ch'ol." In *Luchas 'muy otras', zapatismo y autonomía en la comunidades indígenas de Chiapas*, ed. Bruno Baronnet, Mariana Mora, and Richard Stahler-Sholk. México City: CIESAS.

Ornelas Tavares, Gloria. 2007. *Narraciones míticas y procesos rituales en la escuela y su entorno*. Mexico City: UPN.

Ortega, Florencia. 2006. "Comunidades y trayectorias de lectura en la biblioteca pública." *Revista Mexicana de Investigación Educativa* 11, no. 28: 293–315.

Paradise, Ruth. 1996. "Passivity or Tacit Collaboration: Mazahua Interaction in Cultural Context." *Learning and Instruction* 6, no. 4: 379–89.

————. 1998. "What's Different About Learning in School as Compared to Family and Community Settings?" *Human Development* 41: 270–78.

————. 2002. "Finding Ways to Study Culture in Context." *Human Development* 45: 229–36.

Paradise, Ruth, and Mariette de Haan. 2009. "Responsibility and Reciprocity." *Anthropology and Education Quarterly* 42, no. 2: 187–204.

Paradise, Ruth, and Barbara Rogoff. 2009. "Side by Side: Learning by Observing and Pitching *Ethos* 37, no. 1: 102–38.

Pastrana, Leonor. 2007. "Hacer pueblo en el contexto industrial metropolitano: 1938–2006. Un estudio en Santa Clara Coatitlan, Ecatepec de Morelos en el Estado de México." PhD diss., CIESAS.

Pérez Campos, Gilberto. 2005. "La complejidad de los marcos de interacción en 'educación de padres.'" *Avances en Psicología Latinoamericana* 23, no. 1: 177–92.

Pérez Pérez, Elías. 2003. *La crisis de la educación indígena en el área tzotzil*. Mexico City: UPN.

Pérez Expósito, Leonel. 2010. "¿Estudiar para emigrar o estudiar para transformar?" *Argumentos* 62, 131–156.

Pérez Ruiz, Maya Lorena, ed. 2008a. *Jóvenes indígenas y globalización en América Latina*. Mexico City: INAH.

———. 2008b. "Diversidad, identidad y globalización. Los jóvenes indígenas en la Ciudad de México." In *Jóvenes indígenas y globalización en América Latina*, ed. Maya Lorena Pérez Ruiz. Mexico City: INAH.

Piña, Juan Manuel. 2003. *Representaciones, imaginarios e identidad*. Mexico City: Plaza y Valdés.

Piña, Juan Manuel, and Beatriz Pontón. 2002. *Cultura y procesos educativos*. Mexico City: Plaza y Valdés.

Podestá, Rossana. 2000. *Funciones de la escuela en la cultura oral Nahuatlaca*. Mexico City: SEP.

———. 2006. "La Escuela y sus mundos interculturales. Hacia una propuesta metodológica de autoría infantil." In *Historias, saberes indígenas y nuevas etnicidades en la escuela*, ed. María Bertely. Mexico City: CIESAS.

———. 2007. *Encuentro de miradas. El territorio visto por diversos autores*. Mexico City: CGEIB, SEP.

Podestá, Rossana, and Elizabeth Martínez Buenabad. 2003. "Sociolingüística educativa." In *Educación, derechos sociales y equidad*, ed. María Bertely. Mexico City: COMIE.

Portal, María Ana. 1997. *Ciudadanos desde el pueblo. Identidad urbana y religiosidad popular en San Andrés Totoltepec, Tlalpan*. Mexico City: UAMI.

Quiroz, Rafael. 2000. "Las prácticas de enseñanza como condición de posibilidad del aprendizaje de los estudiantes de secundaria." In *La Investigación Educativa y el Conocimiento sobre los Alumnos*, ed. Juan Eliézer de los Santos. Mexico City: COMIE.

———. 2003. "Telesecundaria: los estudiantes y los sentidos que atribuyen a algunos elementos del modelo pedagógico." *Revista Mexicana de Investigación Educativa* 8, no. 17: 221–43.

Ramos Ramírez, José Luis. 1996. *Educación y etnicidad*. Mexico City: Escuela Nacional de Antropología e Historia (ENAH).

Ramos Ramírez, José Luis, and Janeth Martínez, eds. 2000. *Diversas miradas sobre el juego*. Mexico City: ENAH.

Rebolledo, Nicanor. 2007a. *Escolarización interrumpida*. Mexico City: UPN.

———. 2007b. "Learning with Differences." In *Can School Be Agents for Indigenous Languages Revitalization? Policy and Practice*, ed. Nancy Hornberger. London: Palgrave.

Reguillo, Rossana. 2000. *Emergencia de culturas juveniles*. Buenos Aires: Norma.

Remedi, Eduardo. 2008. *Detrás del murmullo*. Mexico City: Juan Pablos.

Robles, Adriana, and Gabriela Czarny. 2003. "Procesos socioculturales en interacciones educativas." In *Educación, derechos sociales y equidad*, vol. 1, ed. María Bertely. Mexico City: COMIE.

Rockwell, Elsie. 1996. "Keys to Appropriation: Rural Schooling in Mexico." In *The Cultural Production of the Educated Person*, ed. Bradley Levinson, Douglas Foley, and Dorothy Holland. Albany: SUNY Press.

————. 1998. "Ethnography and the Commitment to Public Schooling: A Review of Research at DIE." In *Educational Qualitative Research in Latin America,* ed. Gary L. Anderson and Martha Montero-Sieburth. New York: Garland Press.

————. 1999. "Recovering History in the Study of Schooling." *Human Development* 42, no. 3: 113–28.

————. 2000. "Teaching Genres: A Bakhtinian Approach." *Anthropology and Education Quarterly* 31, no. 3: 260–82.

————. 2001. "The Uses of Orality and Literacy in Rural Mexico." In *The Making of Literate Societies,* ed. David R. Olson and Nancy Torrance. Oxford: Blackwell.

————. 2006. "La lecture en tant que pratique culturelle: concepts pour l'étude des livres scolaires." *Education et Sociétés* 17: 29–48.

————. 2007. "Huellas del pasado en las culturas escolares." *Revista de Antropología Social* 16: 175–212.

————. 2009. *La experiencia etnográfica.* Buenos Aires: Paidós.

————. 2010. "L'appropriation de l'écriture dans deux villages Nahua du centre du Mexique." *Langage et Société* 134: 83-99.

————. 2011. "Recovering History in the Anthropology of Schooling." In *A Companion to the Anthropology of Education,* ed. Bradley Levinson and Mica Pollock. New York: Wiley-Blackwell.

Rockwell, Elsie, and Ana Gomes. 2009. "Rethinking Indigenous Education from a Latin American Perspective." *Anthropology and Education Quarterly* 42, no. 2: 97–109.

Rojas, Angélica. 2010. "Diferentes significados del trabajo de los niños otomíes en Guadalajara." In *Etnicidades urbanas en las Américas. Procesos de inserción, discriminación y políticas multiculturalistas,* ed. Séverine Durín. Mexico: CIESAS.

Rojas Drummond, Sylvia. 2000. "Guided Participation, Discourse and the Construction of Knowledge in Mexican Classrooms." In *Social Interaction in Learning and Instruction,* ed. Helen Cowie and Geerdina Van der Aalsvoort. Exeter: Pergamon Press.

Roth Seneff, Andrew, Elizabeth Martínez Buenabad, and Manuel Sosa Lázaro. 2004. "A nombre de la comunidad: política étnica y reforma neoliberal en la Meseta P'urhépecha." In *Recursos contenciosos,* ed. Andrew Roth Seneff. Zamora: El Colegio de Michoacán.

Rueda, Mario. 2007. "La Investigación etnográfica y/o cualitativa y la enseñanza en la universidad." *Revista Mexicana de Investigación Educativa* 12, no. 34: 1021–41.

Sagástegui, Diana. 2006. "Tecnologías del conocimiento y educación en las sociedades contemporáneas." In *Tendencias de la educación superior en México,* ed. María Alicia Peredo Merlo, Lucía Mantilla, and Patricia García Guevara. Guadalajara: Universidad de Guadalajara.

Sandoval, Etelvina. 2000. *La trama de la escuela secundaria.* Mexico City: Plaza y Valdés.

Saucedo, Claudia Lucy. 2003. "Family Support for Individual Effort." *Ethos* 31, no. 2: 307–27.

Street, Susan. 1996. "Democratization 'From Below' and Popular Culture." *Studies in Latin American Popular Culture* 15: 261–78.

————. 2000. "Trabajo docente y poder de base en el sindicalismo democrático magisterial en México." In *A ciudadania negada: políticas de exclusão na educação e no trabalho*, ed. Pablo Gentili and Gaudêncio Frigotto. Buenos Aires: CLACSO.

————. 2001. "When Politics Becomes Pedagogy: Oppositional Discourse as Policy in Mexican Teachers' Struggles for Union Democracy." In *Policy as Practice*, ed. Margaret Sutton and Bradley Levinson. Westport, CT: Ablex.

————. 2008. "El género como categoría para repensar al sujeto popular: dos generaciones en el activismo femenino del magisterio democrático mexicano." In *Entre imaginarios y utopías*, ed. Luz Elena Galván and Oresta López. Mexico City: CIESAS.

Taboada, Eva. 1998. "Construcciones imaginarias: ritual cívico e identidad nacional." In *Identidad en el imaginario nacional*, ed. Javier Pérez Siller and Verena Radkau. Puebla: Benemérita Universidad Autónoma de Puebla (BUAP).

Urteaga, Maritza. 2000. "Formas de agregación juvenil." In *Jóvenes: una evaluación del conocimiento*, ed. J. A. Pérez Islas. México City, Instituto Mexicano de la Juventud.

————. 2008. "Jóvenes e indios en el México contemporáneo." *Revista Latinoamericana de Ciencias Sociales, Niñez y Juventud* 6, no. 2: 667–708.

Valle, Imuris, and Eduardo Weiss. 2010. "Participation in the Figured World of Graffiti." *Teaching and Teacher Education* 26, no. 1: 128–35.

Vargas, María Eugenia. 1994. *Educación e ideología. Constitución de una categoría de intermediarios en la comunicación interétnica*. Mexico City: CIESAS.

Villanueva, Nancy. 2000. "Cultura, identidad de género y procesos de simbolización en los juegos infantiles." *Temas Antropológicos* 22, no. 1: 25–53.

Vistrain, Alicia. 2009. "Apertura del tercer espacio en las situaciones de enseñanza dentro del salón de clases." *CPU-e Revista de Investigación Educativa* 8.

Weiss, Eduardo, Irene Guerra Ramírez, Elsa Guerrero Salinas, Joaquín González Hernández, Olga Grijalva Martínez, and Job Ávalos Romero. 2008. "Young People and High School in Mexico: Subjectivisation, Others and Reflexivity." *Ethnography and Education* 3, no. 1: 17–31.

§ 4

ANTHROPOLOGY AND EDUCATION IN THE ARGENTINE CONTEXT
Research Experiences in Buenos Aires

María Rosa Neufeld

Introduction

In academic circles, it is frequently and sharply said that anthropologists are used to making statements about what happens in very large areas—countries, cultures—based on the community or village they got to know during their fieldwork. Therefore, I would like to remark, from the very beginning, that this article by no means intends to embrace the large group of researchers who deal with educational issues from an ethnographic approach in Argentina.

With a much more modest scope and taking the questions around which this book was organized as a starting point, I have tried to reflect on the particular ways in which anthropology and education are being developed in our *Programa de Antropología y Educación.*[1]

This chapter also provides the opportunity to discuss how studies in anthropology and education as a research field first saw the light in Argentina and how they were organized, permitting me to systematize the main problems that our closest fellow researchers deal with, as well as to reflect upon a number of issues concerning the context and possibilities for the development of social research in Argentina in the changing political contexts of the past twenty-five years. These questions will situate our research in the context of Argentine anthropology.

Twenty-five years ago in Argentina just a few researchers (anthropologists or education experts, alone or in small groups) focused on the study of educational issues from a point of view we might call "ethnographic." The final moments of the last military government (1976–1983) and its effects on all institutions confronted us with a number of problems to be approached on every educational level. One of these research groups was the one developed at the Facultad de Filosofía y Letras de la Universidad de Buenos Aires (UBA). In this essay I will try to outline the evolution of this group into the Anthropology and Education Program, which Graciela Batallán and I created twenty years ago. Researchers from different disciplines such as anthropology, psychology, educational sciences, and sociology are part of this program. My comments try mainly to reflect this interdisciplinary collective work. I must point out from the very beginning that educational issues have interested researchers throughout Argentina. It is only due to the limits of our knowledge and a lack of space that this essay focuses on our most immediate experience, although it will comment on other researchers whenever possible.

Anthropology and Anthropologists in Argentina: A Brief History

Anthropology developed in Argentina at the same time as anthropological teaching consolidated in the major European and North American culture centers. In Argentina, early research and teaching of anthropology took place in the La Plata Museum and in the Ethnographic Museum of the University of Buenos Aires, the latter created in 1904. The researchers who worked there included some anthropologists from abroad, from France, Italy, and Germany. In 1958 the "Licenciatura en Ciencias Antropológicas" (that is, the first diploma on anthropological sciences) from Universidad de Buenos Aires was finally established. In the old days local anthropology did not follow the mainstream trends of the discipline: atypically, the most important teachers and researchers defined themselves as members of the historical-cultural school or Vienna School. "Social anthropology" or "cultural anthropology"—in fact the ruling trends in anthropology in a great part of the Western countries in which anthropology was developing—were for these researchers unattractive products of Anglo-Saxon countries.

However, it was easy for us to follow courses on sociology at the same Faculty, which allowed us to be in touch with mainstream Anglo-Saxon and French anthropology and to be part of the informal groups in which we complemented our studies by reading Marx's and Gramsci's works (the latter having been translated into Spanish in Argentina at the end of the 1960s). These multiple approaches to the theories of central anthropologies led us to develop a most critical attitude towards so-called classical anthropology.[2]

Our starting point was, you may say, political: we did not feel obliged to follow the anthropological traditions we studied. What we are used to calling "classical anthropology" had originated alongside the processes of European colonial expansion. However, our refusal to follow the heritage did not mean ignoring the fact that we belonged to an international academic community. Comments below on some aspects of Argentina's history might help throw some light on our perspective.

After Perón's overthrow in 1955, political conditions in Argentina were characterized by only brief periods of elected civil governments (presidents Frondizi and Illia) constantly interrupted by military coups, which created an atmosphere of great instability for the development of social sciences as a whole. Nevertheless, those years witnessed strong growth in social sciences, and it was during this period that the first anthropology courses—all of them in state universities—were created.

In 1966, in an event we remember as the *Noche de los Bastones Largos* (Night of the Long Batons), the armed forces took control of the universities, appointing military deans instead of scholars and forbidding researchers to work or books to be read. Finally, during the last military period (1976–1983), thirty thousand people (*desaparecidos*) were kidnapped and killed, many of them teachers and students. Anthropologists were regarded as particularly dangerous individuals, this perception leading to the dismantling of teaching and research teams in those centers where anthropology had had very interesting developments (in the Universities of Buenos Aires, La Plata, Mar del Plata, Rosario, and Salta). This explains why, after 1984, the restoring of research and teaching of sociocultural anthropology at the University of Buenos Aires, to which I principally refer in this work, had characteristics of a new foundation (Neufeld and Wallace 1998; Neufeld 2006; Morey, Perazzi, and Varela 2008).

Those of us who work in anthropology and education in the UBA share with many other colleagues of our institution some general ideas that are evident in the choice of our subject matters: we believe in the university's commitment to study those problems that appear to us as social priorities (Batallán and Neufeld 2004), some of them related to the effects of former dictatorial governments on schools, others related to the impoverishment of large populations in the last decades, especially by the policies developed under the International Monetary Fund and the World Bank's advice and embraced by the governments of Carlos Menem in the 1990s (Grassi 2003). Thus, we and colleagues at our university often study topics such as power relations, conflicts over inequity and resistance, and movements for social change, as well as gender problems associated with AIDS, educational problems and the demands of popular classes in the neoliberal context, the struggles of native populations for land and social recognition, and the so-called trigger-happy police attitude.

We UBA anthropologists also share other criteria: most of us follow the tradition of anthropological research that proposes long-term research in the field, which includes personal participation of the researcher in local contexts, where the anthropologists confront their own knowledge with the knowledge of the subjects (not objects) with whom they work. In all our fields of study, including anthropology and education, some particular issues arise, such as the fact that researchers must establish relationships with a "subject/object" with whom they already have relationships, because usually Argentine anthropology researchers work in their own society (Neufeld and Thisted 2005; Achilli 2005). Also, we must mention the chronic financing difficulties that have affected researching, often resulting in shorter fieldwork periods.

Anthropology and Education in Argentina

In Argentina, establishment of the field known as anthropology and education has taken place in the universities of Rosario (Achilli 1987), Buenos Aires, and La Plata (García and Alaniz 2000) since the end of the last dictatorship (1976–1983). However, there was an antecedent to this development towards the end of the military government, when anthropologists Elena Achilli and Graciela Batallán participated in the RINCUARE (Red de Investigaciones Cualitativas en Educación, or Network of Qualitative Research on Schools) organized by Elsie Rockwell and Rodrigo Vera (Dirección de Investigaciones Educativas, DIE-CIN-VESTAV, Mexico) and financed by the Canadian International Development Research Centre (Batallán and Neufeld 2004). Although Achilli and Batallán could obviously not work in the context of any local university, they had the opportunity to take part in this group. For a short period, this network published a photocopied magazine, *Dialogando*, which offered Spanish translations of some of the most important texts of the "ethnographic" or qualitative approach to investigation produced up to that moment. In some other cases, as happened to me, we were able to complement the exclusively anthropological training we had received at the university with an updated panorama of socio-educational research in a postgraduate Tutorial Mastership at FLACSO (Facultad Latinoamericana de Ciencias Sociales), which in those final years of the military government had a course in "Education and Society."

After 1984, as a part of the process of beginning anew that I described above, I began to work as a professor and researcher at the Social Anthropology Section of the Anthropological Sciences Institute of the Facultad de Filosofía y Letras (UBA). My first research there took place in a very particular region, the delta of the Paraná River. There it was possible to find families of different origins: Italian, Polish, Spanish, French, and also Argentine-born families *(criollos)* (Neufeld 1988, 1992). They were farmers and fruit harvesters, and their children went to the schools scattered around the islands of the delta. There we had our first opportunity to carry out true ethnographical fieldwork in schools and also in family homes. In those days, John Ogbu's text (1981) and Willis (in Spanish 1983) were very important references.

This long-term ethnographic fieldwork allowed us to question some statements that were hegemonic at the time. We questioned, for example, their assumption of "cultural distance" between teachers and students as an explanation of their failures, and also their conception of teachers as part of a bourgeoisie that, paraphrasing Bourdieu, presumed their right to make an arbitrary selection of knowledge so that schools could supposedly teach universal culture when they were actually favoring those privileged groups.

In the following years, we left behind our initial work in those delta schools, and have constituted, from 1994 to the present, a research team composed of graduates and students. We also included a psychologist (Jens Ariel Thisted), a sociologist (Sara Pallma), and two graduates in educational sciences (Montesinos, Pallma, and Sinisi 1998, 1999). We got to know, directly or in the work within the research team, many schools in Buenos Aires and its outskirts. At the same time, at the beginning of the 1990s, Graciela Batallán joined the UBA with her own lines of research, beginning what was to be a long and fruitful relationship. Her arrival led to the creation of the Anthropology and Education Program.

From those days on, the area of confluence between anthropology and education has been organized around a Program in Anthropology and Education that brings together three projects: "Indigenous Children and Migrants: Identification Processes and Formative Experiences" (directed by Gabriela Novaro and Ana Padawer), "Subjects, Institutions and Policies inside and outside School: A Historical-Ethnographic Study on Education and Everyday Life in Social Inequity Contexts" (directed by María Rosa Neufeld, Liliana Sinisi, and Ariel Thisted) and "Children, Youngsters and Public Space: Agency and Belonging to Communities and the Controversy about the Democratization of Institutions" (directed by Graciela Batallán and Silvana Campanini).

There are some regular national meetings, such as the Argentine Congress on Social Anthropology, the Jornadas Rosarinas de Antropología Sociocultural (Facultad de Humanidades y Artes, Universidad Nacional de Rosario) and the Jornadas de Investigación en Antropología Social (Facultad de Filosofía y Letras, Universidad de Buenos Aires), when researchers meet other colleagues who work mainly in national state universities where this type of research is carried out (Universidad Nacional de La Plata, Universidad Nacional de Córdoba, Universidad Nacional de Rosario). Other Latin American meetings such as RAM (Reunión de Antropología del Mercosur) and ALA (Asociación Latinoamericana de Antropología) allow us to situate our work in the context of Latin-American research. In 2006, we at UBA hosted the 11th Inter-American Symposium on Ethnographic Educational Research, the first of these symposia that took place in South America instead of Central or North America.

Our Theoretical-Methodological Perspective. Fieldwork and Theory: The "Uses Of Diversity" in our Research of the 1990s

During the 1990s, we carried out social research in primary schools regularly, and began to follow some problematic developments that concerned us because, although they had their origin outside schools, we found their echoes inside. For example, one day, the city of Buenos Aires woke up covered with posters fixed on the walls accusing immigrant workers of occupying working places that belonged to Argentine workers, at a moment when the level of unemployment was becoming critical. These xenophobic expressions were not common for us in Argentina: a sort of new vision of the "others" was arising, to which the public statements of the "menemist" officers (of President Carlos Menem, 1989–1999) as well as the mass media contributed heavily. The presence of Korean, Chinese, Bolivian, and Peruvian immigrants was considered a threat. People talked about an "invasion"; the "others" were regarded mainly as foreigners, invaders, illegal immigrants, job usurpers (Montesinos, Pallma, and Sinisi 1998, 1999; Neufeld and Thisted 1999).

At the time we became aware of the continuities but also the gaps that existed between practices and representations about anyone who might be considered "different" in primary and secondary schools, and those practices and representations that prevailed in everyday life, e.g., in the words and attitudes of politicians, the media, ordinary people (Sinisi 1999). Also, we began to ask ourselves about the categories and concepts related to these problems (such as diversity, ethnicity, multiculturalism, discrimination, immigration, integration, and intercultural matters), which meant working on the issues and on the historical and national contexts during which these concepts had arisen.

"Diversity" has been studied traditionally by anthropology. However, diversity as "an issue" was brought up during the 1990s in societies driven by neoliberal ideology. Therefore, when talking about diversity at school, we should take into account that what is *diverse* is different from what is *exotic*. And also that when "diverse" is used as a synonym for "culturally different" or "exotic," we fail to recognize the subalternity relationships that rule the lives of "others" who are different or diverse in our societies.

Let us say that in most cases such contexts refer to unequal relations: the migrant condition, or some connotations linked to places of origin or habits of particular ethnic groups, help build these plural and unequal, subordinated relationships.

We needed theoretical concepts that could go beyond simplistic explanations based on "cultural differences." We also needed to recognize that the same actors who might be "victims" of stigmatizing words and practices might also construct and reconstruct identities dynamically, contesting domination and building self-confidence on the basis of those same stigmatizing expressions (Thisted 2006): for instance, *"paraguas"* and *"bolita"*[3] are stigmatizing names for Paraguayan and Bolivian people respectively, and they are frequently heard in our schoolyards. But at the same time, the Bolivianness or the Paraguayanness of migrants is being constructed precisely from the recovery and resignification of categories that were originally degrading. Processes of reinforcement of collective identities arise from these categories. Those identities are not static at all; they undergo continuous processes of transformation.

Our starting point lies in the socio-anthropological approach as a theoretical and methodological perspective, not just as a "technique" (Rockwell 2009). That is why I point out here that our research advances in these issues were accompanied by a number of theoretical and methodological clarifications of terms.

These clarifications came along through interchange among members of the research team, as well as with the rest of the participants in the Anthropology and Education Program. Another sphere where we have tested theoretical categories and their major or minor importance for research has been in graduate and postgraduate thesis direction. In spite of financing difficulties, one of the socio-anthropological research parameters still considered to be in force in our country is long-term fieldwork (in our case, in schools and neighborhoods), and it is carried out strictly in the case of thesis research. Ethnographic thesis research—led by a group of young anthropologists[4]—has called into question the existing body of knowledge within each area studied.

One of the clarifications of terminology mentioned above has to do with the recognition of the need to approach school problems concerning sociocultural diversity/inequity from different points of analysis. Let me introduce some examples. Teachers have been one of our privileged subjects when working at schools. We have often recognized their expert knowledge,[5] which includes not only traditional and settled ways of approaching historical matters, mathematics teaching, and so on, but also a number of so-called concepts-in-use in everyday life at schools. Some of these are key concepts still central to anthropology, mainly the concept of culture, that are used by teachers as part of their knowledge as "technical experts." The word *culture* is used daily at schools to explain diversity and is continually referred to (Neufeld 2005; Achilli 2006). This concept in use at schools has its origins in the concept of culture coined by anthropologists, referring to "a people's entire lifestyle." Another important aspect of this concept of culture is denial of the biological basis of these human behaviors. In school speech it is important to put forward the legitimacy of all cultures: "We are all equal, although we may come from different cultures. ... We live in the same country."

In this school use of the concept of culture, there is an acceptance that "ways of life" may be different and that they are transmitted "from generation to generation" (Neufeld 1986). In this appropriation of the concept of culture within school contexts, the word is used to explain what happens in the presence of children who are thought to be "different" at school (whether because they are migrants or because they belong to extremely poor contexts).

In Argentine schools these "uses of diversity" (Geertz 1996) had already been ensconced when the educational system was organized at the end of the nineteenth century: at the time, with the arrival of large numbers of European immigrants, "positive discrimination" was common and blond children of pale complexion were judged more intelligent than the children of the native families.

However, between 1990 and 2000, the events related to the historical moment characterized by a combination of neoliberalism and unemployment demonstrated that it was not possible to separate cultural "diversity" from the processes of exclusion and social inequity that obviously affect society as a whole. This led us to work on constructions—abundant at school and in everyday life—by means of which sociocultural differences are simplified and generalized. They are part of a process by which, as "diversity" is perceived, the "others" are stigmatized; they are "made unequal" in an attempt to keep them in subordinating working and living conditions. I am referring here to derogatory characterizations of internal and external migrants, or just the poor, as *cabecitas negras* (dark-skinned heads), *tanos* (Italian migrants), *paraguas* (Paraguayan migrants), *bolitas* (Bolivian migrants), *negros villeros* (dark-skinned shantytown dwellers), and *cartoneros* (people picking up and living on rubbish and junk).

Also, there is often a subtle inversion of the meaning of culture, which repeatedly replaces a sense of pliability with a sense of rigidity, implying that these values, norms, or ways of life that keep being transmitted will be adopted and kept immutable. Thus, other qualities are associated with culture: the perpetual reproduction of the same culture and the imperviousness of boundaries between cultures. For example, one quotation from our fieldwork notes records statements from school doctors implying that children who were raised in shantytowns felt "pleasure" in overcrowding at home and that they would reproduce overcrowding even if they had the possibility of better housing. So when reasons for the differences regarding children who are thought to be different are used to justify their learning capacities or learning difficulties—issues that matter to the very core of school activity—it is important to realize whether the original concept of culture or the modified version is being used.

In the period mentioned (1990 to the present) there are many contradictions: for example, in 1990–1992 the Ley Federal de Educación was passed, which emphasized the "acceptance of diversities and differences" in a sociopolitical atmosphere that promoted the opposite; since 2003, in a different context, the government clearly expressed its opinion against the growth of xenophobia and acted accordingly, but its actions by no means ended the practice of discrimination. Neither has the growth of biological explanations for educational issues been stopped, nor have highly fatalistic explanations that blame the families who are victims of exclusion for the educational difficulties of their children been stopped. On the latter issue, the concept of "educability" has emerged as an international revival of this kind of explanation (Menéndez 2002; Neufeld 2005).

A Historical-Anthropological Approach

Although we consider the question of labels to be secondary, we characterize our approach as historical-anthropological. The opportunities we had to share points of view with Elena Achilli, Graciela Batallán, Elsie Rockwell, and the members of our research groups led us to consider that the particular contribution of the ethnographic approach lies in planning studies to reconstruct "the informal logic of real life," as

Malinowski would put it, but within historically built patterns. The ethnographic approach, from this perspective, attempts to understand interactions, events, and discourses in context, according to the horizon of meanings given by the actors themselves.

Quite some time ago, anthropologists rediscovered history and acknowledged conflict in the societies they studied, which they no longer imagine to be in static equilibrium, even as the work of historians such as E. P. Thompson (1979) has come increasingly close to anthropologists' work. Ezpeleta and Rockwell in *Escuela y clases subalternas* (1983) emphasize that "every living social form, every institution, is ... accumulated history, rearticulated. It is ... a synthesis of practices and conceptions originated in different moments of the past; its present appearance is neither coherent nor homogeneous. Making the present intelligible requires searching the meaning of those traces in the past."

An outline of the historicity of institutions will allow us to get into the deep transformations that took place in the area of educational problems in Argentina. In 1983, near the end of the military government, the profound crisis of the Argentine educational system became evident. Schools and their curricula had been the object of political control, and the authoritative ways of the military period had been "naturalized." To make things worse, educational institutions had deteriorated at every level, even in terms of physical infrastructure, and projects on community and adult education had been cancelled. What was happening in schools was woven into the canvas of a country stricken by an economic crisis, which included a period of hyperinflation (1988–89), a turning point in many aspects of social life (Kaufman 2006; Neufeld 2006, 2009). The study of educational events revealed the traces left by these political and economic events on every feature of the educational system, in interpersonal relations at school, on the texts used, and so on.

Another ongoing strategy has been research within newspapers and periodicals, accepting the testimonial quality of this journalistic material. In the Rio Paraná delta, a local newspaper also called *Delta* distributed between the years 1933 and 1990 became a very rich source of information about the migrants of different European origin who peopled this area and its schools, which has helped us to reconstruct the history of the place and situate those who had a voice in it and those who did not.

Educational Research and Social Crisis

Since its association with nation-states, education has been a political matter by definition. In the last twenty-five years of Argentine history, there has been a strong awareness first of social crisis and then of the state as a field of conflicts. That is why members of our research group considered the problems derived from state policies, such as the educational reform of the 1990s[6] (Santillán 2003a), the new constitutional status of native peoples in 1994 and their rights and claims, as well as the reconsideration of the rules related to children's education after the International Convention on Children's Rights. In the following years and in the context of increasing unemployment, especially from 1998 to 2003, and of new social policies (*Plan Trabajar* and similar ones) (Manzano 2004), all of Argentina suffered the tragic and long-lasting effects of the new—neoliberal—model of accumulation, which presupposed the globalization of markets, and of so-called structural adjustment. All kind of inequalities deepened in a crisis that reached spectacular heights in 2001. This happened along with significant redefinitions of the state and its functions, following the advice of the International Monetary Fund (Montesinos 2004).

Anthropologists have approached many of these issues: for example, the problems concerning the education of children living on the streets (Montesinos and Pagano 2006), or of indigenous children living in large cities as a consequence of large-scale rural-urban migrations. The recent processes of rural-urban migration led to such an increase in the number of Toba people in the Gran Rosario (Achilli 2000) and in the suburbs of Buenos Aires (Bordegaray and Novaro 2004) that their populations there are now larger than in Chaco (northeastern Argentina) where they came from originally.

A second issue is the study of the families who send their children to school. Although it appears to be an obvious point of research, it demands renewed efforts of investigation. These efforts include in-depth work with families and their educational stories/background and experiences, as well as their practices and representations in relation to their children's schooling (Cerletti 2006). These scholars also consider the way in which interactions—conflicts, expectations, agreements, and disagreements—take place in everyday life between adults in charge of children and teachers, inside and outside schools.

Other investigations have approached the creation of complementary schooling spaces: Santillán's study on the *"apoyos escolares"* (remedial work spaces that support children's schooling) leads to the recognition of the way in which different agents (of the state, of the church, and of nongovernmental organizations) are concerned with the problem of "poverty," bringing complexity to the educational scenario (Santillán 2003b; Santillán and Woods 2004).

Most recently (2007), because the state has made schooling compulsory up to age seventeen, a number of researchers have focused on issues related to youth and high school education. Through our fieldwork in the south of Buenos Aires City (a poverty-stricken area), anthropologists articulate the question of school attendance at both primary and secondary levels with public policies, and also with the processes of appropriation of urban spaces and institutions (García and Paoletta 2007; Montesinos, Sinisi, and Schoo 2009).

Anthropologists and Policy Implementation

Finally, I will refer to the relation between anthropologists and politicians (officers in ministries and organizations of different levels) in Argentina. As Liliana Sinisi (2005) points out, in recent years, one of the main debates in the arena of educational research in Argentina referred to the possible utility of the knowledge produced by anthropological research for the improvement of educational practices. This trend has stimulated a deep rethinking of the validity of this sort of knowledge.

In 2000 (after the failure of the neoliberal reform), the Ministry of Education created a new Unit of Educational Investigations, which deals with specific problems of interest for the administration of educational policies. The researchers started an evaluation of the design and implementation of educational policies, especially those addressed to schools in a situation of poverty such as the Integral Program for Educational Equality (Programa Integral para la Igualdad Educativa, PIIE) and the Program "Everybody to School" (Programa "Todos a Estudiar"). Nowadays, some members of the team who take part in the design and the processes of evaluation of these programs are anthropologists, called in especially to design the qualitative approach, as experts in the analysis and interpretation of the data gathered in the field, owing to their experience in the knowledge of what happens in schools beyond the statistical data (Cerletti 2007; Padawer 2002; Sinisi 2008; Novaro and Diez 2006; Diez 2004).

However, it cannot be claimed that these contributions are necessarily taken into account when political decisions are made. The application is not always direct; that is to say, the results of educational ethnographic research may not be directly transferred to the field of politics and educational practices. The efforts of these and other anthropologists do not necessarily have a direct impact on policy, but we hope that they help policy makers see the complexity of issues and contribute to a deeper, more nuanced understanding.

As a conclusion, I would like to point out that we are relieved that these researchers are able to keep some distance from the ministry and its policies, because maybe the greatest contribution anthropological research can make to transform everyday school life is to document what is undocumented, as Rockwell (2009) puts it, and this distance is needed to be able to detect problems and conflicts.

Notes

1. In 2005 Kathryn Anderson-Levitt invited me to Chicago to take part in a symposium called "Anthropologies and Ethnographies of Education World-wide" (AERA; 2006), where I presented the first version of this text. Spanish speakers have our own communication networks in Spanish-speaking areas and universities around the world but, as Kathryn Anderson-Levitt pointed out, we are "almost invisible" to the eyes of the English-speaking world. I am therefore very grateful for having the chance to be part of this collective work, which, among other things, will allow us to shorten distances.

2. By *classical anthropology*, we mean the works written in the period between 1922, when Malinowski published *Argonauts*, and 1950, when the structural-functionalist paradigm began to be seriously discussed.

3. In Argentina *"paraguas"* is a derogatory way to refer to *"paraguayos,"* i.e., "people from Paraguay," but the actual meaning of the word *"paraguas"* is "umbrella." Also, *"bolita"* is used for people born in Bolivia but its actual meaning is *"small ball."*

4. Gabriela Novaro, Ana Padawer, María Paula Montesinos, Liliana Sinisi, Laura Santillán, Lucía Petrelli, Mercedes Hirsch, Victoria Gessaghi, Cecilia Diez, Maximiliano Rúa, Javier García, and others have worked or are working on educational problems with socioanthropological methodologies for their thesis.

5. What we say here is related to Rockwell's distinction between social and analytical categories (Rockwell 1987). We also make our own the statements of Eduardo Menéndez and Renée Di Pardo (Menéndez and Di Pardo 1996) about the importance of taking into account not only representations but also (and principally) practices. In his own work, he distinguishes representations, knowledge, and practices of health practitioners; we are thinking about the possibility of considering the problem of teachers' knowledges from this point of view.

6. This Educational Reform gave way to the Ley Federal de Educación (Federal Law of Education) in 1992, which has just been abolished and replaced by the new Ley de Educación Nacional (Law of National Education) (2007).

Bibliography

Achilli, Elena L. 1987. "Notas para una antropología de la vida cotidiana." In *Cuadernos de la Escuela de Antropología,* no. 2: 5–31. Facultad de Humanidades y Artes, Universidad Nacional de Rosario, Argentina.

————. 2000. "Etnografías y diversidad sociocultural. Reflexionando sobre nuestro propio quehacer." Paper presented at the IX Simposio Interamericano de Investigación Etnográfica en Educación Mexico, October.

————. 2005. *Investigar en Antropología Social. Los desafíos de transmitir un oficio.* Rosario, Argentina: Laborde Editor.

————. 2006. "Escuela e interculturalidad. Notas sobre la antropologización escolar." In *Diversidad cultural e interculturalidad,* ed. Aldo Ameigeiras and Elisa Jure, 43–56. Buenos Aires: Prometeo Libros and Universidad Nacional de General Sarmiento.

Batallán, Graciela, and María Rosa Neufeld. 2004. "Presentación." *Cuadernos de Antropología Social,* no. 19 (July): 7–9. Sección Antropología Social, Instituto de Ciencias Antropológicas, Facultad de Filosofía y Letras, Universidad de Buenos Aires.

Bordegaray, Graciela, and Gabriela Novaro. 2004. "Diversidad y desigualdad en las políticas de Estado. Reflexiones a propósito del proyecto de Educación Intercultural y Bilingüe en el Ministerio de Educación." *Cuadernos de Antropología Social,* no. 19: 101–19. Sección Antropología Social. Facultad de Filosofía y Letras. Universidad de Buenos Aires.

Cerletti, Laura. 2006. *Las familias, ¿un problema escolar? Sobre la socialización escolar infantil.* Buenos Aires: Novedades Educativas.

————. 2007. "Educación y (des)igualdad. Un análisis del Programa Integral para la Igualdad Educativa desde la investigación etnográfica." *Revista Runa,* no. 28: 11–28.

Diez, Cecilia. 2004. "El programa de integración escolar *La escuela inclusiva abierta a la diversidad* desde una perspectiva antropológica." Paper presented at VII Congreso Argentino de Antropología Social. (May) Villa Giardino, Córdoba, Argentina. En CD Actas del VII Congreso Argentino de Antropología Social, Córdoba, 2004, ISBN 987–20286–9-9.

Ezpeleta, Justa, and Elsie Rockwell. 1983. "Escuela y clases subalternas." In *Educación y clases subalternas en América Latina,* ed. M. de Ibarrola and Elsie Rockwell. México: Departamento de Investigaciones Educativas, Cinvestav-IPN.

García, Javier, and Horacio Paoletta. 2007. "Avances de una investigación etnográfica en contextos de diversidad sociocultural y desigualdad social: contextualización de escuelas, barrios y políticas estatales en el escenario pos 2002." Paper presented at *II Encuentro Políticas Públicas y pobreza en el escenario pos 2002.* November. Buenos Aires, Argentina.

García, Stella Maris, and Marcela Alaniz. 2000. "Antropología y Educación: estado de conocimiento. Aportes para una discusión." Paper presented at VI Congreso Argentino de Antropología Social, Mar del Plata, Argentina. September.

Geertz, Clifford. 1996. *Los usos de la diversidad.* Barcelona: Paidós Ibérica.

Grassi, Estela. 2003. *Políticas y problemas sociales en la sociedad neoliberal: la otra década infame (I).* Buenos Aires: Espacio Editorial.

Kaufman, Carolina, ed. 2006. *Dictadura y educación.* Buenos Aires: Editorial Miño y Dávila.

Manzano, Virginia. 2004. "Tradiciones asociativas, políticas estatales y modalidades de acción colectiva: análisis de una organización piquetera." In *Intersecciones en Antropología*, no. 5: 53–66. Facultad de Ciencias Sociales de la Universidad Nacional del Centro de la Provincia de Buenos Aires, Olavarría. Argentina.

Menéndez, Eduardo. 2002. *La parte negada de la cultura*. Barcelona: Editorial Bellaterra.

Montesinos, María Paula. 2004. "Construyendo sentidos acerca de los procesos de desigualdad sociocultural en las escuelas: un estudio acerca de los programas educativos focalizados." Paper presented at VII Congreso Argentino de Antropología Social, Córdoba, Argentina. Edited as CD.

Montesinos, María Paula, and Ana Pagano. 2006. "Chicos y chicas en situación de calle y su relación con las políticas y las tramas institucionales." Paper presented at XI Simposio Interamericano de Investigación Etnográfica en Educación. "Niños y Jóvenes dentro y fuera de la escuela. Debates en la Etnografía y la Educación." Facultad de Filosofía y Letras. Universidad de Buenos Aires. March. Edited as CD.

Montesinos, María Paula, Sara Pallma, and Liliana Sinisi. 1998. "Ilegales, Explotadores, Invasores, Sumisos … , Los Otros, quiénes son?" *Cuadernos de Antropología Social*, no. 10: 191–200. Instituto de Ciencias Antropológicas. Sección Antropología Social. Facultad de Filosofía y Letras. UBA.

Montesinos, María Paula, Sara Pallma, and Liliana Sinisi. 1999. "La Diversidad Cultural en la mira. Una reflexión desde la antropología y la educación." *Revista Publicar en Antropología y Ciencias Sociales 7*, no. 8: 149–69. Buenos Aires.

Montesinos, María Paula, Liliana Sinisi, and Susana Schoo. 2009. *Sentidos en torno a la "obligatoriedad" de la educación secundaria*. Dirección Nacional de Información y Evaluación de la Calidad Educativa, Ministerio de Educación, Presidencia de la Nación, Argentina.

Morey, Eugenia, Pablo Perazzi, and Cecilia Varela. 2008. "Construyendo memorias: detenidos-desaparecidos de la carrera de Ciencias Antropológicas 1974–1983)." *Revista Espacios*, no. 39 (November): 122–30. Facultad de Filosofía y Letras UBA.

Neufeld, María Rosa. 1986. "Crisis y vigencia de un concepto: la cultura en la óptica de la antropología." In *Antropología*, ed. Mirta Lischetti, 381–408. Buenos Aires: EUDEBA.

———. 1988. "Estrategias familiares y escuela." *Cuadernos de Antropología Social*, no. 2: 1–6. Sección Antropología Social, Instituto de Ciencias Antropológicas, Facultad de Filosofía y Letras, UBA.

———. 1992. "Subalternidad y escolarización: acerca de viejos y nuevos problemas de las "escuelas de islas." *Cuadernos de Antropología*, no. 4: 67–98. Universidad de Luján, Argentina.

———. 2005. "¿Persistencia o retorno del racismo? Consideraciones desde la antropología de la educación." In *Desigualdad educativa. La naturaleza como pretexto*, ed. S. Llomovate and C. Kaplan, 51–60. Buenos Aires: Ediciones Novedades Educativas.

———. 2006. "Antropología y dictadura." Paper presented at IV Jornadas de Investigación en Antropología Social. Sección Antropología Social, Instituto de Ciencias Antropológicas, Facultad de Filosofía y Letras. August.

————. 2009. "Las *escuelas de islas* al finalizar la dictadura: a 25 años de un trabajo de campo." Paper presented at IV Congreso Argentino y Latinoamericano de Antropología Rural. March. Mar del Plata, Argentina.

Neufeld, María Rosa, and Jens A. Thisted. 1999. "'El crisol de razas' hecho trizas: ciudadanía, exclusión y sufrimiento." In *"De eso no se habla..."* los usos de *la diversidad sociocultural en la escuela,* ed. M. R. Neufeld and Jens A. Thisted. Buenos Aires: EUDEBA.

————. 2005 "Mirando la escuela desde la vereda de enfrente." In *Vivir en la ciudad. Espacios urbanos en disputa,* ed. E. Achilli, 193–200. Rosario, Argentina: Centro de Estudios Antropológicos en contextos urbanos/ Laborde Editor.

Neufeld, María Rosa, and Santiago Wallace. 1998. "Antropología y Ciencias Sociales. De elaboraciones históricas, herencias no queridas y propuestas abiertas." In *Antropología social y política. Hegemonía y poder: el mundo en movimiento,* ed. Mabel Grimberg, María Rosa Neufeld, Sofía Tiscornia, and Santiago Wallace, 15–36. Buenos Aires: EUDEBA.

Novaro, Gabriela, and María Laura Diez. 2006. "Interculturalidad en Educación: ¿un abordaje para la crítica? Reflexiones a propósito de la escolarización de chicos migrantes bolivianos en Buenos Aires." In *Una forma de mirar la educación intercultural en América Latina,* ed. Patricia Melgarejo, 1–10. México: Editorial Plaza y Valdés/Universidad Nacional Autónoma de México-CONACYT.

Ogbu, John U. 1981. "School Ethnography: A Multilevel Approach." *Anthropology and Education Quarterly* 9, no. 1: 3–29.

Padawer, Ana. 2002. "Alternative Educational Projects: Technical Developments and Political Debate in the Everyday Workings of 'Nongraded' Schools in Argentina." In *Ethnography and Education Policy Across the Americas,* ed. Bradley A. U. Levinson, Sandra L. Cade, Ana Padawer, and Ana Patricia Elvir. Westport, CT: Praeger.

Padawer, Ana. 2008. *Cuando los grados hablan de desigualdad. Una etnografía sobre iniciativas docentes contemporáneas y sus antecedentes históricos.* Buenos Aires: Editorial Teseo, 2008.

Rockwell, Elsie. 1987. "Reflexiones sobre el proceso etnográfico, 1982–1985." *Documentos DIE,* Nº13. Departamento de Investigaciones Educativas, México.

Rockwell, Elsie. 2009. *La experiencia etnográfica. Historia y cultura en los procesos educativos.* Buenos Aires: Paidós.

Santillán, Laura. 2003a. "La Experiencia de la reforma educativa en una escuela del conurbano bonaerense: una etnografía del cambio." *Revista del Instituto para el Estudio de la Educación, el Lenguaje y la Sociedad* 1, no. 1 (December): 257–73. Facultad de Ciencias Humanas. Universidad Nacional de la Pampa.

————. 2003b. "Entre 'la casa,' la 'calle' y el 'apoyo escolar': el estatus del 'sujeto/ niño' en contextos de pobreza urbana y educación complementaria." Paper presented at Sextas Jornadas Rosarinas de Antropología Social. Rosario, Argentina.

Santillán, Laura, and Marcela Woods. 2004. "Modalidades de intervención de la Iglesia en la cuestión social. Las demandas de educación, tierra y vivienda en las diócesis de Quilmes y de San Isidro (Gran Bs. As)." Paper presented at Séptimas Jornadas Rosarinas de Antropología Sociocultural. Rosario, Argentina.

Sinisi, Liliana. 1999. "La relación nosotros-otros en espacios escolares multiculturales: estigma, estereotipo y racialización." In *"De eso no se habla…" los usos de la diversidad sociocultural en la escuela,* eds. María Rosa Neufeld and Jens Ariel Thisted. Buenos Aires: EUDEBA.

Sinisi, Liliana. 2008. "Un estudio sobre el Programa de Fortalecimiento Institucional en las escuelas de enseñanza media de la Ciudad de Buenos Aires." In *Gestión de Innovaciones en la Enseñanza Media: Argentina, Brasil y España,* ed. M. R. Almandoz et al., 53–90. Buenos Aires: Editorial Santillana.

Thisted, Jens Ariel. 2006. "El sufrimiento producido en contextos de pobreza, desigualdad y exclusión social, con especial referencia a situaciones escolares." In *Diversidad cultural e interculturalidad,* ed. Aldo Ameigeiras and Elisa Jure, 123–28. Buenos Aires: Prometeo Libros.

Thompson, E. P. 1979. "Tiempo, disciplina de trabajo y capitalismo industrial." In *Tradición, revuelta y conciencia de clase,* ed. E. P. Thompson, 239–93. Barcelona: Editorial Crítica.

Willis, Paul. 1983. *Aprendiendo a trabajar, o cómo los chicos de clase obrera obtienen trabajos de clase obrera.* Madrid: Editorial Akal.

§ 5

ANTHROPOLOGY AND EDUCATION IN BRAZIL
Possible Pathways

Ana Maria Rabelo Gomes and Nilma Lino Gomes

To address the theme of interfaces between anthropology and education in Brazil means to accept the challenge of describing developments that have proven to be extremely mobile and at times scattered during the last thirty years. Indeed, it is a field in progressive consolidation, which can be seen in several initiatives (publications, specific seminars in congresses, research lines in some doctoral and masters programs, among others), even if these initiatives do not yet converge on clearly identifiable lines of theoretical debate. In the congresses of national associations, which bring together researchers in the fields of anthropology and of education (ANPED, ABA and ANPOCS),[1] the last ten years have seen more and more presentations of studies within work groups specifically on anthropology and education,[2] which have a very broad and varied thematic approach, or work groups focusing on themes such as childhood and youth, cultural diversity and education, or even narrower themes such as indigenous education and indigenous children.

The field is also characterized by its several intersections with other disciplines, such as sociology and psychology, where themes similar to those of anthropology and education are dealt with. For example, studies on youth conditions and identity have a strong interface with sociology; studies on childhood are always discussed in psychology and currently seen as themes of investigation in history and sociology; research on black identity is conducted in sociology and social psychology. We will not attempt to review the whole field in detail, due to its scattered nature. Rather, we propose to explore possible theoretical lines of convergence or recurrent themes, analyzing certain Brazilian authors' proposals that have explicitly approached the interfaces between anthropology and education in the last thirty years. Such a review does not aim at presenting an organic body of literature, as it will be marked by theoretical and thematic choices that have proven to be fruitful and promising for analysis, especially for a much-needed theoretical dialogue between the two disciplines.

The first part of the chapter will analyze articles and books that have become recurrent references and that aim to build communication between anthropology and education. In the second part, we approach some research topics of a possible Brazilian anthropology and education, although, as we will see, this overview can be extended into a dialogue including several other disciplines.

Reconstructing a Little-Revealed Dialogue

At the end of the nineteenth century, the work of Franz Boas, followed in the 1930s by the work of Margaret Mead, Ruth Benedict, and others, initiated a dialogue between anthropology and education in the United States, which expanded into many other countries.

In Brazil, the discussions that originated in this period among educators and politicians concerned the internal diversity of the Brazilian people, which was seen as a dualism and a schism—between the *sertão* (backcountry), symbol of the savage and unknown rural zone, and the civilized urban part of Brazil, at that time still a minority of the population (Freitas 2001).

In the 1920s and 1930s, the challenge was to overcome this backwardness, in which problems seen as social and racial overlapped and were fought with different policies, educational and others, aiming at "the whitening of Brazilian society" and the overcoming of traditionalism and regionalism, both seen as obstacles to the consolidation of a new national configuration.

In the 1950s, in another decisive moment in the elaboration of educational policies and the training of education professionals, the need to know the national reality became more relevant and, ironically, to accomplish that it was considered necessary to delve into the uniqueness of each place. In this period, educational research linked up with sociological and anthropological research, in an attempt to understand different expressions of Brazilian culture (Freitas 2001: 15–19).

Many social scientists were involved in the discussion of educational reforms in the 1950s.[3] Therefore, we can consider this period as the beginning of the development of an educational anthropology focused on Brazilian themes, with sociologist Florestan Fernandes as a good example. In the text "As Trocinhas do Bom Retiro" of 1947 (in Fernandes 1979), he recorded the activities of children's play groups (*trocinhas*) in São Paulo, and considered them part of children's socialization process; in "Notas sobre a educação Tupinambá" of 1951, the author approaches what would be considered an unsystematic education in an indigenous population (see also Fernandes 1966 and Saviani 1996). These studies can be seen as precursors of a possible approach to the field, even if at the time of their production, there were controversies concerning the nature of this research.[4]

In this brief indication of precursor studies, some tendencies can already be identified that would mark the development of anthropology and education research in Brazil, such as studies of so-called popular culture and the two ethnic components—Indians and blacks—and which would be the subject of investigations. In the origins of a possible Brazilian anthropology and education, the internal plurality that characterizes Brazilian society—the need to know "Brazils" in the plural—would become a central theme to guide researchers. Less emphasis is found on themes related to school inequalities, even though it is an aspect of socioeconomic inequalities, a strong characteristic of Brazilian society.

According to Consorte (1997), in the 1930s, early in the period of culturalism in Brazil, research dealt with analysis of the formation of the Brazilian people, especially regarding groups from different periods of immigration (Italian, German, Japanese) found mainly in southern Brazil, and African descendants, found throughout Brazil. Such analyses, in the context of the educational system, were marked by two kinds of goals discussed by politicians and educators: "on the one hand, the Brazilianization of immigrant descendants, so that they would not constitute cultural enclaves threatening national unity; on the other hand, the eradication of cultural traditions of African origin, a permanent threat to the project of constructing a white, western and Christian country" (Consorte 1997: 28). Culturalism in Brazil thus assumed very different aspects from culturalism in the United States, where it was based, with Boas, on the affirmation of cultural diversity.

In an analysis of community studies conducted in the 1950s, aiming originally at identifying the educational problems involved in the social changes of that time, Consorte stresses exactly the lack of attention given to educational problems and to the school itself. Dealing with the communities as separate units, and concerned especially with assessing the possible continuity of traditional cultural models—that is, worried about the risk of their disappearance—the research did not consider the insertion of these communities in the broader context to which they belonged. As a consequence, there was no systematic study of the school and the different forms it took in these communities, since it was seen as an unfamiliar institution, separated from local everyday life.

With the country's growing urbanization, in the mid-1950s, the school became one of the issues to be confronted in this new opposition between the rural and the urban. However, the issue gradually evolved from one of cultural diversity into a problem of social class difference. This development should be understood in the broader context of social sciences in Brazil, as an interpretation of the diversity of the formation of Brazilian society. A strong sociological and economic interpretation combined with a political and ideological context marked by the military dictatorship produced, during the 1960s and 1970s, the abandonment of the analysis of ethnic and racial inequalities, which were no longer recorded in the census.[5] During this time, the promotion of a positive interpretation of the ethnic-racial intergroup relationships— under the "myth of racial democracy," a Brazilian image disseminated worldwide in academic circles as well as in popular knowledge—led to a decrease in interest in educational studies on these themes. Likewise, even if indigenous ethnology was then a promising field of research, with some precursor studies on education (Schaden 1962, 1964, 1976), this had no impact on the broader educational and social sciences research. The 1960s and 1970s was marked also by the political invisibility of indigenous people.

However, from the 1970s on, this lack of interest was denounced by social movements and, gradually, new social actors started to be recognized. This change signaled the renewal of interest in gender, ethnic, racial, religious, and age differences, among others (see Sader and Paoli 1986; Sader 1988) as topics studied again by social scientists. The influence of anthropology is undeniable in the 1980s not only in educational research but also in teacher training programs. The creation of schools of education in 1968—resulting from an extensive university reform promoted by the military regime—was marked by a technicist approach, which for a long time silenced interest in anthropology and other social and human sciences. From the 1980s on, this dialogue re-emerges, sometimes advertised as completely new, at a time of reaction and change of paradigms that characterized the period. The end of the 1970s and the early 1980s was a period also marked by the consolidation of graduate research programs in education in the country. As a result, educational research underwent considerable growth, and its publications became more theoretically dense.

Paths and Themes of an Emerging Anthropology and Education

The choice of the authors and texts to be analyzed here is neither exhaustive nor categorical. It is rather an attempt, based on the literature, to outline questions and/or themes that seem interesting and promising for delimiting a possible Brazilian anthropology and education field.

The first text we shall analyze is the book *A Educação como Cultura*, by Carlos Rodrigues Brandão, originally published in 1985. The book was written in the context of Brazil's transition back to a democratic regime, a period in which the debates and actions regarding popular education, associated with the emblematic figure of Paulo Freire, acquired a prominent position. The concept of culture, almost always characterized as "popular culture," would be extensively explored in social sciences and in education.

In the first chapter of the book, Brandão analyzes the "discovery of culture in education" in the field of popular culture. Culture and alienation; mass culture; dominant and nondominant—these are the qualifiers with which the author seeks to problematize and analyze social education movements as an example of a popular culture movement. Brandão then pursues a more direct connection with anthropological theory by introducing the symbolic concept of culture and discussing the relations between symbol, knowledge, and power (compare Brandão 2002b). The author proposes a reinterpretation of "Marshall Sahlins for educators" (1985: 121) as a means of better comprehending the dynamics of culture in the work of educators, in a context of a dominant sociology of education with strong Marxist influences.

In the same book, Brandão takes up Lévi-Strauss's ideas (1986) about the role of creativity in children's education, extending the discussion by introducing the issue of the child at the interface of education, psychology, and anthropology. The author states that one meets a "cultureless child" in the psychological studies, whereas in anthropological studies, one finds a "culture without children." Such themes, which were rarely discussed at the time, experienced significant development in the Brazilian academic production during the following two decades (see also Brandão 2002a).

In the 1990s we highlight two collections of essays by authors who propose an explicit approach to the interface between culture and education. The first collection, organized by Juarez Dayrell (1996), called *Multiple Views of Education and Culture*, is the result of a seminar that occurred in 1994. The discussions presented in this volume draw special attention to the relation between education and culture, focusing on schooling and nonschooling processes. The foreword stresses a reaction against technicism and attention to the diversity of educational actors as the starting point for much of the research found in the book. The book begins with two emblematic essays by the anthropologists Pierre Sanchis and Paula Montero, introducing broad theoretical themes: the relation to the "other" as central in the production of anthropological theory; the diversity and syncretism of cultural forms as problematic or contested concepts. Then follow texts that present studies on ethnographic practice and the field of education, indigenous education, race and youth, schools as sociocultural spaces, and teachers and students as sociocultural subjects.

The second collection, *Anthropology and Education: Interfaces Between Teaching and Research,* is edited by Neusa Gusmão (1997). The volume deals with wide-ranging themes, from the theoretical exploration of anthropology and education to ethnographic research in schools and the teaching of anthropology. Dialogue with the field of urban anthropology, which proved to be very significant since the 1980s, is carried on by Tânia Dauster. This is one of the themes that received the most attention in the following years, especially through studies of youth and children in urban settings as well as studies of different relationships and experiences within schools.

In the volume's introduction, Gusmão (1997) seeks to reconstruct the historical roots of the interface between anthropology and education. She reinforces the importance of the symbolic approach to culture, which is recurrent in Brazilian educational research, and stresses the necessity of taking up a systematic use of ethnography, which was seen "during the 1990s as the common and contentious field in the dialogue between anthropology and education" (1997: 23). More recently, the author has turned to the analysis of the relation between the two disciplines and their connection to cultural studies (Gusmão 2008).

The volume *Anthropology, History and Education: The Indigenous Issue and School,* edited by Aracy Lopes da Silva and Mariana K. L. Ferreira (2001), was a milestone in proposing an anthropology and education in Brazil from a specific point of view: indigenous ethnology. This field has seen a very significant development in our country during the last four decades, achieving international visibility. The introductory essay by Lopes da Silva (2001) has a clearly programmatic character aimed at building a potential "critical anthropology of education," which gives the essay a significant and singular character. Making reference to the various essays in the volume, Lopes da Silva tries to identify the contributions coming from an interdisciplinary analysis of the history and of the great variety of current educational experiences of the indigenous populations in our country.[6]

Lopes da Silva's initial critique focuses on the active commitment of many anthropologists and educators to offer a concrete answer to the demand for schools expressed by the indigenous groups with which they work, which was not followed by a theoretical endeavor in the academic field of anthropology. She retraces ethnological contributions through the specificities of "Amerindian thought": "in the 1980s ... the Nature/Culture opposition becomes insufficient to methodologically and analytically encompass the complexity of indigenous conceptions of the relations between persons, bodies, souls, spirits, animals. In the 1990s, ethics and a symbolic economy were discussed, to ask which kind of 'human nature' it is actually possible to speak about," (Silva 2001: 33).[7] The systematic effort to get at the logic of the Amerindian thought links different disciplines (cognitive sciences, philosophy, aesthetics, psychology) to broad fieldwork, and generates discussion around the concepts of totality and society. The concepts of Nature, as well as Culture, appear then as historic and specific.

This first volume, as the others that followed—*Pedagogic Practices in the Indigenous School* (Silva and Ferreira 2001b), *Indigenous Children* (Silva, Macedo, and Nunes 2002), and *Mathematical Ideas of Culturally Distinct Peoples* (Ferreira 2002)—are a first response presenting systematic historical and anthropological research and offering a clear dialogue with anthropological theory. The training of indigenous teachers (Grupioni 2003) has been another recurrent research subject, due to experiments that have been carried on since the 1980s and that led, more recently, to the opening of degrees in indigenous teacher education in universities in almost all regions of the country.

We intentionally have not dealt here with a wide-ranging and crucial subject: ethnography in studies of the school and educational processes. This choice is justified by the fact that ethnography has not been characterized, in Brazil, as an approach pertaining exclusively to anthropology, but rather as multifaceted zone that also includes research in sociology of education and in language studies (particularly studies on orality and writing). Despite the fact that anthropology's influence is evident in the wide use of ethnography, the authors that analyze the body of ethnographic research repeatedly state that, since the end of the 1980s, it has lacked a more systematic theoretical dialogue. The contributions of Elsie Rockwell (Ezpeleta and Rockwell 1986) and Cláudia Fonseca (1999) are examples of this effort to theorize the practice of field research.

More recently, there have been some collections of essays (Dauster 2007), as well as publications from sessions of the ABA (Gusmão 2003, 2009) and from other international seminars (on childhood and youth, schooling, indigenous education, public policies, and cultural diversity), such as Paladino and Garcia's (2007) publication on indigenous schools and on teaching anthropology in Brazil (Grossi, Tassinari, and Rial 2006). There have also been thematic collections in which one chapter is dedicated to anthropology, such as in collections on childhood (for example, Gomes 2008). And there is the first publication of an introductory approach to the field (Rocha and Tosta 2009). In these publications we can assess the progress, albeit uneven, of the growing body of work in some subfields. We may also assess the character, at the same time heterogeneous and scattered but also quite rich and containing great potential, of a possible research field of anthropology and education in Brazil.

Race Relations and Education

The theme of race relations and education, within anthropology and education, is characterized by works that adopt the case study in schools and nonschool spaces as their main research method. In this context, participant observation and the ethnographic approach are predominant. Oral life history, discourse analysis, and content analysis emerge as additional methodological tools.

In the 1970s and the early 1980s, studies on race relations and education went through strong changes, with advancements and setbacks. From the conceptual point of view, the notion of culture from an interpretive perspective stands out, and Clifford Geertz (1978) is regarded as a preferred source for the analysis. Studies generally emphasize the understanding of practices, meanings, discourses, and representations of race relations made by the various actors from the school and from other educational arenas (family, cultural groups, social movements, religious communities, among others).

Since the 1980s and early 1990s, studies focus more incisively on descendants of Africans as subjects of research. In schools, ever since the second half of the 1990s, research has approached the ethnic-racial relations between black and white teachers and students as a theme, thereby widening the range of such approaches.

Maintaining a deep interface with sociology, most research draws on a conceptual discussion of race, regarding it as a sociological category of analysis and as a social construction (Silva and Hasenbalg 1992, Silvério 2002; Telles 2003, Guimarães 2003). Identity, understood as a process historically built within a society that suffers from an ambiguous racism and from the myth of racial democracy, is also an important theoretical and conceptual topic for analysis. Several studies overlap with social psychology (Bento 2002).

Some research themes stand out: the processes of construction of the black identity (Munanga 1999; Oliveira 1999); racial stereotypes in textbooks (Silva 2004, 2005, 2008); the educational nature of organizations of black men in the nineteenth century (Domingues 2008); the educational dimension of the black movement (Gonçalves and Gonçalves e Silva 2000); silence as a pedagogical ritual/rite that favors racial discrimination at school (Gonçalves 1985); the overlap between social and racial inequalities and how it affects the trajectories of black and white school students (Barcelos 1993; Rosemberg and Pinto 1988); the life and school trajectory of black female teachers (Gomes 1995; Muller 1999, 2008); racial inequalities and the school performance of black and white students (Rosemberg 1987; Carvalho 2005); and childhood and race (Cavalleiro 2000; Fazzi 2004).

Currently, new themes are emerging, such as the training of teachers for ethnic-racial diversity (Gomes and Gonçalves e Silva 2006); blacks in the history of education (Fonseca 2000); black youth (Jovino 2007); whiteness (*branquitude* in Brazil; Bento 2002); African-Brazilian literature (Amâncio, Jorge, and Gomes 2008); and affirmative action (Silvério 2002). These subjects are discussed at the interface of the school, the cultural world, the gender issue, the assertion of black identity, and the policies and practices devised to overcome racism.

The body of academic work on racial relations and education has another characteristic that should be highlighted: the presence of black researchers (men and women). This presence represents a political and epistemological change. Black men and women are no longer the object of "studies of blacks," as they were at the end of the nineteenth century and the beginning of the twentieth century. They are now producers of knowledge about the relations between blacks and whites in Brazil, and their theoretical work carries, in its content and its critique, the mark of the ethnic-racial place from which the discourse originates and of the authors' political commitment to the production of a committed scientific knowledge.

Some scholars, such as Guerreiro Ramos (1957), Oracy Nogueira (1998), Clovis Moura (1983 and 1988), Lélia González (González and Hasenbalg 1982), and Abdias do Nascimento (1982), can be considered the main individuals responsible for the visibility of theoretical studies on the racial issue that parallel the "traditional" literature in the social sciences. These studies can be considered precursors of the current scientific body of work produced by the contemporary generation of black intellectuals who analyze racial relations in education, anthropology, history, sociology, and social psychology.

Youth, School, and Contemporary Education

The subject of youth is a field of study strongly influenced by sociological and anthropological analyses. In terms of methodology, case studies, ethnographic research, participant observation, and quantitative research in dialogue with official statistical data can all be found in this field.

In general, the studies privilege the conceptual understanding of youth as an age category (Debert 2003; Bourdieu 1983) and as a social, historical, cultural, and relational construction that takes on various meanings through different periods of time as a result of historical processes (Peralva 1997; Dayrell 2005). Anthropology and education researchers in Brazil have come to agree that, in order to analyze the different situations young Brazilians have been through, one must consider *youths* by overcoming the notions of the transitory condition and the biologization of the term, both of which still persist in the social imaginary, in public policies, and in the schools. The studies aim to portray the youngster as a person, recognizing that he lives a *youth condition* that possesses its own problems and characteristics.

The subject of youth public policies is highlighted, particularly the shift of policies from the *status quo* to the creation of a public agenda for youth, especially since the 1990s, when youth became an specific object of state intervention (Sposito 2007; Novaes 2008).

The worsening of violence faced by young people in society and school, as well as juvenile unemployment (Abramo 1994; Damasceno 2000; Araújo 2001; Soares 2004) are issues that incite not only public policies, but also educational research. The issues of youth living in poverty and youth denied rights and citizenship require a change of perspective, a shift from understanding young people as sociological problems to understanding them as social actors who are co-responsible for possible changes and transformations in society.

This shift has led to several educational studies and public actions that attempt to understand how young people have become important actors through the idea of juvenile agency or as "strategic agents of development" (Sposito 2007). It is in this set of reflections that the issue of youth and social movements have also been problematized (Sposito 2000). This literature also highlights the relationship among youth, education, leisure, and cultural production (Dayrell 2005; Carrano 2002, 2003) in studies conducted at the interface between education, sociology, and anthropology.

Another focus of research has been the relationship between youth and school, problematizing the role of the institution of schooling in the socialization of contemporary youth, in particular of young people from lower social classes. One research hypothesis is that the tensions and the challenges in the current relationship between young people and school are signs of the deep changes in Western society. These changes interfere with social production of individuals as well as with their time

and spaces, directly affecting the institutions and the socialization processes of the new generations (Dayrell 2007; Camacho 2004; Leão 2006).
In particular, the secondary school level has become a privileged setting to understand the relationship between youth and education.

Educational research in dialogue with juvenile issues has also begun to emphasize topics such as adolescents in conflict with the law
(Grandino 2006), youth and sexual diversity (Mott 2003), young people
in public education programs where they participate alongside adults
(Silva 2009), and young people and the media (Fischer 2005).

Indigenous Education and Childhood

The most recent research on indigenous education emerges from the setting up of indigenous schools in several villages throughout the country, especially after the constitution of 1988 and the 1996 *Lei de Diretrizes
de Bases da Educação Nacional* (National Educational Law) that opened
up the possibility of teaching in native languages and safeguarded the
right of indigenous people to an education in consonance with their
cultural traditions and their own learning processes. The schools were
no longer to be managed by FUNAI (National Foundation for Indigenous People) and, after 1988, the vast majority of the indigenous schools
were founded by NGOs and local associations, with the frequent contribution of researchers (see Ferreira 2001). These schools became publicly
managed beginning in the mid-1990s with the involvement of state and
municipal organizations, closely coordinated by Ministry of Education,
making the issue of indigenous education management itself newly
relevant.

Research development eventually followed, and the body of discipline-
specific and interdisciplinary work is increasing gradually. The field is
developing as one of the most relevant in terms of systematic investigation in anthropology and education (see Silva 2001; Gusmão 2009).[8]

The implementation of school education projects always takes place
within a broader context of issues related to land struggle, self-man-
agement, and environmental and economic sustainability of the territory itself (Pechincha 2005) as well as changes in socialization processes
and internal and external social relationships concerning communities.
However, most of the research refers to topics that are more school related, such as the analysis of pedagogical and curricular projects, pedagogical practices, and teacher training.

The effort to build a "specific, intercultural, diverse, and bilingual
education," as envisioned in the legal text in response to the indige-

nous movement, and the difficulties found in its execution are some of the research's core themes. The concept of interculturality has been repeatedly used to describe the proposal or the practices of indigenous schools, although there is also a strong demand for its revision and problematization (see Silva 2001; Tassinari 2001; D'Angelis 2003; Paladino and Garcia 2007).

The challenge of meeting the specificities of each indigenous people with regard to their territory, language, and symbolic heritage is one of the most salient themes. Therefore, there is discussion of indigenous people as the main agents in the definition of pedagogical projects in their own schools (Gallois 2001); in the formulation and implementation of language policies where the "space and future of Brazilian indigenous languages" (Monserrat 2001) is discussed along with the role of indigenous school in such a project (D'Angelis and Veiga 1997; Oliveira 2000; Franchetto 2001; Veiga and Salanova 2001) and in the proposal of "indigenous authorship" that guides several of the experiences (Monte 2001).

A significant number of the investigations aim to describe the specificities of indigenous school experiences—from ethnic groups, tribes or villages—concerning their relations to the local cultural orientation or local history (see Tassinari 2001; Weigel 2003; Gomes 2006). The case of indigenous people who have refused to develop school is also a topic (see Bergamaschi 2004). Other educational topics, such as socialization or traditional educational processes and the learning of specific cultural practices, have only recently emerged (Nunes 1999; Cohn 2000; Silva, Macedo, and Nunes 2002; Menezes 2004; Tassinari 2007). Comparative analysis of the different experiences of different indigenous schools can be seen as a future aim. Also still incipient is the possibility of a dialogue on school experiences outside the indigenous context, in societies or segments whose schooling process is quite advanced, which points to an enduring "school crisis" (compare Vincent, Lahire, and Thin 1994) as an inherent characteristic of school system itself, which could help to understand many of the recurrent difficulties in developing indigenous education. Likewise, there are still few investigations that see the school as part of a broader change process, a process that includes the introduction of an official and standardized medical assistance, the increase of money in circulation in the indigenous villages, and other changes in the social organization of economic production. These topics are approached by other subfields such as medical anthropology and economic anthropology. Finally, there is discussion of the theme of the inclusion of indigenous students in higher education institutions. This more recent inclusion should lead to an increase in research, such as Taukane (1999), carried out by the indigenous researchers themselves.

Final Considerations: Toward a Possible Brazilian Anthropology and/of Education?

As suggested in the first part of this chapter, to propose a Brazilian anthropology and education would imply, in our view, seeking to identify the "Brazilian themes" that should characterize it—in other words, seeking to verify and understand, in the unique context of our history, the way in which these themes are concretely and symbolically embedded in different components of current Brazilian society. Cultural diversity has always been the mark of Brazil, seen from the inside as well as from the outside. Diversity has long been celebrated, at the same time that contradictions and inequalities have always been hidden. Today, such contradictory movement becomes ever clearer, and this visibility is decisive in promoting further development for both the fields of anthropology and of education.

The dialogue that we seek to outline, using several research subjects, permits us to identify some directions of work that point out to a field very much in tension because of social realities: the problem of persistent violence and the exclusion of children and youth; sharp socioeconomic inequalities with ethnic-racial overtones; a still precarious rule of law in Brazilian society and an incapacity to deal with different cultural traditions in a country that still represents itself institutionally as white, Christian, and monolingual—among other characteristics that mark the current social and historical moment in Brazil. In this scenario, the intention to identify a Brazilian anthropology and education should be seen as a commitment to these issues that are still a challenge for research in all disciplinary fields.

On the other hand, the exercise of pursuing a more specific and dense connection with theoretical themes from the interface of anthropology and education can also offer a wider panorama, in which genuinely "Brazilian" studies can potentially reveal new and undiscovered social dynamics that cross national boundaries. In particular, the history of black identity in Brazil, as well as the unique and rich studies of Amerindian thought, which are becoming better known nowadays, could be seminal subjects that contribute to advancement of the field globally.

Finally, a word about schooling, this institution that has recently been made almost universally available at the obligatory educational level across Brazil. The attempts to implement an education of quality—a very current theme—and the research investment that seeks this goal both have much to gain in developing in close dialogue, as in some cases seen in this chapter, with activities and studies that explore the wider dynamics of Brazilian society. The cultural and symbolic dynamism of the different social and ethnic-racial groups, which comprise the many faces of Brazil, and the peculiar realities and strategies to which these groups give rise in their very own ways of life, are still, in our view, what can contribute to produce new solutions to old problems faced by school systems around the world.

Notes

1. ANPED (National Association for Educational Research); ANPOCS (National Association for Social Sciences Research); ABA (Brazilian Anthropological Association).

2. The sessions were called anthropology *and* education, instead of anthropology *of* education, and we use the former expression to refer to the field of studies.

3. Among the sociologists and anthropologists who worked in some projects of the Brazilian Centre for Educational Research, created in 1955, we can find Marvin Harris, Gilberto Freire, Fernando de Azevedo, Antônio Cândido, Florestan Fernandes, Roger Bastide, Egon Schaden, Darcy Ribeiro, and Josildeth Gomes.

4. Compare Cavalcanti and Vilhena (1990) for the controversy, at that time, about the interfaces between sociology, anthropology/ethnology, and folklore studies, which also involved R. Bastide's evaluation of F. Fernandes's works. Nowadays, in Brazil the term *ethnology* is reserved for research fields that stress local orientations, and we have particularly the identification of the specialized field of indigenous ethnology (*etnologia indígena*). The folklore studies field is associated with the idea of "a national culture," which was strong in the first part of the twentieth century, and in the approaches that give relevance to the idea of a unitary national mixed culture (the miscegenation, *a mestiçagem*), besides an emphasis in the modernization of the country.

5. The racial or "color" classification, using diverse approaches, was a question proposed in the first Brazilian census in 1872. There is no such information in the census of 1900, 1920, and 1970, but with the census of 1980, the racial/color topic returned, with a new category: Indian. Nowadays, the census uses the categories: black, brown (*pardo*), white, yellow, and Indian (Petruccelli 2007: 13–25).

6. A. Lopes da Silva was the coordinator of the Group on Indian Education (MARI—Grupo de Educação Indígena) of the University of São Paulo (USP). The work done by this group between 1995 and 2000 led to the volumes she edited together with Mariana Kawall Leal Ferreira, Angela Nunes, and Ana Vera Lopes da Silva Machado.

7. Compare Eduardo Viveiros de Castro (1998), Philippe Descola, and Joanna Overing, among others.

8. In a survey carried out about the research conducted between 1978 and 2002 (Grupioni 2003), of a total of 74 items (53 master's theses and 21 doctoral dissertations), more than half of them were on education (37), followed by lin-

guistics (13), and anthropology (12). Prior to 1994 there were only 11studies; the significant increase in the production took place only in the mid-1990s, showing how recent the research is. A quick survey of the thesis and dissertations written 2003–2008 reveals more than 90 papers, a significant increase.

Bibliography

Abramo, Helena Wendel. 1994. *Cenas Juvenis: Punks e Darks no Espetáculo Urbano*. São Paulo: Scritta.

Amâncio, Íris, Miriam Jorge, and Nilma Lino Gomes. 2008. *Literaturas africanas e afro-brasileiras na prática pedagógica*. Belo Horizonte: Autêntica.

Araújo, Carla. 2001. "As marcas da violência na constituição da identidade de jovens da periferia." *Educação e Pesquisa* (São Paulo) 27, no. 1: 141–60.

Barcelos, Luiz Cláudio. 1993. "Educação e desigualdades raciais no Brasil." *Cadernos de Pesquisa* (São Paulo), no. 86: 15–24.

Bento, Maria Aparecida Silva. 2002. "Branqueamento e branquitude no Brasil." In *Psicologia do racismo: estudos sobre branquitude e branqueamento no Brasil*, ed. Iray Carone and Maria Aparecida Silva Bento. Petrópolis: Editora/Vozes.

Bergamaschi, Maria Aparecida. 2004. "Por que querem e por que não querem escola os Guarani?" *Tellus* (Campo Grande) 4, no. 7: 107–20.

Bourdieu, Pierre. 1983. "A 'juventude' é apenas uma palavra" In *Questões de sociologia*, Pierre Bourdieu. Rio de Janeiro: Ed. Marco Zero

Brandão, Carlos Rodrigues. 1985. *A educação como cultura*, 2nd ed. São Paulo: Brasiliense.

———. 2002a. *A educação como cultura*, 3rd rev. ed. Campinas: Mercado das Letras.

———. 2002b. "Pensar o saber, pensar o poder." In *A educação como cultura*, 3rd rev. ed. Campinas: Mercado das Letras.

Camacho, Luiza Mitiko Yshiguro. 2004. "A invisibilidade da juventude na vida escolar." *Perspectiva: Revista do Centro de Ciências da Educação* (Florianópolis) 22, no. 2: 325–43.

Carrano, Paulo Cesar Rodrigues. 2002. *Os jovens e a cidade. Identidades e práticas culturais em Angra de tantos reis e rainhas*. Rio de Janeiro: Relume Dumará/FAPERJ.

———. 2003. *Juventudes e Cidades Educadoras*. Petrópolis: Vozes.

Carvalho, Marília Pinto de. 2005. "Quem é negro, quem é branco: desempenho escolar e classificação racial de alunos." *Revista Brasileira de Educação* (Rio de Janeiro) 28: 77–95.

Cavalcanti, Maria Laura, and Luis Rodolfo Vilhena. 1990. "Traçando fronteiras: Florestan Fernandes e a marginalização do folclore." *Estudos Históricos* (Rio de Janeiro: FGV) 5: 75–92.

Cavalleiro, Eliane. 2000. *Do silêncio do lar ao silêncio escolar. Racismo, preconceito e discriminação na educação infantil*. São Paulo: Contexto.

Cohn, Clarice. 2000. "Crescendo como um Xikrin: uma análise da infância e do desenvolvimento infantil entre os Kayapó-Xikrin do Bacajá." *Revista de Antropologia* (São Paulo, Universidade de São Paulo/USP) 43, no. 2: 195–222.

Consorte, Josildeth G. 1997. "Culturalismo e Educação nos anos 50: o desafio da diversidade." *Cadernos Cedes* (Campinas),18, no. 43: 26–37.

Damasceno, Maria Nobre. 2000. "Entre o sonho e a realidade: os jovens e as relações com o mundo do trabalho." *Educação em Debate* (Fortaleza) 21, no. 39: 130–42.

D'Angelis, Wilmar da Rocha. 2003. "Propostas para a formação de professores indígenas no Brasil." *Em Aberto* (Brasília, DF) 76: 34–43.

D'Angelis, Wilmar, and Juracilda Veiga, eds. 1997. *Leitura e escrita em escolas indígenas*. Campinas: ALB: Mercado de Letras.

Dauster, Tânia, ed. 2007. *Antropologia e Educação*. Rio de Janeiro: Forma e Ação.

Dayrell, Juarez T., ed. 1996. *Múltiplos olhares sobre educação e cultura*. Belo Horizonte: Editora da UFMG.

———. 2005. *A música entra em cena. O rap e o funk na socialização da juventude*. Belo Horizonte: UFMG.

———. 2007. "A escola faz a juventude? Reflexões em torno da socialização juvenil." *Educação & Sociedade* (Campinas) 28, no. 100: 1105–28.

Debert, Guita Grin. 2003. "A antropologia e o estudo dos grupos e das categorias de idade." In *Velhice ou terceira idade? Estudos antropológicos sobre identidade, memória e política*, ed. Myriam Moraes Lins de Barros. Rio de Janeiro: Editora FGV.

Domingues, Petrônio. 2008. "Um 'templo de luz': Frente Negra Brasileira (1931–1937) e a questão da educação." *Revista Brasileira de Educação* 13, no. 39: 517–34.

Ezpeleta, Justa, and Elsie Rockwell. 1986. *Pesquisa participante*. São Paulo: Cortez: Autores Associados.

Fazzi, Rita de Cássia. 2004. *O drama racial de crianças brasileiras: socialização entre pares e preconceito*. Belo Horizonte: Autêntica.

Fernandes, Florestan. 1966. Notas sobre a educação na sociedade Tupinambá. In *Educação e sociedade no Brasil*, Florestan Fernandes. São Paulo: Dominus/Edusp.

———. 1979. "As 'trocinhas' do Bom Retiro." In *Folclore e mudança social na cidade de São Paulo*, Florestan Fernandes. Petrópolis, Vozes.

Ferreira, Mariana Kawall Leal. 2001. "A educação escolar indígena: um diagnóstico crítico da situação no Brasil." In *Antropologia, História e Educação. A questão indígena e a escola*, ed. Aracy Lopes da Silva and Mariana Kawall Leal Ferreira. São Paulo: Global Editora/FAPESP/MARI.

———, ed. 2002. *Idéias matemáticas de povos culturalmente distintos*. São Paulo: Global Editora/FAPESP/MARI.

Fischer, Rosa Maria Bueno. 2005. "Mídia e educação : em cena, modos de existência jovem." *Educar em Revista* (Curitiba) 26: 17–38.

Fonseca, Claudia. 1999. "Quando cada caso não é um caso: pesquisa etnográfica e educação." *Revista Brasileira de Educação* (Campinas, SP: Editora Autores Associados) 10: 58–89.

Fonseca, Marcus Vinícius. 2000. *As primeiras práticas educacionais com características modernas*. Rio de Janeiro: Fundação Ford/ANPED.

Foracchi, Marialice M. 1972. *A juventude na sociedade moderna*. São Paulo: Livraria Pioneira.

Franchetto, Bruna. 2001. "Assessor, pesquisador: reflexões em torno de uma experiência em 'educação indígena.'" In *Práticas Pedagógicas na Escola Indígena*, ed. Aracy Lopes da Silva and Mariana Kawall Leal Ferreira. São Paulo: Global Editora/FAPESP/MARI.

Freitas, Marcos Cezar. 2001. *História, antropologia e pesquisa educacional: itinerários intelectuais*. São Paulo: Cortez Editora.

Gallois, Dominique Tilkin. 2001. "Programa de educação Waiãpi: reivindicações indígenas versus modelos de escola." In *Práticas Pedagógicas na Escola Indígena*, ed. Aracy Lopes da Silva and Mariana Kawall Leal Ferreira. São Paulo: Global Editora/FAPESP/MARI.

Geertz, Clifford. 1978. *A interpretação das culturas*. Rio de Janeiro: Jorge Zahar.

Gomes, Ana Maria R. 2006. "O processo de escolarização entre os Xakriabá: explorando alternativas de analise na antropologia da educação." *Revista Brasileira de Educação* 11: 316–27.

———. 2008. "Outras crianças, outras infâncias?" In *Estudos da Infância—Educação e práticas sociai*, ed. Maria Cristina Soares Gouvea and Manuel Sarmento. Petrópolis: Vozes.

Gomes, Nilma Lino. 1995. *A mulher negra que vi de perto*. Belo Horizonte: Mazza.

Gomes, Nilma Lino, and Petronilha Beatriz Gonçalves e Silva. 2006. *Experiênicas étnico-culturais para a formação de professores*. Belo Horizonte: Autêntica.

Gomes, Nilma Lino, and Lilia K. M. Schwarcz, eds. 2000. *Antropologia e história: debate em região de fronteiras*. Belo Horizonte: Autêntica.

Gonçalves, Luiz Alberto Oliveira. 1985. "O silêncio: um ritual pedagógico a favor da discriminação racial na escola." Master's thesis in education, Universidade *Federal* de *Minas Gerais*, Belo Horizonte.

Gonçalves, Luiz Alberto Oliveira, and Petronilha Beatriz Gonçalves e Silva. 2000. "Movimento negro e Educação." *Revista Brasileira de Educação* (Campinas: ANPED) 15: 134–58.

González, Lélia, and Carlos Hasenbalg. 1982. *Lugar de negro*. Rio de Janeiro: Marco Zero.

Grandino, Patrícia Junqueira. 2006. "O paradoxo do atendimento a adolescentes em conflito com a lei em tempos de reconstrução de relações entre crianças, jovens e adultos." *Dialogia* (São Paulo) 5: 101–9.

Grossi, Miriam Pillar, Antonella Maria Imperatriz Tassinari, and Carmen Sílvia Moraes Rial, eds. 2006. *Ensino de Antropologia no Brasil: Formação, práticas disciplinares e além-fronteiras*. Blumenau: Nova Letra.

Grupioni, Luiz. Donizete. B. 2003. "Experiências e Desafios na formação de professores indígenas no Brasil." *Em Aberto* (Brasília) 20: 13–18.

Guimarães, Antonio Sérgio A. 2003. "Como trabalhar com 'raça' em sociologia." *Educação e Pesquisa* (São Paulo: USP) 29, no. 1: 93–10.

Gusmão, Neusa M. M., ed. 1997. "Antropologia e educação. Interfaces do ensino e da pesquisa" (theme issue). *Cadernos CEDES* (Campinas: Cedes/Unicamp), no. 43.

———, ed. 2003. *Diversidade, cultura e educação: olhares cruzados*. São Paulo: Biruta.

———. 2008. "Antropologia, Estudos Culturais e Educação: desafios da modernidade." *Pro—Posições* (Campinas: Unicamp) 19: 47–82.

————. 2009. "Entrelugares: antropologia e educação no Brasil." *Educação* (Santa Maria) 34, no. 1: 29–46. Available at http://www.ufsm.br/revistaeducacao.

Jovino, Ione S. 2007. "Juventude e o hip hop. Escola, juventude negra e hip hop: um ensaio sobre biopotência." In *Educação,* ed. Luiz Alberto Oliveira Gonçalves and Regina Pahim Pinto. São Paulo: Contexto.

Leão, Geraldo Magela Pereira. 2006. "Experiências da desigualdade: os sentidos da escolarização elaborados por jovens pobres." *Educação e Pesquisa* (São Paulo: USP) 32, no. 1: 31–48.

Lévi-Strauss, Claude. 1986. "Palavras Retardatárias Sobre a Criança Criadora." In *O Olhar Distanciado,* 373–386. Lisbon: Edições 70. (translated from *Le Regard Eloigné,* 1983)

Menezes, Ana Luísa Teixeira. 2004. "O corpo 'educado' na dança Mbyá-Guarani." *Tellus* (Campo Grande) 4, no. 7: 93–106.

Monserrat, Ruth Maria Fonini. 2001. *Política e Planejamento Linguístico nas Sociedades Indígenas do Brasil Hoje: o Espaço e o Futuro das Línguas Indígenas, e Linguistas e Indios. Nova Parceria.* Caxias do Sul: Ed. UCS.

Monte, Nietta Lindenberg. 2001. "Textos para o currículo escolar indígena." In *Práticas Pedagógicas na Escola Indígena,* ed. Aracy Lopes da Silva and Mariana Kawall Leal Ferreira. São Paulo: Global Editora/FAPESP/MARI.

Mott, Luiz. 2003. "O jovem homossexual: noções básicas de direitos humanos para professores, professoras e para adolescentes gays, lésbicas e transgêneros." In *Homossexualidade: mitos e verdades,* ed. Luiz Roberto de Barros Mott. Salvador: Editora Grupo Gay da Bahia.

Moura, Clóvis. 1983. *Brasil—Raízes do protesto negro.* São Paulo: Globo.

————. 1988. *História do negro brasileiro.* São Paulo: Ática.

Muller, Maria Lúcia Rodrigues, ed. 1999. *As construtoras da Nação: professoras primárias na Primeira República.* Niterói/RJ: Intertexto.

————, ed. 2008. *A Cor da Escola—imagens da Primeira República.* Cuiabá: EdUFMT.

Munanga, Kabengele. 1999. *Rediscutindo a mestiçagem no Brasil. Identidade Nacional versus Identidade Negra.* Petrópolis: Vozes.

Nascimento, Abdias do. 1982. *O negro revoltado.* Nova Fronteira.

Nogueira, Oracy. 1998. *Preconceito de marca. As relações raciais em Itapetininga.* São Paulo: Edusp.

Novaes, Regina. 2008. *Juventude e sociedade: jogos de espelhos sentimentos, percepções e demandas por direitos e políticas públicas.* http://www.antropologia.com.br/arti/colab/a38-rnovaes.pdf. Accessed 14 June 2008.

Nunes, Angela. 1999. *A Sociedade das Crianças A'uwe–Xavante: por uma antropologia da criança.* Lisboa: Ministério da Educação, Instituto de Inovação Educacional.

Oliveira, Gilvan Muller, 2000. "O que quer a lingüística e o que se quer da lingüística—a delicada questão da assessoria lingüística no movimento indígena" (Theme Issue on Indigenous School Education). *Cadernos Cedes* 49.

Oliveira, Iolanda. 1999. *Desigualdades Raciais: Construção da Infância e da Juventude.* Niterói: Intertexto.

Paladino, Mariana, and Stella M. García, eds. 2007. *Educación escolar indígena. Investigaciones antropológicas en Brasil y Argentina.* Buenos Aires: Antropofagia.

Pechincha, Monica. 2005. "Ensino técnico e sustentabilidade dos povos indígenas." *Tellus* (Campo Grande) 5, no. 8/9: 79–89.

Peralva, Angelina. 1997. "O jovem como modelo cultural." *Revista Brasileira de Educação* (São Paulo: ANPED), no. 5/6: 15–24.

Petruccelli, José. Luiz. 2007. *A Cor Denominada—Estudos sobre a classificação étnico-racial.* Rio de Janeiro: DP&A—LPP/UERJ.

Ramos, Alberto Guerreiro. 1957. *A Introdução Crítica a Sociologia Brasileira.* Rio de Janeiro: Andes.

Rocha, Gilmar, and Sandra F. Pereira Tosta. 2009. *Antropologia e Educação.* Belo Horizonte: Autêntica.

Rosemberg, Fulvia. 1987. "Instrução, rendimento, discriminação racial e de gênero." *Revista Brasileira de Estudos Pedagógicos* (Brasília) 159, no. 68: 324–55.

Rosemberg, Fulvia, and Regina Pahim Pinto. 1988. "Trajetórias escolares de estudantes brancos e negros." In *Educação e discriminação dos negros,* ed. Regina Lucia Couto de Melo and Rita de Cássia Freitas Coelho. Belo Horizonte: IRHJP.

Sader, Eder. 1988. *Quando novos personagens entraram em cena: experiências, falas e lutas dos trabalhadores da Grande São Paulo 1970–1980).* Rio de Janeiro: Paz e Terra.

Sader, Eder, and Maria Célia Paoli. 1986. "Sobre 'classes populares' no pensamento sociológico brasileiro." In *A aventura antropológica: teoria e pesquisa,* ed. Ruth. C. L. Cardoso. Rio de Janeiro: Paz e Terra.

Saviani, Dermeval. 1996. "Florestan e a educação." *Estudos Avançados* (São Paulo: Instituto de Estudos Avançados da USP) 10, no. 26: 71–87.

Schaden, Egon. 1962. *Aspectos fundamentais da cultura Guaraní.* São Paulo: Difusão Européia do Livro (Corpo e Alma do Brasil).

———. 1964. *Aculturação indígena: ensaio sobre fatores e tendências da mudança cultural das tribos índias em contato com o mundo dos brancos.* Tese apresentada para a Cadeira de Antropologia da FFLCH-USP, São Paulo.

———, ed. 1976. "Educação indígena" (theme issue). *Problemas brasileiros* 14, no. 152.

Silva, Ana Célia da. 2004. *A discriminação do negro no livro didático.* Salvador: EDUFBA.

———. 2005. "A desconstrução da discriminação no livro didático." In *Superando o racismo na escola,* ed. Kabengele Munanga. Brasília: MEC.

Silva, Aracy Lopes da. 2001. "Uma 'Antropologia da Educação' no Brasil? Reflexões a partir da escolarização indígena." In *Antropologia, História e Educação. A questão indígena e a escola,* ed. Aracy Lopes da Silva and Mariana Kawall Leal Ferreira. São Paulo: Global Editora/FAPESP/MARI.

Silva, Aracy Lopes da, and Mariana Kawall Leal Ferreira, eds. 2001. *Antropologia, História e Educação. A questão indígena e a escola.* São Paulo: Global Editora/FAPESP/MARI.

———, eds. 2001b. *Práticas Pedagógicas na Escola Indígena.* São Paulo: Global Editora/FAPESP/MARI.

Silva, Aracy Lopes da, Ana Vera Lopes da Silva Macedo, and Ângela Nunes, eds. 2002. *Crianças Indígenas.* São Paulo: Global Editora/FAPESP/MARI.

Silva, Natalino Neves da. 2009. "Juventude, EJA e Relações Raciais: um estudo sobre os significados e sentidos atribuídos pelos jovens negros aos processos de escolarização da EJA." Master's thesis in education, Federal University of Minas Gerais.

Silva, Nelson do Valle Silva, and Carlos A. Hasenbalg. 1992. *Relações raciais no Brasil contemporâneo.* Rio Janeiro: Rio Fundo Editora.

Silva, Paulo Vinícius Baptista da. 2008. *Racismo em livros didáticos.* Belo Horizonte: Autêntica.

Silvério, Valter Roberto. 2002. "Ação afirmativa e o combate ao racismo institucional no Brasil." *Cadernos de Pesquisa,* no. 117: 219–45.

Soares, Luiz Eduardo. 2004. "Juventude e violência no Brasil contemporâneo." In *Juventude e Sociedade: trabalho, educação, cultura e participação,* ed. Regina Novaes and Paulo Vannuchi. São Paulo: Ed. Fundação Perseu Abramo.

Sposito, Marília Pontes. 2000. "Algumas hipóteses sobre as relações entre movimentos sociais, juventude e educação." *Revista Brasileira de Educação* (Rio de Janeiro), no. 13: 73–94.

———. 2007. "Introdução." In *Espaços públicos e tempos juvenis: um estudo de ações do poder público em cidades de regiões metropolitanas brasileiras.* São Paulo: Global.

Tassinari Antonella M. I. 2001. "Escola indígena: Novos horizontes teóricos, novas fronteiras da educação." In *Antropologia, História e Educação. A questão indígena e a escola,* ed. Aracy Lopes da Silva and Mariana Kawall Leal Ferreira. São Paulo: Global Editora/FAPESP/ MARI.

———. 2007. "Concepções de infância indígena no Brasil." In *Tellus* (Campo Grande) 7, no. 13: 11–25.

Taukane, Darlene Yaminalo. 1999. *A história da educação escolar entre os Kurã-Bakairí.* Cuiabá: Governo de Mato Grosso.

Telles, Edward. 2003. "Da democracia racial à ação afirmativa." In *Racismo à brasileira: uma nova perspectiva sociológica,* Edward Telles. Rio de Janeiro: Relume Dumará.

Veiga, Juracilda, and Andrés Salanova, eds. 2001. "Questões de Educação Escolar Lingüística: da formação dos professores ao projeto de escola." Brasília: FUNAI/ Dedoc. Campinas/ALB.

Vincent, Guy, Bernard Lahire, and Daniel Thin. 1994. "Sur l'histoire et la théorie de la forme scolaire." In *L'éducation prisonnière de la forme scolaire? Scolarisation et socialisation dans les sociétés industrielles,* ed. Guy Vincent, Lyon: Presses Universitaires de Lyon. Translated into Portuguese by Diana Gonçalves Vidal, in *Educação em Revista,* 33 (2001): 7–47.

Viveiros de Castro, Eduardo. 1998. "Cosmological Deixis and Amerindian Perspectivism." *Journal of the Royal Anthropological Institute* 4, no. 3: 469–88.

Weigel, Valéria Augusta Cerqueira de Medeiros. 2003. "Os Baniwa e a escola: sentidos e repercussões." *Revista Brasileira de Educação* (Rio de Janeiro), no. 22: 5–13.

§ 6

ETHNOGRAPHIES OF EDUCATION IN THE FRENCH-SPEAKING WORLD

Maroussia Raveaud and Hugues Draelants

The French-speaking world has no tradition of anthropology of education as a specific discipline. To take up a distinction suggested by some of the founders of the discipline (Dell Hymes, Shirley Brice Heath), neither ethnography *in* education nor ethnography *of* education[1] developed as a specific field. A significant indicator of this reality is the fact that in the latest *Dictionnaire de l'éducation*, edited by Agnès van Zanten, the entries "*anthropologie de l'éducation*" and "*ethnographie de l'éducation*" are two of the few articles written by North American authors. Education research is strongly dominated by a sociology of schooling where empirical studies were long shunned in a quest for general macrosociological theories. However, since the 1980s there has been a profound renewal of theoretical analyses, research questions, objects, and methods, which led to a surge of interest for ethnography of education fueled by an exploration of the American and British literature in anthropology and ethnography.

This chapter retraces the original resistance to field research and empirical methods in French-speaking education research due to the dominance of the inequalities and social reproduction macrosociological paradigm. However, the combined effects of critical sociology, shifts in educational policy, as well as the influence of other disciplines brought about an interest in social actors and actual educational processes. Ethnography has played a significant role in this renewal, though rather than being taken up as a new discipline, it has mainly been used within sociology as a set of tools adapted and "creolized," to use Ulf Hannerz's term, to fit with contextual factors, existing research traditions, and national political priorities.

Our review focuses mainly on the French case. In general, work undertaken in other French-speaking spaces has been profoundly influenced by research carried out in France. However we consider three other French-speaking territories that are significant in terms of research activity—French-speaking Belgium, French Switzerland, and Quebec—to highlight some key specificities.

The Age of "Glaciation": Longstanding Resistance to Empirical Approaches

Key to understanding the education system and research traditions in France is the Republican ideology. It was originally devised to unite the nation beyond its linguistic, religious, and local particularisms and later extended to immigrants, the assumption being that minority groups would assimilate into the dominant French culture. In education, it translated into the two founding values of secularism and egalitarianism.

This distinctive ideology has had profound implications on policy, research and successive theoretical analyses of schooling (Duru-Bellat and van Zanten 2006). A structural-functional perspective on socialization long dominated the research agenda, which was shaped by Durkheimian macrosociological issues of integration and socialization. A more conflictual view of social relations developed in the 1960s and 1970s, schools being seen as perpetuating and legitimizing unequal power structures and social positions. Marxist analyses and Pierre Bourdieu's theory of reproduction emphasized schools' potential for dividing as opposed to Durkheim's integrating perspective, but prolonged the Durkheimian heritage insofar as they were general theories of the education system with a focus on its normative foundations—meritocracy, equality, democracy.

The hegemonic macrosociological focus on inequalities until the 1980s has been likened to a phase of "glaciation" characterized by a largely ideological refusal to engage with the English-speaking literature, and disdain or ignorance of empirical studies so that the boundaries between sociology and anthropology remained very rigid. This may appear somewhat paradoxical if we consider that French sociology and ethnology stem from a common base and share founding fathers in the persons of Emile Durkheim and Marcel Mauss, and that Durkheim held the first chair in education at the Sorbonne. But while British social anthropology built upon their heritage of microsociological and monographic methods, Durkheim's French posterity favored the macrosociological heritage with a theoretical and methodological insistence on the externality of social facts and a mistrust of spontaneous thought categories.[2] Furthermore, research on education in France was originally undertaken nearly exclusively by sociologists, while Francophone anthropologists tended to work abroad. It is only very recently that French ethnology has developed a significant voice "at home" and that ethnology and sociology have (re)discovered common interests in their objects and methods.

Ethnography in the Hands of Sociologists: A Paradigm, a Discipline, or a Tool?

In the 1980s sociology shifted away from the quasi-exclusive dominance of macrosociological theories to meso- and microanalyses due to the combination of various factors (Duru-Bellat and van Zanten 2006). Within sociology, an internal critique challenged the limited capacity of macrosociological theories to explain how the phenomena they described were actually playing out in practice. Growing awareness of American and British research as well as the influence of other disciplines such as sociolinguistics developed an interest for smaller units of analysis and more empirical methods, and rigid disciplinary boundaries relaxed considerably. Simultaneously, social and political developments were weakening the power of institutions to regulate the education system and to impose on it a coherent taken-for-granted set of values. Policy reforms in favor of mass education and decentralization were giving local actors new roles and scope for action. Such combined developments led to a profound renewal of research interests: while schools had long been a research *object*, they now became a research *field*, and the focus increasingly turned to social actors, their representations, interactions, and rationales, which required appropriate methods and conceptual frameworks.

Given the dearth of French qualitative empirical or theoretical work to draw upon, researchers turned to the American and British literature, the dissemination of which was ensured in the late 1980s and early 1990s by in-depth literature reviews (e.g., Derouet, Henriot-van Zanten, and Sirota 1987; Forquin 1989; Henriot-van Zanten and Anderson-Levitt 1992) and translations of core texts such as those undertaken by Jean-Claude Forquin (new sociology of education), Patrick Berthier (ethnography), and Georges Lapassade and Alain Coulon (ethnomethodology). The foundational literature review by Jean-Louis Derouet, Agnès Henriot-van Zanten, and Régine Sirota (1987) engaged with a variety of methodologies: "qualitative approaches, microsociological approaches, descriptive methods, comprehensive sociology, interpretive approaches" (91) and various schools of thought ranging from cultural anthropology to the Chicago School through symbolical interactionism, organizational theory, and ethnomethodology, the common point being defined as a reliance on field research. Such work not only made the key concepts of anthropology and ethnography more readily available to French-speaking researchers, they also related findings from the English-speaking world to the French context, highlighting the tensions and adaptations that occurred in such a process. For instance, an inverse process appeared to be taking place in France and North America in the late 1980s: while American anthropology was engaging in the elaboration of global theories after a phase of intense and diverse ethnographic production, French sociology was moving away from the great theoretical constructions of the 1970s in order to examine everyday classroom interactions and local educational contexts (Henriot-van Zanten and Anderson-Levitt 1992).

A fundamental epistemological issue for French sociology relates to the implications of resorting to the English-speaking literature. Some concerns stem from a perception of ethnography as being limited to microlevels of analysis that preclude any claim to representativity, too context bound to achieve universality, lacking in rigor due to excessive reliance on subjectivity, and underplaying the influence of sociological determinants. A degree of confusion seems to reign regarding the very aims of ethnography, occasionally reported as being restricted to description that, however "thick," precludes any attempt at formalization, conceptualization, or theory in any guise. This perception is reinforced by a tendency to dissociate ethnography from its anthropological framework, thus potentially undermining its legitimacy.

It is essentially the methodological dimension of the ethnographic tradition that has been of interest to French researchers who explore the heuristic potential of borrowing ethnographic methodological tools to use within their own discipline. In the case of sociology, much research continues to rest on testing predefined hypotheses within a clearly identified theoretical framework, with an aim to producing generalizable results and generating theory. Rather than adopting the anthropological or ethnographic agenda wholesale and seeking to develop it as a *discipline* in its own right, an ethnographic approach has more frequently been integrated into an existing disciplinary framework as a *tool* with the potential to facilitate access to the insider perspective and to render the representations of social actors. It is significant that the adjectival form "ethnographic" (qualifying "approach," "method," "orientation," etc.) is favored over the noun. Furthermore "ethnographic" tends to be used much less specifically than in the English-speaking tradition (Henriot-van Zanten and Anderson-Levitt 1992), often being loosely extended as an umbrella term to encompass any microsociological or qualitative method involving fieldwork, such as participant observation, case studies, or interviews. Studies claiming to adopt ethnographic methods may actually rest on semistructured interviews alone. Another frequent compromise consists in combining observation with questionnaires, interviews, documentary research, statistical analysis, or other methods.

Extensive methodological discussions have been limited, with some significant exceptions such as Derouet, Henriot-van Zanten, and Sirota (1987). After examining ethnographic approaches to schools, classrooms, and communities, the authors consider "whether such fields constitute levels of analysis enabling a more fine-grained approach to general sociological phenomena such as the reproduction of social inequalities through education, or new objects which are liable to generate specific research issues" (1987: 92). The authors call on sociology to take on the conceptualizing role originally ensured by ethnology and anthropology in the English-speaking world: sociology is to offer a "rearticulation of the microsociological with the macrosociological," and to provide an epistemological guarantee of rigor within which the interpretive potential of ethnographic approaches can deliver its highest yield (1987: 95). Such an attempt is characteristic of how French sociology has adapted ethnographic approaches to the dominant issue of reproduction and inequalities to elucidate the everyday processes and interactions by which inequalities are constructed and perpetuated at the microsociological level; to test out the model of reproduction on new variables such as gender and ethnicity; to substitute an interactionist perspective to previous structural determinism; or to explore the effects on the education system and its actors of the implosion of the meritocratic republican myth. Yet the crucial issue as to whether a sum of individual practices and interactions can explain social inequalities, in other words whether and how the macro- and microlevels of analysis combine, continues to be considered unresolved (Duru-Bellat and van Zanten 2006).

Dominant Research Themes: "Inside the Black Box"

This literature review outlines core research in three areas where microsociological methods have been drawn upon significantly: social actors and educational practices; the local dimension of schooling and segregation; and professional development.

Inside the Black Box and the Turn to the Actor

Since the 1990s research in education has witnessed an explosion of studies exploring what actually goes on inside the "black box" of schools, and turning to social actors. Cross-fertilization across disciplines has accelerated, although the specific intellectual and methodological heritage of different disciplinary approaches continues to bear an influence on research produced and issues raised.

A sociolinguistic and psychological approach underlies the investigations of students' relationship to knowledge, schooling, and language developed by Bernard Charlot, Elisabeth Bautier, and Jean-Yves Rochex (1992). Their research into underachievement aims to account for personal histories and the paradoxical success of some working-class children. It highlights the intersubjective construction through learning situations of a relationship to oneself, to others and to the world. The key variables analyzed in students' relationships to knowledge are not cultural capital, social background, or cognitive competences but personal identity and the significance attributed to the act of learning, while also taking into account the contextual effect of the mobilization of schools, communities, and families.

A more anthropological concern with the way students and teachers construct and make sense of situations through their interactions has led to a reconceptualization of the child or student from being an object of study to an actor in the educational process. While the primary school years are predominantly characterized by a process of integration, children do not simply interiorize and conform to adult categories. Field research in primary classes and playgrounds brings to light the "invisible" socialization processes taking place through everyday routine interactions with adults and with peers and explores how children make sense of situations (Raveaud 2006). Patrick Rayou (1999) uses questionnaires and interviews to explore children's perceptions of their experience of schooling and their understandings of justice and fairness. While these are largely characterized by conformity in the primary school years, he also analyzes the social competences children develop in the playground, away from the adult regulation of the classroom, to regulate the peer group and elaborate their own rules and principles of legitimacy. Ethnologist Julie Delalande (2001) also considers how the playground functions as a microsociety in which children constitute a culture of childhood upon which a collective social identity is constructed. Delalande and Rayou exemplify a thrust to develop a holistic socioanthropology of childhood with a strong symbolical interactionist and ethnographic inspiration.

Secondary education, more marked by tensions and student distancing from the institutional culture, is the level of education that has attracted most attention from sociology. Much French research since the 1990s has moved away from functionalist-style deterministic causal explanations of inequalities to revisit the issue of inequalities under new guises. For instance, learning situations embedded in social relationships are examined to elucidate the everyday processes and interactions by which inequalities are constructed and perpetuated in practice. Anne Barrère's sociological research on student "work" (1997) combines quantitative research methods and in-depth observations in two secondary schools, and reveals an assumption that "work" is defined in a tacitly shared way that masks how such a key concept is not actually preexisting but constructed within the education system and subject to a wide range of practices and of attitudes.

François Dubet's "sociology of experience" (1991) has been particularly influential in offering an alternative to the critical sociology of the 1970s, eliciting student voice while maintaining a broader perspective on the social determinants of educational success in the context of mass access to secondary education. The weakening of schools' institutional function as bearers of universal values and providers of coherent predefined roles for students leads Dubet to replace the Durkheimian concept of socialization with that of the "experience" of the social subject. One major originality of Dubet's work is the use of Alain Touraine's method of "sociological intervention": respondents are not treated as "cultural dopes," in Harold Garfinkel's phrase, but as social actors who discuss their choices, strategies, and emotions in group interviews, and then receive feedback from the researchers and participate in the sociological analysis, both in order to ensure respondent validation and to increase their autonomy as social actors. Such research aims not only to elicit student perspectives but also to analyze institutional developments from a subjective angle and to revisit the central sociological issue of inequalities by exploring the new modalities by which they are played out.

The Local Dimension of Schooling and Segregation

Policy reforms that increase decentralization have led to high demand for understanding the new role of local educational actors such as schools, local authorities, educational priority areas (*Zones d'Éducation Prioritaire*), and communities. The political drive toward decentralization also calls into question the principles guiding public action in the aftermath of the republican claim to universality. Jean-Louis Derouet (1992), inspired by John Rawls's theory of justice, considers how formerly predominant values of equality and citizenship now coexist with competing principles of justice such as a domestic logic emphasizing interpersonal relationships and a market logic grounded in individual freedom within a framework of competition. The task of juggling such principles of justice to guide action falls to schools and local actors in temporary and locally negotiated compromises.

The official recognition of diversity within the education system has also fueled complex individual and collective strategies on the part of school leaders, local authorities, and parents, who articulate instrumental, personal, and broader collective rationales (Duru-Bellat and van Zanten 2006). In research on such issues, concerns with the production of inequalities and social reproduction remain central, but the determinism of social class has given way to an emphasis on strategies, interactions, and negotiations of meaning between socially, culturally, and locally situated actors.

Most qualitative research has focused on schools as their size, visibility, and accessibility makes them an attractive field for ethnographic approaches. It is questionable, however, to what extent this is a relevant level of analysis, particularly in the French context where schools have an administrative existence rather than being characterized by an ethos or a sense of community. One solution has been to firmly locate the analysis of schools in their contextual dynamics, as when Agnès van Zanten (2001) considers fine-grained internal school processes within the remodeled relationship between the center and the "periphery." Based on several years of observations and interviews, she analyzes the subtle ways in which the very nature of teaching and the aims of schooling are renegotiated and adapted to inner-city contexts: where actual circumstances are too far distanced from prescribed norms, new professional, organizational, and relational competences emerge. Emphasizing relationships, valuing minority ethnic cultures, and relaxing strictly academic criteria of success generate ethical tensions as to whether such developments can constitute creative local alternatives to the republican model or only lead to certain categories of students being left behind in the wider educational order.

Microsociological approaches have contributed greatly to understanding mechanisms of segregation and discrimination. In theory, French students enroll at the local school and are randomly grouped to constitute classes. In practice however, parental use of options or of the private sector combined with school strategies turns schools into competitive markets. Jean-Paul Payet (1995) reveals how a significant proportion of lower secondary schools use achievement level to group pupils in an attempt to retain "good" pupils by guaranteeing their parents they will be educated with children from similar social backgrounds. In such cases, avoiding segregation *between* schools leads to segregation *inside* schools.

Working-class and minority ethnic students are particularly concerned by phenomena of educational segregation and discrimination, yet studying the educational fate of the latter constitutes both a political and scientific challenge in the French context. Indeed, legislation restricts the collection of ethnic data in a republican antidiscriminatory logic, which precludes ethnic monitoring, using only nationality and place of birth as official criteria to classify the population.[3] In addition to this legal issue, ethical concerns among French sociologists—in marked contrast to the traditional focus of North American anthropology on ethnicity—long hindered the identification of minority ethnic students for fear of the self-fulfilling discriminatory effects of labeling. Furthermore, highly influential statistical studies within the Ministry of Education concluded that all things being equal, migrant children succeeded as well, if not better, than average, explaining their underachievement by socioeconomic factors, not ethnic origin (Vallet and Caille 1995; INSEE 2005). However, various strategies have been devised to circumvent these political and administrative difficulties and to identify minority ethnic students. For instance, Georges Felouzis's approximation of ethnicity by pupils' first names enabled him to statistically demonstrate the extent of educational segregation in the lower secondary schools of the Bordeaux region. Ethnography was of course available as another avenue, and the combination of ethnographic methods with the sociological inequalities paradigm has produced a powerful challenge to republican complacency (van Zanten 2001). Payet (1995) highlights the discriminatory mechanisms produced through schools' internal mechanisms of selection and routine daily interactions "in the wings" (e.g., in the head teachers' office). In a context of "ethnicization" of social representations, he shows how ethnicity tends to be either essentialized as a single flattening dimension of student identity, or rendered "invisible" in interpretations that reduce students to their social background.

In a ten-year-long ethnographic study of an inner city, Stéphane Beaud (2002) documents the perceptions of new school goers who accessed secondary education as a result of "democratization" policies. The overall picture is that of an experience of humiliation and subjection to processes of labeling, stigmatization, and segregation, where any academic success tends to be paid for by split loyalties and divided identities. Such perceptions of discrimination are conducive to violence, though it is worth noting that there is little evidence in France of an anti-school culture or of collective forms of resistance such as those identified in British research by D. H. Hargreaves, Colin Lacey, and Paul Willis.

Though the traditional French "indifference to difference" in policy and research has given way to a recognition of racism, discrimination, and segregation, the debate remains open as to whether the republican ideal of integration retains any relevance to educational principles and reality, or how far any recognition of community-based identities in education is necessary or desirable.

Practitioners and Action Research

During sociology's phase of "glaciation," other institutional actors likely to be involved in field research were either state actors such as the inspectorate, or teacher-training institutions and departments of education. The inspectorate was long one of the main institutional voices on educational practice, providing school- and classroom-based evidence. However, its validity for use within the social sciences is problematic given the ideological loading of education in France and the tensions between normative and descriptive roles in the inspectorate's brief.

Over time, elements of social science, including anthropology, have been woven in and out of teacher-training curricula. Though they tend to have been reduced to a minimal role, locally teacher-training institutions and departments of "education sciences"[4] have introduced elements of ethnographic and anthropological practice, often involving practitioners in an analysis of their practice and critical self-reflection. Education sciences and teacher training have manifested an interest in phenomenological, interpretive, and reflective perspectives, with action research, autobiographies, and critical reflection featuring as tools for professional training and development. The ambitions of education science research based on ethnography tend to depart from the conceptual and theoretical claims that characterize much sociology, and include issues such as professional development and identity, bridging the gap between research and practitioner knowledge or reclaiming an insider voice on a profession that had felt itself under the attack of critical sociology.

While much work produced within education science departments is geared at practitioners, some engages with epistemological issues. The quest for legitimacy and scientific credibility occasionally leads education science researchers to turn to ethnology or anthropology as a discipline and holistic frame of reference rather than simply borrowing some of its concepts or tools, thus departing from the dominant practice in sociology. One notable instance of a genuine turn towards ethnology and ethnomethodology as a discipline per se is exemplified by "institutional analysis," an emancipatory project developed in the 1960s, which placed the subject at the heart of the knowledge process and conceived research as intervention. It brought together interactionism, action research, and ethnography to question the role and involvement of the fieldworker. Its emancipatory dimension, related to the accountability movement, rested on abandoning a view of the researcher as an external specialist in order to promote ownership of the analytical process by the actors themselves. It drew upon the work of Kurt Lewin, W. F. Whyte, Lawrence Stenhouse, and Alfred Schutz and was promoted in France by Georges Lapassade and his colleagues at the education sciences department of the Paris 8 University (Lapassade 2006). A similar set of references is central to the European Society of Ethnography and Education (SEEE) created in 1999 and presided by Patrick Boumard: SEEE members consider that ethnography cannot be reduced to a mere inquiry method but needs to build on anthropology (Boumard and Bouvet 2007).

More recently, it is significant that researchers with a background in anthropology have joined education science departments, with Jean-Paul Filiod as one such influential and active example spearheading what may eventually develop as a genuine French anthropology of education (Filiod 2007).

Finally, several initiatives have disseminated ethnographic approaches beyond academia. Ethnographers working alongside primary- and secondary-school teachers have introduced children to the discipline to promote a critically distanced view of the familiar reality of their everyday environment.[5] It is also worth noting that alongside the increasing reliance on audiovisual recording as an observation tool, there has been a significant recent output of highly acclaimed films about schooling for the cinema—e.g., *Être et avoir* (*To Be and to Have*) or the 2008 Palme d'Or *Entre les murs* (*The Class*). The boundaries between documentary and fiction have become increasingly blurred with this genre and the wide public interest they generate suggests a demand for the unique insider perspectives on schooling that ethnography has to offer while raising issues about the epistemological risks of divorcing a method from its theoretical framework of reference.

The Situation in French-Speaking Belgium, French Switzerland, and Quebec

To a large extent, the panorama of ethnography and education described for France is also valid for French-speaking Belgium, French Switzerland, and Quebec. Among the similarities between the French situation and those of the larger French-speaking world, let us underscore the influence of the invisible college formed by the international community of sociologists, in particular by French-speaking sociologists, who have met regularly during the annual gatherings of the AISLF (the international association of French-speaking sociologists) and other organizations since 1958. It is especially worth noting the strong hold of the work of Bourdieu and Jean-Claude Passeron during the late 1960s and 1970s. Concerning the case of Quebec, Card writes: "Depending on the ideological persuasion of professors, Bourdieu appears to be one of the most 'worked' and alternatively the most 'worked-over' writers in current Quebec sociology of education" (1976: 10–11). In French-speaking Switzerland, Perrenoud (1992) also points out the impact of Bourdieu and Passeron's thesis on numerous researchers, alternatively viewed as a model or as a countermodel of sociology. Over the past twenty years, the AISLF special interest group on socialization has strengthened the development of a specific sociology of education in the French-speaking world while fostering the dialogue with other linguistic areas, notably by the publication of *Education et Sociétés,* an international review of sociology of education whose scientific committee includes French, Belgian, Canadian, and Swiss researchers. Generally speaking, across the French-speaking world at the start of the 1980s, the paradigm shift was similar: from macro- to microsociological approaches; from the study of structures to the study of agents and agency.

Simultaneously, qualitative methodological approaches and those inspired by ethnography, whose status was originally marginal, are now achieving recognition of their epistemological legitimacy and their specific contribution to research.

However, due to their sociopolitical, institutional, and historical characteristics, important specificities remain attached to these countries and influence the agenda of research in education. We hereafter sketch some of the most prominent differences with France. At the risk of simplifying, and for the sake of brevity, we consider the French-speaking territories of Belgium, Switzerland, and Canada simultaneously. In comparison with France, these territories share some core sociopolitical characteristics, allowing us to draw a common and contrasting picture with the French situation. All three are located in small or sparsely populated countries and divided into linguistic areas of unequal importance where the French-speaking people represent a minority. The political organization of these states strongly differs from that of France: Belgium and Canada are federal states, Switzerland is a confederation. Consequently, these countries do not have a centralized and unified education system.

The Organization of Disciplines from Country to Country

More than in France, where sociology maintains a tradition of relative autonomy in relation to the political authorities, the other French-speaking areas seem characterized by a closer connection between government and some academics in sociology of education (Card 1976; Perrenoud 1992; Van Haecht 1992). The normative orientation of much research is due to the modes of research funding, largely subsidized by the public authorities to evaluate the effect of implemented policies. In French-speaking Switzerland, for example, sociology of education is very unequally developed. Often missing or marginal elsewhere, it is particularly developed in the canton of Geneva, where the Education Department set up a sociological research center in the 1960s without equivalent in the other cantons (Perrenoud 1992). Another reason for practice-oriented research is that sociologists are often, in particular in Quebec and in Switzerland, institutionally attached to faculties of psychology and education sciences where teacher training takes place rather than in faculties of social sciences. Research in education in these countries is thus, more than in France, dominated by research in psychology and pedagogy rather than by sociology.

Who Governs Education?

Considering the nature and organization of public education in Canada, Belgium, and Switzerland, one cannot speak of national systems of education as is the case in France. If researchers have ultimately taken little advantage of this coexistence of various education systems within their country to undertake intranational comparative studies—particularly in Switzerland and Belgium—nonetheless this fragmentation and the decentralization of authority undoubtedly led researchers to focus on real actors' strategies and negotiations. It encouraged a questioning that does not arise in the same way in more centralized countries, namely, "Who governs education?" (Perrenoud 1992). In France, indeed, the Jules Ferry model conveys a myth of educational uniformity that constituted and still sometimes constitutes an ideological obstacle to the objective analysis of the education system. In these countries, even if the republican ideology resonated to a certain extent, none ever believed in a supposed uniformity of the system. Still, that being said, in the Belgian case, even if a multiactor governance has always existed and if the Belgian state, unlike France, never tried to overcome the multiple divisions within its society, other institutional obstacles contributed until recently to slow down the development of data enabling

comparison between the different school boards and education providers. The different institutional actors regard such knowledge with suspicion because it could threaten the very bases of the long-standing yet
fragile consociative[6] compromise that prevails between the main sociological groups (Flemish/French, Catholic/secular, etc.) (Mangez 2009).

Ethnography of Educational Policies

In line with this, ethnographic methods have recently been taken up in
the sociology of education of the French-speaking world to study education policy. During the 1960s and 1970s, the sociology of education
was interested in the structures of education systems in relation with
the economic and social structures or the power struggles within societies; then, the 1980s and 1990s witnessed growing interest in local actors
in classrooms, schools, and districts, and in the analysis of formal and
informal transmission of knowledge, in other words all the fine-grained
processes contributing to the production of inequalities at school. From
then on, since the end of the 1990s, researchers have been considering
policies "in action," with public action as a new field of study, thus
taking into account transformations of frames of reference underlying
current policies (Doray and Maroy 2008). Case studies and ethnography find here a favorable environment. One aim of such research, well
developed in France but also in Belgium, where some scholars play a
leading role fostering comparative research (Maroy 2006), is to study
the reception of educational reforms on the ground, that is to say in
classrooms and schools, from the point of view of the actors and street-
level bureaucrats in charge of their implementation (Draelants 2009).
Such research shows how public policy is not made "once and for all"
by policy makers but undergoes a series of mediations that give rise to
interpretations and recontextualizations in the local contexts of their
implementation.

Far from the "One Language, One School, One Flag" Ideology

Among the historical and cultural specificities affecting key questions
and agendas of research in education, the question of pluralism is also
noteworthy. A sociopolitical reality shared by Canada, Belgium, and
Switzerland, which distinguishes these countries from France, is their
bi- or multilingual and thus bi- or multicultural character, which generates research into intercommunity relationships at the linguistic, ethnic, and cultural, or religious level.

In Canada, especially, throughout the history of the country, the Francophone minority, due to a history as an oppressed minority for over two hundred years, sought to mark its difference and wanted to be recognized as distinct from the other Canadians. Education thus became an essential tool for differentiating itself from the Anglophone world. Today, this holds especially true in the Canadian provinces (Ontario and New Brunswick in particular) where Francophones are a minority. Majoritarian in their province, the Francophones of Quebec dispose of a state that is actively pursuing a policy of preservation of their language. Not being able to claim territorial spaces, the other Francophones in Canada aspire to institutional spaces of autonomy, including French-speaking schools (Boudreau and Nielsen 1994). Another challenge concerned the education of the native communities of Quebec, as well as programs aimed at conserving and protecting Native Canadian language and cultures by and through schooling. Nowadays, as Quebec is still a land of immigration, multicultural education and integration have become very present concerns for qualitative researchers. Several conference-based collections on multicultural education in Canada were published in the 1980s, giving legitimacy to this field of inquiry and practice (e.g., McAndrew 2008).

These pluralist contexts also fostered an interest in the question of identity at school among qualitative researchers. We can mention here the ethnographic work of Diane Gérin-Lajoie studying French-language minority education in Canada in connection with the students' identity-building processes in a pluralist society (Gérin-Lajoie 2006). The interaction between schools and processes of identity building for (ethnic) minority students in relation with stigmatization processes and school violence has also been studied, ethnographically, in Belgium by Philippe Vienne through an intensive participant observation in two underprivileged schools (Vienne 2005). Comparing contrasting secondary schools in French-speaking Belgium and in England, Marie Verhoeven studied how national models of integration influence the degree of acceptance of minority ethnic students' expressions of cultural membership and religious beliefs within school space (Verhoeven 2002). The French model of integration, characterized by a homogenizing ideology, is less conducive to this kind of expression than in the rest of the French-speaking world where other models of integration prevail. Consequently, whereas in France studies tended to focus on the social class heterogeneity induced by increasing access, scholars in the other systems, inspired by the arrival of immigrants, added cultural diversity as another important topic earlier than in France. In France, as mentioned above, this issue long tended to be blotted out by the republican indifference to difference.

These comments should obviously be moderated. For example, the French-speaking Belgian education system can be described as occupying an intermediate position between an Anglo-Saxon model and a French model. Actually, the situation varies within this education system according to the school providers. The schools of the Catholic teaching networks are characterized by a personalist[7] philosophy, sensitive to cultural differences, whereas the schools of the official network display a more universalizing model. Furthermore, on top of cultural differences between countries, it seems that the acceptance of expressions of cultural, religious, or linguistic membership depends on the position and prestige of the school on the local school market. The better the position of a school, the less legitimate the expression of community identification (Verhoeven 2002). Thus, according to Verhoeven, effects related to the functioning of the education system itself could prevail over societal and cultural dimensions.

Conclusion

In France, ethnographies of education grew out of a sociological tradition rather than out of a cultural anthropology. The notion of culture, so central in the American tradition of anthropology of education, is regarded with suspicion. Sociologists have mainly used ethnography as a methodological tool, which they submit to their own research agenda and thus set apart from its epistemological roots. However, this situation is currently evolving with ethnology as a specific discipline making a growing contribution to education research (Delalande 2001; Filiod 2007).

The same seems to apply, to some extent, to the other parts of the Francophone world considered in this chapter: French-speaking Belgium, Quebec, and French-speaking Switzerland. While several significant variations set them apart from research undertaken in France, what is perhaps most striking is paradoxically the extent of similarities in spite of deep sociopolitical, institutional, and historical differences. In these countries, the number of educational sociologists being limited, such small research communities can hardly function as closed-in communities and are readily open to foreign influences, essentially the influence of the French big brother, even though Anglo-American research has not been disregarded.

Notes

1. The expression "ethnography in education" emphasizes that ethnology and education are two interacting fields rather than an instrumentation of the first by the second, as implicit in the expression "ethnography of education" (Winkin 1992), where ethnography is conceived as a method available to the qualitative researcher primarily to approach sociological questions rather than to tackle the issues of cultural anthropology.

2. Bourdieu plays an equally ambiguous role: despite being an accomplished ethnographer himself, he never applied ethnography to his work on schools, and his scathing remarks on ethnomethodology arguably contributed to slowing down the adoption of microsociological methods in education. At the same time he was also interested throughout his career in the key anthropological issue of the transmission of culture, with the "habitus" constituting a mediating concept bridging macro- and individual levels of analysis.

3. A 1978 law restricts the collection of "sensitive" personal data such as ethnic origin, political or religious affiliation, trade-union membership, and sexual orientation.

4. Though education sciences was administratively recognized as a discipline in 1967, it is usually considered multidisciplinary epistemologically, and its researchers draw upon and often stem from a background in sociology, history, psychology, policy studies, or related disciplines.

5. See http://www.ethnoart.org and http://www.ethnokids.net.

6. As a sharply "pillarized" society, Belgium has often been described as a consociational democracy (Mangez 2009). The term "consociational democracy" was first used by Arend Lijphart in the late 1960s to name a type of democratic system in between the Anglo-American and Continental European democracies found, for example, in the Scandinavian Countries, the Netherlands, Switzerland and Belgium. This model of democracy differs from the other two on the criteria of social structure and political stability. It characterizes societies that are fragmented but stable thanks to cooperation among the elites of each of its major social groups (Lijphart, 1969).

7. *Personalism* is a school of thought that can be linked to the Christian Democratic political ideology.

Bibliography

Barrère, Anne. 1997. *Les lycéens au travail*. Paris: Presses Universitaires de France.

Beaud, Stéphane. 2002. *80% au bac ... et après? Les enfants de la démocratisation scolaire*. Paris: La Découverte.

Boudreau, Françoise, and Greg M. Nielsen, eds. 1994. "Les francophonies nord-américaines." *Sociologie et Sociétés* 26, no. 1: 3–196.

Boumard, Patrick, and Rose-Marie Bouvet. 2007. "La Société Européenne d'ethnographie de l'éducation. Histoire et enjeux." *Ethnologie française* 37, no. 4: 689–97.

Card, Brigham Y. 1976. "A State of Sociology of Education in Canada: A Further Look." *Canadian Journal of Education/Revue canadienne de l'éducation* 1, no. 4: 3–32.

Charlot, Bernard, Elisabeth Bautier, and Jean-Yves Rochex. 1992. *École et savoir dans les banlieues et ailleurs*. Paris: Armand Colin.

Dandurand, Pierre. 1992. "L'éducation et la sociologie de l'éducation au Québec de 1950 à 1990." In *Permanence et renouvellement en sociologie de l'éducation*, ed. Eric Plaisance. Paris: INRP, L'Harmattan.

Delalande, Julie. 2001. *La cour de récréation*. Paris: Le Sens social.

Derouet, Jean-Louis. 1992. *École et justice*. Paris: Métailié.

Derouet, Jean-Louis, Agnès Henriot-van Zanten, and Régine Sirota. 1987. "Approches ethnographiques en sociologie de l'éducation: l'école et la communauté, l'établissement scolaire, la classe." *Revue française de pédagogie*, no. 78: 73–108 and no. 80: 69–97.

Doray, Pierre, and Christian Maroy, eds. 2008. "Les nouvelles politiques d'éducation et de formation" (theme issue), *Sociologie et Sociétés* 40, no. 1.

Draelants, Hugues. 2009. *Réforme pédagogique et légitimation. Le cas d'une politique de lutte contre le redoublement*. Brussels: De Boeck Université.

Dubet, François. 1991. *Les Lycéens*. Paris: Seuil.

Duru-Bellat, Marie, and Agnès van Zanten. 2006. *Sociologie de l'école*, 3rd ed. Paris: Armand Colin.

Filiod, Jean-Paul. 2007. "Anthropologie de l'école. Perspectives." *Ethnologie française*, no. 112: 581–95.

Forquin, Jean-Claude. 1989. *École et culture. Le point de vue des sociologues britanniques*. Brussels: De Boeck University.

Gérin-Lajoie, Diane, ed. 2006. "La contribution de l'école au processus de construction identitaire des élèves dans une société pluraliste" (theme issue). *Education et francophonie* 34, no. 1.

Henriot-van Zanten, Agnès, and Anderson-Levitt, Kathryn. 1992. "L'anthropologie de l'éducation aux États-Unis: méthodes, théories et applications d'une discipline en évolution." *Revue Française de Pédagogie*, no. 101: 79–104.

INSEE (Institut national de la statistique et des études économiques). 2005. *Les Immigrés en France*. Paris: INSEE.

Lapassade, Georges. 2006. *Groupe, organisation, institution*, 5th ed. Paris: Anthropos.

Lijphart, Arend. 1969. "Consociational Democracy." *World Politics* 21, no. 2: 207–225.

Mangez, Eric. 2009. "De la nécessité de discrétion à l'État évaluateur." *La Revue Nouvelle*, no. 7–8 (July-August): 32–37.

Maroy, Christian, ed. 2006. *École, régulation et marché. Une comparaison de six espaces scolaires locaux en Europe*. Paris: PUF.

McAndrew, Marie, ed. 2008. "Rapports ethniques et éducation: perspectives nationales et internationales" (theme issue). *Education et francophonie* 36, no. 1.

Payet, Jean-Paul. 1995. *Collège de Banlieue. Ethnologie d'un monde scolaire*. Paris: Méridiens Klincksieck.

Perrenoud, Philippe. 1992. "Aspects de la sociologie de l'éducation en Suisse romande." In *Permanence et renouvellement en sociologie de l'éducation,* ed. Eric Plaisance. Paris: INRP/L'Harmattan.

Raveaud, Maroussia. 2006. *De l'enfant au citoyen. La construction de la citoyenneté à l'école en France et en Angleterre.* Paris: Presses Universitaires de France.

Rayou, Patrick. 1999. *La Grande École. Approche sociologique des compétences enfantines.* Paris: Presses Universitaires de France.

Vallet, Louis-André, and John-Paul Caille. 1995. "Les carrières scolaires au collège des élèves étrangers ou issus de l'immigration." *Education et Formations,* no. 40, 5–14.

Van Haecht, Anne. 1992. "La sociologie de l'éducation en Belgique." In *Permanence et renouvellement en sociologie de l'éducation,* ed. Eric Plaisance. Paris: INRP/L'Harmattan.

van Zanten, Agnès. 2001. *L'école de la périphérie. Scolarité et ségrégation en banlieue.* Paris: Presses Universitaires de France.

Verhoeven, Marie. 2002. *École et diversité culturelle. Regards croisés sur l'expérience scolaire de jeunes issus de l'immigration.* Louvain-la-Neuve: Academia-Bruylant.

Vienne, Philippe. 2005. "Carrière morale et itinéraire moral dans les écoles 'de dernière chance': les identités vacillantes." *Lien social et Politiques,* no. 53: 67–80.

Winkin, Yves. 1992. "L'ethnographie en éducation aux États-Unis: une première cartographie avec une ébauche de projection sur la Belgique." In *Odyssée dans un archipel scolaire,* ed. Marie-Françoise Degembe. Namur: Editions Erasme.

§ 7

ANTHROPOLOGY OF EDUCATION IN ITALY

Francesca Gobbo

In 1997, the newly published *Dizionario di antropologia* listed anthropology of education among the various "anthropologies of." The concise description of the subdiscipline represents an official recognition of its intellectual and research relevance for the Italian context. Studies on enculturation are mentioned as well as the contributions from "culture and personality," from research into the processes of schooling in complex societies, and from initiatives countering the negative impact of foreign educational models on non-Western cultures. The article's concluding lines note how today anthropology of education is confronted by new "problems" arising in schools where "pupils from different cultures" are enrolled and experience "difficulties in communicating, understanding and adapting to interaction with their peers" (Fabietti and Remotti 1997: 65). Those difficulties—at least in Italy—will be at the origin of teachers' demand for anthropological knowledge and of the intercultural educational discourse.

The article's general references do not include the many anthologies and ethnographies of education that had been published internationally. However, two references (Callari Galli 1993; Gobbo 1996) represent the anthropological discourse on education, and suggest to what extent it can interpret the impact of change on Italian classrooms and respond to their new educational needs.[1]

The Early Encounters

However, the conversation between cultural anthropology and education had begun well before Italy started to be described as a multicultural society because of migration. From 1967 to 1969, cultural anthropologists Matilde Callari Galli and Gualtiero Harrison had explored illiteracy in four urban contexts in Sicily. They documented the process of exclusion and discrimination that poverty, lack of work prospects, and schooling itself produced in the underdeveloped parts of the country (Harrison and Callari Galli 1971). They had originally planned to inquire if compulsory education improved people's life opportunities, if not mobility, but had concluded that literacy, far from leading to educational equity through compulsory schooling, created instead a sharp divide between literate and illiterate citizens, and enveloped the latter with "invisible walls," generating what the researchers defined as "illiterate culture."

Though compulsory education had been extended to eight years of schooling in 1962, the still disheartening learning experience of too many pupils of low social status had made a number of educators and linguists worried. They hypothesized that "unsuccessful school results among subordinate social classes were related to the fact that compulsory education, in Italy, did not respond to the social and cultural needs of those classes" (Gobbo 1977: 32). The richly differentiated fabric of languages and cultural ways characterizing Italy had been consistently ignored by educational authorities since the political unification of the country in 1861. Instead, their aims "were deliberately and clearly 'socio-political,' namely, to build feelings of new nationhood, language and culture, against the typically Italian traditions of political fragmentation and plurality of cultural centres" (Simonicca 2007: 244). For almost a century, the pursuit of national unification and the construction of a national culture required that the regional and dialect differences be overcome. For their part, "teachers played their teaching and moral role with an already clear national vocation, as they had learned to incorporate a national culture while attending high school and/or the university" (2007: 244). Consequently, they had not considered that the assimilation path they had followed impeded them from coping with, or understanding, pupils' different ways of thinking, relating, and acting.

Callari Galli and Harrison convincingly criticized the "naturalization" of schooling, reminding readers that it is a cultural invention. In theoretical/political terms they argued that "to state that every form of social life is not natural ... means to state that every way of life—ours included—can change, does change, must change; it means that it can change the way we want. ... If we take others into account, if we do not see their existence as the negative side of ours, if we plan to know them as alternate versions of ourselves, we can reach a new vantage point" (Harrison and Callari Galli 1971: 119) beyond ethnocentrism.

They interpreted educational failure as a form of "violence and oppression" that charged adults and young people with the responsibility for being illiterate, and portrayed them as "culturally deprived." Furthermore, educational disregard of, and irrelevance to, specific sociocultural environments paradoxically intensified those people's ties to their local tight webs of meanings, relations, and expectations generated and strengthened by illiteracy.

The unquestionable connection between social class and school failure had to be complemented by awareness that schooling provoked the self-exclusion of illiterates' children and a belief that they are not fit for school. The anthropologists saw resignation and acceptance of dominant models (such as meritocracy) in families and children, rather than resistance or opposition to schooling. They portrayed the illiterates' cultural ways as homogeneous, and contrasted them with a likewise homogeneous category of "schooled people." Readers might today wonder whether these two anthropologists had the opportunity to notice intracultural differences and hidden agency. However, this kind of question presumably emerges only now, when the risk, and danger, of cultural essentialism is rightly feared, and when it is expected that even members of oppressed groups be reinterpreted as active human beings. Among the Sicilian illiterates, only the decision to migrate and the ability to adapt to new environments indicated their agency.

Callari Galli's *Antropologia e educazione* (1975) is both an examination of the basic relationship between education and cultural anthropology, and a critical reflection on the latter and on her own anthropological work. Culture and education are presented as intrinsically connected since "the tool, not nature, had allowed some animals to establish new relations with the surrounding world ... giving way to a new system of child raising" (1975: 6). Stones transformed into tools modified the pressure for natural selection, hastened the evolution toward *Homo sapiens,* and required that one's own offspring be taught how to make and use tools. In fact, human creativity and civilization would wither away without the cultural transmission that transfers both cultural meanings and society's relational architecture. It is through both of them that diversity is organized and the historical "mutual dependency of social strata" (1975: 113) is made acceptable.

Yet because of Italian cultural heterogeneity and social stratification, neither all meanings nor all social connections can be passed from one social stratum to another. Different social experiences may entail different meanings of schooling. Italy's great old problem "is anthropological and educational at the same time" resulting from "pluriculturalism determined by the historical pre-unification past, the different social conditions of the different regions developing [all] in a differential way, and a social stratification that mixes the class-based antagonism with the otherness of subcultures" (1975: 15). In Callari Galli's view, cultural anthropology can address the refusal to recognize alternative languages and lifestyles, and indicate how to achieve a "multi-linguistic environment" that is able "to transform the élite mono-lingual school environment" (1975: 33). She argues that anthropology guides us in learning about others' cultural diversity. Most importantly, however, it gives us the opportunity to learn something new and something else about ourselves in our interaction with others.

The Recognition of Italian Internal Diversity

At the beginning of the 1990s, the positive recognition of the Italian history of cultural and linguistic diversity was reclaimed in educational thought and practice. Social justice was perceived as a matter of social and economic equity and also an area for serious attention to Italian internal differences. Recognition of diversity led to a new kind of encounter between cultural anthropology and education in the renovation of history teaching in compulsory schooling. The renewal of the discipline of history by academic scholars had given prominence to local contexts and perspectives alongside the official ones.[2] The new scholarship was heeded by members of the Movimento di Cooperazione Educativa,[3] who transferred it to national curricula through their research and writing on history themes and methodology, together with anthropologist Paola Falteri (MCE 1990). The MCE anthology acknowledges that improvement of Italians' socioeconomic conditions, longer compulsory schooling, and easier access to higher education represent a challenge to "the previous model of cultural transmission ... based on the isomorphism between the culture taught by the teacher and that of students' context of origin" (Falteri and Lazzarin 1990: 3). These new conditions are also a prompt for teachers to realize that "they are working within a microcosm where cultural models, behaviors, values are different among students and even within each student" (1990: 3). Since "one kind only of educational discourse" cannot address students' wide diversity, teachers need to know which contents are both educationally effective and a "source of identity" for students (1990: 4). This theoretical and educational renewal also anticipates critical multiculturalism's goals, because it aims to prevent students from remaining embedded in their cultures of origins, and promotes their openness to, and understanding of, an ever-transforming world. The long cooperation of Falteri[4] with MCE members was important for establishing that recognition of the meanings that orient people's thoughts, decisions, and actions was relevant for a new vision and practice of education. Additionally, Falteri explored representations of the non-Western worlds in textbooks for compulsory schooling (Falteri 1993) and reflected on intercultural education initiatives and projects (Falteri 1995).

The Changing Sociocultural Landscape and Intercultural Education

In 1993, Callari Galli resumed her concern for a productive dialogue between anthropology and education. She also reaffirmed her belief that cultural anthropology could both challenge current views of education and schooling and analyze the social transformations that had changed Italy from a country of emigration into one of immigration. In *Antropologia culturale e processi educativi* (1993), her interdisciplinary efforts are "fostered precisely by [contemporary social and communicative] tensions" (146) emerging in classrooms where languages, religious faiths, and everyday meanings are increasingly diverse. The 1993 reflections and hopes that an interdisciplinary approach may promote dialogue and overcome conflicts are written in her usual brilliant and elegant style, and sustained by an ample and thought-provoking scholarship. Yet they remain largely distant from the empirical reality of classrooms with their educational dilemmas, cultural strategies, and misunderstandings (see also Callari Galli 2000.)

My own contribution to anthropology of education can be characterized as a project to introduce into Italian intercultural education the theoretical and methodological reflections elaborated in the United States and Britain during some decades of anthropological debates on schooling, enculturation, and social justice. The political, social, and cultural climate in the United States between the late 1960s and early 1970s had been a relevant learning experience for me. It had prompted me to understand and study those notions (identity, ethnicity, culture, enculturation, among others) that were considered as crucial for the realization of human and educational rights. The "conversation causally begun ... more than thirty years ago" with John U. Ogbu[5] strengthened my inclination for research and for an approach that gave adults and children the opportunity "to tell researchers their views on the social environments where they lived, worked, studied and hoped" (Gobbo 2004c: 349–350).

My earliest effort came out as a book on intercultural education (Gobbo 1992). There I discussed the theoretical perspectives on schooling, and the critical analysis of multiculturalism elaborated by anthropologists of education. I also analyzed the educational recognition of diversity through historical and anthropological references that problematized the notions of minorities' school performance and identity.[6] In continental Europe, intercultural discourse and practice consider diversity as a resource for education rather than something to be silenced, as Italian internal diversity had been silenced. Immigrants' diversity and their cultural, ethnic, and religious identities soon became the focus of teachers' concerns, which were answered by a number of cultural anthropologists (among them Ugo Fabietti, Vittorio Lanternari, and Francesco Remotti). Though theoretically relevant, the anthropologists' occasional contributions referred to their own research and interpretive experience, which rarely focused on educational institutions and their participants. Instead those concerned with the dilemmas and challenges of multicultural classrooms can surely benefit from the knowledge gained through ethnographic findings and anthropologists of education's theorization conducted in educational contexts. Research and theory can furthermore widen the scope of the intercultural debate, enrich it with comparative and methodological rigor, and foster a reflective attitude among future and practising teachers.

The anthology *Antropologia dell'educazione* (Gobbo 1996) discussed such aims and issues in a systematic and comparative way. Its chapters were translations of a number of relevant articles that Ogbu had put together and edited for the *International Encyclopedia of Education,* and could not specifically address the Italian situation. However, they gave readers the opportunity to learn, from a historical and theoretical point of view, about the construction of this anthropological subdiscipline as an independent scholarly realm. They also reminded them that the subdiscipline had developed both as a thoughtful response to the political demands and protests of minorities in the United States, and as a well-founded criticism of educational theories of "cultural deprivation" or "educational disadvantage."

Perhaps assuming the role of the cultural broker, between 1996 and 2001 I invited a number of Italian and European anthropologists and anthropologically oriented educators to the University of Padua—my institution at the time. They presented their theoretical and ethnographic research on various aspects of diversity, and its problematic relation to education and migration (Gobbo 1997; Gobbo and Tommaseo Ponzetta 1999; Gobbo 2003b). Those seminars created opportunities for intellectual exchange and cross-cultural comparison on multicultural school contexts and actors, and challenged widely held educational ideas and practices. Intercultural education is concerned with cultural miscommunication in schools, but it usually ignores the cultural dimension of schools and classrooms with which immigrants and minority pupils have to grapple, and which teachers and principals often take for granted.

Thus it seemed important that those planning to work in the field of education were able to problematize representations of multicultural classrooms, their pupils and teachers, as well as the processes of teaching and learning occurring there, thanks to ethnography. "Making the familiar strange" through daily participant observation, listening, and conversations became a metaphor for challenging intercultural learning experiences (Gobbo 2004b; Gobbo 2007b, Galloni 2007b); some of the studies in this vein have recently been anthologized (Gobbo 2007d).

Pedagogia interculturale (2000b) is my second book on intercultural education. There, through ethnographic findings and anthropologists' theorizations, schools—and Italian schools in particular—are interpreted as problematic cultural environments that are often discontinuous with the surrounding sociocultural context. I argued that teachers involved in fighting indifference, ethnocentrism, prejudices, and even racism through intercultural education would be more effective if they learned how the cultures of the schools, when unexamined, could thwart their efforts.

My proposal that teachers become their own ethnographers of education (Gobbo 2000b and 2004d) stemmed from the awareness that schools' and classrooms' changes do not originate exclusively from the students' cultural, religious, or linguistic diversity but are also produced by educational rules and expectations as well as by students' and teachers' coping strategies. Such dynamic situations have convincingly been interpreted by educators and psychologists with a background in anthropology of education. Based on extensive participant observation in schools, they document the differently enacted agency of children and families, and the relational strategies that teachers choose to promote— not always successfully—migrants' children's learning and integration in school. They also interpret and discuss how processes of inclusion are—or are not—realized through ad hoc projects, how participation in classroom activities and learning is influenced by teachers' and peers' expectations, and how strategic socioeducational functions are carried out through peer interaction and communication (Gobbo and Gomes 2003; Gobbo 2007c, 2008b). Some researchers do not restrict ethnography of education to schooling but widen its scope to include out-of-school contexts and interactions. Understanding the latter is relevant for a comprehensive view of educational processes and intercultural relations that makes young people's agency and projects better visible (Caronia 2003; Costa 2007, 2008; Dallavalle 2008; Galloni 2008b).

These ethnographies challenge teachers' and even educational experts' theories on pupils' and students' relational comfortableness or unease, learning problems or successes, school misadaptation or fit by demonstrating that they are not always influenced by cultural differences. For instance, Galloni's long and sympathetic acquaintance with the Sikh community of Lombardy's rural areas allowed her to interpret (2007a) Sikh children's disruptive behavior in primary school as related to their need for acceptance by Italian peers rather than to their "ignorance" of how to behave properly and perform successfully. Life in small towns of the Po river valley, or in isolated farms,[7] makes having fun with their classmates more important than good grades and teachers' approval. Indeed, those who enroll in vocational schools after compulsory schooling often find themselves marginalized by Italian peers, who dislike their investment in education and their brilliant learning capacities (Galloni 2008a, 2009).

Research on Cultural Diversities and Education

Among cultural anthropologists it has been long established that concepts such as "culture" and "identity" must be declined in the plural. Likewise, diversity can be cultural, religious, linguistic, or ethnic. Its impact on societies and schools can be not only the result of international migration but of internal migration as well. Nations' cultures as well have come to be perceived as multicultural, also because of their historical complexity. Such an awareness was diffused in Italy between the 1980s and the early 1990s when important curricular reforms were enacted. However, it soon receded into the background because of teachers' greater concern with immigrants' diversity. For its part, intercultural education concentrated its focus on the latter and often contributed to defining it in terms of problems and emergency. Yet other cultural, ethnic, occupational, and religious Italian diversities continue to exist besides migrants' diversity and have attracted the attention of anthropologists and anthropologically trained educators.

Cultural anthropologists studying Roma, Sinti and Camminanti[8] have repeatedly been concerned with those children's experiences of schooling, although they would hardly define themselves as anthropologists of education. Their ethnographic research provides educators and teachers with fine theoretical interpretations of the classroom vicissitudes of these minority children, of teachers' expectations and representations of them, and of the cultures of schools. The ethnographies delve into the children's strategies for learning (Gomes 2003; Pontrandolfo 2004) and for identity preservation—interpreted as resistance to schooling—and also examine the processes of fragmented participation in classroom activities, differentiated learning, and dilemmas of adult literacy projects (Gomes 1998; Saletti Salza 2003, 2004; Sidoti 2007; Trevisan 2005, among others). Anthropologist Leonardo Piasere has conducted and coordinated anthropological and historical research on the various Roma groups that is relevant to those engaged in achieving equity in education. This has led him to consider the relationship between cultural anthropology and education (Piasere 2004), and to warn teachers, educators, and policy makers of the risks that, on the one hand, by seeking to chart Roma cultural differences, ethnographic research might contribute to their reification, and on the other, that intercultural education, with its focus on recognition and integration of diversity, might unwittingly support assimilatory expectations (Piasere 2007).

However, some children's school life can be a difficult, painful experience, even when they are not perceived as culturally different, because of the truly nomadic life they live. This is the case with traveling attractionists' families that I studied between 1999 and 2001 in Veneto. Their children's right to education is not fully achieved because schools and teachers do not have the capacity, or the willingness, to question an institutional culture and organization that is unable to answer their needs. Furthermore, teacher-centered pedagogy cannot take into account the social and communication skills those children have learned at home and demonstrate in the classroom (Gobbo 2003a, 2006, 2007a, 2007b, 2009b). Research on traveling attractionists' lifestyle, identity, and schooling can productively interrogate an anthropology of education that, at least in Italy, has been concerned almost exclusively with the effects of migration on educational processes.

The relationship between childhood, schooling, and geocultural environment (*territorio*) is another interesting area where diversities, education, and ethnographic research connect—illuminating, for instance, pedagogical strategies for representing the local environment and daily working activities as well as the correlated "imagined" identities (Falteri 2005). Anthropologist Alessandro Simonicca has studied processes of enculturation and schooling in some areas of Tuscany. He interprets the construction of Siena children's neighborhood identity—so crucial for the famous *Palio* horse races of Siena—when the family moves out of the neighborhood of membership. Based on anthropological and historical knowledge, his findings document new strategies that successfully maintain the prized identity while avoiding its celebration or folklorization. He has also researched the local administrations' investment into cultural and educational projects in the region's urban and classroom contexts, and has produced finely documented portraits of school activities (Simonicca 2007).

Conclusions

Decades ago, it was cultural anthropology in the Anglo-Saxon world that alerted teachers and students that there is education before, during, and after schooling, that school learning does not coincide with the learning of curricular content, and that school success can be defined in many, and opposite, ways. Then, once the subdiscipline of anthropology of education was constructed, anthropologists of education pointed out that notions such as "culture of the school" refer more often to the experience of negotiating meanings and rules than to uncontested sharing of meaning.

In Italy, the encounter between cultural anthropology and education has produced mixed results: Italian cultural anthropologists have stressed some of the above points in an effective manner, and have recognized anthropology of education as an area of theory and research. As I said, in the 1990s individual anthropologists contributed their knowledge to the understanding, and possible solution, of educational dilemmas that teachers were then facing, more in the vein of applied anthropology than of anthropology of education. Yet, only in a limited way did they succeed in promoting research specifically focused on the educational, cultural, and social processes that take place in the various kinds of school and out-of-school contexts. And the hoped-for dialogue and possible cooperation between researchers from the two disciplines has seldom been achieved.

Recently, however, several young educators with a background in anthropology of education have considered the various educational processes, actors, and problems as research issues in their own right. Their attention to questions of social justice, educational performance, and anthropological theory is still very high, but they now examine these questions through empirical research. Considering heterogeneous classrooms mostly in terms of "problems" or "conflicts" to be solved might be understandable. Yet, it will not enable researchers to challenge interpretations that define social and cultural transformation as emergency situations. It will not let them study the construction and negotiation of identities as well as the relational and communication networks in different educational contexts, as it has successfully been done in many school and out-of-school ethnographies. Moreover, new social roles and functions, such as that of cultural mediator,[9] or new words and expressions coined to make sense of the intertwining of differences (cf. Gobbo 2008a, 2009a), deserve to be interpreted against the background of the host society's needs and worries and in dialectic relation with its cultural hegemony—as it can be seen happening these days in Italy. Such research and critical reflections could perhaps contribute to the elaboration of a theory of cultures and educational processes.

Notes

1. The attention of Italian anthropologists to contemporary empirical and theoretical production at the international level arose in post–World War II years, when its prevailing demological tradition was revived by Ernesto De Martino's research in Southern Italy, whose findings and interpretations answered the need to understand the country's geocultural diversity in intellectual as well as political terms, on the one hand, and on the other by the encounter with American cultural anthropology and the work of Lévi-Strauss. The books of the latter were translated and disseminated mostly among philosophers and philosophy students, some of whom were to become the new generation of cultural anthropologists. The impact of Lévi-Strauss was deeply felt by Italian intellectual circles, provoking academic debates on cultural relativism more than ethnographic research, as the French anthropologist's perspective questioned the diffused historicism of Hegelian or Marxist hue. A Marxist or progressive stance remained relevant among cultural anthropologists for many years and promoted interest for the new theoretical and political awareness that was taking place, within the discipline, at the end of the 1960s, especially in the United States. Between the 1970s and the 1980s the works of Marvin Harris and Dell Hymes were translated, published, and widely quoted. In the 1990s, publication followed of texts by Victor Turner, Clifford Geertz, and others that kindled the Italian anthropologists' debate on contemporary directions of cultural anthropology. In Italy, the latter was soon supplemented and enriched by ethnographic research resulting from the newly established doctoral degree that had prompted fieldwork abroad among future cultural anthropologists. More recently, subsectors have been developed (Alpine studies, anthropology of tourism, Roma studies, among others) that produce relevant findings and further theoretical debates. As far as anthropology of education is concerned, however, it has until now been carried out mostly by scholars and young researchers whose institutional affiliation is with the faculties of education.

2. It also promoted different methodological approaches such as life stories when workers and their jobs, women and their place in society became subjects of research.

3. In Italy, the MCE (Movement for Cooperative Education) was founded in the 1950s, and inspired by the pedagogical and social philosophy of Célestin and Élise Freinet (http://www.mce-fimem.it).

4. Personal written communication (9 January 2009).

5. As I have recounted elsewhere (Gobbo 2004c), I met Ogbu in 1972 at Berkeley, where I was attending graduate studies. I registered for a class on urban anthropology that he introduced by speaking about the great Italian internal migration of the 1960s. For the next two years, and under his supervision, I delved into the various aspects of the migration process that had changed my

country, since I would have liked to carry out an ethnographic and comparative research in Turin (Italy) and Bradford (UK) that turned out to be impossible. After I returned to Italy in 1975, the contacts with John Ogbu continued at an irregular pace, but the theory he had in the meantime elaborated seemed to me of particular value, because of his problematization of diversity as well as attention to minorities' epistemologies of educational and social prospects, and the crucial relevance of history and of minority/majority relationships for interpreting minorities' experience and the meaning of schooling and education. To test if Ogbu's category of autonomous minorities could be heuristically useful in a different geohistorical context, I decided to do fieldwork among the Waldensian religious minority that had lived in three neighboring valleys of Piedmont since the fourteenth century. I intended to study how education, religious identity, and minority status had developed, intersected, and were understood in the second half of the 1990s (see Gobbo 2000a). Meanwhile, cultural anthropologist Leonardo Piasere has discussed if the category of involuntary minority status could be applied to Roma (2007). Obgu's theory has been widely tested by the young researchers in anthropology of education I supervise, who have done their fieldwork in classrooms where immigrants' children are enrolled.

6. The issue of minority identity had emerged in the 1970s. As a member of Harrison's and Callari Galli's team that explored local bilingualism, ethnic identity, and schooling (Callari Galli and Harrison 1974, Harrison 1979), I had carried out fieldwork in Calabria, in a small Arbëresh town, between 1975 and 1976. During my stay, I focused on the "imagined" ethnic identity, the complex, intertwined history of the Arbëresh, of Southern Italy, and Italy (Gobbo 1976). Historical and ethnographic data did not support the claim that the Arbëresh language spoken by everyone (and peacefully coexisting with Italian and the Calabrese dialect) matched, or expressed, a specific and homogeneous ethnic and cultural identity rooted in a distant past and place—Albania. Twenty years later, I focused again on the dialectics of identity and schooling among the Protestant Waldensians living in the "diffuse educational environment" of the Piedmont mountain valleys. Findings indicated that their educational identity is fostered by attendance at the only Italian Waldensian high school, while their religious identity is strengthened by participating in activities promoted by lay and religious community's members (Gobbo 2000a).

7. Where their fathers are usually hired to tend cattle.

8. Literally "those who walk." They are not an ethnic group, but rather occupational nomads that live in apartments, mostly in a neighborhood of the Sicilian town of Noto.

9. Minority status might make the construction of a public and professional identity more complicated and emotionally costly, though not impossible. Cf. Gobbo 2004a.

Bibliography

Callari Galli, Matilde. 1975. *Antropologia e educazione. L'antropologia culturale e i processi educativi.* Florence: La Nuova Italia.

————. 1993. *Antropologia culturale e processi educativi.* Florence: La Nuova Italia.

————. 2000. *Antropologia per insegnare.* Milan: Bruno Mondadori.

Callari Galli, Matilde, and Gualtiero Harrison. 1974. *La danza degli orsi.* Caltanissetta-Roma: Edizioni Salvatore Sciascia.

Caronia, Letizia. 2003. "Linguaggio e vita quotidiana come contesti di apprendimento. Uno studio etnografico sulla socializzazione alla lettura in una istituzione educativa." In *Etnografia nei contesti educativi,* ed. Francesca Gobbo and Ana Maria Gomes. Rome: CISU (1st ed. 1999).

Costa, Cecilia. 2007. "Sperimentare l'incontro: giovani migranti e italiani in un centro educativo extra-scolastico." In *Processi educativi nelle società multiculturali,* ed. Francesca Gobbo. Rome: CISU.

————. 2008. "Amicizie interculturali in un contesto extrascolastico: una ricerca etnografica a Torino." In *L'educazione al tempo dell'intercultura,* ed. Francesca Gobbo. Rome: Carocci.

Dallavalle, Chiara. 2008. "Identità molteplici: la seconda generazione di Mazara del Vallo." In *L'educazione al tempo dell'intercultura,* ed. Francesca Gobbo. Rome: Carocci.

Fabietti, Ugo, and Francesco Remotti, eds. 1997. *Dizionario di antropologia.* Bologna: Zanichelli.

Falteri, Paola, ed. 1993. *Interculturalismo e immagine del mondo non occidentale nei libri di testo della scuola dell'obbligo.* Rome: Ministero della Pubblica Istruzione.

————, ed. 1995. *Andata & ritorni. Percorsi formativi interculturali.* Rome: Editoriale Cooperativa MCE.

————, ed. 2005. *"Ho visto i buoi fare il pane." L'immagine del mondo rurale nei libri di testo della scuola primaria.* Rome: Coldiretti.

Falteri, Paola, and M. Giovanna Lazzarin 1990. "Introduzione." In *Storia di segni storia di immagini. Proposte per la formazione storica di base,* Movimento di Cooperazione Educativa/Gruppo Nazionale Antropologia culturale. Florence: La Nuova Italia.

Galloni, Francesca. 2007a. "Alunni sikh a Cremona." In *La ricerca per una scuola che cambia,* ed. Francesca Gobbo. Rome: Carocci.

————. 2007b. "Etnografia: scelta metodologica e non solo." In *La ricerca per una scuola che cambia,* ed. Francesca Gobbo. Padua: Imprimitur.

————. 2008a. "Studenti sikh di fronte alla scelta della scuola secondaria." In *L'educazione al tempo dell'intercultura,* ed. Francesca Gobbo. Rome: Carocci.

————. 2008b. "Che cosa spinge le famiglie sikh a scegliere un centro d'aggregazione?" In *L'educazione al tempo dell'intercultura,* ed. Francesca Gobbo. Rome: Carocci.

————. 2009. *Giovani indiani a Cremona.* Roma: CISU.

Gobbo, Francesca. 1976. "Rapporto sull'identità etnica arbëresh." Unp. ms.

————. 1977. "Decentramento e partecipazione di base: il caso della Black America." *Scuola e Città* 28, no. 1 (January): 32–39.

————. 1992. *Radici e frontiere. Contributo all'analisi del discorso pedagogico interculturale.* Padua: Edizioni Alfasessanta.

————, ed. 1996. *Antropologia dell'educazione. Scuola, cultura, educazione nella società multiculturale.* Milan: Edizioni Unicopli.

————, ed. 1997. *Cultura Intercultura*. Padua: Imprimitur.

————. 2000a. "Ethnography of Education in the Waldensian Valleys: Analysis of the Relationship between a Religious Minority Identity, its Cultural History and Current Educational Experience." In *Educational Research in Europe. Yearbook 2000*, ed. Christopher Day and Dolf van Veen. Leuven: Garant.

————. 2000b. *Pedagogia interculturale. Il progetto educativo nelle società complesse*. Rome: Carocci.

————. 2003a. "C'è una giostra nel futuro? Esperienza scolastica e processo d'inculturazione in una minoranza occupazionale nomade." In *Etnografia dell'educazione in Europa. Soggetti, contesti, questioni metodologiche*, ed. Francesca Gobbo. Milan: Edizioni Unicopli.

————, ed. 2003b. *Etnografia dell'educazione in Europa. Soggetti, contesti, questioni metodologiche*. Milan: Edizioni Unicopli.

————. 2004a. "Cultural Intersections: The Life Story of a Roma Cultural Mediator." *European Educational Research Journal* 3, no. 3: 626–41.

————. 2004b. "Ethnographic Research as a Re/Source of Intercultural Education," *Proceedings of INST International Conference "Das Verbindende der Kulturen"* (Vienna, November 2003), http://www.inst.at/trans/15Nr/08_1/gobbo15 .htm : 1–12.

————. 2004c. "John U. Ogbu: A Personal Recollection." *Intercultural Education* 15, no. 4 (December): 349–58.

————. 2004d. "L'insegnante come etnografo: idee per una formazione alla ricerca." In *L'intercultura dalla A alla Z*, ed. Graziella Favaro, Lorenzo Luatti. Milan: FrancoAngeli.

————. 2006. "Along the Margins, Across the Borders: Teaching and Learning among Veneto *attrazionisti viaggianti*." *Teaching and Teacher Education* 22, no. 7 (October): 788–803.

————. 2007a. "Alunni 'di passo'? Le narrazioni delle insegnanti sulla scolarizzazione dei figli degli attrazionisti viaggianti." In *Processi educativi nelle società multiculturali*, ed. Francesca Gobbo. Rome: CISU.

————. 2007b. "Between the Road and the Town: The Education of Travelling Attractionists. An Ethnographic Research." In *International Handbook of Urban Education*, ed. William T. Pink and George W. Noblit. Dordrecht: Springer.

————, ed. 2007c. *Processi educativi nelle società multiculturali*. Rome: CISU.

————, ed. 2007d. *La ricerca per una scuola che cambia*. Padua: Imprimitur.

————. 2008a. "Sull'uso di alcune metafore in pedagogia interculturale." In *L'educazione al tempo dell'intercultura*, ed. Francesca Gobbo. Rome: Carocci.

————, ed. 2008b. *L'educazione al tempo dell'intercultura*. Rome: Carocci.

————. 2009a. "On Metaphors, Everyday Diversity and Intercultural Education: Some Further Reflections." *Intercultural Education* 20, no. 4: 321–32.

————. 2009b. "Moving Lives. A Reflective Account of a Three Generation Travelling Attractionist Family in Italy." In *Traveller, Nomadic and Migrant Education*, eds. Máirín Kenny and Patrick A. Danaher. London: Routledge.

Gobbo, Francesca, and Ana Maria Gomes, eds. 2003. *Etnografia nei contesti educativi*. Rome: CISU (1st ed. 1999).

Gobbo, Francesca, and Mila Tommaseo Ponzetta, eds. 1999. *La quotidiana diversità*. Padua: Imprimitur.

Gomes, Ana Maria. 1998. *"Vegna che ta fago scriver."* *Etnografia della scolarizza-zione inuna comunità di sinti.* Rome: CISU

———. 2003. "Esperienze di scolarizzazione dei bambini sinti: confronto tra differenti modalità di gestione del quotidiano scolastico." In *Etnografia nei contesti educativi,* ed. Francesca Gobbo and Ana Maria Gomes. Rome: CISU (1st ed. 1999).

Harrison, Gualtiero. 1979. *La doppia identità. Una vertenza antropologica nella minoranza etnicolinguistica arbëresh.* Caltanissetta-Roma: Edizioni Salvatore Sciascia.

Harrison, Gualtiero, and Matilde Callari Galli. 1971. *Né leggere né scrivere.* Milan: Feltrinelli.

MCE/Gruppo Nazionale Antropologia culturale. 1990. *Storia di segni storia di immagini. Proposte per la formazione storica di base.* Florence: La Nuova Italia.

Piasere, Leonardo. 2004. "La sfida: dire 'qualcosa di antropologico' sulla scuola." *Antropologia* 4, no. 4: 7–17.

———. 2007. "Roma, sinti, camminanti nelle scuole italiane: risultati di un pro-getto di ricerca di etnografia dell'educazione." In *Processi educativi nelle so-cietà multiculturali,* ed. Francesca Gobbo. Rome: CISU.

Pontrandolfo, Stefania. 2004. *Un secolo di scuola. I rom di Melfi.* Rome: CISU.

Saletti Salza, Carlotta. 2003. *Bambini del "campo nomadi." Romá bosniaci a Torino.* Rome: CISU.

———. 2004. "Non c'è proprio niente da ridere. Sulle strategie di gestione del quotidiano scolastico di alcuni alunni rom". *Quaderni di sociologia* XLVIII, no. 36: 7–29.

Sidoti, Simona. 2007. "Scuole possibili lungo la strada dei Caminanti di Noto." In *Processi educativi nelle società multiculturali,* ed. Francesca Gobbo. Rome: CISU.

Simonicca, Alessandro. 2007. "Problemi sull'uso pubblico dell'antropologia in settino scolastici." In *Processi educativi nelle società multiculturali,* ed. Fran-cesca Gobbo. Rome: CISU.

Trevisan, Paola. 2005. *Storie e vite di sinti dell'Emilia.* Rome: CISU.

§ 8

Central Europe (Bulgaria, the Czech Republic, Hungary, Poland, Romania, Slovakia)

Gábor Eröss

This chapter could be very short. Not only is it difficult to identify practitioners of anthropology in the formerly socialist countries of Europe (Sárkány 2002), but neither the anthropology of education nor the ethnography of school can be considered well-established fields of study in this region. Anthropology has a particular history in Central Europe: virtually no school of anthropology or any other kind of cultural/social anthropology had existed before the 1970s, or even up to the end of communism. There was another discipline that was stealing the show: ethnography, i.e., folklore studies (the descriptive study of local cultures). However, since ethnography (or folklore studies) has always sought for the "authentic" culture, the "ancestral" tradition (exactly as anthropology had in its beginning), school—as a modern institution—was not in its sights.

But a few important contributions in the past, as well as a multitude of recent publications make it worthwhile to examine this field, even more so because "social scientists of Central and Eastern European countries publish mainly in their own languages" (Sárkány 2002). No publication has tried to cover this heterogeneity so far. In this region of the world, whose countries have never had colonies, "there are possibilities for publication, but specialized cultural anthropological journals do not exist" (Sárkány 2002).

* * *

I will try to puzzle this field together for the first time. I shall present anthropologies and ethnographies of education in six Central European countries in this chapter, current members of the European Union, former members of the "Soviet Bloc" (but not of the former Soviet Union): Bulgaria, the Czech Republic, Hungary, Poland, Romania, and Slovakia. My conception includes two countries usually defined as Southeastern European (Romania and Bulgaria), but excludes several others, such as the three Baltic States and the seven countries originating from the former Yugoslavia. I ignore—more or less—the relatively small number of studies on learning *outside* school (socialization and informal education), for lack of space. Also, I define education as compulsory schooling, and exclude higher education.

To begin, I should note that Central and Southeastern Europe is far from homogeneous. Poland in particular is a separate case, because of its historical past. Polish educational anthropology derives mainly from a "German branch" (Bollnow 1963, 1987; Langeveld 1968); as a result, it concentrates mainly on philosophical issues. Ablewicz's work (2003) is a sort of summing-up of the influence of the German literature in Poland. A new generation of young anthropologists also has emerged, attempting to break (at least partially) with the philosophical tradition (Anna Fitak, Alicja Sadownik, and others), and studying, for example, institutions like vocational schools (Sadownik 2006).

Anthropology without Anthropologists

My central thesis is that—beyond institutional, national, and methodological divergences—a major topic, a common object of studies dominates anthropologies of education in this region: ethnicity in general, and the Roma in particular.

My two additional theses are:

(1) Anthropologies of education possess a double nature in this region: a few authors follow a traditional ethnographic pattern (characteristic of early social sciences in general throughout the region), while the mainstream position can be seen as an applied science, part of global policy initiatives, with more or less explicitly emancipatory—and evidence-based policy making—aspirations (funded by the Soros Foundation, the Roma Education Fund, International Step by Step Association [ISSA], the European Union, Amnesty International, the United Nations Development Program, UNICEF, and others).[1] This applied science transforms knowledge into a policy tool (Delvaux and Mangez 2008). In a further step, however, national institutions internalize that transnational perspective and focus on the issues of Roma, minorities, and migrants in school—especially in Bulgaria, Hungary, and Romania. So, paradoxically, the development of educational anthropology is coupled with this process of "policy learning." In the era of applied knowledge and postbureaucratic regulation, knowledge, and policy evolve more and more inseparably. This results in constellations of knowledge *as* policy, and policy *as* knowledge.

(2) Since no autonomous anthropology of education emerged as an institutionalized, strong academic subdiscipline, sociologists and other social scientists (including educational scientists, social psychologists, Roma studies scholars, and others) divided this field of study among themselves.[2] Which is, again, not a unique phenomenon; sometimes even authors in *Anthropology of Education Quarterly* tend to ignore many of the developments in mainstream anthropology, as Delamont points out in this volume.

***

In a region of the world that gave anthropology some of its most important figures—Bronisław Malinowski, Emil Torday, Aleš Hrdlička, and others—anthropology has, except in Romania, only very late and very gradually became an established academic discipline (Sárkány 2002), unlike ethnography or folklore studies. The descriptive perspective dominates in ethnography, and theorization is rare. Ethnographers (and ethnologists) working in Central and Eastern Europe participated in the construction of independent nation-states. "Consequently, the driving forces behind research activity were an awareness of ethnicity, nationalism, and historical and cultural ties" (Sárkány 2002). Folklore studies are in this respect similar, although (even) narrower in focus.

The dominance of sociology in the field of social sciences, in a context of "Mode 2"-type knowledge production (Nowotny, Scott, and Gibbons 2003), combined with *transnationalization* (Delvaux and Mangez 2008; Eröss et al. 2009), led to the emergence of a new, interdisciplinary topic of research and of policy projects: the "Roma field." Education is a central issue in this field, for a variety of reasons—quite unusual in anthropology. First, researchers, on the basis of their sociological academic background, believe education is key to understanding society, social mobility, reproduction, and symbolic order. Second, those active in this field, far from condemning normative attitudes, are committed to the Roma's case and believe the Roma's situation has to be improved above all through school success (e.g., Equal Access 2007, 2008). Third, school segregation/integration appears to them as the key pattern of both social interactions and power relations (European Commission 2005, 2007).

Evaluation emerges as a major form of (partly) anthropological study of education. Research and evaluation are considered as one,[3] and are both tightly linked to policy. They are also very context sensitive and consist predominantly of local case studies.[4] Sometimes they explicitly declare anthropological objectives: "The evaluation addressed the question: How is the project influencing the quality of the learning environment in the classroom?" (Ulrich et al. 2002: 11).

Action research,[5] deliberative polls (Örkény and Székelyi 2007), policy papers, and good practice guides (Promotion of Roma 2006), are part of this new research-policy mix. Also, cultural studies and community studies play a growing role.

The emergence of the "Roma field" has been followed, more recently, by that of the "migration field": again, research and policy unite and give birth to a multidisciplinary field, where anthropological methods (*active* participant observation) and anthropological theories are applied, among others, but only a few anthropologists (and virtually no ethnographers) are involved. At least not *as* anthropologists.

To a lesser extent, the study of the diverse national minorities contributes to expanding the field. The Hungarian Ombudsman (Parliamentary Commissioner for National and Ethnic Minority Rights) issues a report every year, which is as much a work of lawyers as of social scientists (*Beszámoló* 2000, 2001, 2002, etc.) and is itself based on research papers; it concerns thirteen minority groups living in the territory of Hungary, the large Hungarian minority living in Romania and in Slovakia, a Polish minority in the Czech Republic, a Turkish minority in Bulgaria, and so on. In all of these fields education is a focus of minority research.

The reason I believe it is correct to label this wide range of methods and conceptual frameworks, often very policy oriented, as "anthropological" is that they all put an emphasis on the local. A conviction commonly shared by both policy makers and researchers is that "it's the local, stupid." For the political elite of postcommunist countries, decentralization is a guarantee for democracy, while for researchers, the local level has become the "supreme reality," since territorial fragmentation overwhelms the region and social anomie triumphs. All in all, these are prosperous times for anthropology; but not necessarily for anthropologists.

The Roma

As I will show, both on the societal and the scientific level, the "Roma issue" and more generally the ethnic studies perspective (Roma, migrants, and national minorities) are the focus in five of these six countries (as in some other parts of Europe; compare Gobbo, this volume). Poland is again a separate case, because of its historical past and its small Roma community.

In five of these six countries exists a numerically and—moreover—symbolically important Roma minority. Contrary to the phantasm of an ancestral community, living its nomadic life in freedom, peace, and harmony, the vast majority of the Roma are neither nomadic, nor "aboriginal"-like, but rather settled, seeking social integration and equal schooling. However, important differences among the five countries exist, the Roma in Central European Hungary being probably the most integrated and those living in certain rural areas of Romania and Bulgaria the least.

One of the major contributions of anthropologically oriented research is to show that the essentialist perspective does not get at the complex reality of being Roma, especially in schools. How many Roma have mother tongues different from the official language used in education? In Hungary, for example, virtually every Hungarian Roma speaks Hungarian (with a small group also speaking Beas and another group Lovari in addition to Hungarian), while all underclass or lower-class Roma are identified as having a more general sociolinguistic phenomenon, the problem of the "restricted code."

Is there, nonetheless "a Roma culture"? Is there a (negative) "Roma attitude" toward school as an institution? And, by the way: Who are the Roma? In the Czech Republic, only 12,000 persons identified themselves as of Roma "nationality" in 2001, while their estimated number is between 200,000 and 400,000, about thirty times more. In Hungary, 190,000 declared Roma origin whereas estimates go from around 500,000 to 700,000. There is a fundamental question behind this: Who can say, "This person/this pupil is Roma"? This question generates political and ethical debates, as well as scientific controversies. A debate related to this is: Is it culture or social class that counts? Since the vast majority of Roma are underclass or lower class, the segregation *could* be based on social class, not ethnicity. So, who is Roma? Again, the only solution seems to be to seek the definition on the local level, from the respondents themselves or from their neighbors (Kemény, Janky, and Lengyel 2004), and then to cope with the complexity and volatility of local ethnic settings.

Most countries of the region show high levels of academic inequality (Palečková et al. 2007). Generally, Roma are seen as the first and foremost victims of this problem (see … *all* publications on this topic). The question is: does one select one's school, or is it the school who selects the students, and if so, on what basis—abilities or ethnic markers? A major part of research in school socioanthropology is dedicated to the selection/segregation issue (see details below). Those who wish to understand and also combat segregation (two actions that cannot be separated) need to know the situation village by village, school by school, classroom by classroom, observing, making interviews, and participating in the elaboration of the "Local Desegregation/ Equal Chances Plans."

A specific but major issue related to the segregation/integration topic is that of "special schools" or "remedial schools" (see Eröss et al. 2009 and below, country by country). Many of them, in Hungary, the Czech Republic, or Slovakia, for example, are overwhelmingly filled with Roma students (Amnesty International 2008). Roma students made up 90 percent of the enrollment in Czech special schools, which were abolished by the 2005 amendment of the Education Act.

Preschooling is another major policy and research issue: Roma children seldom attend nursery schools. Although the impact of kindergarten attendance on educational opportunities is easy to show, preschool preparatory programs for the Roma in the Czech Republic or early development and early kindergarten programs for them in Hungary are based on the deficit hypothesis, the implicit assumption that Roma culture is indeed different and that Roma have to be, so to speak, re-socialized or "acculturated" in order to meet mainstream education's requirements and cultural standards.

The very solution-oriented nature of the "Roma issue" produces also a sizeable literature on intercultural or multicultural education: publications range from the review of the rich English-language literature to practical issues such as how to "deal with" Roma in everyday teaching in the classroom (compare Boreczky 1999; Czachesz 1998; Nahalka 2004; Torgyik 2004).

Czech Republic and Slovakia

Czech Republic

International organizations as well as national institutions adopting the transnational agenda (Czech School Inspectorate, Council for National Minorities of the Government, and so on) focus more and more on the Roma issue (and, to a lesser extent, on the migration issue).

Educational anthropology (ethnoecology of school) is one of the branches of pedagogics in the Czech Republic as in Slovakia. There are a couple of publications in English, a few in Slovakian (Svec 1998) and many in Czech, for there exists a group named *Prazska skupina skolni etnografie*—Prague Group of School Ethnography ("What you have ..." 2001; Kučera, Rochex, and Štech 2001), which was maybe the only research community in this field throughout the region for years. (The group is now more or less breaking down, its members joining other research teams; it remains to be seen whether Czech school ethnography will weaken or will spread.)

In the second half of the 1990s, Vladimír Smékal (2003), the renowned psychologist of Marsaryk University in Brno, conducted in-depth research among Roma children, which showed that preschool children from the Roma and other minority environments have in fact the same mental dispositions as their monolingual Czech-speaking age-mates. What he and his colleagues see as the two major obstacles for Roma children are "linguistic competences" and "motivation" — they "have not learnt to learn." In addition, preschool tests disadvantage Roma (and other minority) children.

It is the experience of many teachers, as supported by more in-depth research in Roma communities (e.g., Poledňová and Zobačová 2006), that too many Roma children do not enjoy a supportive environment within their families and the wider communities that would motivate them to better achievements and higher ambitions in school. Perhaps the best known example of ethnographic research done by Plzeň anthropologists (Hirt and Jakoubek 2006) is the latter's general assertion that the Roma "problem" is in fact not an ethnic one, but instead a social class issue (Szalai 2008).

In 1999, The European Roma Rights Centre undertook extensive research in the Ostrava region (ERRC 1999), which resulted in a legal case (*D. H. vs. Czech Republic*). The research showed that Roma children in Ostrava were twenty-eight times more likely to be placed in remedial schools (then called "special schools") for pupils with learning and behavioral disorders than non-Roma children, and that more than half the Roma children were placed in these schools. In November 2007, the legal case was finally closed: the European Court for Human Rights found the Czech authorities guilty of racial discrimination against Roma children. Thus there is only one step from empirical quasi-anthropological research to court cases. And from court cases to policies, and from policies back to local (non-)implementation.

Slovakia

As far as Slovakia is concerned, again, the most significant research findings concerning the role of ethnicity in education can be found in the numerous reports of domestic and foreign nongovernmental organizations (such as the European Roma Rights Centre, the Open Society Institute, the Slovak Governance Institute, and many others). Several studies have been published about the efficiency of "zero-grade" classes (a preparatory school year) and teacher's assistants as compensatory instruments for alleviation of the disadvantaged conditions of children from marginalized Roma communities. Much attention has also been paid to special schooling, its inadequate quality and the overrepresentation of Roma pupils in special schools (Tomatová 2004; Stigmata 2004; Still separate, still unequal 2007; Equal Access 2008).

Tomatová (2004) described various administrative procedures that enable placements and transfers of students from regular to special schools. Detailed field research has been provided by the Slovak Governance Institute under the series of *Interface* reports. These combine the analysis of concrete legislative provisions with microlevel surveys of their implementation in practice. The most relevant reports analyzed the efficiency of social provisions for the increase of school attendance and performance of Roma children (Húšová 2006) and the analysis of transitional classes.

Bulgaria and Romania

Our introductory hypothesis seems validated in the case of Romania and Bulgaria too. The anthropology of education as such does not exist. Instead many social scientists address the issue of Roma in school.

Romania

The literature about Roma in Romania is mainly in three languages, English, Romanian, and Hungarian.

Beginning with the Hungarian language literature, we can state that the Roma topic is not part of the school topic; rather, the school topic— among many others—is part of the Roma topic. Most "school anthropology-like" studies originate in the Roma field. Just as in other countries, school segregation is the focus. But there is also another academic discipline, regional studies, where the Roma issue arises: "Roma and school" is thus defined there as a social and cultural phenomenon embedded in the regional (Transylvanian) and in the local setting (village by village): schooling is dismissed in one Roma community, it is favored in another; Roma are segregated in one village, they learn together with the local majority (the ethnic Hungarians in this case) in another; high Roma drop-out rate characterizes one village, low drop-out rate another (Bodó 2002).

In the Romanian language literature, "Roma and Education" is also a major subject. Research requests often come from the government;

again, research has to be policy oriented, but it is at the same time locally ("anthropologically") embedded since the government is aware of the heterogeneity of local ethnic/school settings. On this basis, the Ministry of Education tries to conceive and adjust its programs for Roma schooling.

The public discourse debates are generated at the meeting point of two major positions, one emphasizing the ethnic nature of the Roma question (the right to learn the Romani language and history, and even to learn all disciplines in Romani and have Roma-only classes or schools), and the other stressing its social character (Roma as a disadvantaged group).

I would like to present a few recent and major studies in this domain in Romania. First, the project "Come Closer: Inclusion and Exclusion of Roma in Present-Day Romanian Society" (Fleck and Rughinis 2008). This was a complex research project, financed by the European Union's PHARE Program, including a vast survey of Roma and one thousand non-Roma households as well as a remarkable thirty-six community studies.

Another case study was conducted in the multicultural southwestern Romanian town of Timişoara (Magyari-Vincze 2007). It pointed out that Roma children's access to school is reduced for the following reasons: lack of birth certificates and identity cards (representing an obstacle in enrolling children in school or kindergarten); financial and housing conditions of the families (increasing the risk of school failure and drop-out); marriage of girls at an early age, followed by giving birth at an early age (especially in the case of traditional Roma groups, in this case Geambaşi and Gabor); prejudices and discriminatory treatment towards Roma children by teachers, other pupils, and parents; temporary migration of parents, who take their children back and forth abroad; school segregation (which goes together with a lower quality of education).

The policy-oriented perspective is dominant in Romania too (for example, Toma 2005), especially among English-language articles and reports. Notwithstanding the EDUMIGROM project (see note 1) and other cross-national/European projects, there are also national-level studies that assess concretely the impact of given policies (for example, the Roma school mediators program).

All disciplines are involved in the "Roma field" — see the extensive bibliography of Roma studies during the 1990–2007 period (Fosztó 2008). But the "Roma field" itself is open for multicultural perspectives. In this respect, the complex community study by Stefania Toma may be typical: she studies a multiethnic village as a whole (employment, social structure, and so on) but addresses the school topic in more than the half of her paper (Toma 2008).

Bulgaria

The anthropology of education—as such—does not really exist in Bulgaria either. Again, we need to understand "anthropology" in a broader sense and include qualitative sociology and any related field, including (but not limited to) the field "Roma (and/or the 'Turkish' minority') and Education."

Valentina Milenkova (2008 and many others) emerges as a central figure of qualitative educational studies. Grekova (2008 and many others), Nunev (2006), and Kjuchukov (2006) have a wider focus, but also use qualitative methods. Earlier, Grekova focused more narrowly, on the "Configurations of Cultural Diversity at School" (2002) and on "Cultural Difference as a Problem of Intercultural Education'" (1999). Dimitrov and Boyadjieva (2009) use qualitative data and discuss the citizenship education in the Bulgarian secondary schools.

The policy perspective and the (local) best-practice approach dominate in Bulgaria too. Donka Panayotova for instance studies a successful grassroots Romani School Desegregation project: "'I have a dream to become a lawyer and I think that my new school will help me achieve that,' Kalcho said. This is how most of the children in the desegregation program feel, despite the challenges facing them in a new school environment" (Panayotova 2007).

Hungary

Hungary seems to be the epicenter of the Central European Roma field, for a variety of reasons. The proportion of the Roma is quite high (which is also the case in Romania and Slovakia); they have been settled early and entirely (which is unique to Hungary); they participated in the formation of Hungarian national identity; social scientists "targeted" them as early as the 1970s (Kemény 1976), and more. Therefore, the presentation of the Hungarian case will be essentially limited to the "really" anthropological approaches, since the entirety of social scientists' works would exceed the limits of this chapter.

Cecilia Kovai's research question—studied through the example of a Roma schoolgirl in a Hungarian city and compared to her previous field, a Roma community—is "Why and how a stable love relationship and school become contradictory. What kind of relationships among

'Roma-ness,' family, love and marriage lead to a situation where school and educational perspectives lose any kind of importance" (Kovai 2008).

A number of other anthropologists (Csongor 1991) and sociologists conduct local inquiries. Havas, Kemény, and Liskó (2002), Zolnay (2007), Neumann and Zolnay (2008), Váradi (2008), Virág (2003), and Havas (2002) study the communities, education, patterns of (school) segregation, and integration village by village, town by town. Paradoxically, the local level is also the only one on which Roma can be observed, for statistics about ethnic identity of pupils are illegal since 1993. Only a local, scientific method can be used. Németh (2006) and her colleagues conduct an important study as part of the country-wide Public Education Integration Network initiative's monitoring.

Sociologists and anthropologists (Eröss 2008a; Domokos 2008) studied the integration/segregation/inclusion interplay in the case of students with special educational needs. The critique of special (remedial) education as a means of segregation is constant in Hungarian social sciences (Csanádi, Ladányi, and Gerö 1978; Loss 1996; Kende and Neményi 2006). The standards of "school readiness" are far from being consensual or even official, yet they are widespread and lead to early selection and tracking. In addition, this process is based on the medicalization and "psychologization" of "learning disabilities" and "behavioral disorders" (e.g., ADHD), thus—despite the experts' and specialists" obvious good will—legitimating tracking and segregation as early as at the age of six (Oblath et al. 2007; Eröss 2008a and many others). The meaning of the various categories is interpreted and the children are diagnosed in the light of local educational opportunities, the municipality's or county's priorities, the committee's or center's own understanding of the context, and the scientific background of special educational needs.

Although the studies addressing the "Roma and School issue" are broad in focus and great in number, one may read them with some dissatisfaction, precisely because of an exaggerated devotion of most authors to quantitative methods; this is why a new perspective is needed (as discussed below).

Immigrants

Immigration has been a minor phenomenon throughout the decades of communism. It has almost exclusively concerned higher education. In the mid-1980s the first immigrants from China arrived, then later, their children. Again, Hungary distinguishes itself with a relatively high level of Chinese immigration in the 1980s and 1990s. There are still almost no migrants from Southern or Southeast Asia (with the exception of Vietnam), the Middle East, or Africa, and even fewer from Latin America.

In Hungary, the law obliging refugees to send their children to Hungarian schools constituted an important turning point at the beginning of the new Millennium (Feischmidt and Nyíri 2006). Illegal migrants or refugees seeking to reach Western Europe but stuck in Hungary and settled in refugee camps are now integrated into Hungarian schools. However, their number is rather small; in other countries of the region, even smaller. In spite of the limited number of mainly East Asian immigrants and Afghani refugee school children, social scientists and among them anthropologists started to study their situation; interestingly enough, the references to the Roma case are frequent (Feischmidt and Nyíri 2006).

Again, research is mainly conducted in the framework of international projects and policy initiatives (such as the Eurydice Network). In the Czech Republic, besides Slovak pupils (who are the most numerous "migrant" group, though culturally and linguistically very close to the "natives"), two immigrant groups attend in significant numbers: Vietnamese and Ukrainians. These three nationalities represent traditional immigrant groups to the Czech Republic: Slovaks for long decades or even centuries; Vietnamese since the 1970s when they were coming as temporary guest workers (many of them having stayed), with a new wave of Vietnamese immigration started after 1990; last but not least, the Ukrainians, who have joined these two groups in the 1990s in a predominantly economic immigration. The numbers are still relatively low, compared to more traditional immigrant countries of Western Europe. Yet this may well change in the years to come as the Czech Republic has recently become a favorite immigration destination, ranking third after Spain and Italy in 2007. Immigrant pupils from Ukraine largely share initial and persistent language problems with the Roma pupils, along with other (sometimes concomitant) problems like bad communication with parents and discontinuous school attendance, although to somewhat lesser extent. In contrast, according to migration researchers Kocourek and Pechová (2007), Vietnamese children start basic education with the most serious language problems, but their family support and motivation help them overcome this barrier relatively quickly. Kocourek and Pechová (2007) provide perhaps the only consistent account of the experience of and with Vietnamese children at schools. And their account indeed does support the popular thesis reproduced above, although these researchers also point to two gaps that may emerge in the Vietnamese children's experience. One is the gap between them and their schoolmates, especially during the first years of basic education, where different cultural habits may lead to feelings of exclusion. The other is that between Vietnamese children and their parents, which may arise especially during later years of formal education, insofar as the children have adopted some habits of the majoritarian society in order to get better accommodated to their peer environment.

"National Minorities"

Sorbs living in the southeastern part of Germany are considered "relatives" by other Western Slavic nations, i.e., the nearby Czechs and Poles. Among other phenomena, the national identity of students of Sorbian (not Serbian!) origin has been studied (Šatava 2007). Central Europe has traditionally been multiethnic; four of the six countries discussed here once belonged to the modern world's first multicultural empire, Austria-Hungary.

While the Roma issue, although very important, has never been a challenge for its respective nation-states, the "national minority" issue has. In all these countries, which are at a relatively early stage of their national development, school and schooling constituted a national issue. This could have led to the rise of educational anthropology as a state science of efficient assimilation through schooling, but it (un?/fortunately) did not.

The national minorities themselves ("ethnic Hungarians" in Slovakia or in Romania, "ethnic Germans" in the whole region), however, contribute to what we called above the ethnographic tradition of educational anthropology. In Romania (Transylvania), during the 1990s, the right to have Hungarian-only schools was contested. The possibility of learning in the Hungarian language at all educational levels is ensured by now and many Hungarian-only schools were (re)established (Papp Z. 1998). In this "hot" context, local/anthropological studies of education are numerous. Turai shows, for example, how different dimensions or layers of time—that of the school, of the church, of the Hungarians as a community, and of the state—interrelate, and that the (Reformist) church and the school can play together a decisive role in maintaining the national (ethnic Hungarian) identity in one village, while, in another village, where the school director is "ethnic Romanian" and the (Baptist) church refuses to play an active role in this domain, the institutional actors of significance are different (Turai 2005).

Beyond Roma Studies as a "Default" Anthropology of Education

Would we not learn more by studying the normal operation of school and success in school? The criticism that there is a kind of obsession with school failure and minority children in this research field echoes a criticism of the US field (Delamont, this volume). Is an anthropology of education not derived from ethnic studies possible in this region? I will try to show that the answer is "yes." A few authors indeed investigated the school as object with qualitative (anthropological) methods without focusing on the Roma. Visual anthropology (Kapitány and Kapitány 2006) and community study (Kovács 2007) are among the approaches used. One of the most ambitious projects is probably that of György Mészáros (2009), employing an epistemology that unites deconstructive, narrativist, and (neo-)Marxist approaches.

The classical and fundamental questions about issues like time, space, and symbolic structures are also asked. Csilla Meleg analyzed hidden curricula—expressed by temporal and spatial arrangements—and its impact on academic achievement: the choreography of delays, ruptures, and waiting (2005: 128). Eszter Neumann conducted research at a secondary school located in the suburb of an industrial town in northeastern Hungary. A young teacher said during an in-class observation when pupils asked him to dictate slower: "I wait, but you will spend the break in class, if I wait! . . . If you pack, I will add one minute to each question [posed by the pupils]. And then you will be in trouble when the break comes!" In this case, affirms the anthropologist, the control over time is used to punish (Neumann 2007). A striking characteristic of the spatial arrangements is the separation of the school's two branches:

> The vocational training school branch expands downwards in the basement, one has to submerge oneself in a badly illuminated labyrinth of corridors to reach the noisy workshop and the classrooms situated in this wing. Altogether it is a somewhat infernal experience. ... Dreary classroom, rundown furniture. The wall is decorated by a mechanical drawing and a small map of Hungary (in fact the advertisement poster of Trilak '98 Co.). (Neumann 2007: 21).

The spatial-symbolic division has been verbalized in the apprentices' focus group interviews as well; as one student put it, "We are in the basement, and the vocational pupils are up on the top!" (Neumann 2007: 23).

Towards a New Political Anthropology of Education

In a decentralized context, anthropology is more than a perspective: it is a necessity. As a matter of fact, the everyday reality of schools is much more complex than that often described by sociological research focusing on negative and general phenomena, such as segregation or early drop-outs. The anthropological perspective (Eröss 2008a, 2008b) focuses instead on the contingency (not the mere variety) of local constellations. As long as the municipalities have a high level of autonomy, the focus put on locality seems to be simply the right approach.

The perspective is an anthropological one in Hungary, simply because there is virtually no state. When my colleagues and I were looking for the locus of power, the relevant level of policy making in Hungary, we found it at the level of the local governments. They have an almost total autonomy in matters of education (curriculum of the local schools, selection, and so on). And these local processes are to be understood through anthropological methods (starting with long-lasting field research and "immersion"), anthropological themes (a focus on symbols, categories, and rituals, as well as on the local), as well as an anthropological perspective—an "epistemological modesty" avoiding generalization.

Having said this, I must insist: the real break consists of not starting with the Roma, but with the village or the district—or the school as a whole. My anthropology of education is an ethnosociology of education, allying cultural and structural analysis; I consider the parents as part of the educational system, and do not limit anthropology's field of investigation to the classroom. The parents interact with the school as much as they interact with their children at home: the way parents are controlling the children's homework, the way the children are questioned at home on the lessons they are studying, should also be part of a comprehensive ethnography of learning.

Inspired by Agnès van Zanten (2001) among others, I consider the analysis of the local sociohistoric context as the key to a better understanding of education: various schools of "type 'a'" can be very different in different contexts. The district we studied is a former workers' district: constant references are made to this past by the actors (especially decision makers), and institutions such as the factory's kindergarten exist even now (Bajomi et al. 2006). Also, children with learning difficulties are considered as a heritage of this past, which is somehow—since workers used to belong rather to the lower middle class than to the underclass—a paradoxical reinterpretation of the past, a semantic shift that transforms the underclass into some kind of residue of the working class.

The anthropological approach also shows that there is a multidimensional system of categories and distinctions, a different one in every single local context. These multidimensional classificatory systems do not result in a nationwide single hierarchy; rather, they are the effect of the cultural, social, and political construction and interpretation of locally embedded meanings. They open the way for local contingency, although without repressing overall inequalities.

In our research[6]—using survey methods, interviews, and participant observation—we witnessed the growing importance of institutions and processes aiming at categorizing, classifying, selecting, and tracking pupils. Admitting, selecting, and grouping go hand in hand. These are the aspects of a threefold categorizing process, leading to the classification of students into various legal and nonlegal, explicit and implicit categories. I would like to show here the multiplicity of categorizing processes and explain the reasons why this phenomenon seems to be developing all around Europe.

Segregation is not about "Roma culture" or about the majority's prejudices. It is about the school system and the political system. A political anthropology of education shows that the interpretation of educational taxonomies in use by various regulatory bodies, from state- to street-level bureaucracy, is context dependent; it also shows that even the global discourses and policies (such as standardized testing, or teacher autonomy) are locally embedded (Anderson-Levitt 2003).

An analysis in terms of "performativity" demonstrates that categories and meanings are not only locally interpreted, but also locally constructed, and permanently reflected, re-presented, exposed, hidden. challenged, and reinvented (Wulf and Zirfas 2001). Local actors often do not know who "is" Roma and who "is not." The boundary of any single ethnicity is "fuzzy": it will vary depending who does the classification, where, and why (Ladányi and Szelényi 2001). In our research we were constantly told, on the one hand, about "mestizos," "half-Gypsies," "different Gypsies" by the interviewees (teachers, parents, and others), and, on the other, about (non-Roma) underclass, alcoholic parents neglecting their children. Notwithstanding the predominantly "ethnic" composition of the segregated group, we must insist on the fact that not all lower-class pupils get excluded from mainstream schooling, and that working-class and middle-class children are as much affected by the multiple and never-ending categorizing, classifying, and grouping processes as others. In a word, this is not (only) about labeling the poor in order to exclude them.

School choice is a mutual, dynamic, and performative process: in a way, schools and parents choose each other, and their choice can only be predicted to a certain degree. What is "more" middle class: a class specialized in math or in English? It depends. Are lower-status pupils welcome into "good" schools? In some cases, yes. Let us take a concrete example of a category such as the "national minority classes" (for example, the German minority). In different local spaces it is used very differently. In one village, it serves the purpose of identity preservation for the German-speaking minority; in another one, it serves the purpose of intraschool segregation and keeps the local elite from "fleeing" (the Roma being excluded from the "German" class); in yet another village, with no "ethnic Germans," it simply guarantees better financial conditions for the school and the whole village, including the Roma (extra funds being directed to these "minority" classes, even if there is not a single "ethnic German" enrolled). Van Zanten explains the needed approach in qualitative educational sociology, or anthropology: the study of "contrasting sites" shows "the degree to which local reinterpretation of policy can vary depending on local social class configurations," ethnic configurations, and other contextual variables (van Zanten 2002: 290).

Conclusion

The analysis of a highly decentralized school system such as the Hungarian one shows that there is a need in education research for a political anthropology that attempts to explain the various processes reproducing, in the end, school inequalities after the age of (nation-)states, in somehow different ways from one local context to another. This anthropology has to be political, because decision-making bodies do not disappear: they change and become more and more local and or transnational. It has to be an anthropology, because the meaning in a given context of the various categories that coexist results from a social and cultural, dynamic and performative construction process; the categories and their meanings are reinterpreted at the moments of school rituals (such as entrance exams) and in the process of everyday interaction between street-level bureaucrats, the parents, the pupils, and other stakeholders. The constant and contradictory categorizing of pupils is a never-ending, locally embedded process and seems to emerge as the key phenomenon of postnational school systems.

The high sensitivity of Central European social scientists, including anthropologists, to the Roma (and other minority) issues, and the richness of publications makes the region without doubt a field with very high potential. The risk exists, however, that the essentialization of the minority groups on the one hand, and the policy-driven research focus on the other, inhibit both the autonomous research initiatives and the establishment of an autonomous field of educational anthropology/ethnography.

Acknowledgments

I wish to thank Eszter Neumann, Mária Neményi, Veronika Domokos, György Mészáros, Judit Gárdos (Hungary), Radim Marada, Katerina Sidiropulu Janku, Martina Haltufová, Lucie Jarkovska (Czech Republic), Anna Fitak (Poland), Zita Skovierova (Slovakia), Liliana Eskenazi, Valentina Milenkova, Pepka Boyadjieva, Maya Grekova (Bulgaria), Adél Kiss, Hajnalka Harbula (Romania), as well as Dariush Ehsani (USA) and Christoph Wulf (Germany).

Notes

1. One good example of the numerous EU-projects is the EDUMIGROM project: http://www.edumigrom.eu/.
2. A representative, encyclopedic volume of Hungarian (cultural) anthropology divided into numerous thematic chapters contains no chapter on education (Kézdi Nagy 2008). Sárkány's introduction to Eastern and Central European anthropology does not mention education/school at all, either (Sárkány 2002).
3. For example, "Research and Evaluation" is a single web page, http://www.osi.hu/esp/rei/research.html.
4. See the Bulgarian, Slovakian, and especially the Hungarian evaluation reports at http://www.osi.hu/esp/rei/research.html.
5. A Serbian example: "Participatory Research of the Roma needs, main problems and potentials in education in Vojvodina." http://www.nshc.org.rs/eng_nshc/eng_ref_research.htm.
6. (1) The "Reguleduc" project (http://www.girsef.ucl.ac.be/europeanproject.htm), (2) studies funded by The Hungarian Scientific Research Fund "OTKA" and the Fund for Social Studies Research of National Priority "OKTK," and (3) the ongoing "KNOWandPOL" research (http://www.knowandpol.eu).

Bibliography

BU = Bulgarian
CZ = Czech

EN = English
FR = French
GER = German
HUN = Hungarian
POL = Polish
RO = Romanian
SK = Slovakian

Ablewicz, Krystyna. 2003. *Teoretyczne i metodologiczne podstawy pedagogiki antropologicznej.* [The Basics of Pedagogical Anthropology's Theory and Methodology]. Kraków: Wydawnictwo Uniwersytetu Jagiellońskiego. (POL)

Amnesty International. 2008. "A Tale of Two Schools: Segregating Roma into Special Education in Slovakia." http://www.amnesty.org/fr/library/asset/EUR72/007/2008/en/c0c45cb3–58d7–11dd-a0f9–8dfec124dda9/eur720072008eng.html. (EN)

Anderson-Levitt, Kathryn, ed. 2003. *Local Meanings, Global Schooling: Anthropology and World Culture Theory.* New York: Palgrave Macmillan. (EN)

Băican, Eugen. 2005. *Research Report: Educational Measures for the Roma Minority in Romania. The Effectiveness of Integrated and Segregated Education. Case Study of Pata-Rât, Cluj-Napoca.* Cluj: CERGE-Ei. (EN)

Bajomi, Iván, Eszter Berényi, Gábor Eröss, and Anna Imre. 2006. "Ahol ritka jószág a tanuló. Oktatásirányítás, cselekvési logikák és egyenlőtlenségek Budapesten" [Where Pupils Are Scarce. Educational Regulation, Logics of Action and Inequalities in Budapest], Research Reports Series. Budapest: OKI [Institute for Higher Education]. (HUN)

Beszámoló a nemzeti és etnikai kisebbségi jogok országgyűlési biztosának tevékenységéről [Reports on National and Ethnicity Minority Rights by the Parliamentary Commissioner], 2000, 2001, 2002, 2003, 20004, 2005, 2006, 2007, 2008. Budapest: Budapest: Országgylési Biztosok Hivatala. (HUN)

Bodó, Julianna, ed. 2002. *Helykeresők. Roma lakosság a Székelyföldön* [The Roma Population in Transylvania]. Csíkszereda: Pro-Print. (HUN)

Bollnow, Otto Friedrich, 1963. *Mensch und Raum* [Man and Space]. Stuttgart: W. Kohlhammer. (GER)

———. 1987. *Crisis and New Beginning: Contributions to Pedagogical Anthropology.* Translation by Donald Moss and Nancy Moss of *Die Anthropologische Betrachtungsweise in der Pädagogik* (originally published by Neue deutsche Schule Verlagsgesellschaft, 1965). Pittsburgh, PA: Duquesne University Press. (EN)

Boreczky, Ágnes. 1999. "Multikulturális pedagógia - új pedagógia?" [Multicultural pedagogy? New pedagogy?]. *Új Pedagógiai Szemle* no. 4 (1999): 26–38. (HUN)

Csanádi, Gábor, János Ladányi, and Zsuzsa Gerő. 1978. "Az általános iskolai rendszer belső rétegződése és a kisegítő iskolák" [The Internal Stratification of the Elementary School System and the Special Education Schools]. *Valóság* 6. (HUN)

Csongor, Anna. 1991. "A cigány gyerekek iskolái" [The Schools of Roma Children]. In *Cigánylét-Műhelytanulmányok*, 179–200. Budapest: Magyar Tudományos Akadémia Politikai Tanulmányok Intézete. (HUN)

Czachesz, Erzsébet. 1998 *Multikulturális nevelés. Szöveggyűjtemény tanító- és tanárszakos hallgatók számára* [Multicultural Education: Textbooks for Teachers and Teacher Trainees]. Szeged: Mozaik Oktatási Stúdió. (HUN)

Delvaux, Bernard, Eric Mangez, et al. 2007. "Literature Reviews on Knowledge and Policy." http://www.knowandpol.eu/fileadmin/KaP/content/Scientific_reports/Literature_review/Know_Pol_literature_review.pdf. (EN)

Dimitrov, Georgi, and Pepka Boyadjieva. 2009. "Citizenship Education as an Instrument for Strengthening the State's Supremacy: An Apparent Paradox?" *Citizenship Studies* 13, no. 2: 151–67. (EN)

Domokos, Veronika. 2008. "Képességzavarok és a 'családi körülmények': (halmozottan) hátrányos helyzet és 'romaság' a tanítói narratívában" [Ability Disorder and "Family Conditions": (Multiple) Social Disadvantage and "Gipsyness" in Teachers' Narratives]. In *Túl a szegregáción. Kategóriák burjánzása a magyar közoktatásban* [Beyond Segregation: The Proliferation of Categories in Hungarian Public Education], ed. Gábor Erőss and Anna Kende. Budapest: L'Harmattan. (HUN)

Equal Access to Quality Education for Roma, vol. 1 and 2. 2007, 2008. Open Society Institute. (EN)

Erőss, Gábor. 2008a. "Categorization, Tracking and 'School Readiness': Towards a New Political Anthropology of Education." In *Proceedings of the Paris International Conference on Education, Economy and Society, 2008*, 581–91. Paris: Paris International Conference on Education, Economy and Society. (EN)

———. 2008b. "Különbség és szórás. Kategorizációs és szelekciós finommechanizmusok az oktatásban: SNI-k, lókötők és társaik" [Difference and Variance: Categorization and Selection in Public Education: Special Educational Needs Children, Lókötők and the Others]. In *Túl a szegregáción. Kategóriák burjánzása a magyar közoktatásban* [Beyond Segregation: The Proliferation of Categories in Hungarian Public Education], ed. Gábor Erőss and Anna Kende. Budapest: L'Harmattan. (HUN)

Erőss, Gábor, et al. 2009. *All Against Misdiagnosis*. KNOWandPOL Report, http://www.knowandpol.eu. (EN)

European Commission, Directorate-General for Employment and Social Affairs. 2005. *The Situation of Roma in an Enlarged European Union*. ec.europa.eu/employment_social/publications/2005/ke6204389_en.html. (EN)

European Commission, Directorate-General for Employment and Social Affairs. 2007. *Segregation of Roma Children in Education*. ec.europa.eu/employment_social/fundamental_rights/pdf/legnet/seg07_en.pdf. (EN)

European Roma Right Center. 1999. *A Special Remedy: Roma and Schools for the Mentally Handicapped in the Czech Republic*. ERRC. http://errc.org/publications/reports/. (EN)

Feischmidt, Margit, and Pál Nyíri, eds. 2006. *Nem kívánt gyerekek? Külföldi gyerekek magyar iskolákban* [Unwanted Children? Foreign Children in Hungarian Schools]. Budapest: MTA NKI. (HUN)

Fleck, Gabor, and Cosima Rughinis, eds. 2008. *Come Closer: Inclusion and Exclusion of Roma in Present-Day Romanian Society*. Bucharest: Human Dynamics. (EN)

Fosztó, László. 2008. "Bibliografie cu studiile şi reprezentările despre romii din România—cu accentul pe perioada 1990–2007." *Working Papers in Romanian Minority Studies.* http://www.ispmn.gov.ro/docs/Foszto_Laszlo.pdf. Cluj-Napoca: The Romanian Institute for Research on National Minorities. (RO)

Greger, David, Jiří Kotásek, and Ivana Procházková. 2004. *Požadavky na školní vzdělávání v České republice (Národní zpráva pro OECD)* [Requirements for School Education in the Czech Republic (National Report OECD)]. Prague: Charles University. (CZ)

Grekova, Maya. 1999. "Cultural Difference as a Problem of Intercultural Education." In *Bulgaria—Facing Cultural Diversity,* ed. G. de Keersmaeker and Pl. Makariev. Sofia: IPIS, ACCESS. (EN)

——— (in collaboration with Pl. Makariev). 2002. "Configurations of Cultural Diversity at School." *Strategies of Educational and Scientific Policy.* Special Issue: "Educational Policy and Cultural Diversity." (BUL)

——— (in collaboration with four students). 2008. *Roma in Sofia: From Isolation to Integration?* Sofia: East/West. (BUL)

Havas, Gábor. 2002. "The School as Breakout Point." In *The Gypsies/the Roma in Hungarian Society,* ed. Ernő Kállai, 79–106. Budapest: Teleki László Foundation. (EN)

Havas, Gábor, István Kemény, and Ilona Liskó. 2002. *Cigány gyerekek az általános iskolában* [Gypsy Children in Elementary Schools]. Budapest: Oktatáskutató Intézet, Új mandátum Kiadó.

Hirt, Tomáš, and Marek Jakoubek, eds. 2006. *"Romové" v osidlech sociálního vyloučení* ["Roma" in the Confines of Social Exclusion]. Plzeň: Aleš Čeněk. (CZ)

Húšová, Mária. 2006. "Ako sa zmenila situácia v absencii rómskych detí v školách v dôsledku vládnych opatrení za obdobie rokov 2002 – 2005" [How the Situation of Roma Children's School Absence Schools Has Changed as a Result of Government Measures over the Period 2002 to 2005]. *Interface* (Slovak Governance Institute) no. 1 (2006). (SK)

Kapitány, Gábor, and Ágnes Kapitány. 2006. *Intézménymimika II* [Institutional Mimetism II]. Budapest: ÚMK. (HUN)

Kemény, István. 1976. *Beszámoló a magyarországi cigányok helyzetével foglalkozó 1971-ben végzett kutatásról* [Report on the Status of Gypsies in Hungary: 1971 Research]. Budapest: MTA Szociológiai Intézet. (HUN)

Kemény, István, Béla Janky, and Gabriella Lengyel. 2004. *A magyarországi cigányság 1971–2003* [The Roma Population of Hungary 1971–2003]. Budapest: Gondolat Kiadó–MTA Etnikai-Nemzeti Kisebbségkutató Intézet. (HUN)

Kende, Anna, and Mária Neményi. 2006. "Selection in Education: The Case of Roma Children in Hungary." *Equal Opportunities International* 25, no. 7: 506–22. (EN)

Kézdi Nagy, Géza. 2008. *A magyar kulturális antropológia története* [History of Hungarian Cultural Anthropology]. Budapest: Nyitott Könyvműhely Kiadó. (HUN)

Kjuchukov, Hristo. 2006. *Desegregation of Roma Pupils.* Sofia: C.E.G.A. (BUL)

Kocourek, Jiří, and Eva Pechová, eds. 2007. *S vietnamskými dětmi na českých školách* [With the Vietnamese Children in a Czech School]). Jinočany: Nakladatelství H&H Vyšehradská. (CZ)

Könczei, Csongor. 2008. "A kalotaszegi cigányzenészek társadalmi és kulturális hálózatáról" [The Social and Cultural Network of Gipsy Musicians in the Kalotaszeg Region]. PhD diss., Eötvös Loránd University, Budapest. (HUN)

Kovács, Éva, ed. 2007. *Közösségtanulmány. Módszertani jegyzet* [Community Study: Methodological Note]. Budapest: Néprajzi Múzeum—PTE. (HUN)

Kovai, Cecília. 2008. "Az iskola és a család. Kizáró és megengedő viszonyok" [The School and the Family: Exclusive and Inclusive Relations]. *Beszélő* 13, no. 5. http://beszelo.c3.hu/cikkek/az-iskola-es-a-csalad. (HUN)

Kučera, Miloš, Jean-Yves Rochex, and Stanislav Štech, eds. 2001. *The Transmission of Knowledge as a Problem of Culture and Identity*. Prague: Karolinum. (EN)

Ladányi, János, and Iván Szelényi. 2001. "The Social Construction of Roma Ethnicity in Bulgaria, Romania and Hungary during Market Transition." *Review of Sociology* 7, no. 2: 79–89. (EN)

Langeveld, Martinus J. 1968 [1960]. *Die Schule als Weg des Kindes: Versuch einer Anthropologie der Schule* [School as the Way of the Child: Attempt at an Anthropology of the School]. Braunschweig: Westermann. (GER)

Loss, Sándor. 1996. "Egy csapásra. Cigány gyerekek útja a kisegítő iskolába" [All of a Sudden: The Road of Gypsy Children to Special Schools]. *Beszélő* 6. (HUN)

Magyari-Vincze, Enikő. 2007. *Social Exclusion of Roma. Case Study from Timisoara*. http://adatbank.transindex.ro/vendeg/htmlk/pdf7060.pdf. (ROM)

Meleg, Csilla. 2005. "Iskola az időben" [School and Time]. *Iskolakultúra*, no. 2: 127–34. (HUN)

Mészáros, György. 2009. "The Role of Youth Subcultures in the Educational Process School Ethnography." PhD diss., Eötvös Loránd University, Budapest. (HUN) [English-language abstract: http://ppk.elte.hu/images/stories/_UPLOAD/DOKUMENTUMOK/Nevelestudomany_Phd/2009/meszaros_gyorgy_tezisek_2009_phd.pdf.]

Milenkova, Valentinas. 2008. "Roma Dropping Out and Rural School." In *Mobility, Vulnerability, Sustainability*, 147–60. Sofia: Publishing House Alia. (BUL)

Nahalka, István. 2004. "A roma gyerekek kognitív fejlesztését meghatározó sajátosságok" [Roma Children and the Cognitive Development of Defining Characteristics]. In *Megközelítések. Roma gyermekek nevelésének egyes kérdései* [Approaches: Certain Questions about Roma Education], ed. István Nahalka and Judit Torgyik. Budapest: Flaccus. (HUN)

Németh, Szilvia. 2006. *Integráció a gyakorlatban* [Integration in the Practice]. Budapest: OKI. (HUN)

Neumann, Eszter. 2007. "School in the Shadows of the Closed Steel-Mill. The Hidden Curriculum in a Hungarian Secondary School." Master's thesis, Eötvös Loránd University, TáTK, Budapest. (EN)

Neumann, Eszter, and János Zolnay. 2008. *Esélyegyenlőség, szegregáció és oktatáspolitikai stratégiák Kaposváron, Pécsen és Mohácson* [Equality, Segregation and Educational Strategies in Kaposvár, Pécs, and Mohács]. Budapest: EÖKIK. (HUN)

Nowotny, Helga, Peter Scott, and Michael Gibbons. 2003. "Introduction: 'Mode 2' Revisited: The New Production of Knowledge." *Minerva* 41, no. 3: 179–94.

http://www.prescott.edu/faculty_staff/faculty/scorey/documents/Nowot nyGibbons2003Mode2Revisited.pdf. (EN)

Nunev, J. 2006. *Roma and the Process of Desegregation in Education.* Sofia: Kuna. (BUL)

Oblath, Márton, Balázs Berkovits, Gábor Eröss, et al. 2007. *Unhealthy Data, Competing Sciences. 2nd Part: The Field of Special Educational Needs.* http://www .knowandpol.eu/fileadmin/KaP/content/Scientific_reports/Orientation1/ O1_Final_Report_Hungary_health.pdf. (EN)

Örkény, Antal, and Mária Székelyi. 2007. *Deliberatív közvélemény-kutatás a magyarországi romák és nem romák viszonyáról* [Poll on the Relationship between Roma and Non-Roma in Hungary]. Budapest: Ulpius Ház. (HUN)

Palečková, Jana, et al. 2007. *Hlavní zjištění výzkumu PISA 2006. Poradí si žáci s přírodními vědami?* [Document of the Institute of Information on Education. The Main Finding of the PISA Research for 2006]. Prague: ÚIV. (CZ)

Panayotova, Donka. 2007. *Successful Romani School Desegregation: The Vidin Case.* http://www.errc.org/cikk.php?cikk=1630. (EN)

Papp Z., Attila. 1998. "A romániai magyar oktatás helyzete 1989 után" [The Situation of Hungarian Schools in Romania after 1989], *Magyar Kisebbség* no. 3–4 (1998): 13–14. http://www.jakabffy.ro/magyarkisebbseg/index.php?actio n=cimek&cikk=m980321.htm. (HUN)

Poledňová, Ivana, and Jarmila Zobačová, eds. 2006. "Romské děti předškolního věku a jejich příprava na zahájení školní docházky" [Roma Children of Preschool Age and Their Preparation for School Attendance]. In *Sborník referátů z konference Multikulturní výchova v dnešní společnosti* [Multicultural Education in Contemporary Society—Conference Volume]. Brno: Pedagogická fakulta. (CZ)

Promotion of Roma/Traveler Integration and Equal Treatment in Education and Employment Project, 2005–2006, 2007. *Conclusions and Good Practices Identified in the International Seminar. Handbook.* Madrid. (EN and six other languages)

Sadownik, Alicja. 2006. "The Paradox of Special Vocational Schools." http:// changeandresistance.blogspot.com/2006/12/paradox-of-special-vocational-schools.html. (EN)

Sárkány, Mihály. 2002. "Cultural and Social Anthropology in Central and Eastern Europe." In *Knowledge Base Social Sciences Eastern Europe.* GESIS (Leibnitz Institute for the Social Sciences). http://www.cee-socialscience.net/archive/ anthropology/article1.html. (EN)

Šatava, Leoš. 2007. "Etnická identita a vztah žáků lužickosrbské školy k jazykové kultuře (porovnání let 2001/02 a 2005/06)" [Ethnic Identity and Language/ Culture Attitudes among Students of a Sorbian Grammar School 2001/02 and 2005/06—A Comparison]. *Lětopis* (Journal for Sorbian Language, History and Culture) 54, no. 2: 20–38. (CZ)

Smékal, Vladimír. 2003. *Rizikové a protektivní faktory v utváření osobnosti dětí různých etnik* [Risk and Protective Factors in the Shaping of Character in Children of Different Ethnic Groups]. Brno: Barrister and Principal. (CZ)

Stigmata: Segregated Schooling of Roma in Central and Eastern Europe. 2004. Budapest: European Roma Rights Center. (EN)

Still separate, still unequal: Violations of the right to education of Romani children in Slovakia. 2007. Bratislava: Amnesty International. (EN)

Svec, Stefan, et al. 1998. *Metodológia vied o vychove* [Methodology of Science Education]. Bratislava: Vydavatelstvo IRIS. (SLO)

Szalai, Júlia. 2008. *Ethnic differences in compulsory education. Policy Brief.* Budapest: Center for Policy Studies, Central European University. http://www.edumigrom.eu/download.php?oid=T32a26879c15267f25561a03fd82f1f2; aid=T12928899e17277424524eb06f34284a;file=;download. (EN)

Toma, Stefania. 2005. *Research Report: Educational Measures for the Roma Minority in Romania. The Effectiveness of Integrated and Segregated Education. The Case of Odorheiu-Secuiesc, Hargita County.* Cluj: CERGE-Ei—Global Development Network, CCRIT. (EN)

———. 2008. "Roma/Gypsies and Education in a Multiethnic Community in Romania." *Working Paper in Romanian Minority Studies*, no. 6. http://www.ispmn.gov.ro/docs/Toma_Stefania.pdf. (EN)

Tomatová, Jana. 2004. *Na vedľajšej koľaji* [Side-Tracked]. Bratislava: Slovak Governance Institute. (SLO)

Torgyik, Judit 2004. "Modellértékű roma nevelési programok és elterjedésük gátjai" [Exemplary Educational Programs for Roma Children]. In *Megközelítések. Roma gyermekek nevelésének egyes kérdései* [Approaches: Certain Questions about Roma Education], ed. István Nahalka and Judit Torgyik, 83–93. Budapest: Flaccus. (HUN)

Turai, Tünde. 2005. "A szilágysomlyói kistérség nemzeti identitásának komponensei (magyar kulturális és oktatási intézmények működése az elmúlt másfél évtizedben)" [The Components of National Identity in the Szilágysomlyó Region]. In *Magyarlakta kistérségek és kisebbségi identitások a Kárpát-medencében* [Hungarian-Speaking Minority and Micro Identities of the Carpathian Basin], ed. Boglárka Bakó and Szilvia Szoták. Budapest: Gondolat—MTA ENKI. (HUN)

Ulrich, Catalina, Alexandru Crisan, Simona Moldovan, and Nancy Green. 2002. *Evaluation Report for the Project "Equal Opportunities for Roma Children through School Development Programs and Parents' Involvement."* http://www.osi.hu/esp/rei/Documents/EvaluationRomaniaFinalDraftcolumbiareport2002.doc. Bucharest: Roma Education Initiative, Open Society Foundations. (EN)

Van Zanten, Agnès. 2001. *L'école de la périphérie* [School on the Periphery]. Paris: PUF. (FR)

———. 2002. "Educational Change and New Cleavages between Head Teachers, Teachers and Parents: Global and Local Perspectives on the French Case." *Journal of Education Policy* 17, no. 3: 289–304. (EN)

Váradi, Mónika. 2008. "Kistelepülések és kisiskolák—közoktatási tapasztalatok a kistérségi társulásokban" [Small Towns, Small Schools. Public Education in the Multipurpose Micro-regional Corporations]. In *Függőben: közszolgáltatás-szervezés a kistelepülések világában* [Dependence: The Organizing of Public Services in Small Towns], ed. Katalin Kovács and Edit Somlyódyné Pfeil, 155–82. Budapest: KSZK. (HUN)

Virág, Tünde. 2003. "Gettósodó térség, gettósodó iskolarendszer" [Ghettoization of a Territory, Ghettoization of Education]. *Kisebbségkutatás* 2. http://www.hhrf.org/kisebbsegkutatas/kk_2003_02/cikk.php?id=750. (HUN)

What you have learned in the years of your youth ("Co se v mladi naucis ..."). 2001. Prague: Charles University, Faculty of Pedagogics, Group of School Ethnography. (CZ)

Wulf, Christoph, and Jörg Zirfas. 2001. "Das Performative als Focus Erziehungswissenschaftlicher Forschung. Zur Bildung von Gemeinschaften in Ritualen" [The Performative as a Focus in Educational Research: For the Formation of Communities through Rituals]. In *Anthropologie pädagogischer Institutionen* [Pedagogical Anthropology of Institutions], ed. Eckart Liebau, Doris Schumacher-Chilla, and Christoph Wulf. Weinheim: Deutscher Studien Verlag. (GER)

Zolnay, János. 2007. "Kirekesztés, szegregáció, vákuumhelyzet a drávaszögi kistérség iskolakörzeteiben" [Exclusion, Segregation and Entrapment in the School Districts of the Drávaszög Microregion]. *Műhelytanulmány* no. 31. Budapest: Európai Összehasonlító Kisebbségkutatások Közalapítvány. (HUN)

§ 9

EDUCATIONAL ANTHROPOLOGY IN A WELFARE STATE PERSPECTIVE
The Case of Scandinavia

Sally Anderson, Eva Gulløv, and Karen Valentin

The subfield of educational anthropology in Scandinavia is quite new. Before 1990, only a handful of anthropologists focused their research specifically on education and socialization. Education (*uddannelse*) as a topic does not figure in review articles on Scandinavian anthropology (Gullestad 1989), nor is it indexed in Scandinavian anthropology readers (Hastrup and Ovesen 1985; Eriksen 1993). The present chapter draws together three strands of research—school ethnography,[1] the anthropology of children and youth, and anthropological development studies—all of which contribute to the subfield of *educational anthropology* presently under construction in Scandinavia. We focus mainly on research trends in Denmark, as representative of Scandinavia, but note relevant research from Sweden and Norway where pertinent.[2] We argue that irrespective of country, any educational anthropology developing in this region inevitably resonates with the cultural norms and political priorities of Scandinavian welfare societies.

Before sketching the field, a brief presentation of Scandinavia is in order. The three countries of this region—Denmark, Norway, and Sweden—are closely tied linguistically,[3] politically and culturally. Located on Europe's northern perimeter, they share an interlocking history, and their present political systems, ideological foundations, and social organization bear strong resemblances. All three countries are characterized by Social Democratic traditions of universal welfare. Governments employ high levels of taxation, state regulation of markets, and universal welfare provision to stabilize economies, level incomes, and ensure universal basic human rights. The cornerstones of this model—social security, free health care, and free public education—entail an expansive public sector with a range of public institutions such as nurseries, kindergartens, after-school care, schools, hospitals, and nursing homes. Resonant notions of social similarity and equality permeate political discourses and interests as well as broader cultural perceptions of sociality (Gullestad 1984, 2002; Liep and Olwig 1994). These factors have greatly influenced educational studies. Universal provision of free education at all levels, viewed in Scandinavia as the ultimate guarantor of social equality, has particularly shaped research questions posed by educational ethnographers and anthropologists.

Anthropology in Scandinavia

The history of anthropology in Scandinavia is fairly similar to that of other places. Following the German tradition of *Kulturgeschichte*, anthropology was connected with national museums, first becoming a university-affiliated academic discipline[4] after World War II. In the 1960s, many anthropologists turned away from museum-based ethnography, and led by Norwegian anthropologist Frederik Barth, turned toward processual studies of individuals and societies. Identifying largely as social anthropologists, Scandinavian anthropologists have drawn eclectically on the major French, British, and American anthropological traditions.

Several parallel trends have influenced the development of educational anthropology. First, Scandinavian anthropology grew explosively over the last three decades. As graduates far outnumbered academic positions available at established anthropology departments at major, old universities, young scholars looked for appointment elsewhere. Their obvious choices were newer universities, which in looking to gain academic relevance and political legitimacy, housed a variety of interdisciplinary programs prioritizing studies of welfare institutions. Incoming anthropologists began to fill the ranks of interdisciplinary research units focusing on education and children.

Second, growing numbers of anthropologists dovetailed with growing numbers of immigrants and refugees, classic objects of anthropological study, whose encounters with Scandinavian welfare institutions (and vice versa) posed new challenges. Scandinavian states play an extensive role in socialization and education through universal provision of child-care and schooling. Viewing the educational system as the most proficient site for integrating children of immigrants, governments have channeled much public funding into research that investigates the role educational institutions play in integrating (as well as marginalizing) immigrant populations.

Third, global emphasis on education as a vital factor for economic growth, nationally and internationally, has increased political interest and public investments in educational research across the board. National research councils generously support ethnographic studies of education at all levels, and national aid programs to countries in the Global South place a high priority on educational programs. Thus, anthropologists are engaged in interdisciplinary research projects aimed at improving educational efficiency in countries dependent on development aid.

Finally, as doing "anthropology at home" became more accepted, many graduate students and younger anthropologists chose critical study of public institutions as a pragmatic alternative to fieldwork abroad while raising young children.[5] Scandinavian anthropology of education has taken form within the context of these parallel trends.

Problems of Translation

That many hesitate to call the growing body of research "educational anthropology," in Danish *uddannelsesantropologi*, is connected to problems of translation into Scandinavian languages, systems of education, and traditions of educational research. The English term "education" translates easily enough as *uddannelse*, yet the Danish term puts emphasis squarely on practical, systemic, and political issues of schools and schooling, and tends to exclude more philosophical matters of pedagogy and *Bildung*, or *dannelse* in Danish. Focusing on the moral, social, and cultural formation of educated persons, pedagogy (as both academic discipline and profession) has been central to Scandinavian educational studies. The term *uddannelse* tends to exclude studies of particular *pedagogical sites*—day-care centers, leisure clubs, or juvenile detention centers—and particular *pedagogical practices*—public health campaigns and workplace safety programs—extending well beyond the bounds of public schooling. These sites and practices fit more easily within *pedagogical anthropology,* a term presently coming into use.

While the Scandinavian breakdown of education into *uddannelse, dannelse,* and *pædagogik* may be quite different from some traditions, the institutional tensions posed by an "anthropology of education" in both departments of education and anthropology may be more easily recognized. Some tensions arise from the focus on education that tends to fix research in schools and install anthropologists in broad interdisciplinary research networks. Other tensions arise from the encounter between anthropology per se, with its own research interests, cross-cultural comparison, and relativity, and more traditional educational research agendas employing ethnographic methods to develop curricula and shed critical light on national school systems. In a sense, the "anthropology of education" has no home base. It has little chance in small anthropology departments organized around classical anthropological themes and regions, and it is an interloper among the established research fields in departments of education. There are thus many "problems of translation" to take into account in developing an anthropology of education that both looks and moves across the national, regional, institutional, disciplinary, and thematic borders dividing the field.

School Ethnography—The Progressive Beginning

Although research leading to the institutionalization of educational anthropology per se first appeared in the 1990s, a focus on other disciplines reveals a growing use of ethnographic methods in educational research. In Scandinavia, as elsewhere, the contribution of educational ethnography to educational anthropology is significant. Below, we present a brief overview of the development of educational ethnography over the last four decades and its coalescence with broader anthropological studies of educational questions and settings at the turn of the century.

Structures of Dominance

Initiated in the 1970s, ethnographic classroom studies in Denmark were informed by progressive, left-wing ideology. Researchers viewed educational systems as critical components of prevailing structures of dominance. Studies focused on the reproduction of class and on unequal access to public resources and political influence. They confronted the goals and pedagogies of existing public schooling, challenged the uncritical orientation of prevailing educational research, and placed general issues of social inequality squarely on the research agenda. This critical approach was predominantly inspired by sociology, specifically neo-Marxist and structuralist traditions (see Berner, Callewaert and Silberbrandt 1977; Callewaert and Nilsson 1974). Jackson's concept of the hidden curriculum (1968) was also particularly influential, launching a general critique of public schooling (Bauer and Borg 1976). Using microethnography to inform macrostructural analyses, early school ethnographies were characterized by a strong interest in revealing how structural relations of dominance and stratification penetrate the classroom (Lindblad and Sahlstrøm 2006). This work was explicitly critical, and while ideological indignation has since been tempered, much subsequent educational research in Scandinavia has maintained comparable critical ambitions.

Ironically, the interests of scholars who critiqued "established society" in the 1970s resonated with Social Democratic ideologies. As Scandinavian governments vastly expanded universal welfare, they began to pay particular attention to educational institutions as agents for overcoming class inequality. Thus while many researchers donned critical perspectives, the moral horizon of much critical school ethnography was thoroughly permeated by welfare state ideology.

Everyday Processes of Stratification

In the 1980s, earlier efforts to understand the power structures of educational systems and society as a whole through classroom observation met with criticism. Following a general critique of Marxist and deterministic structural approaches in Scandinavian social science, educational ethnography was criticized for sociological reductionism, and particularly for reducing social actors such as teachers to passive reproducers of power structures (Bjerrum Nielsen 1985). Inspired by Basil Bernstein's code theory and his dual focus on communicative competence and social stratification (1975), linguistically trained scholars argued for more fine-grained studies of social interaction in classrooms to capture individual difference in class-specific socialization processes (Bjerrum Nielsen 1985). Inspired by Paul Willis (1977), classroom studies of the 1980s investigated gender relations to expose patterns of male dominance (Kryger 2004: 125).

In contrast to an earlier focus on oppression, school ethnographers of the 1980s explored modes of resistance and meaning making among variously positioned actors. Shifting from an explicit interest in the role of schools in processes of social reproduction, and drawing more on sociolinguistics, cultural studies, and social anthropology, classroom studies of this decade focused directly on modes of communication, interactional genres, and cultural forms produced in daily classroom interaction (Lindblad and Sahlström 1999; Klette 1998).

An Ethnographic Turn toward Broader Horizons

By the late 1980s, it is fair to speak of an "ethnographic turn." Qualitative methods began to enjoy widespread popularity (Borgnakke 2000: 16), and up through the 1990s, school ethnography moved from the margins to the mainstream of educational research. Shifting from attempts to identify the institutional mechanisms of social reproduction writ large, ethnographic studies now asked more modest questions of everyday life in institutions. Although most ethnographic research was

still carried out in public schools, studies were increasingly being conducted in other sites as well (see Madsen 1994). Subsequently, as scholarly interest in "the institution in society" waned, growing interest in
"persons in various culturally constructed institutionalized relations"
opened for studies of pedagogical agendas and practices in an array of
institutions.

This is approximately where trained anthropologists stepped in.
Conducting fieldwork "at home" on questions and in settings pertinent to the field of education, anthropologists added their voices to
an emerging subfield of educational anthropology. Their work was
inspired by American anthropologists[6] and by the work of Bourdieu,
Foucault, Vygotsky, and the Birmingham school. Motivated by anthropological questions of the late 1990s, they brought broad interests in
cultural and social organization, practical cultural knowledge, categorization, social learning, cultural notions of the educated person, and
processes of meaning and knowledge production to their studies. The
settings they studied included Danish kindergartens (Gulløv 1999; Palludan 2005), public schools (Anderson 2000; Gilliam 2006), university
physics departments (Hasse 2002), construction sites (Baarts 2004),
schools for the blind (Lundberg 2005), hospitals and children's homes
(Højlund 2002, 2006), officer training schools (Nørgaard 2004), and
sport associations (Anderson 2008). Not all of these studies found a
home alongside traditional school ethnography, nor was this body of
work consolidated as an "anthropology of education" per se. Studies
carried out in more traditional educational sites—schools, day care,
and kindergartens—became seminal works in the emerging subfield of
educational anthropology. Studies investigating the processes through
which construction workers learn safety rules or how young officers
learn humanitarian "Danish" soldiering have not yet been recognized
as belonging to this subfield.

A broadening and merging of research approaches and sites in educational ethnography and anthropology in the first decade of the twenty-
first century has been accompanied by a striking continuity in central
research interests. Vigorous ideals of social and economic *equality* intrin-
sic to welfare societies continue to inspire strong interest in structures
and processes of domination. Ongoing political efforts to overcome inequality and promote social integration through universal welfare provision inform ongoing research interests in the production of similarity
and difference and inclusive and exclusive *fællesskaber* (roughly, groups
or communities) as they play out in educational settings.

Equally vigorous ideals of personal *autonomy* continue to inform and
inspire research on social control, more specifically on the pursuit and

practice of authority and discipline in educational institutions. Inspired by neo-Foucauldian approaches, studies investigate forms of authority, mechanisms of control, and disciplinary practices in new pedagogical regimes in public schools and day care (see Hultqvist and Dahlberg 2001). Research on higher education explores new modes of governance and systems of management and control in universities undergoing re-form (Wright 2008). These and similar studies are exploring new ways of conceptualizing discipline through a focus on management agendas, training programs, and everyday sociality in educational institutional settings.

Massive enrollment in public day care has also continued to prompt research on institutionalized processes of child rearing. While some studies have focused specifically on the consequences of public peda-gogical regimes in institutional settings, many focus more broadly on the perspectives and experiences of children and youth in their every-day lives. Discussed below, these form the second strand of research presently contributing to the configuration of educational anthropol-ogy in Scandinavia.

Children and Youth—Proper Childhoods and Future Generations

The emerging anthropology of education is informed by policy, ped-agogy, and research critically concerned with the provision of "good childhoods" and with the construction of socially safe (*tryg*) environ-ments deemed crucial for inculcating moral human-beingness and good citizenship. This is in part due to the high value contemporary Scandinavian societies place on children, childhood, and child-centered pedagogy (Einarsdóttir and Wagner 2006). It is also in part due to the fact that research interests are inevitably linked with public concerns with upbringing, growing up, learning, and education. Thus, despite their distinct development in different eras, the anthropology of educa-tion and the anthropology of children and youth are not as divergent as they may seem. The aim of this brief presentation is to show the pertinence of the anthropology of children and youth for an emerging anthropology of education within and beyond schools.

New Childhood Studies

Early ethnographic studies of children focused traditionally on play and culturally informed models of "growing up" in families, villages, and institutions (Berentzen 1980; Ehn 1983; Broch 1990; Åm 1989; Norman 1991). Developing in the 1980s and 1990s, the "new childhood studies" (Qvortrup et al. 1994; James, Jenks, and Prout 1998) had a major impact on Scandinavian research on children (Kampmann 2003). Child research expanded from a predominant focus on child rearing and development to one on children's welfare, rights, perspectives, and participation in society, a perspective resonating well with contemporary Scandinavian understandings of children (Einarsdottir and Wagner 2006).

Adoption of the United Nations' Convention on the Rights of the Child (1989), along with the new scholarly interest in children as social actors, led to a range of ethnographic studies of children's perspectives, experiences, and agency (Markström and Halldén 2008), children's rights (Lidén and Kjørholt 2004; Valentin and Meinert 2009), and children's community participation (Kjørholt 2004). High enrollment in public institutions meant that many studies were carried out in these settings (Brembeck, Johansson, and Kampmann 2004), exploring how children make sense of their institutional environments and how their actions contribute to the ongoing production of social orders and cultural understandings. Scholars have shown a keen interest in kindergartens and schools as primary arenas for the everyday construction of social identity, with a specific focus on constructions of gender and ethnic difference, and how various forms of categorization marginalize children (Palludan 2005; Gitz-Johansen 2006; Bundgaard and Gulløv 2008; Gilliam 2006).

The new focus on young people as social actors also led to research into the lives of children and youth in many noninstitutional settings.[7] While studies of formal educational settings investigated the impact of institutional life and pedagogical regimes on children's experiences and identities, the other studies examined children's participation in society as individuals and members of new generations. Research into how young people engage with work (Gullestad 1992; Solberg 2001) and communication technology, popular culture, and consumption (Olesen 2003; Rysst 2008) has specifically investigated the impact of markets on the sociality, morality, and identity formation of future citizens. Research into family, home, neighborhood, and leisure venues (Lidén 1997; Halldén 2003; Winther 2006) has shed light on patterns of sociality and processes of belonging, and specifically on how children and youth navigate and mediate between multiple domains of belonging (Larsen 2005). Research into the lives of children of immigrants and refugees has highlighted processes of parallel enculturation and identity formation, as well as efforts to incorporate "foreign" children as legitimate members of society (Howell 2002; Norman 2005).

Taken together, new ethnographic child studies have broadened the scope of educational anthropology. By focusing on the social experiences and agency of children and youth in a wide range of settings, these studies illustrate parallel processes of enculturation and identity formation that impact more formal educational settings.

Proper Childhoods—In Scandinavia and Beyond

Many of the research themes noted above link to larger questions of "lost," "new," or "rightful" childhoods. Governments and researchers are concerned with questions of whether children are growing up in environments that provide them with opportunities to grow as moral beings and obtain the necessary skills to support themselves and take active part in democratic society. Strongly focused on the well-being of generations growing up in Scandinavia, the thrust of much of Scandinavian child research is to critically inform national policies that shape the kinds of childhoods society offers children, as young human beings and as citizens. Yet child research in Scandinavia is invariably informed by international research trends and the global child rights movement.[8] This has inspired international collaboration, and studies comparing children's rights, activities, and opportunities in Scandinavia to those in other European countries (Clark, Kjørholt, and Moss 2005).

Anthropologists have found a focus on children and youth conducive to addressing broad comparative questions regarding conceptualizations of "children" and "youth," the impact of migration and mobility on processes of enculturation and belonging, and the various ways in which global forces of conflict and change impinge on young lives (Olwig 2002; Olwig and Gulløv 2003; Gilliam, Olwig, and Valentin 2005). While focusing on the interplay between children and their environments, anthropologists have not generally viewed children as "natives of childhood." Rather, they have seen "children" as windows through which to engage critically with anthropological theory and to critically inform theories and policies shaping the worlds that concrete children encounter as natives of particular settings and conceptual frameworks.

As already suggested, the coupling of educational anthropology with the anthropology of children, is, to some extent, inevitable. We see this convergence in our own work, and as participants in the emerging field of educational anthropology encourage cross-fertilization on the premise that isolating the sociocultural child from "education" makes as little anthropological sense as isolating "education" from multiple sites and activities of children's lives. Further convergence of these two subfields will undoubtedly prove productive, as more and more children's lives become structured by universal schooling and educational aims. Turning our gaze to anthropological studies of education in the Global South, concerns for equal access to universal education and attempts to make new and "proper" childhoods (and educated citizenries) through schooling become more directly pronounced.

Education and Planned Development in a Global Perspective

A third strand of studies informing the emerging field of educational anthropology was conducted by anthropologists working on education and planned development. In line with dominant global development paradigms, education plays a significant role in Scandinavian development aid, both as an end in itself and as a means to other development goals. During the 1980s and 1990s, departments of education were among the first institutions to engage with the role of education in planned development. Several studies integral to ongoing school development and teacher training programs in Africa and Asia served as critical commentaries on ideological constructs of Western educational export to developing countries, and the problems inherent in value transmission (Schnack 1994; Holst et al. 1996). A few ethnographically oriented studies have investigated the meaning of school for social relations in everyday life in Mongolia (Madsen 1996), parental attitudes towards education in Nepal (Conrad 1997), and local socialization systems in Senegal (Daun 1985).

Since the mid-1990s, a small number of anthropological studies have engaged with development-related education research. These studies represent a shift in the conceptualization of schooling, largely inspired by the American tradition of educational anthropology. Acknowledging that notions of "education" and "the educated person" are culturally produced called into question singular notions of "school" and drew attention to coexisting and competing forms of education, and thus to the struggles over values and knowledge obtained from different sites of learning (Levinson and Holland 1996). In contrast to ethnographic studies of education and children and youth conducted primarily in Scandinavian settings and often within the bounds of formal institutions, the emergent field of educational anthropology in a development perspective was, in its initial stages, characterized by studies conducted outside schools and away from home, a legacy of classical fieldwork and comparative perspectives inherent to the discipline of anthropology. Over the last fifteen years, a growing number of anthropological studies of education have been carried out primarily as doctoral research in Asia and Africa.

One major theme is the relationship between mass schooling in postcolonial, developing states and the varied experiences and expectations of children and their families towards education in Zambia (Boesen 2000), Uganda (Meinert 2009), and Nepal (Valentin 2005). Other important themes are the interplay of schooling, nation-building, citizenship, and conflict in Sri Lanka (Sørensen 2008), political socialization and mass education in Vietnam (Valentin 2007), and the coexistence of schooling as a culturally distinct and universally dominant form of education with other more or less institutionalized forms of education, such as religious training among young Muslims in Ghana (Ihle 2003), informal, kin-based medical training between grandparents and grandchildren in Kenya (Prince and Geissler 2001), health communication and child-to-child learning in Kenya (Onyango-Ouma 2000), and the relationship between mothers' education and child health in Uganda (Katahoire 1998).

Moving out of formal educational settings, concretely as well as analytically, is both a consequence of and a precondition for exploring the kinds of questions raised by anthropological studies of education in these particular settings. By shifting the ethnographic gaze beyond public educational institutions and their "inner logics," these studies attempt to place and comprehend the dynamics of schooling in relation to other competing forms of education and to wider societal processes. This has shed light on the tension between politically defined standards of education in international and national arenas and the ways in which education is interpreted and given meaning by social actors themselves. A key question addressed by studies is the ambivalence with which both pupils and their families meet schools. Studies show how schooling in contexts of poverty and political destabilization is tied to promises of social mobility and respectability, which makes a schooled status an important identity marker for both pupils and their families. Studies also show that school education in many cases leads to new experiences of exclusion and marginalization, when the certificate obtained cannot be translated into a job, money, or a higher status.

Not confining studies to schools allows for fieldwork in a variety of settings—families, work places, political organizations, NGOs, churches and temples—where "education" takes place and where ideas of the "educated person" are developed parallel with, and often in response to dominant notions. With the spread of mass schooling in the Global South over the last three decades, many children do in fact go to school,

yet, as a category, they are often represented as being more loosely attached to specific educational institutions when compared to children
in Scandinavia. This is perhaps one explanation for the tendency to focus on children *between* rather *within* institutions in studies conducted
in the Global South.

The recent development of anthropological studies oriented towards a broad range of educational issues has several merits for the
field of educational anthropology and, from a more practical perspective, for current development policy. First, by providing a comparative
perspective, the increasing number of studies conducted in the Global
South has contributed to a critical exploration of basic constructions of
"school" and "pupil," which were often left unquestioned and uncon-
textualized as such in much ethnographic research focusing solely on
public schools in Scandinavia. Second, while the recent research agendas mentioned above have to some extent been shaped by, and oriented
toward, current development policy priorities, many scholars engaged
in potentially controversial research issues also use their research as a
platform for criticizing these same development aid policies. For example, studies on education in the Global South funded by the Danish Ministry of Foreign Affairs also question the somewhat naive and
uncritical assumptions guiding much development thinking on education as a means to development. While not denying the transformative capacities of formal education, they call into question the kind of
changes it brings about by shedding light on the role schooling plays
in people's imaginations of new possibilities and identities as educated
persons (see Levinson and Holland 1996; Stambach 2000), which itself
may work as a driving force for social mobility.

Conclusion

This chapter represents an attempt to flesh out an emerging field of educational anthropology in contemporary Scandinavia. The three strands
of research outlined above—school ethnography, the anthropology of
children and youth, and anthropological development studies—have
evolved separately and still form independent fields of research, not
least due to ongoing research traditions and institutional affiliations.

The critical approach developed in ethnographic school research
highlights the ways in which mechanisms of dominance subtly play
out in everyday practices. That most of these studies were conducted in
classrooms proved too narrow a focus, yet their emphasis on learning

and socialization as social processes goes to the heart of educational anthropology. By paying attention to children's meaning constructions, anthropological child research highlights the need to take processes of sensemaking from different actor-positions into account when investigating a range of educational settings, pedagogical regimes, and processes of transforming children into proper and properly educated persons and citizens. We have argued that an anthropology of children and youth provides a starting point for further discussions within educational anthropology of where and when transformative processes are thought (and ought) to take place and how they play out in peoples' lives.

Research on education and development in a global perspective challenges taken-for-granted assumptions about institutional necessity. Systematic comparative perspectives force the hand of educational studies that implicitly privilege schools as central sites of educational processes. Moving out—geographically and institutionally—affords broader perspectives on transformative processes yet also reminds us that these processes are invariably related to dominant educational institutions, which at once serve as symbols and gatekeepers of future opportunities.

The three strands of research drawn together here underline the importance of broad anthropological perspectives for the study of educational processes, a perspective that includes schools, but does not work from preconstructed notions of schools as the most important sites of learning and tutorage. Educational anthropology in Scandinavia has by and large emerged from the research interests, themes, and institutional affiliations presented, but has not yet synthesized them to any great extent. These strands of research, however, presently provide a platform for educational and research programs in "pedagogical anthropology."

As noted, the Scandinavia term for "education," *uddannelse*, does not cover the moral and social education central to pedagogical institutions of this region. Pedagogical anthropology potentially offers a broader focus on "education" than *uddannelsesantropologi* (educational anthropology). Encompassing educational anthropology, it links to a traditional Scandinavian focus on *dannelse* (*Bildung*) and to a tradition of training pedagogues as professional caretaker-educators of the young, the elderly, and others categories of people in need of care and tutorial support. Pedagogical anthropology highlights processes of learning, formation, transformation, and the creation of personhood in a wide range of social relations, while maintaining a focus on the influence formalized institutions have as mental and social points of references in people's lives. Pedagogical anthropology opens a whole range of formal and informal sites where "education" may take place. This makes the emerging study "pedagogical anthropology" potentially productive in broadening the bounds of educational anthropology as this subfield of anthropology grows and matures.

Notes

1. *Ethnography* refers to methodology employed to study particular forms of social interaction.

2. Spanning four decades, three countries, and a broad range of disciplines employing ethnographic methods forces us to select work we feel best represents the strands of research we chose as our focus. Because we know this work best, our selection has a Danish bias. For this pragmatic solution to problems of time and space, we apologize to those who may feel passed over.

3. The common beginning of Scandinavian languages in Old Norse, the language of the Vikings, has been reinforced by a long history of trade, occupation, and union. Despite shifting royal powers and repeated war, the Scandinavian languages, are still, particularly in written form, mutually intelligible to inhabitants of Sweden, Norway, and Denmark.

4. There are thirteen anthropology departments: three in Denmark, four in Norway, and six in Sweden. Two sister disciplines—ethnology and folkloristics—have focused respectively on European peasant life and expressive folk culture.

5. Scandinavian graduate students are often more established with partners and children than graduate students elsewhere.

6. For example, Jean Lave, Jean Briggs, Ray McDermott, Barbara Rogoff, and Bradley Levinson.

7. Anthropologists are also working beyond the bounds of Scandinavia, for example Åm 1991; Howell 1985, 2002; Gilliam 2003; Meinert 2009; Rabo 2008; Rydstrøm 2003.

8. The Norwegian Center for Child Research publishes *Childhood* and is one of the key institutions in *Childwatch International*, a global network promoting children's rights and well-being.

Bibliography

Åm, Eli. 1989. *På jakt etter barneperspektivet*. [In Search of the Child Perspective]. Oslo: Universitetsforlaget.
———. 1991. *Japansk barnehage*. [Japanese Kindergarten]. Oslo: Universitetsforlaget.
Anderson, Sally. 2000. *I en klasse for sig* [In a Class of Their Own]. Copenhagen: Gyldendal.

————. 2008. *Civil Sociality. Children, Sport, and Cultural Policy in Denmark.* Charlotte, NC: Information Age.

Baarts, Charlotte. 2004. "Viden og Kunnen—en antropologisk analyse af sikkerhed på en byggeplads" [Knowledge and Skill—An Anthropological Analysis of Safety in Construction Work]. PhD diss., Department of Anthropology, University of Copenhagen.

Bauer, Mette, and Karin Borg. 1976. *Den skjulte læreplan. Skolen socialiserer, men hvordan?* [The Hidden Curriculum. Schools Socialize, but How?]. Copenhagen: Unge Pædagoger.

Berentzen, Sigurd. 1980 [1969]. *Kjønnskontrasten i barns lek* [Gender Construction in Children's Play]. Bergen: University of Bergen.

Berner, B. Boel, Staf Callewaert, and Henning Silberbrandt. 1977. *Skole, ideologi og samfund.* [School, Ideology, and Society]. Copenhagen: Munksgaard.

Bernstein, Basil. 1975. *Class, Codes and Control,* vol. 3, *Towards a Theory of Educational Transmission.* London: Routledge and Kegan Paul.

Bjerrum Nielsen, Harriet. 1985. "Pædagogiske hverdagsbeskrivelser—et forsømt område i pædagogisk forskning." [Pedagogical Descriptions of Everyday Life—A Neglected Field in Pedagogical Research]. *Tiddskrift for Nordisk Förening för Pedagogisk Forskning* 5, no. 2: 27–42.

Boesen, Inger. 2000. "Growing Up as an Educated Zambian. Primary Education and Cultural Identity in the Context of Change. A Study of Four Local Communities in the Copperbelt." PhD diss., RDSES, Copenhagen.

Borgnakke, Karen. 2000. "Empirisk forskning, læringsbegreber med (livs)bredde og etnometodologiske inspirationer." In *Læringslandskaber—artikler om læring og fagdidaktik.* [Landscapes of Learning—Articles on Learning and Didactics], ed. Mads Hermansen, Kirsten Hastrup, and Henning Salling Olesen. *Forskningstidsskrift fra Danmarks Lærerhøjskole* 4, no. 5: 13–37.

Brembeck, Helene, Barbro Johansson, and Jan Kampmann, eds. 2004. *Beyond the Competent Child: Exploring Contemporary Childhoods in the Nordic Welfare Societies.* Frederiksberg: Roskilde Universitetsforlag.

Broch, Harald Beyer. 1990. *Growing up Agreeably. Bonerate Childhood Observed.* Honolulu: University of Hawai'i Press.

Bundgaard, Helle, and Eva Gulløv. 2008. *Forskel og fællesskab. Minoritetsbørn i daginstitution.* [Difference and Community: Minority Children in Day Care]. Copenhagen: Hans Reitzels.

Callewaert, Staf, and Bengt A. Nilsson. 1974. *Samhället, skolan och skolans inre arbete.* [Society, School and the Inner Workings of Schools]. Lund: Lunds bok og tidskrifts AB.

Clark, Alison, Anne-Trine Kjørholt, and Peter Moss. 2005. *Beyond Listening. Children's Perspectives on Early Childhood Services.* Bristol, UK: Policy Press.

Conrad, Joan. 1997. *The Impact of Educational Policy on Local Communities and on Parental Attitudes towards Education. A Study from Eastern Nepal.* Copenhagen: University of Copenhagen.

Daun, Holger. 1985. *Primary Learning Systems in Sub-Saharan Africa. Cases from Senegal.* Stockholm: University of Stockholm.

Ehn, Billy. 1983. *Ska vi leka tiger? Daghemsliv ur kulturell synsvinkel.* [Shall We Play Tiger? Day Care from a Cultural Perspective]. Stockholm: Liber.

Einarsdóttir, Johanna, and Judith T. Wagner, eds. 2006. *Nordic Childhoods and Early Education: Philosophy, Research, Policy and Practice in Denmark, Finland, Iceland, Norway and Sweden.* Charlotte, NC: Information Age.

Eriksen, Thomas Hylland. 1993. *Små steder, store spørgsmål. En innføring i socialantropologi.* [Small Places, Large Issues: An Introduction to Social Anthropology]. Oslo: Universitetsforlaget.

Gilliam, Laura. 2003. "Restricted Experiences in a Conflict Society: The Local Lives of Belfast Children." In *Children's Places. Cross-cultural Perspectives,* ed. Karen Fog Olwig and Eva Gulløv. London: Routledge.

———. 2006. "De umulige børn og det ordentlige menneske. Et studie af identitet, ballade og muslimske fællesskaber blandt etniske minoritetsbørn i en dansk folkeskole." [Impossible Kids and the Decent Human Being. A Study of Identity, Troublemakers and Muslim Solidarity in a Danish School]. PhD diss., Danish School of Education, Copenhagen.

Gilliam, Laura, Karen Fog Olwig, and Karen Valentin, eds. 2005. *Lokale liv. Fjerne forbindelser.* [Local Lives, Distant Connections: Studies of Children, Youth, and Migration]. Copenhagen: Hans Reitzels.

Gitz-Johansen, Thomas. 2006. *Den Multikulturelle Skole. Integration og sortering.* [The Multicultural School: Integration and Sorting]. Frederiksberg: Roskilde Universitetsforlag.

Gullestad, Marianne. 1984. *Kitchen-Table Society.* Oslo: Norwegian University Press.

———. 1989. "Small Facts and Large Issues. The Anthropology of Contemporary Society." *Annual Reviews of Anthropology* 18: 71–93.

———. 1991. "The Scandinavian Version of Egalitarian Individualism." *Ethnologia Scandinavica* 21.

———. 1992. "Children's Care for Children." In *The Art of Social Relations: Essays on Culture, Social Action and Everyday Life in Modern Norway.* Oslo: Scandinavian University Press, 113–36.

———. 2002. "Invisible Fences: Egalitarianism, Nationalism and Racism." *Journal of the Royal Anthropological Institute* 8, no. 1: 45–63.

Gulløv, Eva. 1999. *Betydningsdannelse blandt børn.* [Sensemaking among Children]. Copenhagen: Gyldendal.

Halldén, Gunilla. 2003. "Children's Views on Family, Home and House." In *Children in the City: Home Neighborhood and Community,* ed. Pia Havdrup Christensen and Margaret O'Brien. London: Falmer.

Hasse, Cathrine. 2002. *Kultur i bevægelse.* [Culture in Motion]. Copenhagen: Forlaget samfundslitteratur.

Hastrup, Kirsten, and Jan Ovesen. 1985. *Etnografisk grundbog* [Ethnographic Reader], 2nd ed. Copenhagen: Gyldendal.

Højlund, Susanne. 2002. *Barndomskonstruktioner. På feltarbejde i skole, SFO og på sygehus.* [Constructions of Childhood: Fieldwork in School, After School and Hospital]. Copenhagen: Gyldendal.

———. 2006. "Hjemlighed som pædagogisk strategi" [Hominess as a Pedagogical Strategy]. In *Mellem omsorg og metode,* eds. Ole Steen Kristensen, 95–135. Viborg: Forlaget PUC.

Holst, Jesper, Chresten Kruchov, Ulla Ambrosius Madsen, and Ellen Nørgaard, eds. 1996. *School-Development in Mongolia 1992–94*. Copenhagen: RDSES.

Howell, Signe. 1985. "From Child to Human: Chewong Concepts of Self." In *Acquiring Culture: Cross Cultural Studies in Child Development*, ed. Gustav Jahoda and Ioan M. Lewis. London: Croom Helm.

———. 2002. *Kinning of Foreigners*. London: Berghahn.

Hultqvist, Kenneth, and Gunilla Dahlberg, eds. 2001. *Governing the Child in the New Millennium*. New York: Routledge/Falmer.

Ihle, Anette Haaber. 2003. "'It's all about Morals.' Islam and Social Mobility among Young and Committed Muslims in Tamale, Northern Ghana." PhD diss., Copenhagen University.

Jackson, Phillip W. 1968. *Life in Classrooms*. New York: Holt, Rinehart and Winston.

James, Allison, Chris Jenks, and Alan Prout. 1998. *Theorizing Childhood*. Cambridge: Polity.

Kampmann, Jan. 2003. "Barndomssociologi. Fra marginaliseret provokatør til mainstream leverandør." [Childhood Sociology: From Marginalized Provocateur to Mainstream Supplier]. *Dansk Sociologi* 3: 79–93.

Katahoire, Anne. 1998. "Education for Life: Mothers' Schooling and Children's Survival in Eastern Uganda." PhD diss., Institute of Anthropology, University of Copenhagen.

Kjørholt, Anne-Trine. 2004. "Childhood as a Social and Symbolic Space. Discourses on Children as Social Participants in Society." PhD diss., NTNU, Trondheim.

Klette, Kirsti. 1998. *Klasserumsforskning—på norsk* [Classroom Research—in Norwegian]. Oslo: Ad Notam Gyldendal.

Kryger, Niels. 2004. "Mesterfortællinger og pædagogisk feltforskning i Danmark fra 1970 erne til idag" [Master Stories and Pedagogical Field Research in Denmark from the 1970s until Today]. In *Pædagogisk Antropologi*, ed. Ulla Ambrosius Madsen, 122–48. Copenhagen: Hans Reitzel.

Larsen, Birgitte Romme. 2005. "Afviste flygtningebørn i kirkeasyl: Om 'normalitetet,' 'unormalitet' og rollen som mediatorer mellem forældre og samfund" [Refused Refugee Children in a Church Asylum: About Normality, Abnormality and the Role of Mediator between Parents and Society]. In *Lokale liv. Fjerne forbindelser*, ed. Laura Gilliam, Karen Fog Olwig, and Karen Valentin, 233–48. Copenhagen: Hans Reitzel.

Levinson, Bradley A., and Dorothy C. Holland. 1996. "The Cultural Production of the Educated Person: An Introduction." In *The Cultural Production of the Educated Person: Critical Ethnographies of Schooling and Local Practice*, ed. Bradley A. Levinson, Douglas E. Foley, and Dorothy C. Holland, 1–54. Albany: SUNY Press.

Lidén, Hilde. 1997. "Growing up in Urban Norway." In *Growing Up in a Changing Urban Landscape*, ed. Ronald Camstra. Amsterdam: van Gorcum and Comp.

Lidén, Hilde, and Anne Trine Kjørholt. 2004. "Children and Youth as Citizens: Symbolic Participants or Political Actors?" In *Beyond the Competent Child*, ed. Helene Brembeck, Barbro Johansson, and Jan Kampmann. Roskilde: Roskilde Universitetsforlag.

Liep, John, and Karen Fog Olwig. 1994. "Kulturel kompleksitet" [Cultural Complexity]. In *Kulturel mangfoldighed i Danmark*, ed. John Liep and Karen Fog Olwig. Copenhagen: Akademisk.

Lindblad, Sverker, and Fritjof Sahlström. 1999. "Gamla mönster och nya gränser. Om rammefaktorer och klassrumsinteraktion" [Old Patterns and New Borders: On Framing Factors and Classroom Interaction]. *Pedagogisk Forskning i Sverige* 4, no. 1: 73–92.

———. 2006. "Classroom Research and Classroom Interaction: Changes in Theory and Practice." Paper presented at seminar 2006–02–08. Göteborg: Pedagogiska Institutionen.

Lundberg, Pia. 2005. "Blindhed: Antropologisk analyse af de blindes verden fra renæssancen til i dag" [Blindness: An Anthropological Analysis of the Blind from the Renaissance to the Present]. PhD diss., Department of Anthropology, University of Copenhagen.

Madsen, Ulla Ambrosius. 1994. "Hverdagsliv og læring i efterskolen." [Everyday Life and Learning in Folk Boarding Schools]. PhD diss., RDSES, Copenhagen.

Madsen, Ulla Ambrosius. 1996. "School and Everyday Life." *School-development in Mongolia 1992–94*, ed. Jesper Holst, Chresten Kruchov, Ulla Ambrosius Madsen, and Ellen Nørgaard. Copenhagen: RDSES.

Markström, Ann-Marie, and Gunilla Halldén. 2008. "Children's Strategies for Agency in Preschool," *Children and Society* 23, no. 2: 112–22.

Meinert, Lotte. 2009. *Hopes in Friction: Schooling, Health, and Everyday Life in Uganda*. Charlotte, NC: Information Age.

Nørgaard, Katrine. 2004. "Tillidens teknologi. Den militære ethos og viljen til dannelse" [The Technology of Trust: The Military Ethos and the Will toward *Bildung*]. PhD diss., Department of Anthropology, University of Copenhagen.

Norman, Karin. 1991. *A Sound Family Makes a Sound State. Ideology and Upbringing in a German Village*. Stockholm Studies in Social Anthropology. Stockholm: Almqvist and Wiksell International.

———. 2005. "Changing Family Relations and the Situation of Children: Kosovo Albanian Asylum Seekers in Sweden." In *The Asylum-Seeking Child in Europe*, ed. Hans E. Andersson, Henry Ascher, Ulla Björntorp, Marita Eastmond, and Lotta Mellander. GRACE: University of Gothenburg.

Olesen, Jesper. 2003. *Det forbrugende barn* [The Consuming Child]. Copenhagen: Hans Reitzel.

Olwig, Karen Fog. 2002. "'Displaced' Children? Risks and Opportunities in a Caribbean Urban Environment." In *Children in the City*, ed. Margaret O'Brien and Pia Havdrup Christensen. London: Falmer.

Olwig, Karen Fog, and Eva Gulløv. 2003. *Children's Places. Cross-cultural Perspectives*. London: Routledge.

Onyango-Ouma, Washington. 2000. "Children and Health Communication. Learning about Health in Everyday Relationships among the Luo of Western Kenya." PhD diss., Institute of Anthropology, University of Copenhagen and Danish Bilharziosis Laboratory.

Palludan, Charlotte. 2005. "Når børnehaven gør en forskel." [When the Kindergarten Makes a Difference]. PhD diss., Institute of Educational Anthropology. Copenhagen, Danish University of Education.

Prince, Ruth, and P. Wenzel Geissler. 2001. "Becoming 'One Who Treats': A Case Study of a Luo Healer and Her Grandson in Western Kenya." *Anthropology and Education Quarterly* 32, no. 4: 447–71.

Qvortrup, Jens, Marjatta Bardy, Giovanni Sgritta, and Helmut Wintersberger, eds. 1994. *Childhood Matters. Social Theory, Practice and Politics*. Aldershot, UK: Avebury.

Rabo, Annika. 2008. "Doing Family': Two Cases in Contemporary Syria." *Hawwa* (Leiden: Brill) 6, no. 2: 129–53.

Rydstrøm, Helle. 2003. *Embodying Morality: Growing Up In Rural Northern Vietnam*. Honolulu: University of Hawai'i Press.

Rysst, Mari. 2008. "'I want to be me. I want to be *kul*': An Anthropological Study of Norwegian Preteen Girls in the Light of a Presumed 'Disappearance' of Childhood." PhD diss., Department of Social Anthropology, University of Oslo.

Schnack, Karsten, ed. 1994. *Export of Curriculum and Educational Ideas*. Studies in Educational Theory and Curriculum, vol. 13. Copenhagen: RDSES.

Solberg, Anne. 2001. "Hidden Sources of Knowledge." In *Hidden Hands: International Perspectives on Children's Work and Labour*, ed. Angela Bolton, Phillip Mizen, and Christopher Pole. London: Routledge/Falmer.

Sørensen, Birgitte Refslund. 2008. "The Politics of Citizenship and Difference in Sri Lankan Schools." *Anthropology and Education Quarterly* 39, no. 4: 423–43.

Stambach, Amy. 2000. *Lessons from Kilimanjaro. Schooling, Community, and Gender in East Africa*. London: Routledge.

Valentin, Karen. 2005. *Schooled for the Future? Educational Policy and Everyday Life among Urban Squatters in Nepal*. Greenwich, CT: Information Age.

———. 2007. "Mass Mobilization and the Struggle over the Youth: The Role of Ho Chi Minh Communist Youth Union in Urban Vietnam." *YOUNG Nordic Journal of Youth Research* 15, no. 3: 299–315.

Valentin, Karen, and Lotte Meinert. 2009. "The Adult North and the Young South: The Civilizing Mission of Children's Rights." *Anthropology Today* 25, no. 3: 23–28.

Willis, Paul. 1977. *Learning to Labour: How Working Class Kids Get Working Class Jobs*. Aldershot, UK: Gower.

Winther, Ida Wenzel. 2006. *Hjemlighed. Kulturfænomænologiske studier*. [Homeyness. Phenomenological Cultural Studies]. Copenhagen: University of Education.

Wright, Susan. 2008. "Autonomy and Control: Danish University Reform in the Context of Modern Governance." *Learning and Teaching. The International Journal of Higher Education in the Social Sciences* 1, no. 2: 27–57.

§ 10

THE DEVELOPMENT OF ETHNOGRAPHIC STUDIES OF SCHOOLING IN JAPAN

Yasuko Minoura

In Japan, studies on culture and education were initiated in 1955 by the Research Institute for Comparative Education and Culture, newly founded as an annex to the Faculty of Education, Kyushu University. The fortieth-anniversary publication of the Institute (Kyushu daigaku 1996) has a long list of its works such as *Education and Culture in Thai Rural Community, A Comparative Study of Education for National Identity in Developing Countries, A Comparative Study of Education for Alien Children,* and others, indicating that their ethnographic studies had been conducted outside of Japan except those dealing with cultural minority groups in Japan. The institute offered a graduate course in educational anthropology from 1968 to 1997, and some graduates wrote an introductory article to educational anthropology (Ebuchi 1982), or related books (Harajiri 2005; Sakamoto 2006). Very few Japanese anthropologists have been interested in the field of education except those related to this institute and some trained by graduate schools in North America, although the Intercultural Education Society of Japan founded in 1981 included anthropology as one of its subfields. Therefore this review, which attempts to introduce ethnographic studies of schooling written mostly in Japanese by Japanese scholars, includes scholars in related fields rather than limiting itself to educational anthropology.

Ethnographic studies of schooling in Japan were carried out in the beginning by American educational anthropologists such as Singleton (1967) and Rohlen (1983), both once affiliated with the institute previously mentioned, and by the sociologist Cummings (1980). The latter two books, translated into Japanese, influenced Japanese to conduct fieldwork in their own schools, as did the British new sociology of education (Karabel and Halsey 1977, translated into Japanese in 1980). In the 1980s through the 1990s ethnographic studies of education have been produced both by Japanese (Minoura 1984; Ikeda 1985; Shimizu and Tokuda 1991) and by non-Japanese scholars (Tobin, Yu, and Davidson 1989; Goodman 1990). A textbook on fieldwork was published first by Sato (1992) and then by Kinoshita (1999). Minoura has taught field-work as part of a regular methodology courses in the School of Education, University of Tokyo, since 1993, the content of which has been published (Minoura 1999). This book has been widely read by psychologists, probably because of its focus upon microethnography. Many kinds of textbooks on fieldwork have been produced by sociologists, anthropologists, and psychologists in the 2000s, helping ethnographic studies to proliferate.

The Japan Society of Educational Sociology had the first consecutive panel discussions on ethnographic studies in its annual meetings of 1996 and 1997. In 2006 and 2007, recognizing the dramatic expansion of ethnographic studies during the past ten years, this society again organized a panel to examine the present state and future possibilities of ethnographic studies in education. The Japanese Society of Educational Psychology had a session on fieldwork in 1999.

This review, covering works after 1980, is divided into three sections: (1) Ethnographic Studies of Ordinary Schools, (2) Studies Focusing upon Children with Cultural Background Different from Those in the Mainstream, and (3) Ethnographic Studies of Atypical Educational Institutions.

Ethnographic Studies of Ordinary Educational Institutions

Focusing on Ordinary Educational Practices in Middle Schools

Shimizu Kokichi is probably the first Japanese scholar who published an ethnography of a school, and since then he has led ethnographic studies in Japan's educational sociology (Shimizu 1998, 2003). Shimizu did his first fieldwork at Nanchu during three years beginning in 1987 (Shimizu and Tokuda 1991). This school used to be notorious for school vandalism, but has carried out various kinds of reforms to normalize education under the strong leadership of a principal, who contributed one chapter to Shimizu's book together with other two teachers, main informants to Shimizu's study. The first part, "Daily Life of Nanchu," is written by teacher-collaborators and the principal, while the second part is Shimizu's ethnographic report.

Shimizu (1992) discussed the three kinds of *shido* (guidance) — *gakushu shido* (study guidance), *seito shido* (student guidance), and *shinro shido* (career guidance) — prevalent in Japanese middle schools. *Gakushu shido* aims at raising the academic abilities of students. *Seito shido*, a unique Japanese educational practice, aims at helping students think, decide, and act themselves through teachers' relations with students at homerooms, extracurricular clubs, and various kinds of school events. Another face of *seito shido* is a group of operations relevant to disciplinary problems, a sort of crackdown to control the students. *Shinro shido* includes a process of assigning individual students to the future courses available for them. In his ethnography Shimizu describes how each teacher carries out three kinds of *shido* in what context and discusses how *shido* affects the socialization of students.

Socialization at the middle school is done not only in daily classroom and extracurricular activities but also on special occasions such as *gasshuku* (off-campus training). In *gasshuku* students stay at an educational institution off campus for few days to receive *seikatsu shido* (life guidance, in literal translation) that cannot be taught in the classroom. Kuwayama (1996) described how the three-day *gasshuku* mandatory to all first-year students was carried out and analyzed how Japanese values such as empathy, cooperation of group members, and the sense of belonging were ingrained in various *gasshuku* programs.

Fujita and his associates (1995) did fieldwork in elementary and middle schools, besides conducting a questionnaire survey with two thousand teachers. This study shows how Japanese teachers' work is composed of a variety of different tasks and activities, not just teaching but also various consultative, administrative, and coordinating tasks. It also reveals how the job of teaching has been intensified in recent years, due to the extraordinary variety and multidimensionality of teaching activities and the overloaded schedule of teachers, resulting in the feeling of teachers that they are too busy to spend their time and energy for teaching itself.

During the 1990s, the structural changes in Japanese society, triggered by the decrease in number of children, the transformation of the youth labor market after the collapse of bubble economy, the development of information technology, changes in the values or moral standards shared by people, and other factors have shaken the foundations of the Japanese educational system (Ichikawa 2002). The school system has become the focus of increasing discontent because of its rigidity, uniformity, and exam centeredness, which led to a series of educational reform proposals and policy measures in the 1990s. Local governments and individual schools have been given wider discretionary powers. In return, demands for accountability have increased, resulting in more paperwork for documentation. Consequences of reforms have been studied by Japanese as well as non-Japanese.

Seito-shido with "*kaunseringu maindo*" (disciplinary guidance flavored by the psychological understanding of students) was emphasized throughout the 1990s rather than controlling students' appearance and behavior coercively. Along with this line of discourse, the Ministry of Education, Culture, Sports, Science and Technology (hereafter, Ministry of Education) decided in 2001 to place a counselor in every public middle school. One of the ways to realize this new ideology of *seito shido* is to open a room where students drop by anytime during recess and after school to consult with a counselor or to spend time merely doing nothing or doing what they want. Seto (2006) explores how each user perceives the function of such a room by observing users in the open counseling room, and concludes that this type of ambiguity offers a sort of comfort to students.

Yoshida (2007) explores how the concept of accountability has changed the styles of *seito shido* by investigating the control system and teachers' survival strategies in a low-rank senior high school in 2005–2006 where she worked as a full-time teacher. Her study reveals newly developed indirect ways of controlling students' behavior without real confrontation with an individual student, which she calls "*osewa* (caring) mode." This device consists of the recording of absence time in five-minute intervals together with treating students who violate school regulations softly to avoid an outburst of students' rage. The maximum amount of absence that still allows credits towards graduation is announced in the beginning of the school year. In this way teachers managed to keep their classes in order and avoid direct confrontation with students, still getting accountability when students had to be punished or were forced to leave school. Yoshida's ethnography depicts quite a different picture of *shido* compared with that in the 1980s described by Shimizu and Tokuda (1991).

Ochiai (2009) observed how teachers were exhausted at the school where she served as a counselor. She identified six factors responsible for exhaustion: (1) an increase of immature and difficult students; (2) teachers being forced to undertake some of parental role because of the weakened child-rearing function of families; (3) increasing demands for accountability to defend one's school, resulting in more paperwork; and (4) intensification of bureaucratic management of schools. Combined with (3) and (4), two additional factors—(5) differences in educational beliefs between younger and older generations and (6) exclusion from decision-making processes of one's own school—have led to the decline of mutual support among teachers, resulting in isolation. The loss of a sense of autonomy derived from factors such as (4) and (6), when coupled with a sense of isolation, precipitated teacher burnout. Ochiai's fieldwork revealed that, in addition to these recent changes, the culture of the Japanese teaching profession itself was the breeding ground for burnout.

In order to alleviate teachers' stress and to regain mutual support among colleagues, Sato (2006) has proposed his vision of and design for activities to make a school a community of learning that places more emphasis upon what a child has learned than upon how much a teacher has taught. Sato first helped Hamanogo Elementary School to implement his vision and design and to observe outcomes. He did the same with other elementary as well as middle schools.

The Japan Exchange and Teaching program introduced in 1987 by the government to improve foreign-language education in secondary schools and to promote international exchange has brought approximately six thousand Assistant Language Teachers (ALTs) to Japan every year. They saw Japanese schools in a comparison with their own at home. Asai (2006), building on McConnell (2000), examined how ALTs' cultural identities were redefined in the interaction with the culture of Japanese schools, which was quite different from what they experienced in their home countries.

Teaching Practices in Elementary Schools

Schooling in elementary schools has been studied by both Japanese and non-Japanese, but I introduce only three such studies here.

Shimahara and Sakai (1995) conducted classroom observations and interviews with teachers in public elementary schools both in New Jersey and in Tokyo in order to explore how teachers motivated students towards learning. They found Japanese teachers believed that the development of an emotional bond with a teacher motivated students to work at learning more eagerly and to reflect critically on their own behavior because students did not want to betray teachers' expectations. Thus Japanese teachers tried to foster caring and supportive relationships with students during recess and after school, whereas American teachers believed that it was their responsibility to motivate students towards learning through their teaching per se, by constructing effective teaching materials and classroom presentations. Shimahara and Sakai call the Japanese emphasis on human relationships as a source of motivation "ethno-pedagogy."

Watanabe (2001) examined how individuality and creativity were understood and taught in Japanese and American fifth- and sixth-grade classrooms by observing language arts lessons, particularly writing instruction. In order to achieve creativity, American teachers gave strict guidance in composition, stressing techniques for choosing the style best fitting the individual objective among several different ones, while Japanese teachers encouraged students to freely express their feelings.

And yet Japanese students' compositions were found to be remarkably similar, while American instructional methods produced variety in students' writing. Watanabe discusses the great differences in teachers' view of individuality and creativity between Japan and the United States, which influenced teaching practices and their outcomes.

Shimizu (2003) did fieldwork at Nunose Elementary School where *buraku*-liberation education had been successfully carried out to empower disadvantaged children. *Buraku* is literally a "hamlet," but sometimes refers to a hamlet of those historically stigmatized due to particular occupations. Shimizu described how teachers supported each other as a team to raise the academic and social competence of children who grew up there. Teachers strictly scolded even the first graders who hurt others physically and psychologically and let older children interview their parents to gain insight into the reality of their families' history. Immediate intervention by teachers as a whole helps to build reliable human relations in this school. An educational ethnography of *buraku* children initiated by Ikeda (1985) was followed by Kuraishi (2001) as well.

Extracurricular School Clubs

Bukatsudo (the school club) makes up an intensive part of the middle- and high-school experience. Once class ends around 3:30 PM, almost all students head for *bukatsudo* of either sports or culture clubs (chorus, brass band, painting, and others) and are engaged in practice until dusk. The lengthy and informal interaction during *bukatsudo* facilitates the personal teacher-student relationships, on the basis of which teachers sometimes do *seito shido* for students' personal growth. In *bukatsudo* students encounter for the first time the role of *senpai* and *kohai* (senior and junior) and the expectation that they defer to those in older year-groups. Cave (2004) made an important suggestion that self-chosen long-term commitment to a single club is conducive to the emotional engagement and resultant attachment to an organization that is a crucial instrument of order in schools.

The role of gender in a judo club was discussed by Hatano (2004), who did fieldwork at a middle school. In contrast to other sports clubs, boys and girls always practiced together, following the same practice schedule. However, the judo training space was divided, with two-thirds assigned to boys and one-third to girls. Hatano clarified the mechanism for the reproduction and sustenance of the social belief that males were superior to females in physical capabilities through her analysis of *randori* (technical training in pairs). When choosing a *randori* partner, weaker players must ask the stronger players. Hatano noticed that boys would only ask girls who were their senior since, even if the boy was defeated, he could mentioned her technical seniority so that he could sustain his male physical superiority.

Preschools: Half-Day Kindergartens (Youchien) and Full-Day Childcare Centers (Hoikuen)

Compulsory education in Japan begins at age six, but about 95 percent of children attended at least two years of pre-elementary education, options for which include both *hoikuen*, geared to the needs of working parents, and half-day *youchien*.

Ethnographers noticed that, along with the emphasis upon a group-oriented mentality, assigning a day monitor (*toban*) and turning over various class management duties to a child, practices prevalent in Japanese elementary schools through which teachers deliberately weaken their authority over children, cultivated the children's power of self-control. This was so even with preschoolers (Hendry 1986; Tobin et al. 1989; Lewis 1995). Foreign ethnographers conclude that the preschool education is the very basis of Japan's collectivism.

Complementing their works, Yuuki (1998) conducted an ethnographic study of a private kindergarten in 1991 and clarified the educational and social significances of learning and growing up in a group as well as how order in the kindergarten is maintained. The uniqueness of her study lies in her focus upon the function of both visible groups and invisible groups, whereas all foreign ethnographers have paid attention only to visible groups such as *kumi* (a small group). Yuuki discerned ten visible groups in her *youchien*, while an invisible group emerged instantly when a teacher recognized deviant children who do not follow her instruction. Teachers addressed "those who are still fooling around" without calling the names of particular children and without labeling them as bad, producing an invisible group of bad children. By this sort of temporal expulsion, teachers waited for children to become aware of their wrongdoings by themselves. Japanese teachers believed that children best learn to control their behavior when the impetus to change comes spontaneously from the realization that they have to conform to their group in order to avoid expulsion.

What happens if a foreign child enters a group-oriented Japanese *hoikuen* or *youchien*? This topic has been explored by several Japanese scholars, but I take up just two of them.

Shibayama (1995) observed a five-year-old Chinese boy who was placed in a four-year-old class of a *hoikuen*. She had begun fieldwork two months prior to his entry and recognized that there were scripts practiced by children when they join into play and when they had lunch. In order to explore the process of his incorporation of these scripts (*hoikuen* culture), she closely monitored this Chinese boy's cognition, behavior, and feelings. Shibayama found that he became able to follow most of lunchtime scripts in four months and to start expressing his wishes in one or two Japanese words in three months, although he failed to acquire the rule of sharing toys with other children even after seven months. She discusses the mechanism of cultural learning observed in this case. Shibayama (2001) expands her research to include two- and three-year-old foreigners in Japanese *hoikuen* to explore the development of actions and utterance.

Sato (2005), based on her fieldwork in 2003 at a *youchien* to which many foreign students sent their children, observed that three-year-olds began to notice foreign children's differences such as skin color and language through daily contacts. Four-year-olds understood that foreign children were different from the beginning and, when influential children took care of an Egyptian child, other classmates tended to imitate their attitudes. Upon noticing this boy's strategy of using his tears to manipulate people, the teacher began treating him in the same way as Japanese children, although the teacher encountered protest from his classmates who regarded him as "a sort of baby much below them" who needed handling with care.

Focusing upon Children with Cultural Background Different from Those in the Mainstream

Japan was once considered as a homogeneous society, but with the inflows of new types of foreigners, non-Japanese passport holders reached over two million, constituting 1.6 percent of the total population by the end of 2005. They include Koreans (30 percent), Chinese (24 percent), Brazilians and Peruvians (17 percent), Filipinos/as (10 percent), and Americans (3 percent). School-aged foreign children who attend a local Japanese public school must learn the Japanese language as a second language. The number of such children rose from 5,463 in 1991 to 25,411 in 2007 (Monbu kagaku sho 2008). Forty percent of this population was Portuguese speakers, while 20 percent were Chinese speakers.

Ethnic Japanese Returnees from Mainland China

There were children and women who were obliged to stay behind even after the completion of massive evacuation of Japanese nationals from then-colonized China at the end of World War II. They were descendants of Japanese immigrants to Manchuria, which had been colonized by Japan, stranded in China. One of their parents was Japanese legally, but their children grew up culturally as Chinese. The establishment of diplomatic relationships between Japan and China in 1972 opened a way to restore their legal rights to live in Japan. These people started coming back to Japan from 1980 on.

The school-aged children had to face discrimination and indifference in their schools, stresses generated from encounters in everyday life, and an identity crisis because they fell in-between Chinese and Japanese. Some schools set up a special class to relieve their difficulties, especially in the learning of the Japanese language. As time passed, they proceeded from primary to middle to high school. There are no ethnographic studies with this population in the 1980s. Most researchers are now doing fieldwork in high schools. Here I take up one study.

Kaji (2000) worked with returnees from China for a long while, which resulted in several insightful papers. He found linguistic and cultural capacity varied greatly depending upon the age of entry and upon socioeconomic status attained in China before migrating to Japan. Some had excellent academic records in China but could not do well in Japanese school because of their lack of fluency in Japanese. They managed to enter a low-rank high school. After lonely and alienated days in high schools, they obtained an admission to a university within a special quota designated for those of the foreign-born with limited ability in Japanese. By that time they had acquired Japanese fluency and were headed for creating a hybrid culture that refused to define them as either Chinese or Japanese. Others who had a poor academic record while in China easily gave up schooling. Dropouts tended to flock together and sometimes become delinquent or formed reckless biker gangs. Still another type of youth has good oral fluency, but limited ability in reading and writing in both Japanese and Chinese. Most of them came to Japan when they were very young or were born in Japan.

Ethnic Japanese Returnees from Brazil

The first explosive growth in the employment of foreign workers occurred in the latter half of the 1980s. The prospect of high salaries along with the deteriorating economy in Brazil attracted 302,000 *nikkeijin* (immigrants who have Japanese ancestry) to Japan by 2006. After the parents settle, children are taken into Japan and are enrolled in a nearby school, but they are occasionally left unenrolled for a few months or even years.

By now more than twenty researchers have carried out ethnographic studies on Brazilian children. Studies that adopt the assimilation-reproduction model regard the Japanese Brazilian (hereafter referred to as "Brazilians") as a passive recipient of the acculturative pressure of Japanese society. Osanai (2003) found that attendance at a Brazilian school shaped children's prospect for the future and led to an identity that differed from those attending a Japanese school. Brazilians who attended a Japanese school lost proficiency in Portuguese and said that they no longer felt as Brazilian after living Japan for so many years.

Children's problems were linked directly with parents' lifestyle, which was characterized by insecure employment with hourly wages and no secure plan for the family's future. Most Brazilians planned to return to Brazil when they saved the desired amount of money. Some parents bounced back and forth between Brazil and Japan. This sojourners' mentality had a detrimental effect upon children's prospects for the future, since children could not decide which country they would live in. Most Brazilian parents who were eager to work overtime could hardly find time for their children, leaving them frustrated and lonely at home. Under weak parental supervision some children failed to discover the meaning of going to school and eventually quit, gathering to play soccer, hanging out in a shopping mall, and occasionally engaging in delinquencies.

In contrast to the assimilationist studies, a considerable number of studies adopt a critical stance that assumes subjects as active agents who negotiate their position in a society. Yamanouchi (1999) describes "deviant behavior" such as the rejection of schoolwork, wild sexual expression, and excessive conspicuous consumption observed among Brazilian teenagers as tactics of resistance. Japanese middle schools are full of petty regulations about what to wear and how to behave, to which Brazilian students cannot adapt easily. The disciplinary policy of most Japanese schools is to deal with students as equally as possible. However, when it comes to dealing with a specific deviant behavior such as bringing a mobile phone to school and wearing perfume and earrings, teachers tended to avoid the reprimand that is usually given to Japanese students, saying that it cannot be helped because the Brazilians' culture is different (Kojima 2006). Brazilians playfully deviated from school rules in an attempt to place themselves in a higher position than Japanese students, whom they considered as pathetic victims and as childish. The differential treatments sometimes brought about antagonism between Brazilian and Japanese students, resulting in more marginalization of Brazilians in schools. The researchers of critical stance believe schools should respond to the needs not only of Brazilians but also of every student, since troubles caused by Brazilians may give an impetus to renovate the rigid culture of Japanese middle schools.

Children of Indochinese Refugees

In contrast to the voluminous influx of Brazilians, the total number of Indochinese is just over 11,000—8,656 Vietnamese, 1,357 Cambodians, and 1,306 Laotians settled in Japan through the governmental refugee assistance program.

The biggest source of stress for them is the Japanese language. At home Indochinese children speak their mother tongue and, upon entering school, they have to learn Japanese. After exit from the special Japanese language class, they face difficulties in understanding academic subjects. Teachers are not aware of a big gap experienced by nonnative speakers between basic interpersonal communicative skills and academic language needed to do class work. In primary school they can manage to do the work. When they enter a middle school, however, they tend to be left out, are unable to understand, and are gradually pushed towards the verge of dropping out.

Shimizu Mutsumi (2006), an educational sociologist, concluded after ten years of fieldwork that dropping out of school and delinquent behavior, which appeared to be related to the students' low cognitive/academic language proficiency, became prominent in either the eighth or ninth grade. The students could not enjoy school and were not able to have a positive self-image. That problem combined with poor parental supervision drove them to hang out in the streets instead of going to school. Similar types of youngsters got together to form a gang with a slogan of "We strong Vietnamese" with the intention of showing off their power by drinking alcohol, shoplifting, sniffing paint thinner, and hitting people in the street, while looking down at other Vietnamese boys who do not join them as "coward Japanized guys." These unlawful deeds caused them to be arrested and sent to a juvenile detention home.

Kawakami (1999, 2006) did in-depth interviews with young people who left their homeland before the age of three or who were born and have grown up in either Japan or Australia. What he found as suffering common to both groups are: (1) gaps in ways of thinking, especially regarding the parents' wish for the children to marry a Vietnamese, between parents who tend to idealize Vietnam and children who do not have any memories of it; and (2) discomfort with being in their father's land, feeling awkward and out of place. In addition he found that most young Vietnamese in Japan had a negative self-image, while their counterparts in Australia were very positive about themselves and their future, believing that they contributed to building Australian society. Vietnamese growing up in Japan were annoyed by feeling suspended in the middle, which may have come from incongruence between what they had incorporated culturally and their recognition of their racial origin.

The Vietnamese name was another source of discomfort that made their foreignness salient, especially in the case of primary-school children. However, ethnicity came to have different meanings when they reached high-school age. When young people found a positive meaning for their ethnicity in relation to their future work, they made efforts to learn their mother tongue and culture (Shimizu 2006).

The Korean Minority and the Development of Multicultural Education in Japan

Koreans are the biggest minority group in Japan, with a long history. When World War II was over, the majority of Koreans went back to Korea, but about 600,000 chose to stay in Japan and came to be called *zainichi* (residing in Japan) Koreans. As Japan's nationality is based on the principle of ancestry, not territoriality, the second and later generations of *zainichi* Koreans (hereafter, just "Koreans") remain as such unless they apply for naturalization or marry a Japanese national. Korean children attend either Japanese or Korean ethnic schools. Although legally Koreans, as the third or fourth generation they are culturally more Japanese and most of them speak Japanese as their mother tongue. Therefore, the education given in Korean ethnic schools is immersion-type bilingual education (Motani 2002). Relegating political, sociohistorical issues and various kinds of discrimination related to Koreans to other sources (Motani 2002; Harajiri 2005), this review deals only with the fact that multicultural education in Japan has developed in close connection to the Korean minority.

Koreans in Japanese schools are invisible since they use Japanese names, speak fluent Japanese, and act like other Japanese. Korean ethnic study classes, which were offered by Korean lecturers to help Korean children develop a positive ethnic image by teaching their language and culture, were set up first as an extracurricular activity in the 1950s in some public schools attended by many Koreans. Kishida (1997) examined the historical transition in relationships between Korean lecturers and Japanese teachers and found Korean lecturers were isolated from the rest of a school until the 1970s. They felt that Japanese teachers were prejudiced towards them. Most Japanese teachers, however, believe in equal treatment of Korean students, disregarding ethnicity, as the best educational practice. In reality it sometimes resulted in making inequality wider.

Changes gradually took place in the 1970s under the influence of *buraku*-liberation education, which aimed at leveling academic competence and at finding a career path for each student, overcoming discrimination from the perspective of human rights (Nakajima 1993). Teachers concerned formed the research society for *buraku*-liberation education. Some of these teachers expanded their horizon to include education for Koreans as a human-rights issue, resulting in cooperation between Korean lecturers and concerned Japanese teachers in order to eradicate racial prejudice of Japanese students toward Koreans and at the same time to develop ethnic awareness among Korean students. Some universities opened a new course to focus upon better understanding of *zainichi* Koreans as a part of pre-service teacher-training program (Tabuchi 1991). Encouraged by the guidelines of the Osaka prefectural board of education, Korean lecturers now played a role in making Japanese students aware of the sociohistorical roots of the Korean presence and familiarizing them with Korean culture (Kishida 1997). In other words they challenged Japanese to change their attitude towards the Koreans through intercultural education. However, Korean teachers still felt that there was a firm wall between them and Japanese teachers.

Additional changes occurred after the mid-1980s as globalization brought various types of newcomers into Japanese schools. The first book that dealt with multicultural education was published (Kobayashi and Ebuchi 1985). Several local boards of education, upon acknowledging the importance of multicultural education, renewed their guidelines. The guidelines for education of resident foreigners issued in 1986 by Kawasaki City aimed at the improvement of education to Koreans, who made up 86 percent of about ten thousand foreigners, while the guidelines of 1996 emphasized the creation of a multicultural society living with people of different cultures, reflecting the changing composition of what had become twenty thousand foreign residents. Assimilation ideology, formerly dominant, has been replaced by an emphasis on multiculturalism from the 1990s on, reflecting increased awareness of the value of cultural diversity.

Japanese Children Growing Up Overseas

The global economy has produced a large number of Japanese families residing abroad as a result of their fathers' overseas assignment. In

2007 about 59,000 Japanese children attended schools outside Japan. The Saturday School in Los Angeles, for example, was established in 1969 with 68 students, and the number of its students increased dramatically, reaching 2,947 as of 1991. Children go to a local American school, and then most of them go to a Japanese school for supplementary education every Saturday in order to keep up their ability to do a Japanese curriculum. The phenomenon of children educated overseas has attracted research interest from the 1970s to the present, some of which I review.

Minoura (1984) investigated children growing up in Los Angeles in 1977–1982 and followed up to do interviews after their return to Japan. She realized that discrepancies among behavior, cognition, or affect were an essential feature of the intercultural experience, which offered an invaluable opportunity to assess how and when culture-specific meaning systems were incorporated. From her observation and interviews with children as well as their mothers, she concluded that there was a sensitive period for the incorporation of cultural meaning systems that mediated interpersonal relations among peers, and that this sensitive period appeared to be between the ages of nine and fifteen years old (Minoura 1992). Minoura's work was complemented twenty-five years later by Sato and Kataoka (2008), who did fieldwork in the 2000s with Japanese children living in the United States.

Goodman (1990) concluded that returnees constituted a privileged group and that the so-called returnee problem was exaggerated. Compared to studies by Japanese scholars who focused more upon individual's experiences, he used the phenomenon of "returnee" as a strategic lens to explore changing Japanese society in the globalizing age. Shibuya's study (2001) was also quite different in terms of her employing Stuart Hall's conceptualization of identity as positioning, through which she interpreted data obtained from her fieldwork in a returnees' class in 1997.

Ethnographic Studies at Atypical Educational Institutions

There are two kinds of schools operated in Japan: schools under Article 1 of the School Education Law observe the curriculum guide prescribed by the Ministry of Education, and the other, called non-Article 1 schools or *kakushu gakko*, are free from the Ministry curriculum guide. This section deals mainly with the latter type, atypical schools under Article 1, and informal learning places not regulated by the School Education Law.

The category of *Kakushu gakko* includes international schools, seminaries, language schools, preparatory schools for entrance examinations, and schools for nursing, cooking, dressmaking, bookkeeping, and so on that are covered by Article 134 of the School Education Law.

International Schools

There are twenty-three international schools, whose language of instruction is English, and most of them are authorized as *kakushu gakko* under the School Education Law. Willis (1992) explored cultures prevailing in a polyethnic international school in Kobe, and found that students of this school came to possess a wide range of learned cultural competencies and productive achievements through profound personal transformation enhanced by particular sociocultural contexts that school offers. Some Japanese students in international schools are returnees from overseas who did not want to go to a Japanese school, while others had always lived in Japan but nonetheless chose an international school, although acknowledging various disadvantages attached to non-Article 1 schools. Nakamura (1999) examined the families that sent their children to such international schools despite these disadvantages. Interviews with parents revealed that they felt their private space was enriched and balanced by being free from demands in the Japanese public education and that enabled them to measure their children by multiple yardsticks.

Part-Time Evening High Schools and In-Hospital Schools

Both part-time evening high school and in-hospital school are under Article 1 of the School Education Law, but they cater to special situations. The part-time evening high school was established after World War II to serve a variety of working students diverse in age and in career so that they might attain universal high school education. In recent years students of part-time evening schools consist of those who have failed an examination at a fulltime school or who dropped out once but have come back, hoping to obtain a high school diploma.

Kidokoro and Sakai (2006) investigated the role of these schools, analyzing students' narratives, which revealed how the setting of such schools itself helped students to redefine their self-concept and to make a new commitment to their schools and society in general. This redefining process and the recovery of self-esteem were promoted by: (1) a student population that was very heterogeneous in terms of age and background, (2) working experiences and interpersonal relations with adults in a work place during the daytime, and (3) the greater degree of freedom allowed by such a school, which at the same time encouraged students to observe the minimum discipline. The researchers clarified how part-time evening high school enabled adolescents once in trouble and out of school to renew their identities.

An in-hospital school for children who are hospitalized for a long while is administratively operated as a branch of a nearby school. Taniguchi (2009) carried out fieldwork at such an in-hospital school to explore invisible meaning systems behind the daily practices observed there. Her study revealed that the teachers not only taught academic subjects but also performed various other functions that are usually not played by the teacher, such as substituting a parental and a playmate role, family care, medical care, social work, and counseling.

Likely Places of Learning outside Formal Schools

There are many informal learning places in Japan but here we take up only two such places that are not illustrated by Singleton (1998).

Free schools are for *futoko ji* (children who have become unable to attend any schools for various reasons), with whom many ethnographic studies are done. Asakura (1995) did fieldwork in the biggest free school, established in 1985 and run by a nonprofit organization, which was used by two hundred people aged six to twenty. The purpose of this school was to offer a place where children and youth were allowed to be themselves. Therefore, although various programs were offered upon users' requests, an individual was not forced to attend. Relationships between staff and users are horizontal as symbolized by calling staff not by *"sensei"* (the categorical name for a teacher), but by their name or nickname.

Problematic symptoms such as stomachache, vomiting, compulsive cleanliness, or violence usually went away as students regained self-esteem when they felt accepted, as they were in this school. Asakura illustrated various ways in which staff enhanced users' recovery of their positive feeling towards themselves and treated children's intense guilty feelings about not going to school or their anxiety about an uncertain future. Staff of the free school treated each user as an autonomous agent, while teachers of ordinary schools treated students as objects for education.

As the number of foreigners residing in Japan increased, numerous classes operated by volunteers emerged to support Japanese language learning. The Intercultural Education Society published a special issue focusing upon this movement and the networks of these classes (Noyama et al. 2003). This issue revealed that the key persons of successful volunteer groups tried to have the foreigners raise their own voices rather than play the role of passive learners. They arranged for collaborative learning by both the Japanese volunteers and the foreigners, who planned and carried out various projects in which the foreigners were teachers, such as a language class and an ethnic cuisine class, beside Japanese language classes for foreigners taught by Japanese, resulting in empowering all participants.

Concluding Remarks

Japanese ethnographers of education have been concerned mainly with studying problems caused by school nonattendance, minority children, and teachers' burnout and with daily interactions among children and teachers in and out of classrooms, along with studying atypical educational institutions. Non-Japanese ethnographers, whose works were regrettably omitted from this review, studied ordinary schools as a means to understand Japanese society and to explore the origins of so-called Japanese culture. In contrast, when Japanese researchers undertook ethnographic studies in ordinary schools, they had more specific focuses such as exploration of factors that made a school effective (for example, Shimizu 2003). There was a demarcation between Japanese and non-Japanese as mutual citations are relatively few. Few Japanese anthropologists have been interested in education, but those few manifested a particular interest in minority groups. Thus most ethnographic studies of Japanese schools were produced not by anthropologists but by sociologists, to some extent by psychologists interested in human development or by foreign Japanologists.

This review does not reflect either trends in educational research or realities of Japanese education, because structural problems such as those related to policies and a widening gap between public and private education are not addressed properly by ethnographic studies. Moreover, studies on higher education were not much included because there are few ethnographic studies except those related to foreign students. Thirty years' development of ethnographic studies, however, reveals shifts in topics reflecting changes in Japan's educational realities as well as a shift in theoretical stance from positivism to constructionism tinged with a critical flavor.

Bibliography

Japanese journals cited more than once with their English title in parentheses:
IKK represents *Ibunka kan kyouikugaku* (*Intercultural Education*, Bulletin of the Intercultural Education Society of Japan)
KSK represents *Kyouiku shakaigaku kenkyu* (*The Journal of Educational Sociology*, Bulletin of the Japanese Society of Educational Sociology)

Asai, Akiko. 2006. *Ibunka sesshoku niokeru bunkateki aidenthithi no yuragi* [Intercultural Experience and Cultural Identity Redefined: The Case of Assistant Language Teachers in Japanese Schools]. Kyoto: Mineruba Shobo.

Asakura, Kageki. 1995. *Toukoukyohi no esunogurafi* [Ethnography of School Refusal]. Tokyo: Sairyuu Sha.

Cave, Peter. 2004. "*Bukatsudo*: The Educational Role of Japanese School Clubs." *Journal of Japanese Studies* 30, no. 2: 383–415.

Cummings, William K. 1980. *Education and Equality in Japan*. Princeton, NJ: Princeton University Press.

Ebuchi, Kazuhiro. 1982. "Kyouiku jinruigaku" [Educational Anthropology]. In *Gendai no Bunka jinruigaku* [Modern Cultural Anthropology], ed. Takao Sofue, 133–230. Tokyo: Shibundo.

Fujita, Hidenori, Sachiko Yufu, Akira Sakai, and Yoshiki Akiba. 1995. "Kyoushi no shigoto to kyoushi bunka ni kansuru esunogurafi-teki kenkyu" [An Ethnographic Research on Teachers' Work and Culture of Teaching]. *Tokyo Daigaku Kyouikugaku Kennkyuka Kiyou* [The Bulletin of Graduate School of Education, University of Tokyo] 35: 29–66.

Goodman, Roger. 1990. *Japan's "International Youth": The Emergence of a New Class of Schoolchildren*. Oxford: Oxford University Press.

Harajiri, Hideki. 2005. *Mainorithi no kyouiku jinruigaku* [Educational Anthropology of Minorities]. Tokyo: Shinkansha.

Hatano, Keiko. 2004. "'Shintaitekina dansei yui' shinwa wa naze iji sarerunoka-supotsu jessen to jenda-no saiseisan" [How is the Myth of 'Male Physical Superiority' Sustained?: Mechanisms of Gender Reproduction in a Junior High School Judo Club]. *KSK* 75: 105–25.

Hendry, Joy. 1989. *Becoming Japanese: The World of the Preschool Child*. Manchester, UK: Manchester University Press.

Ichikawa, Shogo. 2002. "90 nenndai—kyouiku shisutemu no kouzo hendou" [Structural Changes in the Japanese Educational System in the 1990s]. *KSK* 70: 5–20.

Ikeda, Hiroshi. 1985. "Hisabetsu buraku niokeru kyouiku to bunka" [Education and Culture in a Village Discriminated as *Buraku*]. *Osaka Daigaku Ningen Kagakubu Kiyou* 11: 247–71.

Kaji, Itaru. 2000. "Chuugoku kikoku seito to koukou shingaku: gengo, bunka, minzoku, kaikyuu" [On Entry of Returnees from China to High Schools]. In "*Chugoku kikokusha" no seikatsu sekai* [The Life-World of Returnees from China], ed. Shinzo Araragi. Kyoto: Kourosha.

Karabel, Jerome, and A. H. Halsey. 1977. "Educational Research: A Review and an Interpretation." In *Power and Ideology in Education*, ed. Jerome Karabel and A. H. Halsey. New York: Oxford University Press.

Kawakami, Ikuo. 1999. "Ekkyousuru Kazoku: Zainichi betonamujin no net-towa-ku to seikatsu senryaku" [Families Crossing Borders: Vietnamese and Their Life in Japan.]. *Minzokugaku Kenkyu* [The Japanese Journal of Ethnography] 63, no. 4: 59–381.

———. 2006. "Ekkyousuru Kazoku: Zaigo betonamukei jyuumin to zainichi betonamukei jyuumin no hikaku kenkyu" [Families Crossing Borders: A Comparison between Vietnamese Residing in Australia and Vietnamese Residing in Japan]. In *Beyond "Japan,"* ed. Junzo Koizumi and Hideyo Kurimoto. Osaka: Osaka daigaku 21seiki COE Puroguramu.

Kidokoro, Akiko, and Akira Sakai. 2006. "Yakan teijisei koukousei no jiko no saiteigi katei ni kansuru shitsuteki kenkyu" [Qualitative Research on the Process of Self-Redefinition among Part-Time Evening High School Students]. *KSK* 78: 213–33.

Kinoshita, Yasuhito. 1999. *Guraundedo seori apuro-chi* [Grounded Theory Approach]. Tokyo: Koubundo.

Kishida, Yumi. 1997. "Ibunka kyousei kyouiku toshiteno zainichi kankoku/Chousenjin kyouiku" [Education for Korean Residents as an Education for Producing Ethnocultural Harmony]. *IKK* 11: 141–55.

Kobayashi, Tetsuya, and Kazuhiro Ebuchi, eds. 1985. *Tabunka kyouiku no hikaku kenkyu: Kyouiku ni okeru bunkateki douka to tayouka* [Comparative Studies of Multicultural Education: Cultural Assimilation and Diversity in Education]. Fukuoka: Kyushudaigaku Shuppankai.

Kojima, Akira. 2006. *Nyu-kama-no kodomo to gakkou bunka: Nikkei buraziru jin seito no kyouiku esunogurafi* [Children of Newcomers and School Culture: Ethnography of Education for Japanese-Brazilian Students]. Tokyo: Kaiso Shobo.

Kuraishi, Ichiro. 2001. "<I> narumono e no apurouchi no kansei: Buraku kaiho kyouiku toiu kagami ni terashite" [On the Pitfall of Educational Approach to the <Other>: Mirrored by the Buraku-liberation Education]. *IKK* 15: 188–97.

Kuwayama, Takami. 1996. "*Gasshuku*: Off-Campus Training in the Japanese School." *Anthropology and Education Quarterly* 27, no. 1: 111–34.

Kyushudaigaku Kyouiku-gakubu fuzoku Hikakukyouiku bunka Kenkyu-shisetsu, ed. 1996. *Kyouiku bunka no hikaku kenkyu: Kaiko to tenbo* [Comparative Studies of Education and Culture: Retrospect and Prospect]. Fukuoka: Kyushudaigaku Shuppankai.

Lewis, Catherine. 1995. *Educating Hearts and Minds: Reflections on Japanese Preschool and Elementary Education.* New York: Cambridge University Press.

McConnell, David L. 2000. *Importing Diversity: Inside Japan's JET Program.* Berkeley: University of California Press.

Minoura, Yasuko. 1984 [2003 for enlarged edition.]. *Kodomo no ibunka taiken* [Intercultural Experience during Childhood]. Tokyo: Shisaku Sha.

———. 1992. "A Sensitive Period for the Incorporation of a Cultural Meaning System: A Study of Japanese Children Growing Up in the United States." *Ethos* 20, no. 3: 304–39.

———. 1999. *Fi-rudowa-ku no gihou to jissai* [Ethnographic Fieldwork: Basics and Applications]. Kyoto: Mineruba Shobo.

Monbu kagaku sho. 2008. Ministry of Education Home Page. http://www.mext.go.jp/.

Motani, Yoko. 2002. "Towards a More Just Educational Policy for Minorities in Japan: The Case for Korean Ethnic Schools." *Comparative Education* 38, no. 2: 225–37.

Nakajima, Tomoko. 1993. "Nihon no tabunka kyouiku to zainichi kankokujin/chousenjin kyouiku" [Multicultural Education in Japan and Education for Zainichi Koreans]. *IKK* 7: 10–20.

Nakamura, Hiroko. 1999. "Kyouiku ridatsu no sentaku ni miru futatsu no shijika" [Two Cases of Privatization in the Choice of Nonpublic Education: Families That Chose International Schools]. *KSK* 65: 5–23.

Noyama, Horoshi, Michiko Sugisawa, Haruko Yonese, Mika Fujita, Maki Shibuya, Takaya Kawamura, and Kotaro Takagi. 2003. "Chiiki nettowaku to ibunkakan kyoiku" [Regional Networking and Intercultural Education]. *IKK* 18: 4–67

Ochiai, Mikiko. 2009. *Baan auto no esunogurafi* [Ethnography of Burnout]. Kyoto: Mineruba Shobo.

Osanai, Toru. 2003. *Zainichi brazirujin no kyouiku to hoiku* [Education and Child Care of Japanese Brazilians in Japan.]. Tokyo: Akashi Shoten.

Rohlen, Thomas P. 1983. *Japan's High Schools*. Los Angeles: University of California Press.

Sakamoto, Ikko. 2006. *Ajia no kodomo to kyouiku bunka* [Asian Children in Education and Culture]. Fukuoka: Kyushudaigaku shuppankai.

Sato, Chise. 2005. *"Gaikokujin" no seisei to ichizuke no purosesu* [The Process of Japanese Children's Perception of 'Foreigner' and the States of Foreign Children in the Classroom]. *IKK* 21: 73–88.

Sato, Gunei, and Yuko Kataoka, eds. 2008. *Amerika de sodatsu nihon no kodomo tachi* [Japanese Children Living in the United States]. Tokyo: Akashi Shoten.

Sato, Ikuya. 1992. *Fi-rudowa-ku* [Fieldwork]. Tokyo: Shinyosha.

Sato, Manabu. 2006. *Gakko no chousen: Manabi no kyoudoutai wo tsukuru* [Schools' Challenge: Making a Community of Learning]. Tokyo: Shougakkan.

Seto, Ruka. 2006. "Opun ru-mu ni okeru sukuuru kaunnseringu ruumu toiu basho" [What Is the Structure of the Counseling Room in Schools?]. *Kyouiku shinrigaku kenkyu* [The Japanese Journal of Educational Psychology] 54: 174–87.

Shibayama, Makoto. 1995. "Aru 5 saiji no hoikuen sukuriputo kakutoku katei" [Implications of Scripts Acquisition Processes: From a Case Study of a Five-Year-Old Chinese Boy]. *Nyuyouji kyouikugaku kenkyu* [Japanese Journal of Infant Care and Early Childhood Education] 4: 47–55.

———. 2001. *Koui to hatsuwa keisei no esunogurafi* [The Development of Actions and Utterances]. Tokyo: Tokyodaigaku Shuppankai.

Shibuya, Maki. 2001. *"Kikokushijyo" no ichidori no seiji* [The Politics of Positioning by Returnees]. Tokyo: Keiso Shobo.

Shimahara, Nobuo, and Akira Sakai. 1995. *Learning to Teach in Two Cultures: Japan and the United States*. New York: Garland Publishing.

Shimizu, Kokichi. 1992. "Shido: Education and Selection in a Japanese Middle School." *Comparative Education* 28, no. 3: 109–29.

———, ed. 1998. *Kyouiku no esunogurafi* [Ethnography of Schooling]. Kyoto: Sagano shoin.

————. 2003. *Kouritsu shougakko no chousen: Chikara no aru gakko towa* [Challenge of a Public School: What Is an Effective School]. Tokyo: Iwanami Shoten.

Shimizu, Kokichi, and Kozou Tokuda, eds. 1991. *Yomigaere kouritsu chuugaku: Amagasaki shiritsu minami chugakkou no esunogurafi* [Bringing Middle School Back to Life: Ethnography of Minami Middle School in Amagasaki]. Tokyo: Yushindo.

Shimizu, Mutsumi. 2006. *Nyu-kama- no kodomo tachi* [Children of Newcomers: The Life World in-between Schools and Families]. Tokyo: Keiso Shobo.

Singleton, John. 1967. *Nichū: A Japanese School*. New York: Rinehart and Winston.

————, ed. 1998. *Learning in Likely Places: Variables of Apprenticeship in Japan*. Cambridge: Cambridge University Press.

Tabuchi, Isoo. 1991. "Zainichi kankokujin/chousenjin rikai no kyouiku naiyou" [An Exploration of Curriculum toward Better Understanding of Korean Residents in Japan]. *IKK* 5: 123–34.

Taniguchi, Akiko. 2009. *Chouki nyuuinji no shinri to kyouikuteki enjyo* [Psycho-educational Support for Long-term Hospitalized Children]. Tokyo: Tokyo-daigaku Shuppankai.

Tobin, Joseph J., David Y. H. Wu, and Dana H. Davidson. 1989. *Preschool in Three Cultures: Japan, China, and the United States*. New Haven, CT: Yale University Press.

Watanabe, Masako Ema. 2001. "Sakubun shido ni miru kosei to souzouryoku no paradokkusu" [A Paradox of Individuality and Creativity through Composition Lessons: A Comparison of Japanese and American Elementary Schools]. *KSK* 69: 23–42.

Willis, David B. 1992. "A Search for Transnational Culture: Ethnography of Students in an International School in Japan" [Part II]. *International Schools Journal* 24 [Autumn]: 29–41.

Yamanouchi, Yuko. 1999. "Zainichi Nikkei burazirujin tiinaijya no 'teikou'" [The Resistance of Japanese-Brazilian Teenagers as the Practice of Everyday Life]. *IKK* 13: 89–103.

Yoshida, Miho. 2007. "Osewa mo-do to butsukaranai tousei shisutemu" [Osewa Mode and Control Systems to Avoid Conflict with Students]. *KSK* 81: 89–109.

Yuuki, Megumi. 1998. *Youchien de kodomo ha dou sodatsuka-shuudankyouiku no esunogurafi-* [First Group-Life in Japan: Ethnographic Studies of Kindergarten]. Tokyo: Yuushindo.

BAMBOO SHOOTS AFTER RAIN
Educational Anthropology and Ethnography in Mainland China

Huhua Ouyang

This chapter introduces the development of educational anthropology in mainland China. (Throughout this chapter I restrict the word "China" to mainland China, excluding Hong Kong, Macao, and Taiwan). After a general introduction to anthropology with its secondary status vis-à-vis sociology in mainland China, I will report theoretical works that help to construct Chinese educational anthropology as a discipline, then turn to research on ethnic minorities' education by three key national research centers, and finally to research on Han majority group education by scholars from departments of education, sociology, and foreign-language education. Most of the research reviewed here used long-term fieldwork and ethnography, or qualitative methods such as narrative inquiry.

China's Anthropology and Its Secondary Status vis-à-vis Sociology: An Overview

In China, educational anthropology is mostly called "*minzu jiaoyu xue*," which translates literally as "educational ethnology," or more specifically as "studies of ethnic minorities." To the dismay of many Chinese scholars engaged in the field, ethnology is placed under the discipline of legal studies, as a second-class discipline, while anthropology is a second-class discipline under sociology, with the result that educational anthropology is not in the domain of anthropology (Teng 2002: 2). This confusing situation requires clarification of the historical background on anthropology's development in mainland China.

Anthropology was initially introduced into mainland China during the 1920s and 1930s, by the then academic leader and authority Cai Yuanpei,[1] president of Peking University; he happened to have studied in

Germany, where he was influenced by the Russian school of anthropology, which defined the subject as ethnology. Slightly later after Cai, also during the 1930s, the other schools of anthropology, namely that of British functionalism and American historicism, found their way into China through Wu Wenzao and later his renowned students Fei Xiaotong and Lin Yaohua, who used the anthropological approach and methodology to study sociological issues of mainstream communities like villages and towns (Zhu 2006; Harrell 2001). During the Cultural Revolution, from the early 1950s to the late 1970s, the anthropology of the British and American schools was labeled "bourgeois social sciences" and the whole discipline of anthropology was banned, with its scholars and researchers assigned to pursue ethnology in the Russian tradition in remote areas of the country where the ethnic minority groups live, far removed from the center of power and metropolitan life (Zhu 2006).

Deng Xiaoping, in his 1978 Open Door and Reform policy document, advocated that sociology must be revived to offer advice to govern the large-scale national reform process, and this mission has gained the discipline much support from the government, triggering its swift and prosperous development. Many institutions from overseas, particularly from the United States and Hong Kong, have been helpful in establishing courses and research in the social sciences for Chinese universities, resulting in forty-odd joint programs (Hvistendahl 2009). Some of the most fruitful research findings such as those published in the top journals of sociology have been translated into English and published by Sharpe Publishing as articles in the journal *Chinese Sociology and Anthropology.*

Unfortunately, anthropology was not mentioned by Deng and thus was not given a grand status similar to sociology. Still categorized as a second-class discipline under sociology, it did not enjoy much support from the government. The Chinese anthropology association did not come into existence until 1981 in Xiamen University, and in the same year the first department of anthropology was founded in Zhongshan University in Guangzhou. The real advancement of the discipline in its social status did not happen until the 1990s when anthropology was introduced into universities in Beijing, the capital, by a young generation of scholars represented by Wang Mingming, returning from the West (e.g., Wang from University of London, like his senior colleague Fei Xiaotong). About the same time many researchers and scholars moved from ethnology centers to independent anthropology institutions, with the landmark event of the renaming of the sociology school of Peking University as the school of sociology and anthropology, as urged by the anthropology Professor Fei Xiaotong.

Anthropology began its full-scale development in the 1990s. In Harrell's (2001) comprehensive review of the reform and recovery of anthropology in China over a twenty-year span, about two hundred publications cover urban, rural, and migrant communities and the daily life of individuals, including gender and sexuality, family and marriage, childhood and education, and consumption and leisure. Such research findings have been particularly useful to the government to the extent that any policy related to peasants in China's vast landscape of the countryside has been informed by anthropological fieldwork (Zhu 2006: 98).

The Development of Educational Anthropology in Mainland China

As an independent discipline, educational anthropology has a relatively recent history, about thirty years or so (Teng 2006). It was introduced into mainland China in the mid-1980s, with translation and introduction of the classics of anthropology and education from the West, including books on the historical development of educational anthropology and its major theories, methodologies, and research studies characteristic of historical and cultural anthropology schools (Feng 1986; Feng 2001; Zhuang 1989). For instance, J. U. Obgu's macroethnography theory (1981), with an emphasis on the ecology of education closely related to history and culture, was particularly influential (Chen P. 2007: 6). In addition, over twenty classic monographs of Western educational anthropology will be published for graduate student courses, translated by researchers in Central University of Nationalities (Teng 2006).

In the 1990s, as more and more scholars returned from studying in the West, they brought back with them empirical research methods, including various kinds of research methods from educational anthropology, which have been adopted by their colleagues at home. Among these leading scholars of national influence is Chen Xiangming (2000), whose book on qualitative research methods with ethnography as its central tenet worked an effect of "subversive consequence" for China's educational research (Feng 2006: 101). Chen's 521-page book is a classical introduction to qualitative research, covering everything from epistemological origins to research methods and ethics. It is widely used as textbook for research students throughout the country. Chen earned her PhD from Harvard University, and her work on a two-year longitudinal study (1998) scrutinizing the intercultural and interpersonal contacts of a group of Chinese overseas students in the United States is one of China's earliest attempts at using qualitative research methods.

Professor Wu Kangning of Nanjing Normal University has supervised and published a few very high-quality PhD dissertations and edited two series of books on sociology of education, many of which used ethnographic methodology (Wu K. 1999, 2003, more below). Professor Ding Gang, from East China Normal University, has not only promoted narrative theories in many papers of his own, but more importantly edited a large-scale collection of narrative inquiry papers on grassroots classroom research in *China's Education: Research and Review* (2001–2009) (more below), which has created an expectation that "almost any educational research has something to do with narrative" (Feng 2006: 101).

There have also been some conferences, exchange programs, or mutual academic visits, between Chinese researchers and their counterparts in Europe, Japan, and America, and more and more educational anthropologists are coming to do fieldwork in the mainland from the West. In addition, there is a continual increase in joint programs through which some of the universities from the United States and Hong Kong are coming to help China to establish more social science courses and train researchers or social workers (Hvistendahl 2009).

Some of the best fieldwork studies on ethnic minorities' education are achieved by PhD students supervised by Hong Kong professors. Yuan Tongkai (2004) from Nankai University, supervised by professors at the Chinese University of Hong Kong, has demonstrated that the backward school education in the Tuyao ethnic minority is rooted in their limited political influence in the local government and the resulting uneven distribution of educational resources. His work is generally considered as one of the earliest efforts using longitudinal fieldwork-based ethnography, and sets an example of how to conduct ethnography by participating in the target community and living together with the local people under harsh conditions. Luo Huiyan (2009), from the Education Institute of Hong Kong, has conducted high-quality fieldwork in a Miao ethnic minority region in Guizhou Province, which reveals the incongruities between compulsory basic education practice and the local realities. It is widely acclaimed as an outstanding work in that it follows the practical process of basic education, displays the everyday life of the country students, and makes the disadvantaged community's voices heard.

It was not until 2007 that the first National Symposium of Educational Anthropology was held in Northwest China Normal University. Participants exchanged their views on the difficulties in and the future development of educational anthropology and ethnic education in

China with respect to their international counterparts. The second Symposium took place in Guangxi Normal University, the host of which has produced a research-based volume exploring the local practices of education in this province of Guangxi Zhuang ethnic minority members (Sun and Xu 2007; Chen Z. 2007; Gao and Xie 2007). The year 2012 will witness the opening of the third Symposium, held by Yunan Normal University, where field work has been conducted fruitfully by a group of anthropologists headed by Professor Wang Ling, who taught local residents potato planting techniques which helped every household increase their annual incomes.

All these efforts, individual and institutional, have led to the founding of China's Educational Anthropology Society on 26 December, 2010, with *China's Educational Anthropology Review* as its official journal in book form.

Theoretical Construction of Educational Anthropology in China

There have been some important efforts undertaken by Chinese scholars in educational anthropology to establish theoretical frameworks that would guide research in China. These scholars are mainly working in the Han-majority ethnic group, the largest population in China, in so-called mainstream educational institutions. They believe that the key factor for the development of educational anthropology in China is that the discipline must start from the local context and address the core issues encountered in the process of China's educational modernization (Feng 2006: 102). This local context of Chinese education includes difficulties caused by its thousand-year-long educational conservatism for curriculum reforms (Ding 1990; Hayhoe 1996).

With such efforts, the epistemological defining elements for China's educational anthropology are commonly agreed to include that: (1) education should be centered on human beings and their needs, not treating learners as the target of labor personnel training; (2) the core concept is "culture," with regard to its legacy, acquisition, choice, and other similar notions; (3) diversity should be valued and preserved; (4) ethnic and mainstream cultural values should be given equal respect; (5) first-hand evidence through ethnography and fieldwork should replace armchair studies as bases of decision making; (6) equal access to education should be given to all ethnic groups, especially the underprivileged; and (7) educational anthropology should study both formal and informal schooling, including that in family and community (Teng 2006: 6; for a similar discussion see Yue 2008).

Ethnographic Studies of Education: Bamboo Shoots after Rain

Most publications in China's educational anthropology focus on theoretical discussions like the ones introduced above, and there is consensus that the field lacks seriously high-quality ethnographic research (Teng 2006; Feng 2006). This is confirmed by the review where Harrell observes, "What actually happens in schools is the subject of few ethnographic studies" (2001: 149).

Nevertheless, the last ten years have witnessed rapid increase in solid ethnographic studies, often the output of serious and longitudinal fieldwork by PhD students. In the section below I shall report ethnographic studies that are found at (1) three national key research centers focused on ethnic minorities, (2) departments of education and/or sociology in some elite or normal universities, and (3) universities of foreign studies.

Ethnic Minority Studies in Three Key National Research Centers

The three most renowned key universities that have research centers and departments focusing on ethnic minorities and their educational reality have been very active in promoting educational anthropology and ethnography. They are Central University of Nationalities[2] (CUN), Northwest Normal University[3] (NNU), and Southwest University[4] (SU) (Feng 2006), offering BA and MA programs, and in particular, PhD degree courses in educational anthropology in the first two. As their names suggest, the three universities form a central-local bond with CUN located in Beijing, the capital of China, taking the most comprehensive role in ethnological and anthropological studies, NNU specializing in cultivating ethnic teachers for the western regions of China, and SU focusing on the ecological resources and cultures of southwest ethnic minorities. This introduction is partly based upon each university's web site, which has a version in English.

Central University of Nationalities (CUN) is the top institution of higher education for Chinese ethnic minorities, founded in 1941 originally as Yan'an Institute of Nationalities by the Chinese Communist Party. Famous sociologists including Fei Xiaotong and Wu Wenzao taught at CUN, contributing to a solid research foundation. Since the 1950s, CUN has been an important source and point of reference for the Central Government of China's ethnic policy making. There are altogether fifty-one research institutes affiliated with different faculties or departments, including an Institute for Research on Ethnology and Anthropology, an Institute for Research on Ethnic Language and Literature, Institute for Ethnic Religious Studies, and Institute for Ethnic Education.

Their cultural contributions mainly lie in the concrete efforts to investigate ethnic cultures, improve ethnic writing systems, and compile ancient ethnic books. Since 2002, CUN has published 2,177 papers in national publications, and 470 books (including translations, textbooks, and theses collections), such as *History of Chinese Religions* and *Chinese Ethnic Mascots* [totems], *An Anthology of Historical Materials in Tibet,* and *Cultural Change and Bilingual Education.*

In recent years, the researchers at CUN have been playing an increasingly active role in providing evidence and consultations for Chinese leaders in forming ethnic economic and social development policies. Studies such as *A Survey on Population Migration and Cultural Adaptation of Ethnic Minorities along Qing-Zang Railway, A Survey on Establishing the Sino-ASEAN Free Trade Zone and the Economic Development in Yunan,* and *A Survey on Owenke People's Efforts on Casting Off Poverty for Their Well-being* were commended highly by the State Ethnic Affairs Commission.

One of the prominent researchers, Teng Xing from the Institute for Ethnic Education, has done seminal work (2001) on the Yi ethnic group in Daliang Mountains in Sichuan Province, where he traced fifty years of change in language and education, and the social transformation that went along it. Using multiple voices to construct the ethnography, it is widely acknowledged as a pioneer work of cultural anthropology in mainland China. Professor Teng also has edited the *Series of Educational Anthropology* with its second volume totally devoted to ethnographic research reports.

Ba Zhanlong's (2008) PhD study, supervised by Professor Teng Xing, is a masterpiece of educational ethnography. With fieldwork of over five months and oral histories and other documents, Ba has construed the historical narrative of four periods from 1907 to 2007 of a multi-ethnic community called Minghua. With rich ethnographic evidences and with particular reference to its educational practices in which Yoghur, Tibetan, and Han languages as well as Gelug Tibetan Buddhism, Shamanism, and devout ancestor worship coexist, his argument that success of education depends heavily on how much the administration respects and makes use of the local culture legacy is well supported.

Ethnic Education Study, published by CUN, is the principal journal in the field of ethnology in mainland China and has been published for fifteen years. *Educational Anthropology Research Newsletter (EARN),* released monthly by the Institute for Research on Basic Ethnic Education since the end of 2005, is another key journal promoting the development of educational anthropology in China for scholars and research students. For instance, the fifth *EARN* issue (2006) reprinted the research of Li Xiaomin (2003), a former research student of CUN, who has explored the conflicts that an ethnic rural society is undergoing in the course of nationalization and globalization and the dynamics between the contending powers behind knowledge distribution and transmission, through a three-month investigation in a multiethnic village in southwest China. The following sixth *ERAN* issue published the reviews written by seven CUN PhD students who considered Li as a highly qualified anthropologist "with sharp eyes able to dig out the deep meanings behind the taken-for-granted" and her work as a model for research students to follow (He et al. 2006).

CUN has initiated, participated in, or sponsored many academic conferences that have facilitated national and international academic exchanges and scientific research, such as the first National Joint Conference of Teaching and Academic Institutions of Ethnology and Anthropology with participants from mainland China, Taiwan, and Hong Kong; the International Seminar on Manchu History; and the Forum for Ethnology, Anthropology, and the Chinese Experience.

Northwest Normal University (NNU) is the second university highlighted here. One of the fundamental missions of NNU is to promote education in the poverty-stricken rural area and minority-inhabited area in northwest China. In 1985, the Research Bureau for the Education of Ethnic Minorities was established, the predecessor of the current Research Center for the Educational Development of the Minority Peoples. Since 2000, dozens of famous full-time or part-time educators, sociologists, and anthropologists from home and abroad have been working at the center, including Ma Rong from Peking University, Yang Shengmin and Teng Xing from Central University of Nationalities, James Banks from George Washington University, Gerard Postiglione from Hong Kong University, Emily Hannum from the University of Pennsylvania, and John Berry from Queen's University, strengthening the power of academic research and forming an academic team with high standing. The center was authorized as a Key Research Center of Humanities and Social Science by the Ministry of Education in 2004.

Wang Minggang, Meng Fanli, He Bo, and their colleagues probed into the relationship between Tibetan Buddhism, Islam, and local modern school education development; the ethnic and national identification of local youth; and curricular development, bilingual education, and local ethnic realities. The resulting research reports include *The Religious World of Hui Ethnic Minority Youth* and *Study of Religious Value of Hui Ethnic Young Females*. Wang Jian and Zhang Xueqiang, and others, have compared the Western multicultural education history and policies and those of Chinese ethnic education and published a seven-volume collection on the theme of Multicultures and Northwest Ethnic Education.

Contemporary Education and Culture is the periodical published by the center since 2008. The center also has published a six-volume series on education of the minority peoples in northwest China and textbooks on educational anthropology and classroom research. The academic conferences held by the center include the International Symposium of Women and Education of Minority People in 2002, the Summit Forum of Northwest Ethnic Minority Education in 2005, and the first National Symposium of Educational Anthropology in 2007. The center has maintained cooperative relationships with educational research centers or departments in the University of Toronto, George Washington University, the University of London, and the University of Manchester.

Southwest University (SU) is the third highlighted university. Located in the southwest China region inhabited by thirty-six ethnic minority nationalities, which accounts for two-thirds of all nationalities in China, SU becomes an ideal base for ethnological and anthropological studies. The Research Center for Education and Psychology of Southwestern Ethnic Groups was founded in SU in 1984 and was authorized as a Key Research Center of Humanities and Social Science by Ministry of Education in 2004.

The center attaches particular emphasis to fieldwork investigations and has set up research field sites in six southwest ethnic minority regions with representative ecological cultural features and differing educational practices, covering ten ethnic minorities. These sites have provided "lived education" for researchers who have joined horseback transportation teams, slept by the fire, and trekked through snow-covered mountains, vast grasslands, deep gorges, and over rope bridges.

With such an entrée, Wu Xiaorong (2003) explored the educational implications of the Moso's rite of puberty based upon in-depth interviews, field notes, and local documents; Wu's ethnography is generally acknowledged as an early and exemplary work. Similarly, Li Shanze's (2003) fieldwork in Zhanyi County with the Yan-fang Miao ethnic minority lays out the educational significance of the reproduction of local culture. Their work reveals the socialization functions and educational connotation of local customs, something hardly recognized by the Han-majority formal education administration. It argues powerfully that without adequate respect for and use of the cultural legacies of such hundred-year-long customs and without integrating them into local education, the top-down Han-style education could actually create a sense of dislocation and thus deprive the ethnic young people of equal opportunities to participate and survive in the world immediately outside the local community.

The other major fruit of their hard work is the successive publication of nineteen books complied as the *Southwest Research Series* by Zhang Shiya (2003), the center director. *Southwestern Education Review* is the periodical published by the center since 1985, containing columns such as ethnic education, cultural origin investigation, and fieldwork reports. The center has held many academic conferences including the recent International Symposium on Multicultural Education in a Globalizing World in 2006 and the Symposium on Fieldwork Investigations in Ethnic Education and Psychology in 2007.

There are two other centers that are also very important in this line of research on ethnic minorities' education: Xinjiang Normal University and Zhongshan University of Guangzhou.

Sociology of Education with Ethnography and Narrative Inquiry

The second major group of Chinese researchers using anthropological or ethnographic approaches to study educational contexts and issues are scholars working in some of the elite comprehensive universities or best resourced normal universities. Their focus is mostly on the Han majority group, often with sociology as their theoretical framework.

Sociology of education in mainland China has just spent thirteen years to complete a process of recruiting students from undergraduate level (1982) to PhD (1989) and postdoctorate level (1999), and the present orientation is towards more fieldwork and in-depth ethnography on the social reality of education (Wu K. 2003). Professor Wu Kangning, from Nanjing Normal University, has organized a series of books on the sociology of schools published by this university's press; they cover many aspects of school institution or community, such as the *Sociology of School Life, Sociology of Curriculum, Sociology of Classroom Teaching, Sociology of Family Schooling,* and the forthcoming *Sociology of Ethics Education, Sociology of Class, Sociology of Testing,* and *Sociology of Teachers* (Wu K. 1999).

One classical example of school ethnography is *Sociology of School Life* by Liu Yunshan of Nanjing University (2001). To make the familiar Chinese school routines and rituals strange, Liu conducted a yearlong participant observation in a typical Chinese middle school of seventy years' history located in northern Jiangshu province, where she used the local dialect and a humble manner to make herself an inner group member well accepted by the students and teachers there. Her narrative captures the routines and rituals of the school and class, identities of modal students, folklore stories and fables in the textbooks for ethics molding, the teacher's authority exercised at the front and back stage of classroom teaching; it illuminates much of the taken-for-granted tradition and norms, as well as the changes experienced in schools.

Another fine-quality school ethnography is by Qi Xuehong of Beijing Normal University, published as a two-year postdoctorate work under Wu Kangning's supervision (2005), in the series "Research on Contemporary Sociology of Education," again edited by Wu (2003). Using sociology of knowledge as framework, and symbolic interaction, phenomenology, and ethnomethodology, Qi scrutinized the process of how teachers and learners construct their individual knowledge about education. His data provide a thick description of textbook functions, parental influences, head teachers' interaction with students, and practices of bodily docility.

Some educational sociologists have incorporated anthropological research methods to unravel the educational life of marginalized groups. For instance, after spending one month with the migrant teachers in a school for migrant workers, He Xiaoxing and his student (Yang and He 2009) have observed that these teachers are like rootless "strangers" psychologically yearning for the rural life and physically sojourning in the urban area; their life world and teaching practice are characterized by "mobility," which leads to instability in interpersonal relationships, difficulty in achieving consistency in teaching, and an intensified financial pressure.

He (2006; He and Zhang 2008) has also investigated the issue of deaf education reform. Based on school visits, where he audio recorded classroom teaching and conducted ethnographic interviews, He argues that the deaf represented a different culture or an intercultural existence, and advocates bilingual and bicultural deaf education that prioritizes sign language and culture of the deaf people.

Along with ethnography, narrative inquiry is welcomed at least as if not more aggressively by researchers interested in general and teacher education, thanks in particular to the persistent endeavors of Professor Ding Gang[5] from East China Normal University. Ding has founded an internationally referred journal—*China's Education: Research and Review*—in 2001 and has been its chief editor since then, assisted by eleven internationally renowned researchers in Chinese education in the reviewer committee, including Barry Keenan, Marianne Bastid, Heidi Ross, Juergen Henze, Kai Ming Cheng, Lan Ye, Lynn Webster Paine, Mingyuan Gu, Nai Kwai Lo, Nina Borevskaya, Paul Bailey, Qiquan Zhong, Ruth Hayhoe, Stanley Rosen, Stig Thogersen, and Yutaka Otsuka. The journal is in book form, in fact, due to the tight control on journal issuing in China. It not only introduces many classical studies done outside China but also publishes for each volume three to four vigorously conducted narrative inquiries. So far, fourteen volumes have been released with focus on specific individuals, their lives, and their voices. These include, for instance, a middle-school female teacher (Geng 2002), a primary-school headmaster (Huang 2002), a male kindergarten teacher (Liu X. 2007), a private tutor (Liu Yunshan 2002), Shanghai primary students' parents participating in school education (Ma 2005), migrant workers' children living in the city with their parents (Ai 2005), and those left by their parents and staying in the hometown village (Ren 2007). It is an excellent representation of the best research in this field across geographic regions and academic disciplines.

Narrative action research, which has been actively promoted by Liu Lianghua from South China Normal University, has now gained great popularity among Chinese primary- and middle-school teachers. Liu has been using blogs[6] to communicate with and encourage teachers to record and reflect upon their daily teaching life. In 2006, he published *Educational Autobiography* as an effort to resonate with his readers through well-written stories.

Ethnography and Narrative Inquiry in Foreign-Language Education

The third important group of scholars using ethnography or narrative inquiry is from foreign-language schools of universities in mainland China. Many of them have written their research in English or other foreign languages and most of them studied for their PhD degrees in institutions outside the mainland, which provided them easier access to recent literature and qualified supervision, as well as an outsider-insider perspective when examining the issues that they are so familiar with. Teacher education in foreign-language education is one of the focused areas of their research.

The author, who is from Guangdong University of Foreign Studies, Guangzhou, studied for his PhD at City University of Hong Kong under Dr. David Li, and Ron Scollon (his lifetime mentor). Using oral history and a letter from a hinterland teacher, he traced a seven-year-long journey of one teacher "migrating" from the more traditional modes of teaching toward West-imported learner-centered teaching (Ouyang 2000). With the metaphor of a "one-way ticket," he revealed the highly complex dynamics of education reform and its sociopolitical impact upon the unprepared teachers, who are thus caught in a process of identity split/changes, a sense of dislocation, and constant conflicts with communities that are not ready to accept their new teaching principles. In a larger account, Ouyang (2004), using his twenty-some years of membership in a university of foreign studies informed by societal transformation theories of the mainland sociologists (Cao and Chen 1997), described the community of practices (Lave and Wenger 1991) of a university as a typical state-owned work unit (*danwei*) featuring central planning, paternalistic leadership, little mobility, and long-term relationships; he situated curriculum reform as a site of conflicts between this *danwei* system and that of the civil society.

His supervisee, Liu Yongcan, followed this line of studying Chinese teacher education in the state-owned *danwei* community of practices in his PhD study in Cambridge University. With ethnomethodology, narrative inquiry, and case study methods, and one year of participant observation of how teacher-reformers tackle challenges in the workplace caused by the coexistence of traditionalism and liberalism, he examined cultures of learning (at the institutional level), discursive practices (at the interpersonal level), and teachers' identities (at the personal level) (2009). Xu Yueting, a very young teacher who was one of Liu Yongcan's informants in the English-education school of Guangdong University of Foreign Studies, has coauthored with Liu a paper published in *TESOL Quarterly* (Xu and Liu 2009) on teachers' knowledge construction of assessment.

In the faculty of English language and culture of Guangdong University of Foreign Studies, ethnographic methodology or an anthropological approach was also readily accepted by undergraduate students in the author's course on argumentative writing over the last ten years. The students have applied it to examine various aspects of their learning and life in the university as a community: the way they set up various hierarchies among themselves and how such hierarchies discriminate among them, how they argue and quarrel in the dormitory and deal with conflicts, how they deconstruct reliance on teachers' feedback, their dating practices, their sexual concepts, their first work experience off campus and the social pressure they encounter from harassment and in identity formation, and strategies of the beggars outside the campus. They have learned how to establish rapport with informants such as migrant workers and beggars through use of beer or of dialects. As a result, the students have developed a more positive attitude towards life and a more active participation in social activities, with an enhanced sensitivity to details of facts and of the conflicting viewpoints of stakeholders. Part of their work has been published by Peking University Press (Ouyang 2003).

Such "snowball effect" diffusion of ethnography of education as in the Guangzhou case above is also seen in Zhejiang province. Wu Zongjie, from Zhejiang University, did his PhD study in Lancaster University, UK, supervised by Dick Allwright and Norman Fairclough. His study (2005) explores the emerging perspectives in language teacher development that view teacher learning as the nourishment of life rather than the mastery of expertise, and curriculum innovation as the reclaiming of authentic discourse instead of rational manipulation of school systems. It synthesizes a wide range of contemporary Western theories and puts them under Eastern philosophical scrutiny, which results in fresh views of major issues relating to education, institutional change, and East/West relationships. Ethnography combined with discourse analysis is used as the research methodology for this study. Most of the findings are presented in narratives.

Influenced by Wu, Ying Danjun from Zhejiang Normal University did her PhD study at the University of Hong Kong. Drawing on sociocultural theories of learning and discourse theories, her study (2010) examines the discourses of a cross-institutional teacher community in China and its annual events to explore the discursive construction of teacher learning in terms of knowledge, social relations, and identity. Ethnographic observation, conversational interviews, and documentation were adopted for data collection. A narrative approach and a discourse approach were combined for analyzing spoken, written, and visual data. The findings provide useful insights into the conceptualization of teacher learning in communities; for example, teacher learning is considered as relation building that uses storytelling as a tool of inquiry to dialogue with the self, others, and context, or again, teacher learning in communities is aimed not to seek sameness or become someone else, but to attain "harmony in diversity."

Wu, Ying, and Huang Aifeng (a senior teacher greatly loved by her students in Zhejiang Normal University) have collaborated in teacher development programming, using storytelling to reflect and constitute learning as dialogue in a community of real life activities (Wu and Huang 2007; Ying and Huang 2008).

Another young scholar, Li Xiaobo, from Shenzhen University's foreign-language school, did her PhD study with Dr. Aoki Naoko, a pioneer in Japan using qualitative research methodology in Osaka University. With a lot of fine narrative details and a humble tone, Li (2011) told a most touching story of Riyoko, a Japanese female teacher, and her struggles with how to help a group of Chinese students of limited proficiency in Japanese and low self-confidence. Riyoko in the end decided to give up the "updated and advanced" task-based project learning approach and resumed the most traditional rote learning approach of vocabulary and grammar—a most courageous act in a collectivist culture of Japan, at risk of offending her superiors—in order to let the students feel secure and gain some sense of achievement with the learning method that they are familiar with and good at. This change brought a sense of recognition and then shining smiles and joy that lit up the classroom to the students, and eventually by chain effect created a more positive attitude among the group when they worked and interacted with others in the Japanese community.

Before this section concludes, it must be pointed out that the development of ethnography as a research methodology and education philosophy is accelerating so rapidly that even during the process of writing this chapter, many new publications have appeared. The sampling given here thus is by no means exhaustive.

Challenges, Changes of the Landscape, and the Future

The following section is mainly composed of my personal observations. There are some challenges or obstacles that would impair anyone who intended to venture into the realm of ethnographic inquiry in mainland China. Firstly, many academics fear that it is for its very strength of revealing the insider knowledge of a community of practice that ethnography could be frowned on or resisted by authorities. Ethnography draws heavily on true stories from grassroots teachers and learners, and offers in-depth contextualized insights based on longitudinal and field observation. Such disclosure of how members move from the periphery to the center of the community often challenges the position of those in power, who would feel disturbed to see equal access to truth by their juniors or outsiders. And thus ethnography is often marginalized, especially in communities such as Chinese state-owned workplaces of *danwei*, given their dearth of mobility in work or residence and perennial interpersonal relationships (Ouyang 2004; Scollon and Ouyang 1998).

Furthermore, scholars are afraid of being labeled "betrayers." Granted that most Chinese communities do not change quickly in their infrastructure, their memberships, and their "wall culture" (Townsend and Womack 1986), communication in the public sphere is not for truth inquiry or information exchange, but for ranking and maintaining differentiation, in sharp contrast with communication in Western civil society (Gao, Ting-Toomey, and Gudykunst 1996). Probing into a community and publishing the findings would thus be very easily interpreted as "disclosing and spreading one's own family scandal" (*jia chou wai yang*). And if one takes credit from committing such "betrayal," the consequences could be very substantial.

The nightmare from historical tragedies still haunts many intellectuals today. Only three decades ago during the Cultural Revolution, millions of intellectuals were exiled to destitute villages for doing exactly what they had been invited to do—offering criticism and suggestions to the newly founded Chinese government. To change anything, even to suggest a new textbook, would be interpreted as an implied critique of the old decision makers (Dzau 1990). These memories die hard. Playing safe is still a major concern for many teachers and researchers, and thus most research in language education dwells on the technical aspects of teaching, the controlled variables of experiments, or the literature of the past two centuries, rather than on critical examination of the sociological ramifications of the teaching and learning environment.

Worse perhaps, the criteria for publication in most Chinese journals dismisses qualitative or ethnographic research, which is often falsely accused of lacking "solid scientific evidence," of being "anecdotal," or of being "overinterpretative." This has left many academics questioning the value of the methodology. Besides, the journals are limited in number in general. For example, journals for English-language education are scarce even though the profession constitutes the largest population among subject knowledge fields. Specifically, there are only around twenty "key journals" (he xin qi kan) by which one's publication can be recognized for professional promotion, while English teachers in the country number around one million (Xia Jimei, vice director of the national board of college English teaching for eight years, personal communication). Such a per capita quota on publishing by English teachers is partly due to political control, as are the difficulties of forming organization or associations for scholars in educational anthropology.

Nevertheless, the political landscape of China is undergoing a major shift from centralization to local autonomy, with central planning being dramatically replaced by marketization with Chinese characteristics. The *danwei* system is following this momentum: short-term contracts have been introduced; evaluation is increasingly based on individual talents and professionalism such as research output rather than seniority; a social security system is replacing the old *danwei*-supported welfare. These have changed the interaction among people from long-term to short-term and from affective to instrumental, and have encouraged more mobility. Technologization such as ubiquitous internet access and the free speech of blogs has indeed led to more democratization, as Norman Fairclough theorized (1992). Being ruled by law, not by leaders, is on the agenda of current legal reform. Above all, individuals, regardless of sociopolitical background, find it much easier nowadays to voice their concerns and to fight for their rights.

Such changes will provide larger spaces for teachers to empower themselves and for researchers to seek truth. Many of them—not those who still believe in the "hard and scientific" research of psychometric tradition, though—have very much realized that lived stories and ethnographic accounts of their community are more accessible and applicable than quantitative research. It can be anticipated that eventually teachers will see that they need not wait for some benign leaders to rescue them from deep water and burning fire, but to take actions to empower themselves by doing what works for them as groups of mutual support (as proven in the case of Ouyang 1996). More and more journals and channels are opening up to ethnographic research (see Chen X. 2008, for an example of using the format of the book series to publish qualitative research, following Ding Gang's successful example with *China's Education: Review and Practice*). The recentness of the above reported research is surely an encouraging evidence for this change.

As the social reform of China is in full swing in favor of more democracy and mobility, the future of anthropological and ethnographic studies of education in China will certainly be prosperous.

Acknowledgments

This chapter has been supported by the National Center for Linguistics and Applied Linguistics, and English Education Research Center, Guangdong University of Foreign Studies. I would also like to express thanks to individuals including Feng Zengjun, Wu Yian, Gao Yihong, Chen Xiangming, Li Xiaobo, Ying Danjun, Wei Liqui, Mai Xiaoling, and in particular Lu Linqiong for their most generous assistance.

Notes

1. Editor's note: Throughout Dr. Ouyang's text, the family name precedes the given name, as is the norm in Chinese.

2. For more information, see its English web site: http://www.cun.edu.cn/.

3. For more information, see its English web site: http://www.nwnu.edu.cn/cate.do?cate=0038&version=en.

4. For more information, see its English web site: http://www.swnu.edu.cn/english/index.html.

5. For more information, please visit Ding Gang's personal web page: http://www.ses.ecnu.edu.cn/xsdw/dinggang/index.html.

6. Liu presides over two blogs: http://teacher.cersp.com, http://xueshi,cersp.com.

Bibliography

Note: Most Chinese-language journal articles or books are published with an English title and abstract, thus English titles are used below with a mark (C) indicating the original reference is in Chinese.

Ai, Qiong. 2005. "From the Countryside to the Margin of City—An Ethnographic Study on the Education for Rural Workers' Children" (C). In *China's Education: Research and Review*, vol. 9, ed. Ding Gang: 181–225. Beijing: Educational Science Press.

Ba, Zhanlong. 2008. "An Anthropological Perspective of Schooling and Local Knowledge—A Hundred Year Journey of Modernization of a Rural Community in Northwest China" (C). PhD diss., Central University of Nationalities.

Cao, J. Q., and Chen Z. Y. 1997. *Walk Out the "Ideal Castle": The Research about the Phenomena "Chinese Living in Units"* (C). Shenzhen: Haitian Press.

Chen, Peizhao. 2007. "Country Development and Cultural Selection of Schooling—A Case Study of Xiaomaopoying Miao Village in Southwest Hubei" (C). Master's thesis, Guangxi University for Nationalities.

Chen, Xiangming. 1998. *Sojourners and "Foreigners—Study on Chinese Students' Intercultural and Interpersonal Contacts in the United States* (C). Changsha: Hunan Education Press.

———. 2000. *Qualitative Research in Social Sciences* (C). Beijing: Educational Sciences Press.

———, ed. 2008. *Qualitative Research: Reflection and* Review, vol. 1 (C). Chongqing: Chongqing University Press.

Chen, Zhenzhong. 2007. *The Sociology of Education among Disadvantaged Groups* (C). Guilin: Guangxi Normal University Press.

Ding, Gang, ed. 1990. *Culture: Continuity and Transformation* (C). Shanghai: Shanghai Education Press.

———, ed. 2001–2009. *China's Education: Research and Review* (C). Beijing: Educational Science Press.

Dzau, Y. F., ed. 1990. *English in China*. Hong Kong: API Press.

Fairclough, Norman. 1992. *Discourse and Social Change*. Cambridge: Polity Press.

Feng, Zengjun. 1986. "Introducing Educational Anthropology" (C). *Contemporary Graduate Student Journal* 4.

———. 2001. *Educational Anthropology* (C). Nanjing: Jiangsu Education Press.

———. 2006. "Anticipation of the Future of Educational Anthropology" (C). *Journal of South China Normal University (Social Science Edition)* 2: 98–110.

Gao, Ge, Stella Ting-Toomey, and William B. Gudykunst.1996. "Chinese Communication Processes." In *The Handbook of Chinese Psychology*, ed. Michael Harris Bond, 280–93. Hong Kong: Oxford University Press.

Gao, Jinling, and Xie Dengbin. 2007. *A Cultural Study of Educational Reforms* (C). Guilin: Guangxi Normal University Press.

Geng, Juanjuan. 2002. "Educational Belief: Narrative Inquiry from a Female Teacher" (C). In *China's Education: Research and Review*, ed. Ding Gang, vol. 2, 181–232. Beijing: Educational Science Press.

Harrell, Stevan. 2001. "The Anthropology of Reform and the Reform of Anthropology: Anthropological Narratives of Recovery and Progress in China." *Annual Review of Anthropology* 30: 139–61.

Hayhoe, Ruth. 1996. *China's Universities 1895–1995: A Century of Cultural Conflict.* New York: Grune & Stratton.

Hayhoe, Ruth. 2001. "The Spirit of Modern China: Life Stories of Influential Educators" (C). In *China's Education: Research and Review,* ed. Ding Gang, vol. 1, 1–74. Beijing: Educational Science Press.

He, Xiaoxing. 2006. "What Is the Best Way to Teach the Deaf People: A Sociological Survey on Teachers' Perspectives" (C). *Educational Sociology Research in Taiwan* 2: 58–124.

He, Xiaoxing, and Zhang Yuan. 2008. "A Sociological Thinking on Deaf Education Reform: The NGO's Effort for the Bilingual and Bicultural Education" (C). *Journal of Educational Studies* 4, no. 14: 51–57.

He Xuan, Wei Li, Ma Xiaoyi, Zhang Shuang, Li Sumei, Hai Lu, and Ba Zhanlong. 2006. "Book Reviews of 'Village Knowledge Resources and Cultural Power Space—A Fieldwork Investigation of Tuozhi Village, Yongning Country'" (C). *Educational Anthropology Research Newsletter,* no. 6: 25–31.

Huang, Xiangyang. 2002. "School Years: A Principal's Memories" (C). In *China's Education: Research and Review,* ed. Ding Gang, vol. 2, 233–29. Beijing: Educational Science Press.

Hvistendahl, Mara. 2009. "Renewed Attention to Social Sciences in China Leads to New Partnerships with American Universities." *Chronicle of Higher Education* 55, no. 23: A35.

Lave, Jean, and Étienne Wenger. 1991. *Situated Learning: Legitimate Peripheral Participation.* Cambridge: Cambridge University Press.

Li, Shanze. 2003. *Educational Anthropological Interpretations of the Reproduction Culture of Zhanyi County Yan-fang Miao Ethnic Minority* (C). Chongqin: Southwest Normal University Press.

Li, Xiaobo. 2011. *A Classroom "Where Hearts Can Interflow": A Narrative Inquiry of a Japanese Language Teacher's Practical Knowledge* (C). Beijing: Foreign Language Teaching and Research Press.

Li, Xiaomin. 2003. "Village Knowledge Resources and Cultural Power Space—A Fieldwork Investigation of Tuozhi Village, Yongning Country" (C). In *China's Education: Research and Review,* ed. Ding Gang, vol. 5. Beijing: Educational Science Press. Reprinted in 2006: *Educational Anthropology Research Newsletter,* no. 5: 4–23.

Liu, Lianghua. 2006. *Educational Autobiography.* (C). Chengdu: Sichuan Education Press.

Liu, Xuan. 2007. "Narrative Inquiry into the Professional Development of a Male Kindergarten Teacher" (C). In *China's Education: Research and Review,* ed. Ding Gang, vol. 11, 155–263. Beijing: Educational Science Press.

Liu, Yongcan. 2009. "Learning as Negotiation: An Ethnographic Study of Teachers' Learning in the Workplace in a University Department of English Education in China." PhD diss., School of Education, Cambridge University.

Liu, Yunshan. 2001. *Sociology of School Life* (C). Nanjing: Nanjing Normal University Press.

————. 2002. "A Teacher's Life under the Empire's Power: On a Teacher's Story in Private School" (C). In *China's Education: Research and Review,* ed. Ding Gang, vol. 3, 143–73. Beijing: Educational Science Press.

Luo, Huiyan. 2009. *Education and Social Development—A Case Study in Guizhou Province, China* (C). Beijing: Nationalities Press.

Ma, Tianyu. 2005. "Left Hand and Right Hand: Investigation and Analysis on Parent Involving of Shanghai's Elementary School" (C). In *China's Education: Research and Review,* ed. Ding Gang, vol. 5, 73–157. Beijing: Educational Science Press.

Ogbu, John U. 1981. "School Ethnography: A Multilevel Approach." *Anthropology and Education Quarterly* 12: 3–29.

Ouyang, Huhua. 1996. "Things That Don't Work in the Office Might Work at Home: Teachers Develop through Teachers' Chat-in-Private." In *Directions in Second Language Teacher Education,* ed. G. Tinker Sachs, M. Brock, and R. Lo, 186–201. Hong Kong: City University of Hong Kong Press.

————. 2000. "One Way Ticket: A Story of an Innovative Teacher in Mainland China." *Anthropology & Education Quarterly* 31, no. 4: 397–425.

————. 2003. *Writing to Learn as a Community: Voices from Students in Guangwai.* Beijing: Peking University Press.

————. 2004. *Remaking of Face and Community of Practices.* Beijing: Peking University Press.

Qi, Xuehong. 2005. *On the Way Home* (C). Beijing: Beijing Normal University Press.

Ren, Yunchang. 2007. "Staying Alone at the Empty Nest: A Case of Rural Home-Left Children in Nanchuan, Chongqing" (C). In *China's Education: Research and Review,* ed. Ding Gang, vol. 11, 1–72. Beijing: Educational Science Press.

Scollon, Suzanne, and Ouyang Huhua. 1998. "Taijiquan as Intellectual Property: Secrecy, Tradition, Theory and Practice," paper presented at the 97th annual meeting of the American Anthropology Association, Philadelphia, 2–8 December.

Sun, Jieyuan, and Xu Li. 2007. *The Anthropology of Educational Autonomy* (C). Guilin: Guangxi Normal University Press.

Teng, Xing. 2001. *Cultural Transformation and Bilingual Education* (C). Beijing: Educational Science Press.

————. 2002. "Preface to Educational Anthropology Research Series" (C). In *Cultural Transformation and Educational Choices,* ed. Wang, Jun, 1–3. Beijing: Nationalities Press.

————. 2006. "Developing Progress of Educational Anthropology in China—and a Comparison between Educational Anthropology and Educational Sociology" (C). *Journal of South-Central University for Nationalities (Humanities and Social Sciences)* 26, no. 5: 5–12.

Townsend, James R., and Brantley Womack. 1986. *Politics in China,* 3rd ed. Boston: Little, Brown.

Wu, Kangning. 1999. "General Preface" (to the series *Sociology of Education*) (C). In *Sociology of School Life,* Liu Lianghua, 1–6. Nanjing: Nanjing Normal University Press.

————. 2003. "General Preface" (to the series *Research on Contemporary Sociology of Education*) (C). In *On the Way Home*, Qi Xuehong, 1–4. Beijing Normal University Press, 2005.

Wu, Xiaorong. 2003. *Education in the Rituals of Lushuo Ethnic Minority* (C). Chongqin: Southwest Normal University Press.

Wu, Zongjie. 2005. *Teachers' Knowing in Curriculum Change: A Critical Discourse Study of Language Teaching* (C). Beijing: Foreign Language Teaching and Research Press.

Wu, Zongjie, and Huang Aifeng. 2007. "Exploratory Foreign Language Curriculum: RICH Teacher Development" (C). In *Research on English Teacher Education and Development in Chinese Institutions of High Education*, ed. Y., 242–66. Beijing: Foreign Language Teaching and Research Press.

Xu, Yueting, and Liu Yongcan. 2009. "Teacher Assessment Knowledge and Practice: A Narrative Inquiry of a Chinese College EFL Teacher's Experience." *TESOL Quarterly* 43, no. 3: 493–513.

Yang, Canjun, and He Xiaoxing. 2009. "The Life-World and Educational Practice of Migrant Teachers in Schools for Migrant Workers' Children" (C). Journal of Nanjing Normal University *(Social Science Edition)*, no. 5: 69–75.

Ying, Danjun. 2010. "In Search of Self: Understanding Teacher Learning in a Cross-institutional Teacher Community." PhD diss., University of Hong Kong.

Ying, Danjun, and Huang Aifeng. 2008. "Narratives in Interaction: Co-constructing Teacher Identity within Classroom Discourse." In *Verbal/Visual Narrative Texts in Higher Education*, ed. Martin Solly, Michelangelo Conoscenti, and Sandra Campagna, 89–113. Bern: Peter Lang.

Yuan, Tongkai. 2004. *Blackboard in the Bamboo Fences: An Ethnographic Study of the Schooling among the Tu Yao* (C). Tianjin: Tianjin People's Press.

Yue, Tianming. 2008. "On Discipline Orientation and Discipline Spirit of Educational Anthropology in China" (C). *Journal of Research on Education for Ethnic Minorities* 19, no. 1: 35–41.

Zhang, Shiya. 2003. *Stepping into the Southwest—Investigations into the Education in the Southwest.* (C). Chongqing: Southwest University Press.

Zhu, Dongliang. 2006. "The One Hundred Year's Development and Interaction between Sociology and Anthropology in China" (C). *Journal of Xiamen University (Arts & Social Sciences) General Serial* 176, no. 4: 92–99.

Zhuang, Kongshao. 1989. *Educational Anthropology* (C). Haerbin: Heilongjiang Education Press.

§ 12

ETHNOGRAPHY OF EDUCATION IN ISRAEL

Simha Shlasky, Bracha Alpert, and Naama Sabar Ben-Yehoshua

Israeli Society, Anthropology, and Ethnography of Education

As a society of Jewish immigrants, Israel has undergone rapid development and change. The Jewish population has grown from hundreds of thousands of Jews in pre-state Israel to over 5.7 million Jews (75 percent of the current state) alongside about 1.5 million Arabs (20 percent). Immigration of Jews to Israel, in Hebrew *aliyah* or "going up," has been and remains a central value in Zionism, the Jewish national movement, for it marks the return of the Jewish people from exile up to reestablished Jewish sovereignty in their ancient homeland.

Until the State of Israel was established in 1948, the majority of the Jewish population was of European origin (*Ashkenazim*). Since 1948, millions of Jews have immigrated to Israel, many from Muslim countries. The relative cultural cohesion of the pre-state period gave way to multiculturalism. The *Ashkenazi* hegemony failed in its attempts to use the education system and other means to create a homogeneous culture based upon that of the European immigrants.

Although a single national religious group, the Jewish people, comprises three-quarters of Israel's population, highly charged conflicts among the country's diverse national, ethnic, religious, economic, and political groups threaten its unity and cohesion (Lissak and Horowitz 1989; Semyonov and Lewin-Epstein 2004). Israel must also contend with internal and external threats to its security in the form of terrorism and wars. Nevertheless, Israeli society is relatively young; dynamic; extremely creative in technology, economics, and culture; and quite self-critical, all factors that call for extensive social research.

However, due to personal or academic rivalry (Abuhav 2010), until the late 1960s academic anthropology was almost nonexistent in Israel. University courses in anthropology and academic research projects were instituted only towards the end of the 1960s (with particular help from Max Gluckman of Britain's Manchester University; Marx 1975;

Shokeid 2004; see also Abuhav 2010; Deshen and Shokeid 1998; Hertzog et al. 2010).

When comprehensive anthropological research got underway in Israel, functionalist sociological research was already flourishing. One of its main subjects was immigration and absorption, including in schools. "Its primary tendency was to examine how the immigrants adapted to existing social patterns in Israel, emphasizing the advantages of assimilation into the majority 'mainstream' culture and openness to modernization" (Deshen and Shokeid 1998: 19). For the new Israeli elites, this cultural and ideological approach was the obvious road to a new Israeli culture to replace the Jewish Diaspora culture they had left behind. As a modern Western culture, it aimed also to replace the traditional Oriental culture of the immigrants from Muslim countries.

In contrast, in the 1970s and 1980s anthropologists "presented a counter ideology; they championed a discipline intended to highlight, if not glorify, the plurality of cultures and the varied social experiences of the newcomers" (Shokeid 2004: 390). In particular they focused on immigrant groups whose cultures were regarded as traditional, such as those from North Africa and Yemen. These groups aroused curiosity due to their otherness, the sense that their culture needed to be documented before it disappeared, and the desire to understand the process of their encounter with modernization (e.g., Deshen 1977; Shokeid 1971). Similarly, anthropologists began studying the Arabs in Israel, particularly urbanization among Bedouin Arabs (Marx and Shmueli 1984). In spite of their critical approach toward the institutional sociology of the time, the works of the anthropologists of the first generation were criticized later on as expressing the point of view of the hegemony (Kunda 1992a; Van Teeffelen 1978), and as contributing to the constitution of the Oriental Jew (*Mizrahi*) as the Other of the Israeli society (Forum 2002).

Since the 1980s, the scope of anthropological research has broadened to cover diverse sectors in Israeli society, among them deprived groups, hegemonic groups, neighborhoods, work, immigration, and other topics. Israeli anthropology is focused mostly on local issues; nevertheless, there are also some Israeli anthropologists who have studied different cultures abroad (e.g., Bird-David 1990; Kunda 1992b), including one who studied preschool in Japan (Ben-Ari 1997).

The first ethnographic studies of schools and learning in Israel were published in the late 1970s and early 1980s by anthropologists (Shokeid 1980; Halper, Shokeid, and Weingrod 1984; Lewis 1979, 1981). These studies focused on school integration, a major topic of interest in educational sociological research at the time. Yet the bulk of ethnographic research in education developed separately from anthropology. These ethnographic studies, which began in the late 1970s, were carried out by educational sociologists, first from university education departments and later also from academic colleges specializing in teacher training.

The first sociologists who engaged in ethnographic research in education were functionalists who had turned to interpretive approaches in the 1970s. They were influenced by ethnographic studies of schools in the United Kingdom and the United States, among them studies by Hargreaves (1967), Jackson (1968), Willis (1977) and Ball (1981). Thus, ethnographic examination of education in Israel is rooted primarily in interpretive educational sociology, and the most frequent theoretical stances presented are constructivist, critical, or feminist, relating to post-modernist and poststructuralist literature. The primary distinction made in sociological research in Israel is the one between qualitative-interpretive research and quantitative-positivist research rather than between ethnographic research and other genres of qualitative research. Indeed, the lines between qualitative sociology and anthropology are blurred. Nonetheless, in our review we have attempted to remain faithful to the common attributes of ethnographic research, in particular investigation of the culture up close through observations and interviews.

In the mid-1980s, qualitative academic research and writing in education began to be taught on the college level at Tel-Aviv University. The first publication in Hebrew to focus exclusively on anthropological research methods was issued in 1986 as a unit in a series of textbooks for students on research methods (Ashkenazi 1986). The first, and for years the only, textbook in Hebrew on qualitative research was published in 1990 (Sabar Ben-Yehoshua 1990). More recently, several others have been published (Kacen and Krumer-Nevo 2010; Sabar Ben-Yehoshua 2001; Shkedi 2003; Shlasky and Alpert 2007), and reference materials in English have also been recommended to students. Qualitative research and teaching activities have been gradually expanding in Israel; research centers, associations, and societies have been founded; conferences are held in this field; and the number of studies published is steadily growing. Though Hebrew is the native language of the Jews in Israel as well as the language of studies in all the Jewish institutions in the country, many academic publications are published both in English and in Hebrew. Publications in other languages such as French and German are rarer, but still exist. The reasons for the preference of English are that academic promotion and international recognition are more easily achieved by publication in academic journals and publishing houses in this language.

The new Israeli anthropology first examined ethnic groups living within their own communities. This research involved spending a lot of time in the setting being studied, or even living there, as in classical anthropological studies (Shokeid 2004). Nevertheless, as anthropological research began to investigate cultural settings closer to the researchers, participant observations became less intensive. Lack of research funds might be one of the reasons (Shokeid 2004). However, the justification for less-intensive observation was that the investigator was familiar with the field of observation even without long and consecutive stays. Indeed, from certain perspectives, it was important for the researcher to maintain some distance. The difference between ethnography on the one hand and qualitative research based on life stories and interviews on the other was diminished, though not completely eliminated. Ethnography became a qualitative-interpretive sociological research genre in its own right rather than simply a product of classical anthropology. Moreover, it became evident that studying culture can sometimes be well done by using additional research tools such as narrative inquiry, based on interviews, if it includes a detailed description and analysis of the cultural context.

Israeli ethnographers studying minority groups always report their own ethnic or cultural origin in order to indicate their proximity to (e.g., Abu-Rabia-Queder 2008) or remoteness from (e.g., El-Or 2002; Weiner-Levy 2006) the culture investigated.

The growing number of ethnographic studies in education to date focus mainly on schooling: integration in the classroom and in school, immigrants and their absorption, classroom or kindergarten behavior, and national ceremonies in educational settings. These topics reflect the concerns and trepidations of Jewish Israeli society. Conspicuously fewer ethnographic studies have focused on Arab education and education in the ultra-Orthodox community, perhaps due to restricted accessibility or limited interest. Ethnographic research on issues other than schooling has recently been focused on informal youth activities.

Ethnographic studies of education in Israel focus primarily on the following question: How do students from different ethnic origins or social strata cope with schooling processes aimed at formulating an identity, whether national or sectoral, in a reality marked by divisiveness and conflict? Israel is a relatively young society consisting of immigrants and their descendants, along with a large minority of Arabs who have ethnic, religious, and cultural ties to Israel's enemies. As such, it grapples with questions of identity. Indeed, how this identity should be defined and how Israel's territorial borders should be determined are ongoing sources of political, cultural, ethnic, and religious conflicts.

The Israeli educational system reflects the social reality, for it is divided into different sectors, each with its own separate curriculum. The primary division is into Jewish and Arab sectors. The Jewish sector is split into a secular sector and a number of religious sectors, each distinguished by degree and type of religious orthodoxy as well as ethnic origin. The religious sectors are further divided by gender into schools for boys and schools for girls. Within the Arab sector, education is separated into Christian schools, Muslim schools, Druze schools, and Bedouin schools. Moreover, within each sector socioeconomic or ethnic segregation plays a substantial role, particularly in local politics, in debates over school organization, and over student-body composition. This split in the Israeli educational system not only reflects conflicts in Israeli society over identity and distribution of power, but is also responsible for preserving and perpetuating these conflicts.

School and Classroom

From Integrating the Exiles to Educational Integration

For several decades, educational researchers invested their efforts in studying school integration as a policy charged with the hope of narrowing gaps in education, employment, and social status among the various social groups in Israel, particularly between those of Asian and African origin (*Mizrahim*) and those from Europe and America (*Ashkenazim*). However, even through a succession of reform efforts, the findings of the many studies on integration indicated limited achievements, and the gap between the different socioeconomic and ethnic groups remained wide (Adler 1986; Ayalon and Shavit 2004).

Most of the studies of educational integration and reform were quantitative-positivist studies examining macrosocial processes. However, a few ethnographic studies closely observed interactions within schools and between schools and their feeder communities. Some of them (Shokeid 1980; Halper, Shokeid, and Weingrod 1984; Kashti and Yosifon 1985; Lewis 1979) indicated that *Mizrahi* parents saw education as the primary path to social mobility and therefore supported the policy of integration, yet these parents were not always able to cope with the poor image of their children as perceived by school staff. Both the *Ashkenazi* parents who possessed superior political resources and the school principals who were seeking to improve their schools' public image wished to limit integration. A more recent study by Goodman and Mizrachi (2008) explores the implications of ethnic (*Ashkenazi/Mizrahi*) division of high school classes for the educational discussions taking place in them and their impact on the reproduction of the hegemonic order.

A number of studies (Alpert and Bechar 2008; Kashti et al. 1997; Yosifon 2004; Yosifon and Kashti 1998) examined how integrated schools regarded as successful according to various parameters attempted to cope with heterogeneous student bodies by reorganizing teaching and learning and introducing differential pedagogical approaches in order to meet the diverse needs of their students.

The Israeli Classroom and Preschool: Interactions and Discourse

The studies above included description of classroom processes, but research was also conducted specifically on classroom interactions. Among the factors studied were implications of where children sat in the classroom for their learning (Kashti, Arieli, and Harel 1985), the ways in which rules forbidding chat are constructed (Arieli 1995b), the lesson as an asymmetrical speech event in which language reflects as well as constructs social reality (Vardi-Rat and Blum-Kulka 2005), and the ways in which different school cultures encourage or discourage gender differences among students (Klein 2000). Katriel and Nesher (1986) showed how Israel's unique classroom structure and culture construct social cohesion (*gibush*) as a key Israeli symbol.

Some ethnographic studies focused on the Israeli preschool. Most of them dealt with the educational messages transmitted by teachers and their relevance to the Israeli ethos and culture. Furman (1994) describes violence among children on the one hand, and the cultivation of obedience and submission on the other. Shamgar-Handelman and Handelman (1986, 1991) note that preschool classroom ceremonies play a role in promoting a collective ethos and in meeting the bureaucratic demands of the state, while Furman (1999) shows how ceremonies and holiday celebrations in kindergartens transmit ideals of heroism in war and the image of the masculine warrior. Golden (2006) deals with the double message transmitted by the "structured looseness" that governs everyday kindergarten routines. In another study Golden (2005) describes teacher's talk with children about body vulnerability and keeping it from harm, relating it to a suicide attack that occurred at the time. Soker (1992) focuses on children's "As If" play as means to find out whether they have partners to share their views and experiences, and Alpert (2010) describes interactions and attitudes of kindergarten teachers regarding gender equality.

The various studies on preschools, schools, and classrooms examine issues of control, authority, and power in interactions among teachers, pupils, and parents in the daily life and culture of schools and preschools.

Autonomy, Choice, and Unique Schools

Towards the end of the 1970s, new educational trends developed in the wake of widespread public opposition to school integration and the conviction that it had failed, particularly among the higher middle class. A new policy of autonomy empowered parents to establish schools with unique ideological characteristics. Horowitz (1990, 1997) describes one elementary school based on values of the Labor movement, and another school fostering traditional values in the spirit of moderate Judaism. Bekerman (2004) describes two Palestinian-Jewish joint schools, while Bar-Shalom (2006) describes five different unique schools that attempted quite successfully to bridge social and cultural differences, among them a joint school for Jews and Arabs and a joint school for religious and secular pupils. Autonomy in education also found expression in the establishment of community schools. Weil (1985) examined three such schools and found that with respect to their ties to the community, they were not different from regular schools.

Along with this trend toward autonomy, processes of privatization also gained a foothold in Israeli schools in the late 1990s and at the beginning of the twenty-first century. However, the effects of privatization on equity, on the commodification of knowledge, and on the status of teachers have not yet been subject to comprehensive ethnographic examination.

Teachers and Their World

Numerous quantitative studies in Israel have focused on teachers and examined their perceptions and views. Among the few ethnographic studies, one focuses on the existential experience of discontent in teaching (Arieli 1995a) and identifies hurtful actions of students. Some others examine the discourse of the staffroom, an environment that is the site of information and know-how exchange, discussions of professional and school culture, and competitive as well as cooperative relations (Ben-Peretz and Schonmann 2000; Kainan 1994, 1997).

Immigrants in the Schools and in the Community

As mentioned, Israeli sociology has devoted significant attention to immigrant absorption. Functionalist educational researchers examined the school's contribution in transforming immigrants into Israelis. In contrast, ethnographic research sought to examine the young immigrants' world from their own perspective and to describe the immigrant experience in terms of coping with a new and not always welcoming culture.

Ethnographic studies of immigrants from non-Western cultures focused on social rejection and the labeling of young immigrant students (Eisikovits and Varda 1981; Karnieli 2004). Both Shabtay (2001a, 2001b) and Anteby-Yemini (2003) examined social alienation among young Ethiopian immigrants and their serious identity crisis over their skin color. While young immigrants from the former Soviet Union who arrived in masses in the 1990s prefer to preserve their ethnic Russian culture, and view the major role of school as instruction rather than social integration (Eisikovits 1995), many young immigrants from Ethiopia identify either as Ethiopians or as members of the global "imagined community" of blacks (Anteby-Yemini 2003; Shabtay 2001b). Girls of Russian origin tend to be more adept than boys in crossing cultural boundaries (Eisikovits 2000).

Eisikovits and Beck (1990) identified two models for immigrant absorption in school: the assimilation model, which seeks to shorten the time needed in moving to the new culture and requires a quick transition to Hebrew conversation and learning, and a second model that does not limit the amount of time needed to adapt. Each model is marked by distinct learning organization and interaction between teachers and pupils.

School Ceremonies

Ceremonies are a major component of the civil religion in a modern state (Liebman and Don-Yehiya 1983). As a young country that has absorbed numerous immigrants from diverse cultures, Israel is in need of national ceremonies to establish its ongoing relationship to Jewish history and the Land of Israel, as well as to help its citizens identify with the state and establish a common culture. In a comparative study from the late 1960s, Israel ranked first among nine democratic countries in its use of national ceremonies in school (Torney, Oppenheim, and Farnen 1975). It is not surprising that quite a number of ethnographic studies in Israel have focused on this topic.

Israeli children are exposed to holiday and birthday ceremonies in preschool as early as age one or two. These ceremonies also play a role in encouraging children to accept state values (Shamgar-Handelman and Handelman 1986, 1991).

Memorial ceremonies for those who have fallen in Israel's wars and Holocaust Day commemorations have assumed a central and powerful status in Jewish school ceremonies. Indeed, these ceremonies are part of the official school curriculum. As described in ethnographies (Ben-Amos and Bet-El 1999, 2003; Feldman 2001; Furman 1999; Weiss 1997), they stress military and nationalistic themes, advocate the ethos of sacrifice, and emphasize the depersonification of grief. Recently, ties to the local community (Lomsky-Feder 2004) and to the ethos of individual suffering (Lomsky-Feder 2005) have begun to appear in these ceremonies. The attempt to bridge cultural and national gaps by establishing Jewish-Arab bilingual and bicultural schools could not avoid the Jewish hegemonic dominance in those school ceremonies and holiday celebrations (Bekerman 2004).

Another ceremony, added in recent years, is the memorial ceremony marking the assassination of Prime Minister Yitzhak Rabin. Yet, while there is a great deal of consensus within Jewish society regarding war memorial and Holocaust memorial ceremonies, the memorial ceremony for Rabin has been met with reservation in the religious schools (Harrison 2002), and schools in general have avoided discussing the political nature of the assassination (Vinitzky-Seroussi 2001).

Note that these diverse studies have hardly mentioned the situation in non-Jewish schools, even though ties and loyalty to the state in the non-Jewish sector have often been presented in the media as problematic.

Idiosyncratic Educational Settings

The Israeli educational system has many sectors and subsectors, and ethnographic research has not examined all its components. Over the years, educational research has shifted its focus from one sector to another. For example, in the past, kibbutz education and its then unique childrearing methods were of major interest in Israel and worldwide (Bettelheim 1969; Shepher 1983; Spiro 1958). Most studies were quantitative-positivist in nature, but in an ethnographic study, Sabar (2000) examined the connection between school experiences and the decision to live away from the homeland among kibbutzniks who decided to live in Los Angeles. Today kibbutz schools are not different from ordinary schools attended by middle-class students, and probably therefore attract less interest.

The following section surveys ethnographic research on idiosyncratic educational settings in Israel. These studies, while limited in number, reflect the diversity of these settings.

Religious Education

Unlike in most Western countries, state public education in Israel includes a separate religious educational system serving about 20 percent of Jewish elementary school pupils. In addition, there are also two ultra-Orthodox semipublic educational systems, one *Ashkenazi* and the other

Mizrahi. These systems are in large part funded by the state, but at the same time they have almost total autonomy in formulating curricula, organizing learning, and selecting pupils, with limited governmental supervision.

The first ethnographic studies of the religious sector were published in the 1990s and focused on the questions of how schools confront temptations of a free modern society (Gordon et al. 1992; Rapoport 1999); how they try to achieve a balance between the acquiring of religious knowledge and of general scientific and humanistic knowledge (Horowitz 1997; Meirav, Sabar-Ben Yehoshua, and Olshtein 2007); how they promote loyalty to national values and the commitment to act on these values (Rapoport, Penso, and Garb 1994); and how they maintain the special position of women in religious society in view of modern trends toward gender equality (Rapoport 1999; Rapoport and Garb 1998). Parental involvement ranges from a demand for greater orthodoxy that enhances school prestige (Gordon et al. 1992) to increased openness and liberalism (Horowitz 1997).

In recent years, more people have turned to the ultra-Orthodox schools, particularly among the lower classes, many of them of Oriental origin (*Mizrahi*). In 1990, 6.3 percent of all Jewish elementary school pupils attended ultra-Orthodox schools. By 2010, this number had risen to 24.7 percent (CBS 2010, Table 8.9). Because ultra-Orthodox education is suspicious of researchers and does not welcome them, ethnographic studies of these schools are quite rare. Social knowledge misses a lot here, since their curricula and learning processes as well as the knowledge and ways of life of their graduates are very different from those of the state schools. A slight change as to research opportunities in this educational sector can recently be seen. Spiegel's (2011) extensive description, based on ethnographic study, of the ultra-Orthodox educational system for boys in Jerusalem, includes historical background, organizational structure and pedagogical and cultural characteristics. Bilu's (2006) anthropological study associates school initiation ceremony of boys in ultra-Orthodox community to their first haircut ritual as well as their circumcision ritual, and indicates the effect of these rituals on the construction of masculine as well as religious identity. The construction of the feminine identity of the ultra-Orthodox young girl was also studied (Yafeh 2007, 2009).

Arab Education in Israel

As mentioned, Arabs comprise about 20 percent of Israel's population and for the most part live in their own towns and villages. Education rates among the Arab population have gradually risen since the State of Israel was established, and today school attendance of Arabs is equal to that of Jews at the elementary school level, and is only a few percentage points below Jews at the high school level (90 percent compared to 92 percent—CBS 2010, Table 8.20). Most Arab pupils attend Arab public state schools, which offer a curriculum in Arabic and religious studies. Arab education in Israel enjoys linguistic, cultural, and religious autonomy, though the curriculum does not cover the national dimension of their identity.

Until recently, research on Arab education was positivist. It focused primarily on the issue of whether this system offered equal opportunity in social and economic integration compared to schools in the Jewish sector (Al-Haj 1995; Mazawi 1994). The few ethnographic studies we found (Afifi-Agbaria 2007; Gordon et al. 1992; Mari 1975) featured questions regarding the preservation of customs versus modernization and discussed the worth of democratic as opposed to traditional values. Based on ethnographic interviews and narratives, the studies of Abu-Rabia-Queder (2006, 2008) and Pessate-Schubert (2004, 2005) on Bedouin women, and Weiner-Levy's study on Druze women who acquired higher education (2006), describe how by using their education as a personal asset and a profession, and their position as educators in their communities, those women struggled, not without paying sometimes a personal cost, to empower women's position in the community and to introduce some changes in traditional culture.

Residential Education

In the past, residential schools played a prominent role in Israeli education. This education sector was established as part of the Zionist revolution, in answer to the need—and the accompanying feelings of national responsibility—to save young Jews who had been persecuted in their countries of residence just for being Jews. These young people were also seen as reinforcements who would help bolster Jewish settlement in Israel and assist in establishing a firm foothold on what was considered national territory. From the 1970s onward, when the number of immigrants diminished, the residential school system absorbed youngsters from the lower classes as part of the integration project. The educational objective today, then, is to improve its students' chances for social mobility.

A great deal of pedagogical, documentary, and functionalist-sociological literature has been devoted to this educational system. Ethnographic studies from the 1980s (Arieli 1988; Bernstein 1987; Kashti et al. 1991),while relating strongly to Goffman's total institution concept (1961), focused on the tension between the right to preserve one's identity and the supervision and control found in a total educational system such as the residential school.

Ethnographic studies published in the 1990s examined the work of the educational staff (Arieli 1997; Arieli and Aviram 1987; Grupper and Eisikovits 1992), particularly the unique role of the residential youth care workers (*Madrichim*). Questions were raised about the professional identity and training of these workers (Eisikovits 1997).

Several studies published in the first decade of the twenty-first century discussed the world of the residential school students (Grupper, Malkmo, and Nudelman 2003; Shamai 2003; Shlasky and Shlasky 2000). These studies also considered cultural passage among new immigrants, absorbed again in relatively large numbers in residential schools, and the clash between preserving one's culture and encountering a new identity.

Informal Education

A sphere of social research that contributed in the past to local and international educational knowledge and changed its focus and approaches in the last decades is informal youth culture. Before the establishment of the state and in its first decades, most Jewish youths were organized in youth movements. Those movements were the most influential instrument in inculcating political values and recruiting for national missions, such as agricultural settlement. Thus, from the 1950s to the 1970s the main interest of youth culture research was in organized youth movements and their socializing effects, and its theoretical approach was functional-structural (e.g., Eisenstadt 1956; Shapira et al. 1979). The only ethnographic study on Israeli youth movements we found was Katriel's (1987) on one of their ceremonies. In the last decades youth movements attracted fewer members, changed their nature, and became more flexible as well as much less influential politically.

A growing interest in informal youth subcultures can be traced recently among educational anthropologists (Anteby-Yemini 2003; Karnieli 2004; Shabtay 2001a, 2001b). These ethnographic studies deal mainly with street-corner subcultures of immigrant non-Ashkenazi youth that are regarded as subversive by the establishment.

Adult education can be represented by the ethnographic work of Golden (2001), who studied Hebrew-language classes (*Ulpan*) for adult Russian immigrants, and the anthropological studies of El-Or (2002, 2006), which describe the acquisition of different kinds of informal religious and secular knowledge by Orthodox women and its effects on their religious and feminine identity.

Gender in Education

There is a growing interest in gender issues in the Israeli qualitative research on education, especially concerning teachers' work and career. However, ethnographies relating to gender issues focus mainly on students' experience at school. Most of them were mentioned above under different headings (Alpert 2010; Bilu 2006; Eisikovits 2000; Furman 1999; Klein 2000; Lomsky-Feder 2005; Rapoport 1999; Rapoport and Garb 1998; Shlasky and Shlasky 2000; Yafeh 2007, 2009), and they represent different aspects of gender identity construction.

Of special interest are the anthropological studies of El-Or (1994, 2002, 2006) and the narrative studies of Abu-Rabia-Queder (2006, 2008), Pessate-Schubert (2004, 2005) and Weiner-Levy (2006). These researchers studied the complicated situation of young women who acquired further or higher education while living in traditional communities and accepting their basic precepts, and its impact on their identity and social position.

Summary and Conclusions

Ethnographic research in Israel, like qualitative research in general, is quite young. It began in the late 1960s, when positivist-functionalist sociological research was already well established in Israel. This functional research claimed it could explain the macrosocial processes involved in building the nascent Israeli society. It even proposed ways to promote integration in all areas, particularly in education.

Academic ethnographic research sought to give voice to and understand the diverse and conflicting cultures composing the relatively small Israeli society. Hence, this research is spread across many fields, and tends to be critical toward the hegemony. The transition from a nascent society, where social scientists regarded as one of their functions to encourage consensus and cohesion, to a more mature and reflexive society, contributed to the academic recognition of anthropological and qualitative research methods, and to the introduction of critical and postmodernist approaches (Ram 1995).

With respect to education, ethnographic research has focused its attention on the encounter in the school and the classroom between students from diverse ethnic origins and social classes, and between immigrants and native-born students, and has also examined the role of national ceremonies in the school culture. These diverse topics reflect the problem of identity, which has increasingly occupied Israeli society over the last decades. For various reasons, ethnographic research has not directed as much attention to the separate education of idiosyncratic social groups such as Orthodox people and Arabs, even though these too are matters concerning identity and relate to relatively large social groups.

Moreover, more comprehensive ethnographic studies are needed that examine whole educational institutions and their local culture. These studies should focus on the interactions within these institutions and with external factors influencing them, as well as on the worlds of their teachers and students. It can be assumed that as qualitative study expands in Israel, additional ethnographic studies will relate to these issues. These studies will perhaps be able to explain why the educational system has had so much difficulty coping with students' changing attitudes to knowledge and to those representing knowledge, as well as why people are so disenchanted with the way the school system functions today.

Bibliography

Abu-Rabia-Queder, Sarab. 2006. "'They Felt I Raped a Role That Was Not Supposed to Be Mine': First Woman Principal in a Bedouin Tribal Society." In *Women Principals in a Multi-Cultural Society: New Insights into Feminist Educational Leadership,* ed. Izhar Oplatka and Rachel Hertz-Lazarowitz. Rotterdam: Sense Publishing Company.

———. 2008. "Does Education Necessarily Mean Enlightenment? The Case of Higher Education among Palestinians-Bedouin Women in Israel." *Anthropology and Education Quarterly* 39, no. 4: 381–400.

Abuhav, Orit. 2010. *In the Company of Others: The Development of Anthropology in Israel.* Tel Aviv: Resling (Hebrew).

Adler, Chaim. 1986. "Israeli Education Addressing Dilemmas Caused by Pluralism: A Sociological Perspective." In *Education and the Integration of Ethnic Minorities,* ed. Dietmar Rothermund and John Simon, 64–87. London: Pinter Publishers.

Afifi-Agbaria, Dima. 2007. "A Unique Experimental School in the Arab Sector." Master's Thesis, School of Education, Tel-Aviv University (Hebrew).

Al-Haj, Majid. 1995. *Education, Empowerment, and Control: The Case of the Arabs in Israel.* Albany: SUNY Press.

Alpert, Bracha. 2010. "Developing Awareness of Gender Equality among Early Education Student-Teachers through Field Work." In *At Teachers' Expense: Gender and Power in Israeli Education,* ed. Esther Hertzog and Zsvia Walden, 289–310. Jerusalem: Carmel (Hebrew).

Alpert, Bracha, and Shlomit Bechar. 2008. "School Organisational Efforts in Search for Alternatives to Ability Grouping." *Teaching and Teacher Education* 24: 1599–612.

Anteby-Yemini, Lisa. 2003. "Urban Ethiopia and Black Culture: New Models of Identity among Immigrant Youths from Ethiopia in Israel." In *On Cultural Boundaries and Between Them: Young Immigrants in Israel,* ed. Rivka A. Eisikovits, 11–31. Tel Aviv: Ramot (Hebrew).

Arieli, Mordecai. 1988. "Cultural Transition through Total Education: Actors' Perspectives." In *Cultural Transition: The Case Of Immigrant Youth,* ed. Meir Gotessmann, 103–20. Jerusalem: Magnes Press.

———. 1995a. *Teaching and Its Discontents.* Tel Aviv: Ramot (Hebrew).

———. 1995b. "Forbidding Chat During the Class Time: On the Circumstances and the Emergence of School Disciplinary Rules." In *Education toward the 21st Century,* ed. David Chen, 461–74. Tel-Aviv: Ramot (Hebrew).

———. 1997. *The Occupational Experience of Residential Child and Youth Care Workers: Caring and its Discontents.* New York: Haworth Press.

Arieli, Mordecai, and Ovadia Aviram. 1987. "Staff Roles in a Total Living Situation: The Case of an Israeli Residential School." *Child and Youth Services 8,* no. 3/4: 67–88.

Arieli, Mordecai, Yitzhak Kashti, and Simha Shlasky. 1983. *Living at School: Israeli Residential Schools as People Processing Organizations.* Tel Aviv: Ramot.

Ashkenazi, Michael. 1986. "Ethnographic Research in Anthropology." In *Research Methods in the Social Sciences,* unit 4, ed. Ruth Beyth-Marom. Tel Aviv: Everyman's University (Hebrew).

Ayalon, Hanna, and Yossi Shavit. 2004. "Educational Reforms and Inequalities in Israel: MMI Hypothesis Revisited." *Sociology of Education 77,* no. 2: 103–20.

Ball, Stephen. 1981. *Beachside Comprehensive: A Case Study of Secondary School.* Cambridge, UK: Cambridge University Press.

Bar-Shalom, Yehuda. 2006. *Educating Israel: Educational Entrepreneurship in Israel's Multicultural Society.* Palgrave Macmillan.'

Bekerman, Zvi. 2004. "Potential and Limitations of Multicultural Education in Conflict-Ridden Areas: Bilingual Palestinian-Jewish Schools in Israel." *Teachers College Record 106,* no. 3, 574–610.

Ben-Amos, Avner, and Ilana Bet-El. 1999. "Commemoration and National Identity: Memorial Ceremonies in Israeli Schools." In *Between "I" and "We": The Construction of Identities and Israeli Identity,* ed. Azmi Bishara, 129–52. Jerusalem: Van Leer Jerusalem Institute (Hebrew).

———. 2003. "Educating to Militarism and Commemoration: National Commemoration Ceremonies in Israeli Schools." In *In the Name of Security: Sociology of Peace and War in Israel in Era of Change,* ed. Majid Al-Haj and Uri Ben-Eliezer, 369–400. Haifa: Haifa University Press and Pardess Press (Hebrew).

Ben-Ari, Eyal. 1997. *Body Projects in Japanese Childcare: Culture, Organization and Emotions in a Preschool.* London: Curzon.

Ben-Peretz, Miriam, and Shifra Schonmann. 2000. *Behind Closed Doors: Teachers and the Role of the Teachers' Lounge.* Albany: SUNY Press.

Bernstein, Frida. 1987. "The Socialization of Girls in an Ultra-Orthodox Institution." In *Residential Settings and the Community: Congruence and Conflict*, eds. Yitzhak Kashti and Mordecai Arieli, 13–33. London: Freund.

Bettelheim, Bruno. 1969. *The Children of the Dream*. New York: Macmillan.

Bilu, Yoram. 2006. "Circumcision, the First Haircut and the Torah: Ritual and Male Identity Among the Ultraorthodox Community of Contemporary Israel." in *Imagined Masculinities: Male Identity and Culture in Modern Middle East*, eds. Mai Ghoussoub and Emma Sinclair-Webb, 33–64. London: Saqi Books.

Bird-David, Nurit. 1990. "The Giving Environment: Another Perspective on the Economic System of Gatherer-Hunters." *Current Anthropology* 31: 189–96.

Central Bureau of Statistics (CBS). 2010. *Statistical Abstract of Israel* no. 61. Jerusalem.

Deshen, Shlomo. 1977. "Ethnic Boundaries and Cultural Paradigms: The Case of Southern Tunisian Immigrants in Israel." *Ethos* 4: 40–54.

Deshen, Shlomo, and Moshe Shokeid. 1998. "Notes on One Hundred Years of Anthropology." In *The Intercultural Experience: Readings in Anthropology*, ed. Moshe Shokeid and Shlomo Deshen, 7–27. Jerusalem and Tel Aviv: Schocken (Hebrew).

Eisenstadt, Shmuel N. 1956. *From Generation to Generation*. New York: Free Press.

Eisikovits, Rivka A. 1995. "'I'll Tell You What School Should Do for Us': How Immigrant Youths from the Former USSR View Their High School Experience in Israel." *Youth and Society* 27, no. 2: 230–55.

———. 1997. *The Anthropology of Child and Youth Care Work*. New York: Haworth Press.

———. 2000. "Gender Differences in Cross-Cultural Adaptation Styles of Immigrant Youths from the Former USSR in Israel." *Youth and Society* 31, no. 3: 310–31.

Eisikovits, Rivka A., and Robert H. Beck. 1990. "Models Governing the Education of New Immigrant Students in Israel." *Comparative Education Review* 34, no. 2: 177–95.

Eisikovits, Rivka, and Adam Varda. 1981. "The Social Integration of Immigrant Children from the Caucasus in Israeli Schools." *Studies in Education* 35: 76–84 (Hebrew).

El-Or, Tamar. 1994. *Educated and Ignorant: On Ultraorthodox Women and Their Life*. Boulder, CO: Lynne Rienner.

———. 2002. *Next Year I Will Know More. Literacy and Identity of Young Orthodox Women in Israel*. Detroit: Wayne State University Press.

———. 2006. *Reserved Seats: Religion, Gender and Ethnicity in Contemporary Israel*. Tel Aviv: Am Oved (Hebrew).

Feldman, Jackie. 2001. "In the Footsteps of the Israeli Survivor." *Theoria Ubikoret* 19: 167–90 (Hebrew).

Forum for Studying Society and Culture. 2002. "Mechanisms of Constituting and Producing Canonical Knowledge on Mizrahim in Israel." In *Mizrahim in Israel: A Critical Observation into Israel's Ethnicity*, ed. Hannan Hever, Yehouda Shenhav, and Pnina Motzafi-Haller, 288–305. Jerusalem: Van Leer Institute and Hakibbutz Hameuchad Publishing House (Hebrew).

Furman, Mirta. 1994. *The New Children: Violence and Obedience in Early Childhood.* Tel Aviv: Hakibbutz Hameuchad Publishing House (Hebrew).

———. 1999. "Army and War: Collective Narratives of Early Childhood in Contemporary Israel." In *The Military and Militarism in Israeli Society,* ed. Edna Lomsky-Feder and Eyal Ben-Ari, 141–68. New York: SUNY Press.

Goffman, Erving. 1961. *Asylums: Essays on the Social Situation of Mental Patients and Other Inmates.* New York: Anchor Books.

Golden, Debora. 2001. "'Now, Like Real Israelis, Let's Stand Up and Sing': Teaching the National Language to Russian Newcomers in Israel." *Anthropology and Education Quarterly* 32, no. 1: 52–79.

———. 2005. "Childhood as Protected Space? Vulnerable Bodies in an Israeli Kindergarten." *Ethnos* 70, no. 1: 79–100.

———. 2006. "Structured Looseness: Everyday Social Order at an Israeli Kindergarten." *Ethos* 34, no. 3: 367–90.

Goodman, Yehuda C., and Nissim Mizrachi. 2008. "'The Holocaust Does Not Belong to European Jews Alone': The Differential Use of Memory Techniques in Israeli High Schools." *American Ethnologist* 35, no. 1: 95–114.

Gordon, David, Michal Katz, Menachem Avisar, and Walter Ackerman. 1992. *Schooldays: Portraits of Eight Israeli High Schools.* Beer-Sheva: Ben-Gurion University (Hebrew).

Grupper, Emanuel, and Rivka Eisikovits. 1992. "Child-Care Workers Who Require Moratorium: A Study of the Professional Development Needs of New Residential Child-Care Workers." In *Residential Schools: Their Staffs and Communities,* ed. Mordecai Arieli, 80–94. Tel Aviv: Massada Press (Hebrew).

Grupper, Emanuel, Yaakov Malkmo, and Anita Nudelman. 2003. "Rites of Passage of Immigrant Youths from Ethiopia Entering Residential Schools in Israel." In *On Cultural Boundaries and Between Them: Young Immigrants in Israel,* ed. Rivka A. Eisikovits, 33–63. Tel Aviv: Ramot (Hebrew).

Halper, Jeff, Moshe Shokeid, and Alex Weingrod. 1984. "Communities, Schools and Integration." In *School Desegregation,* ed. Yeuda Amir and Shlomo Sharan, 47–62. Mahwah, NJ: Lawrence Erlbaum.

Hargreaves, David H. 1967. *Social Relations in a Secondary School.* London: Routledge and Kegan Paul.

Harrison, Jo-Ann. 2002. "The Social Structuring of Civil Memorial Ceremonies in Israeli Schools." In *Values Education in Various Teaching Contexts,* ed. Nava Maslovaty and Yaacov Iram, 351–74. Tel Aviv: Ramot (Hebrew).

Hertzog, Esther, Orit Abuhav, Harvey E. Goldberg, and Emanuel Marx. 2010. "Introduction: The Israeli Social Anthropology—Origins, Characteristics, and Contributions." In *Perspectives on Israeli Anthropology,* ed. Esther Hertzog et al., 1–15. Detroit: Wayne State University Press.

Horowitz, Tamar. 1990. *Between Ethnic Community and Ideological Community.* Jerusalem: *Henrietta Sold Institute* (Hebrew).

———. 1997. "Parental Choice as a Factor in Educational Change." *Education and Society* 15, no. 1: 33–47.

Jackson, Philip W. 1968. *Life in Classrooms.* New York: Holt, Rinehart and Winston.

Kacen, Lea, and Michal Krumer-Nevo, eds. 2010. *Data Analysis in Qualitative Research*. Beer Sheva: Ben-Gurion University of the Negev Press (Hebrew).

Kainan, Anat. 1994. *The Staffroom, Observing the Professional Culture of Teachers*. Aldershot, UK: Ashgate Publishing.

———. 1997. "The Role of Teachers' Stories in the Staffroom of a Religious School." *Anthropology and Education Quarterly* 28, no. 2: 163–81.

Karnieli, Mira. 2004. *"Teacher, Don't Say That We Are Fucked Up": The Place of the Educational System and the Community in the Development of Oppositional Sub-Culture*. Tel Aviv: Mofet Institute (Hebrew).

Kashti, Yitzhak, Bracha Alpert, Margalith Yosifon, and Ehud Manor. 1997. *School Heterogeneity: Unity and Variety*. Tel Aviv: Ramot (Hebrew).

Kashti, Yitzhak, Mordecai Arieli, and Yeudit Harel. 1985. "The Classroom as a System of Meanings." *Megamot* 29, no. 1: 7–21 (Hebrew).

Kashti, Yitzhak, Ovadia Aviram, Hagai Ben-Zvi, and Yona Sagi. 1991. *Residential Schools: The Daily Realities Ethnographies*. Tel Aviv: Ramot (Hebrew).

Kashti, Yitzhak, and Margalith Yosifon. 1985. *Education as Bargaining*. Tel Aviv: Hakibbutz Hameuchad Publishing House (Hebrew).

Katriel, Tamar. 1987. "Rhetoric in Flames: Fire Inscriptions in Israeli Youth Movement Ceremonials." *Quarterly Journal of Speech* 73: 444–59.

Katriel, Tamar, and Perla Nesher. 1986. "'Gibush': The Rhetoric of Cohesion in Israeli School Culture." *Comparative Education Review* 30: 216–31.

Klein, Esther. 2000. "The Process of Gender Construction in Junior High Schools." In *Sexuality and Gender in Education*, ed. Simha Shlasky, 113–34. Tel Aviv: Ramot (Hebrew).

Kunda, Gideon. 1992a. "Critique Examined: Ethnography and Critique of Culture in Israel." *Theoria Ubikoret* 2: 7–24 (Hebrew).

———. 1992b. *Engineering Culture: Control and Commitment in a High-Tech Corporation*. Philadelphia: Temple University Press.

Lewis, Arnold. 1979. *Power, Poverty and Education: An Anthropology of Schooling in an Israeli Town*. Ramat Gan: Turtledove.

———. 1981. "Minority Education in Sharonia, Israel, and Stockton, California: A Comparative Analysis." *Anthropology and Education Quarterly* 12: 30–50.

Liebman, Charles S., and Eliezer Don-Yehiya. 1983. *Civil Religion in Israel*. Berkeley: University of California Press.

Lissak, Moshe, and Dan Horowitz. 1989. *Trouble in Utopia: The Overburdened Polity of Israel*. Albany: SUNY Press.

Lomsky-Feder, Edna. 2004. "The Memorial Ceremony in Israeli Schools: Between State and Civil Society." *British Journal of Sociology of Education* 25, no. 3: 291–305.

———. 2005. "The Bounded Female Voice in Memorial Ceremonies." *Qualitative Sociology* 28, no. 3: 293–314.

Mari, Sami. 1975. "School and Society in the Arab Village in Israel." *Iyunim Bechinuch* 4: 85–103 (Hebrew).

Marx, Emanuel. 1975. "Anthropological Studies in a Centralized State: The Bernstein Research Project in Israel." *Jewish Journal of Sociology* 17: 131–50.

Marx, Emanuel, and Avshlom Shmueli, eds. 1984. *The Changing Bedouin*. New Brunswick, NJ: Transaction Books.

Mazawi, Andre. 1994. "Palestinians in Israel: Educational Expansion, Social Mobility and Political Control." *Compare: A Journal of Comparative Education* 24, no. 3: 277–84.

Meirav, Nurit, Naama Sabar-Ben Yehoshua, and Elite Olshtein. 2007. "Hassidic Discourse in the Shaping of an Ideological-Cultural-Social Curriculum: Curriculum Planning in an Elementary School for Girls in the Chabad Community." In *Innovations and Renewal in Jewish Education*, ed. David Zisenwine, 135–60. Tel-Aviv: School of Education, Tel-Aviv University (Hebrew).

Pessate-Schubert, Anat. 2004. "'The Sky is the Limit': Higher Education, Gender and Empowerment in the Bedouin Community in the Negev in Israel." *Compare* 34, no. 3: 329–40.

———. 2005. "Retelling Herstory: To Be a Female Bedouin Teacher Differently." *Comparative Education* 41, no. 3: 247–66.

Ram, Uri. 1995. *The Changing Agenda of Israeli Sociology.* Albany: SUNY Press.

Rapoport, Tamar. 1999. "The Pedagogical Construction of Traditional Woman: An Ethnographic Study of 'Holiness Class.'" *Megamot* 39, no. 4): 492–517 (Hebrew).

Rapoport, Tamar, and Yoni Garb. 1998. "The Experience of Religious Fortification: Coming-of-Age of Religious-Zionist Young Women." *Gender and Education* 10, no. 1: 5–21.

Rapoport, Tamar, Anat Penso, and Yoni Garb. 1994. "Contribution to the Collective by Religious-Zionist Adolescent Girls." *British Journal of Sociology of Education* 15, no. 3: 375-388.

Sabar, Naama. 2000. *Kibbutzniks in the Diaspora.* Albany: SUNY Press.

Sabar Ben-Yehoshua, Naama. 1990. *The Qualitative Research in Teaching and Learning.* Givatyim: Massada Press (Hebrew).

———, ed. 2001. *Genres and Traditions in Qualitative Research.* Or Yehdua: Dvir (Hebrew).

Semyonov, Moshe, and Noah Lewin-Epstein. 2004. "Introduction—Past Insights and Future Directions: Studies of Stratification in Israel." In *Stratification in Israel: Class, Ethnicity, and Gender*, ed. Moshe Semyonov and Noah Lewin-Epstein, 1–13. New Brunswick, NJ: Transaction Publishers.

Shabtay, Malka. 2001a. "Living with a Threatened Identity: Life Experiences with a Different Skin Color among Young and Adolescent Ethiopian Immigrants in Israel." *Megamot* 41, no. 1–2: 97–112 (Hebrew).

———. 2001b. *Between Reggae and Rap: The Integration Challenge of Ethiopian Youth in Israel.* Tel Aviv: Tcherikover (Hebrew).

Shamai, Shalom. 2003. "'Of Course I would Like to be Integrated . . . and Maybe It Will Happen Some Day …': Styles of Cultural Adaptation of Immigrant Adolescents from the Former Soviet Union." In *On Cultural Boundaries and Between Them: Young Immigrants in Israel*, ed. Rivka A. Eisikovits, 65–100. Tel Aviv: Ramot (Hebrew).

Shamgar-Handelman, Lea, and Don Handelman. 1986. "Holiday Celebrations in Israeli Kindergartens: Relationships between Representations of Collectivity and Family in the Nation-State." In *The Frailty of Authority (Political Anthropology, vol. 5)*, ed. Myron J. Arnoff, 71–103. New Brunswick, NJ: Transaction Books.

————. 1991. "Celebration of Bureaucracy: Birthday Parties in Israeli Kindergarten." *Ethnology* 30, no. 4: 293–312.

Shapira, Rina, Haim Adler, Miri Lerner, and Rachel Peleg. 1979. *Blue Shirt and White Collar.* Tel Aviv: Am Oved (Hebrew).

Shepher, Israel. 1983. *The Kibbutz: An Anthropological Study.* Norwood, PA: Norwood Editions.

Shkedi, Asher. 2003. *Words of Meanings: Qualitative Research—Theory and Practice.* Tel Aviv: Ramot (Hebrew).

Shlasky, Simha, and Bracha Alpert. 2007. *Ways of Writing Qualitative Research: From Deconstructing Reality to its Construction as a Text.* Tel Aviv: Mofet Institute (Hebrew).

Shlasky, Simha, and Sharona Shlasky. 2000. "How Residential Care Workers Relate to Sexual Behavior of Inmates." In *Sexuality and Gender in Education,* ed. Simha Shlasky, 135–74. Tel Aviv: Ramot (Hebrew).

Shokeid, Moshe. 1971. *The Dual Heritage: Immigrants from the Atlas Mountains in an Israeli Village.* Manchester, UK: Manchester University Press.

————. 1980. "An Ethnographic Perspective on the Problem of Integration—Events at a Regional School." *Megamot* 26, no. 1: 56–70 (Hebrew).

————. 2004. "Max Gluckman and the Making of Israeli Anthropology." *Ethnos* 69, no. 3: 387–410.

Soker, Zeev. 1992. "Playing and Learning: What Do Children Really Want to Learn through Play?" *Megamot* 34: 497–520 (Hebrew).

Spiegel, Ehud. 2011. *"And Learning Torah in Front of Everything Else": Ultra-Orthodox Education for Boys in Jerusalem.* Jerusalem: Jerusalem Institute for Israel Studies (Hebrew).

Spiro, Melford E. 1958. *Children of the Kibbutz.* Cambridge, MA: Harvard University Press.

Torney, Judith V., Abraham N. Oppenheim, and Russell F. Farnen. 1975. *Civic Education in Ten Countries: An Empirical Study.* New York: John Wiley and Sons.

Van Teeffelen, Toine. 1978. "The Manchester School in Africa and Israel: A Critique." *Dialectical Anthropology* 3: 67–83.

Vardi-Rat, Esther, and Shoshana Blum-Kulka. 2005. "The Lesson as an Asymmetrical Speech Event: A Look at the Participation Structure in the Israeli Classroom." In *Discourse in Education: Researching Educational Events,* ed. Irit Kupferberg and Elite Olshtain, 385–417. Tel Aviv: Mofet Institute (Hebrew).

Vinitzky-Seroussi, Vered. 2001. "Commemorating Narratives of Violence: The Yitzhak Rabin Memorial Day in Israeli Schools." *Qualitative Sociology* 24, no. 2: 245–68.

Weil, Shalva. 1985. *The Dynamics of Community Schools in Israel: An Ethnography.* Jerusalem: Hebrew University, The Research Institute for Innovation in Education (Hebrew).

Weiner-Levy, Naomi. 2006. "The Flagbearers: Israeli Druze Women Challenge Traditional Gender Roles." *Anthropology and Education Quarterly* 37, no. 3: 217–35.

Weiss, Meira. 1997. "Bereavement, Commemoration, and Collective Identity in Contemporary Israeli Society." *Anthropological Quarterly* 70, no. 2: 91–100.

Willis, Paul E. 1977. *Learning to Labour.* Farnborough, UK: Gower.

Yafeh, Orit. 2007. "The Time in the Body: Cultural Construction of Femininity in Ultraorthodox Kindergartens for Girls." *Ethos* 35, no. 4: 516–54.

———. 2009. "Female Pedagogical Authority and its Limits." In *Leadership and Authority among the Ultra-Orthodox Society in Israel,* ed. Kimmy Caplan and Nurit Stadler, 31–56. Tel Aviv: Hakibbutz Hameuchad Press and Van Leer Jerusalem Institute (Hebrew).

Yosifon, Margalit. 2004. "Empowerment as Inspiring Change and as Its Product: New Faces in Professional Development at the School." In *Teachers in a Changing World: Trends and Challenges,* ed. Sarah Guri-Rosenblit, 38–73. Ra'anana: Open University of Israel (Hebrew).

Yosifon, Margalit, and Yitzhak Kashti. 1998. "Restructuring Teaching Patterns through Curricular Planning." In *Curriculum as a Social Construction,* ed. Hanna Ayalon, 109–36. Tel Aviv: Ramot (Hebrew).

§ 13

Sociological and Ethnographic Research in French-Speaking Sub-Saharan Africa

Boubacar Bayero Diallo

In sub-Saharan Africa, the 1960s and 1970s were marked by widespread progress in the expansion of schooling (Pilon, Gérard, and Yaro 2001; UNESCO 1995). This movement was slowed in the 1980s mainly by the "economic crisis" and structural adjustment plans, which led in many countries (especially the French-speaking nations) to a sharp slowing of growth or even to a decrease in school-attendance rates (Lange 1998; Mbilinyi 2000; N'Doye 2001; Diallo 2004). However, the 1990s saw strong resurgence in the growth of schooling due to several factors, including a strong mobilization and participation of a wider variety of educational actors: the state, donors, civil society—including national and international non-governmental organizations (NGOs)—and families (Lange 1998; Pilon, Gérard and Yaro 2001; UNESCO 2005).

To support these efforts at developing education, numerous research networks (ERNWACA, FASAF, ADEA, FAWE, CREA, etc.) also appeared at the end of the 1980s and beginning of the 1990s.[1] They aimed to reinforce the national or regional capacity for educational research, notably by financing new projects; to improve the quality of existing research; to develop exchanges and collaborations; and to diffuse and publish the work. Their research supplemented work by existing research institutions, such as the Council for Social Science Research Development in Africa (CODESRIA), created in 1973.

It is in this context that we can ask about the nature of the research on education in sub-Saharan Africa, especially in the French-speaking nations: How did anthropological, sociological, ethnographic, and ethnological research that preceded this educational research develop? Who has conducted the educational research, what were its main themes, and what kinds of questions underlay those themes? Was it inspired by pioneer research or by local historical and social experiences? Was it sociological, anthropological, or ethnographic? Has it been published? If so, in what languages?

Methodology

My intention is not to answer all these questions comprehensively, but simply to launch a reflection, the beginning of an answer based on documentary research carried out principally on the internet. Several books and articles assessing the state of sociology and of anthropology in French-speaking Africa inform this chapter. I also made use of the few mémoires and theses from anthropology or sociology departments of African and foreign universities that I was able to find.[2] This chapter relies primarily on the works of ERNWACA, particularly those carried out in French-speaking countries of West and Central Africa. It refers frequently to the documents of ROCARE summarized by Maclure (1997), a synthesis of 1,056 documents (mémoires or research essays, theses, published manuscripts, reports, and more) produced in the field of education from 1960 to 1991 in seven ERNWACA countries, of which five are French-speaking (Mali, Togo, Cameroon, Burkina Faso, and Benin) and two are English-speaking (Sierra Leone and Ghana). I have added to that several other works from French-speaking West Africa, including those found through FASAF (Pilon and Yaro 2001).

Supplementing the literature studied is an analysis of my own research and that of several colleagues in the Department of Sociology of the University of Sonfonia (DSUS, which belonged until recently to the University of Conakry), as represented by the content of the curriculum vitae of eleven (out of twenty-one) department members.

This work is likewise admittedly limited by methodological questions that it raises. Should one consider works carried out by multidisciplinary teams composed of sociologists, demographers, statisticians, and educational specialists? Should one limit the review only to work accomplished exclusively by African researchers working in Africa? Can studies that use both qualitative and quantitative methods in fieldwork lasting several months be considered ethnographic? Such questions are all the more relevant because most recent work except mémoires and theses has been carried out by multidisciplinary teams, in which expatriates (French and French-speaking Canadians) participate as researchers and provide training in research methods. Another difficulty is that authors of certain works do not specify their discipline and do not describe their research methods with enough detail to determine whether to define them as ethnographers.

Finally, let me note that the definition of *ethnography* used here is the study of everyday life, in context, with an emphasis on longitudinal studies that permit the researcher to follow situations or settings for fairly long periods (Beach et al. 2004). Given that definition and the constraints above, I have included works by sociologists, anthropologists, or ethnologists, whether carried out alone or in the context of multidisciplinary research, as long as they took place in French-speaking countries of Africa, whatever the researcher's nationality.

The Historical Context of Anthropology and Sociology

This section provides a rapid historical sketch of the practice and the positioning, the identity debate and the conditions of production of sociological and anthropological research in French-speaking Africa.

The Weight of Precolonial and Colonial History

The first ethnographic and anthropological studies in Africa were undertaken essentially during the colonial conquest (1860–1920) and the colonial period (1920–1945) by colonial administrators, ethnographers, and ethnologists, and consisted of applied anthropology in the service of colonization (Diop 1963; Copans 1971). However, publication in the 1950s of works in "dynamic anthropology," especially Georges Balandier's *Sociologie des Brazzavilles noires* (1956), represented more or less a "cultural revolution" (Hirschhorn and Tamba 2010). These works demonstrated that all societies are located within history and experience transformations, and that there are thus no societies oriented toward tradition and the past (Abé 2008). They planted the idea of the birth of an African sociology (Diop 2007; Essè 2008; Kolle 2007). Thus, if "in Europe, sociology was the daughter of the Revolution, in Africa sociology was the daughter of Independence" (Hirschhorn and Tamba 2010).

The Influence of Postcolonial National Policies

During the same period, anthropology—accused of the double sins of primitivism and colonialism—was rejected by the new universities or was buried within departments of sociology (Nkwi 1998 and 2006 cited by Bonhomme 2007), except for Diop (2007), who pursued anthropological research during the 1960s and 1970s in the framework of Marxist anthropology among others. That said, in the years following African independence, development of sociology was stalled in many countries either by the establishment of authoritarian regimes or by armed conflict. Certain regimes outlawed the teaching of sociology. For example, the Department of Sociology at the University of Dakar was closed in 1968 and not reopened until 2004 (Diédhiou 2010). In other countries, departments were not closed but teaching of the discipline was tightly controlled, as in the Central African Republic and Cameroon (Nga Ndongo 2010). Elsewhere, it was not totalitarian regimes but rather civil war that put a brake on the development of sociology, as in Congo-Brazzaville and in Chad (Hirschhorn and Tamba 2010).

The Value Placed on Action Research Since the 1990s

Beginning in the 1990s, sociology and anthropology felt a new impetus explained mainly by the democratization of certain regimes and by a strong social demand for training in action research, the latter emanating from development agencies, NGOs, and governments. The demand for action research was driven in good part by the conclusion that failures during the preceding decades were due largely to the fact that policies had not been based on local realities (Hirschhorn and Tamba 2010). This new dynamic led to the creation of new departments of sociology. For example, in Burkina Faso, the sociology, philosophy, and psychology track was split into separate degrees and a department of sociology created in 1992 (Sawadogo 2010). New discussion forums and publications for sociologists and anthropologists emerged: the Pan African Anthropological Association (PAAA) in 1989, the African Sociological Association in 2000, as well as the *African Sociological Review* (semi-annual publication of CODESRIA) and the *African Anthropologist* (the PAAA's biannual journal), both publishing articles in French and in English.[3] These new structures joined CODESRIA (Council for the Development of Social Science Research in Africa) and CAMES (African and Malagasy Council for Higher Education), which already contributed to the impulse for a French-language African sociology and anthropology.

Inequalities between Sociology and Anthropology in the Region

Thus, sociology became, step by step, the "daughter of independence," the "enemy" of authoritarian regimes, and the "new tool for development." Anthropology, the "daughter of colonialism," barely held its own. Within universities, one often counts just four anthropology courses, as at the University of Yaoundé I (Nga Ndongo 2010) or the University of Conakry. There are very few autonomous departments of anthropology in French-speaking African universities. Thus it is only in 1993 and 1997 respectively that the University of Yaoundé I in Cameroon and the University of Oumar-Bongo in Gabon opened departments of anthropology (Bonhomme 2007).

Inequalities from One Country to Another

There are also considerable differences from one country to another within sociology. For example, in Chad, sociology has a history of less than a decade and is taught only in the first two years of university, whereas in Cameroon, sociology goes back to the 1960s, it is taught in five universities, and students can pursue their studies to the doctoral level, with eight doctoral theses having been defended at the University of Yaoudé I from 2003 to 2006 (Nga Ndongo 2010). Similarly, the Democratic Republic of the Congo has many teacher-researchers at the senior level in sociology, whereas in Congo, the department of sociology at Marien Ngouabi University in Brazzaville has only one senior professor at the moment and in Guinea, the University of Sonfonia and the University of Kankan have none (Condé et al. 2005). In the realm of sociological research, in Cameroon Nga Ndongo can speak of schools of thought organized around key figures (2010); Burkina Faso is also relatively productive, having published 189 works from 1995 to 2000, and 171 works from 2000 to 2006, with 32.2 percent and 43.6 percent respectively appearing in peer-reviewed journals (Sawadogo 2010). However, these situations are exceptions, contrasting with countries like Ivory Coast, Senegal, and Madagascar.

Current Debate about the Identity of These Disciplines

Meanwhile, certain sociologists (Malela 1980; Nga Ndongo 2003; Munanga 2008; Nze-Guema 2010) and certain anthropologists (NDiaye 2010) are calling for a sociology or an anthropology that is truly African, emancipated from Western themes, models, research problems, and schools of thought. On the other hand, Abé (2008) proposes rather a sociology of bridges, which builds connections across themes, methodologies, theories, and research programs. For him, this would be a globalized sociology that would be nourished by connections, both here and elsewhere, all the while carrying on the decolonization of African research and scientific production.

This stance in favor of a sociology of bridges is practiced by public spaces of social anthropology in French-speaking Africa — specifically in Niger in the Laboratoire d'Études et de Recherches sur les Dynamiques Sociales et le Développement Local (LASDEL, the Laboratory of Research and Investigations on Social Dynamics and Local Development). Again according to Abé (2008), this new approach operates on the assumption that explanation of the social depends on the construction of a bridge between sociology and anthropology (Olivier de Sardan 2005:

4). It is inspired by the Chicago School and pays particular attention to the construction of knowledge through ethnographic fieldwork as practiced by researchers like Park, Blumer, Redfield, Hughes, and later Goffman, Freidson, or Lemert. This does not mean that the theoretical assumptions of the Chicago School have been appropriated on the local scale, but rather than the LASDEL researchers have built on them to construct new tools of research.[4]

Constraints on Conducting and Disseminating Research

Despite the infatuation with action research beginning in the 1990s, research in French-speaking Africa, especially basic research, takes place under difficult conditions. Examining these issues leads to two observations:

First, there are difficulties at the level of politics, infrastructure and finances, and access to documents—and at the human level (Pilon and Yaro 2001; Diarra 2002; Diallo 2004; ROCARE 2009). For the period 1960–1991, Maclure (1997), writing specifically about educational re-search, underlines the lack of financing and infrastructure, the absence of an environment that encourages research and facilitates training for research, collaboration, and diffusion. Several works since 2000 confirm these constraints. For example, in Mali, Diarra notes the "contradiction between the government's political will to make education a priority and the paucity of means devoted to research in this sector" (2002: 3). Khelfaoui (2009) points out the exodus of researchers to foreign coun-tries and emphasizes the fact that studies in West Africa have shown that the exodus of scientists is of massive scale in contexts marked not only by the material conditions of a difficult life, but also by exclusion, marginalization, and noninvolvement in the future of institutions and of their country in general. In the 1980s and 1990s, countries like Ivory Coast were soaking in opulence, but saw real bleeding of intellectuals, whereas Burkina Faso, counted among the five poorest countries in the world but which practiced a policy of openness to the scientific com-munity, saw little of that phenomenon.

Moreover, researchers (particularly in the French-speaking areas) have limited access to the internet; in fact, in this region there is just one internet user per 5,000 inhabitants compared to the world average of 1 in 40 (Valérien et al. 2001). This restricts their access to research conducted in sub-Saharan Africa and elsewhere that is published in scientific journals and in reports financed by and/or produced by inter-national development agencies.

In addition, according to Tounkara (2005), the notion that decision-making might be systematically enlightened by research results does not break easily into the values of West African educational systems. It runs into several constraints pointed out by researchers, including mistrust by political actors of the critical spirit of some researchers, the difficulty that some researchers have in responding to decision-makers' expectations for results, researchers' fear of being seen as nothing but a "sounding board" for decision-makers, and the material and institutional dependence of researchers on decision-makers. On their side, decision-makers reproach researchers for, among other things, shutting themselves in their "ivory towers," for making recommendations that are too general instead of pragmatic and operational propositions, and for providing support for the conditions imposed by donors.

Second, the lack of functional and dynamic publishing houses and of scientific diffusion across the national or regional level is a major constraint on publication and on the dissemination of research results, particularly in French-speaking countries (Maclure 1997; Diarra 2002; Pilon and Yaro 2001). In contrast to Latin America, sub-Saharan Africa has no large publishing houses, neither for European languages nor for the most widespread African languages (Hausa, Fula, Swahili, Lingala, and others), each of which is spoken by several million people. Most sub-Saharan countries are still obliged to use European languages to gain access to modern technical and scientific knowledge (Teimtoré 2006). As a result, the so-called gray literature is clearly overrepresented within indigenous scholarship. For example, only 8 percent of the 1,056 educational studies identified by Maclure (1997) were published, and the rest were almost completely unknown (Table 13.1).

According to Diarra (2002), the same tendency can be seen in Mali today. The results of my analysis of the eleven curriculum vitae of the researchers of the DSUS likewise show the phenomenon. In the latter, I found 21 mémoires; 2 theses; 110 reports of studies conducted by development agencies, the government, and/or NGOs; and 11 articles or other publications.

Indeed, it is a fairly complicated thing for national authors to publish abroad because of unfamiliarity with the norms of journals of the North, as well as because of the lack of attention paid by such journals to research conducted, sometimes in very different contexts, within African countries. There is also the isolation of researchers, including linguistic isolation, even within the same country or the same region. My examination of the bibliographies of the synthesis of Maclure (1997) revealed that references to English-language publications barely exist in the works of French-speaking researchers, and that English-speaking researchers do not cite French-language studies. Moreover, to publish in a foreign language proves particularly difficult for French-speaking authors in Africa, who have not always mastered languages of the

Table 13.1 | *Nature of West and Central African Research Produced 1960 to 1991*

Percentage of whole	Cameroon	Mali	Togo	Benin	Burkina Faso	Ghana	Sierra Leone	Total
Mémoires	40.6	59.7	53.6	49	82.7	71.9	–	52.8
Theses	6	11.8	1.6	0.5	3.8	–	6.7	8.3
Published documents	15.2	5.6	0.8	4.3	5.4	–	44.4	8
Government reports	16.1	21.5	24.8	14.4	4.2	16.1	–	13.8
Unpublished documents	12	–	4	11.1	–	12	42.2	7.6
Reports of foreign organizations	6.9	–	10.4	10.6	1.2	–	4.4	5.2
Joint reports of governments and foreign organizations	0.5	0.7	2.4	0.5	–	–	2.2	0.7
Seminar papers	2.8	0.7	2.4	9.6	2.7	–	–	3.5

Source: Author's analysis of information from Maclure (1997)

North beyond French. Since English is the dominant language, English-speaking African authors have greater access to publications and to publishing. At the same time, English-speaking countries are more populous, particularly Nigeria. Thus "[i]n sub-Saharan Africa, 75 per cent of academic publications in the Web of Science database come from South African, Nigerian and Kenyan social scientists, and from only a few universities" (UNESCO and ISSC 2010), and in the publications of CODESRIA (*Revue Africaine de Sociologie, Revue de l'Enseignement Supérieur Africain, Afrique et Développement*), English-language articles are clearly more numerous than French-language articles.

The Practice of the Sociology, Anthropology, Ethnography, and Ethnology of Education

Focusing now only on educational research, this section first presents sociological, anthropological, ethnographic, and ethnological studies of education before the 1990s, and then the research achieved by ERNWACA in French-speaking Africa since 1990. The section also comments on the role of international donors in educational research, and illustrates a study that used ethnographic methods.

Promising Beginnings but Late Take-Off of the Sociology and Anthropology of Education

The first studies on education in Africa appeared in the 1920s, but such studies developed especially after independence (around 1960). They came mainly from sociology, and to some extent from history and anthropology (Bouche 1966; Lange 2003) and from the ethnology of education (Marone 1969; Erny 1972). Nonetheless, the sociology of education, in contrast to social anthropology, remained very marginal and benefited from hardly any research except privately conducted studies whose isolation did not permit recognition or diffusion. As a result, despite its promising beginnings, Africanist research in education took off only fairly recently, at the beginnings of the 1990s.

Nevertheless, the predominance of sociology over anthropology influenced the choice of theories, concepts, and themes over the development of this period. The first sociological works in French-speaking Africa fairly often describe African systems from a perspective that is critical (Soulez 1968) and diachronic (Lange 2003). They have enabled us to see, among other things, the new schools of Africa as exogenous and imposed, inherited from colonial school systems (Martin 1971), and the already highly unequal structure of the latter, due notably to the effect of cultural capital (Clignet 1997), gender, region and ethnicity on schooling (Soulez 1968). Thus, Soulez shows that differences in schooling among the different ethnic groups of Ivory Coast was linked to their different visions of the vocational futures of their children and that unequal schooling among girls depended on the conception of social roles for women held by their particular ethnic group.

Much less numerous, the earlier studies, conducted from the 1950s to the 1980s, laid a base for research on African educational systems (themes, methods, or concepts). Thus, in anthropology as in ethnology, studies examined, among other things, traditional foundations of education (Marone 1969; Erny 1972) and Quranic schooling (Santerre 1968). Santerre's studies of Quranic schooling in sub-Saharan Africa led to a theory on the modalities of the transmission of knowledge. Still, it was not until the 1990s that one saw real development of education as a field for research (Lange 2003).

More globally, from 1960 to 1991, according to Maclure (1997), educational research generally focused on the following themes: (1) educational finance and administration; (2) learning and attrition in formal education systems: factors affecting content, quality, and effectiveness; (3) education and socioeconomic integration: employment, community schooling, and social inequality; (4) nonformal and traditional education (burgeoning fields of inquiry); (5) educational reform; and (6) teachers and teaching (with many qualitative studies on this theme).

Development since the 1990s

As indicated above, the preceding decades were marked by a retrenchment of sociology and anthropology in general, by the effects of structural adjustment programs, and by retrenchment of education. In contrast, starting with the 1990s, anthropological research and especially sociological research have been in demand in the domain of education among development agencies, governments, and NGOs, and in civil society. In this new context, ERNWACA has produced many qualitative studies that rely on observation and interviews to report on both classroom education and traditional education (Maclure 1997).

Beginning in the 1990s, studies of the barriers to formal education became most numerous. Inequality of access and of academic success — notably factors limiting girls' access or the continuation of their studies, such as economic constraints (poverty, indirect and direct costs of education), sociocultural factors (gendered socialization, religious beliefs, early marriage), and distance from school — are the most common research themes since 1990. Thus, in Guinea, these factors are treated by a variety of sociological studies (Diallo 1990; Sow 1994; Tambo et al. 1997; Barry, Diallo, and Baldé 1999; Diallo 2004) and by anthropological research (Belle-Isle and Condé 1996; Anderson-Levitt, Bloch, and Soumaré 1998).

The collective work edited by Lange (1998) is likewise focused on various aspects of the education of girls in different countries of French-speaking West Africa, including the educational trajectories of girls in Bamako, Mali (Zoungrana et al. 1998); women, education, and development in Burkina Faso (Gérard 1998); and schooling strategies of girls in Ivory Coast (Proteau 1998). Proteau's study seems to me particularly interesting, revealing that "sexual discrimination impinges as a second level after discrimination which is first and foremost about social class, and which can be illustrated by a series of sharp contrasts in the academic paths of children from different social origins" (1998:. 68). In Mali, let us note in particular the anthropological study of girls' schooling by Gérard (1992).

Since 2000, if the inequalities between boys' and girls' academic careers, focusing more and more on higher education, remain a dominant theme in the studies of ERNWACA, increasing attention is also shown to new information and communication technology, AIDS, distance learning, peace and civic education, the development of competences and employment, African languages, education and culture for regional development and education, alternative schools, and armed conflicts (ROCARE 2004, 2005a, 2005b, 2006, 2008, 2009). For example, note the studies financed by ERNWACA's small grant program aimed at young researchers in Table 13.2 above, as well as the transnational study of information technology conducted in five countries (in thirty-six schools and several internet cafés), whose results were published by a group of nineteen researchers, including sociologists, from Africa, Europe, and North America (Karsenti, Toure, and Tchombe 2009).

The Role of International Donors

The influence of international development agencies in the ERNWACA countries is considerable, and it takes a variety of forms: financing of studies; methodological training for researchers; production of national, transnational, and longitudinal studies; scholarships for advanced degrees; and more. For example, ERNWACA's initial research, the state-of-the-art reviews of research in seven countries, was synthesized and published by a professor at the University of Ottawa (Maclure 1997) and funded by Canada's development agency. Currently, development partners contribute significantly to the program of small grants for research in education and training, and to dissemination and publication of the results of the recipients of this program (Table 13.2). ERNWACA's manual for action research was developed by African and Canadian researchers (ROCARE and UQAM 2003), and several of its transnational studies have been supported in the same way (Maclure 1997; Karsenti, Toure, and Tchombe 2008). This influence by the North can also be observed in the *Revue Africaine de la Recherche en Éducation* (of which volume 1 appeared in 2009), where three of the nine members of the editorial committee are professors at Canadian or American universities, and in the composition of the editorial committee of CODESRIA's *Revue africaine de sociologie,* where seven of its members are from Africa and thirteen from Europe and the United States.[5]

Also beginning with the 1990s, the studies examined suggest that the dominant research themes seem to be increasingly dictated by the institutions that financed the research. According to Samoff and Carrol,

Table 13.2 | *Research Themes, Projects, Researchers, and Funding of Recent Research*

2002	
Funded projects	11 projects by 40 researchers from 11 countries
Research themes and number of projects funded (in parentheses)	How to improve the quality of science courses? (2) To what extent can information technology contribute to improving the quality of education? (3) How to reduce the gender gap in educational attainment? (3) How to reduce the drop-out rate in schools? (1) How to reduce the impact of HIV/AIDS on the quality of education? (1)
Source of funding	International Research & Development Center of Canada and Senegal; Academy for Educational Development (AED); USAID-Washington

2006	
Funded projects	24 projects funded by more than 100 small grants to 80 researchers from 12 countries
Research themes and number of projects funded	The impact of HIV/AIDS on secondary and higher education (4) Contributions of instructional technology to higher education (6) Gender in higher education (2) Corruption and the education of girls (1) The relation between the development of competences and finding employment (1)
Source of funding	Program for Support and Development of Centers of Regional Excellence (PADCER) of the West African Economic and Monetary Union (UEMOA) and the Ministry of Foreign Affairs of the Netherlands (MAEPB)

2007	
Funded projects	21 funded projects by 95 researchers from 14 countries
Research themes and number of projects funded	The role of universities in the development of society in Africa: values higher education (8) Quality and evaluation of teaching innovations (ICT, LMD, e-learning), orientation in higher education (7) Issue of relocation of settlements, cultural heritage of higher education (3) Crises and violence in academia (2) Science education of girls in higher education (1).
Source of funding	PADCER/UEMOA and MAEPB

2008

Funded projects	28 funded projects by 111 researchers from 15 countries
Research themes and number of projects funded	African languages, education, and culture for development and regional integration (5)
	Peace and citizenship education (11)
	Education, development of competences, and employment (11)
	Ecocitizenship and education (1)
Source of funding	PADCER/UEMOA and MAEPB

2009

Funded projects	25 funded projects by 92 researchers from 16 countries
Research themes and number of projects funded	Challenges of the millennium and education for development (7)
	Education and socioeconomic integration (women and development) (5)
	Curricular reform and reinforcement of learning (10)
	Nonformal education: the traditional methods for teaching the Quran (3)
Source of funding	MAEPB

Source: Constructed from information available at http//www.rocare.org/.

"the contemporary World Bank may usefully be understood as a bank, as a development agency, and as a development research institute simultaneously" (2004: 7; compare Anderson-Levitt and Alimasi 2001), and "research on education has become one of the major forms of influence on education in Africa" (2004: 49).

Lange, too, argues in the same direction. According to her, "the timing of publication as well as the institutional origins of studies conducted on girls' schooling reveal the weight of international organization in the production of the discourse on girls' schooling. A large portion of the literature on girls' schooling was produced in the 1990s, principally under the rubric of UNESCO, the World Bank, or UNICEF" (1998: 10–11). Similarly, in their study of educational policy and current educational systems in Burkina Faso, Kaboré et al. note that the majority of the sociological studies "concern, explicitly in their titles, girls' schooling," a real problem but also a topic pursued "for the sake of efficiency in the pursuit of economic development, the education of women having a multiplier effect on other issues (family planning ...)" (2001: 108).

According to Tiemtoré (2006), the expansion of the choice of themes related to information technology in recent years is likewise tied to an international obsession with technology as a lever of development, a means to catch up with more advanced countries.

I would like to nuance analysis of the North's influence, without completely questioning it, in the cases of ERNWACA and of the DSUS. First, ERNWACA does not simply solicit or submit to the influence of universities and external donors, even if it does not yet self-fund the majority of its activities. It seems rather to have developed a strategy of autonomy in broadly diversifying its sources of funds and in orienting its research themes toward the important local preoccupations. To the IDRC (Canada), its first and principal donor, it has added many other partners: USAID, the African Development Bank, the Ministry of Foreign Affairs of the Netherlands, the Association for the Development of Education in Africa (ADEA), SDC (the Swiss Agency for Development and Cooperation), Plan International, FASAF, the West African Economic and Monetary Union, Ecobank Foundation, UIE (UNESCO Institute for Education), OSIWA (Open Society Initiative for West Africa), the University of Montreal, the University of Toronto, the University of Ottawa, and CODESRIA (ROCARE 2005a, 2009).

Furthermore, ERNWACA is becoming more and more a key player in matters of educational research in sub-Saharan Africa. According to ERNWACA,

> the network has succeeded, through its training and through its transnational studies on subjects of importance to education (HIV/AIDS, nonformal education, information technology, literacy campaigns, employment, decentralization, quality ...), in stimulating an African expertise, and in thus creating a community of practice in educational research in West and Central Africa. (Diarra 2009: 13)

In addition, ERNWACA contributes to the development of capacity for educational research among researchers who are its members and within postsecondary institutions, notably through the training and support of multidisciplinary teams of young researchers who receive its program of small grants (ROCARE 2006; see Table 13.2). In fact, there seems to be a strategy of autonomy behind ERNWACA's development, specifically to ask increasingly that its members contribute to funding it and to open itself to other regions and institutions of the North and the South (ROCARE 2009).

It bears repeating that, in the domain of education, the intervention of the North takes place in the context of research that lacks infrastructure, funding, and real support from national governments. Quite clearly, each donor has its own model and interests to promote, but it nonetheless remains true that donors are also sought out, and that ultimately evaluating the total impact of a donor is difficult.

The same is true of the North's contribution to the development of training and research in sociology at the DSUS, at least as I have experienced it. In fact, if the content of the CVs analyzed show that researchers in the department respond quite often to requests from donors (the World Bank, USAID, Germany's GTZ, the European Union, UNICEF, Coopération Française, and others), I notice as well that the contribution of researchers and foreign donors has a significant impact on the development of teaching and research within the department and beyond. Back at the point when I was educated in the DSUS, none of the tenured instructors had received university training at the level of the doctoral or even the DEA (doctoral candidacy), the department of sociology had no research center, and fieldwork was barely mentioned in courses on research methodology. Guinea, which had remained under a revolutionary regime for a long time, opened to Western nations in 1984, and the first scholarships obtained by the department of sociology date only from the first half of the 1990s. Since then, several researchers from the department have obtained a DEA or a master, and a few the doctorate, even though the need for further training still remains substantial. In 2005, the DSUS and the sociology department of the University of Kankan developed a program for a bachelor's degree in sociology in collaboration with consultants from the University of Quebec at Montreal and from other specialized institutions.

As for research, thanks to support from Coopération Française (France's development agency), a Center for the Study of the Student Population and the Employment of Graduates was established at the then-University of Conakry. Its computer equipment was provided by the Canadian Embassy, at the initiative of certain researchers from the department, and its first study was financed by the university itself. The center has contributed to the training of students from the department of sociology, notably through studies developed in the context of research methods courses and through the center directly (Barry, Diallo, Conté, and Diallo 1999; Barry et al. 2000).

As a result, since 2000 the department has included a number of young researchers, of whom some are already preparing their theses overseas. The content of the CVs shows that several of them have participated in studies financed by European or North American institutions or by NGOs or government ministries, and some of them have even succeeded in publishing in foreign French-language and English-language journals.

One Example of Ethnography Learned
and Conducted in an African Context

Compared to my experience as a student and researcher, there has been a very significant development of training and research. Like most other students of my generation, I had no experience of fieldwork, no funding, and no support structure to carry out my thesis at the end of my undergraduate studies. I prepared myself by participating in two studies, one on transportation in Conakry (with a Belgian firm) and the other on domestic energy (for the World Bank under a Danish consultant). The experience and the income from these studies as well as the excellent support from my thesis director, who himself had worked with various foreign researchers, contributed to better preparing me to conduct my first basic research study (Diallo 1990). Afterwards, I participated in several action research projects conducted by researchers in the department (Sow 1994) or by foreign researchers (Cochin, Diallo, and Camara 1994; Hamadache, Diallo, and Baldé 1997; Lacasse et al. 1998). These different collaborations contributed to augmenting my income and to growing and diversifying my experience, particularly in qualitative research. For example, it was by participating in the study Inside Classrooms in Guinea: Girls' Experiences (Anderson-Levitt, Bloch, and Soumaré 1998), that I discovered and practiced the ethnographic approach.

This participation had an impact on my research for my doctoral thesis, which examined the academic careers of girls (particularly those with successful careers) in Africa, specifically in Guinea. In that research, if I used a double quantitative and qualitative approach, the latter was more prominent and essentially ethnographic: observation of living and studying conditions of the students, interviews recorded on audiocassette with students and members of their families, interviews with teachers and academic leaders, focus groups with local leaders, and examination of archives. The quantitative aspect, a questionnaire, served mainly to measure the contribution of the students to family activities (domestic work, work in the fields, small business, and so on) and to assess their socioeconomic status. The idea of observing the interaction of students in class and their conditions at home (lodging, distance traveled to school, distance traveled to get water) and the idea of extending interviews to other members of the family or the community were inspired by an ethnographic approach. I chose not to use a camera due to prior experience (too many hours of viewing!). On the other hand, I made the effort to remain very open to everything that had a connection to schooling, the surrounding community, the students, and the teachers, and to remain in the field as long as I could, making up for a lack of time in the field by recruiting four sociologists as research assistants, and by making two trips, one to prepare work in the field and the other for the principal data gathering, that is, two days and eight to ten days respectively in each site.

Finally, my experience likewise suggests that collaboration between researchers from the North and African researchers on donor-funded studies is not always limited to data collection or the production of reports to the international donors. This kind of research sometimes simulates other projects with independent funding as well as academic publications, as was the case in my later collaborations (Anderson-Levitt and Diallo 2003).

Summary

In short, the emergence of new Africanist studies in education (ethnography and ethnology, school demography) is relatively recent. They are characterized both by a diversity of approaches, fields, and research themes, and by the arrival of new disciplines. The preponderance and the influence of the sociology of education still continues, such that classic concepts from sociology such as field, strategy, representation, actors, game, stakes, and reproduction are appropriated by disciplines such as history and demography (Lange 2003).

Nonetheless, according to UNESCO and ISSC (2010), sub-Saharan Africa's portion of research in sociology and anthropology remains small. In terms of copublications with other parts of the world, from 2004 to 2008, sub-Saharan Africa ranked fifth out of nine in anthropology and seventh out of nine in sociology, nonetheless ranking above South Asia, the Arab states, and Oceania in anthropology. Moreover, the Africanist field of education remains very much centered on the continent and has only rarely managed to develop comparative analyses like those produced in other continents (Lange 2003).

Conclusion

Obviously, no global conclusion on educational research in the French-speaking countries of Africa can be drawn from this chapter, given its limits, but the chapter can contribute toward clarifying the theme of this volume. Despite all the obstacles to their development during the colonial period and after it (the establishment of authoritarian regimes, the social and economic problems), teaching and research have developed significantly in almost all the French-speaking countries of Africa (Hirschhorn and Tamba 2010). Nonetheless, this overview remains in half tones, given the weak production of basic research in those countries.

The literature review reveals the existence of serious national studies that have been carried out under very difficult circumstances, particularly during the 1990s, which address critical educational questions linked to educational policies of the French-speaking nations that belong to ERNWACA. However, these studies have rarely been published, for linguistic reasons and because of the absence of African publishers, and their results have been little used in the development and implementation of government policies.

This literature review also shows that contributions of international development agencies have contributed toward improving the situation. Moreover, the participation of international development agencies has become substantial and varied, to the extent that it increasingly influences the choice of research themes. In fact, international development agencies promote and finance primarily the research themes that interest them, as was the case for the study of girls' schooling in the 1990s and, more recently, for the study of information technology and distance education.

However, analysis of the development of research at ERNWACA and, to a lesser extent, of research and training at the DSUS shows, on the one hand, that the intervention of development agencies has been sought out and responds to a real need, that of filling the long-standing gap in funding and state policy for educational research. In fact, according to Lange (2003), although the first studies of African education appeared in the 1920s, it was above all with national independence that research developed, coming mainly from sociology. However, the sociology of education, as opposed to certain other branches of African research (such as social anthropology, economics, and history) remained very marginal, and has hardly benefited beyond a few studies by individuals whose isolation did not lead to recognition, as attested by the feeble number of publications, mostly in the 1960s. As a result, Africanist research in education would see growth only very recently, since the beginning of the 1990s (Lange 2003).

As for the nature of the research conducted, I did not find ethnographic research as defined by Beach et al. (2004). In general, the studies combined several methods, quantitative and qualitative, and fieldwork did not last as long as envisaged by those authors. The works are generally sociological or multidisciplinary. Nonetheless, several studies surveyed are anthropological or show an ethnographic sensibility.

To conclude, I contend that the independence of an indigenous or national research in the French-speaking countries of Africa is a question of great urgency, given the lack of real state support (in the form of national policies, infrastructure, and its continued funding). Action research, which is often practiced, is quite dependent on financial and scientific support from the North. At the same time, ERNWACA's apparent strategy of seeking autonomy of research vis-à-vis donors is worth emphasizing, although the strategy remains a hypothesis that needs to be pursued by other research.

Acknowledgments

I am grateful to Monsieur Daouda Koman, former director of the department and currently a doctoral student at the University of Laval, for his precious assistance with collecting CVs from my colleges. I also thank Yves Gingras, UQAM, for recent data from UNESCO.

Notes

1. ERNWACA, known in French as ROCARE (Réseau Ouest et Centre Africain de Recherche en Éducation), counts as active members more than 400 researchers in sixteen countries, of which four are English-speaking countries of West Africa (Gambia, Ghana, Sierra Leone, Nigeria) and twelve are French-speaking countries in West Africa (Benin, Burkina Faso, Guinea, Ivory Coast, Mali, Mauritania, Niger, Senegal, and Togo) and in Central Africa (Cameroon, Central African Republic, Congo) (ROCARE 2009). FASAF (Famille et scolarisation en Afrique, or Families and Schooling in Africa) is a thematic network of the Union for the Study of the African Population. ADEA is the Association pour le développement de l'éducation en Afrique, or the Association for the Development of Education in Africa. FAWE is the Forum for African Women Educationalists. CREA is the Consortium pour la recherche économique en Afrique, or the Consortium for Economic Research in Africa.
2. A mémoire is a research report defended before a faculty jury in order to obtain a DES or DEA degree, which are roughly equivalent to advancement to doctoral candidacy in the United States. Here, thesis or dissertation are terms used interchangeably to refer to significant pieces of research defended before a faculty jury to obtain a doctorate.
3. See http://www.codesria.org/spip.php?rubrique1&lang=en.
4. See http://www.lasdel.net.
5. See http://www.codesria.org/spip.php?rubrique42&lang=en.

Bibliography

Abé, Claude. 2008. "La globalisation de la sociologie en situation africaine: entre résistances et dynamiques de structuration." *Canadian Journal of Sociology/Cahiers canadiens de sociologie* 33, no. 3: 575–606.

Anderson-Levitt, Kathryn M., and Ntal-I'Mbirwa Alimasi. 2001 "Are Pedagogical Ideals Embraced or Imposed? The Case of Reading Instruction in the Republic of Guinea." In *Policy as Practice*, ed. Margaret Sutton and Bradley A. Levinson. Norwood, NJ: Ablex.

Anderson-Levitt, Kathryn M., Marianne Bloch, and Aminata Maiga Soumaré. 1998. "Inside Classrooms in Guinea: Girls' Experiences." In *Women and Education in Sub-Sahara Africa*, ed. Marianne Bloch, Josephine A. Beoku-Betts, and B. Robert Tabachnick. Boulder, CO: Lynne Rienner.

Anderson-Levitt, Kathryn M., and Boubacar Bayero Diallo. 2003. "Teaching by the Book in Guinea." In *Local Meanings, Global Schooling*, ed. Kathryn Anderson-Levitt. New York: Palgrave Macmillan.

Balandier, Georges. 1955. *Sociologie des Brazzavilles noires*. Paris: Cahiers de la Fondation nationale des sciences politiques.

Barry, Alpha Amadou Bano, Mamadou Gando Barry, Alhassane Baldé, Thierno Souleymane Sow, Aïssata Bamaba, Mohamed Diaby, Michèle Sona Koundouno. 2000. *Profil des étudiants de première année de l'université de Conakry (année universitaire 1999-2000)*. Conakry: Observatoire de la population étudiante et sur l'insertion professionnelle de l'Université de Conakry.

Barry, Alpha Amadou Bano, Boubacar Bayero Diallo, and Mercedes Baldé. 1999. *La participation des femmes à l'enseignement supérieur et à la recherche en Guinée*. Conakry, Guinea: PADES.

Barry, Alpha Amadou Bano, Boubacar Bayero Diallo, Ibrahima Moriah Conté, and Mamadou Cellou Diallo. 1999. *Rapport d'évaluation des programmes offerts par les institutions d'enseignement supérieur de Guinée*. Conakry, Guinea: Observatoire de la population étudiante et sur l'insertion professionnelle de l'Université de Conakry.

Beach, Dennis, Francesca Gobbo, Bob Jeffrey, Geri Smyth, Geoff Troman, and the ECER Ethnography Network Coordinators. 2004. "Ethnography of Education in a European Educational Researcher Perspective. Introduction." *European Educational Research Journal* 3: 534–38.

Belle-Isle, Lucie, and Kéfing Condé. 1994. *Monographie de la femme en Guinée*. Conakry Banque africaine de développement, Fonds africain de développement, département central des projets, Unité femme et développement.

Bonhomme, Julien. 2007. "Anthropologue et/ou initié l'anthropologie gabonaise á l'épreuve du Bwiti." *Journal des anthropologues* 110–11 (2007): 207–26.

Bouche, Denise. 1966. "Les écoles françaises au Soudan à l'époque de la conquête, 1884–1900." *Cahiers d'Études africaines* 6, no. 22: 228–67.

Clignet, Rémi. 1997. *Sociologue entre Afrique et États-Unis. Trente ans de terrains comparés*. Paris: Éditions Karthala.

Cochin, Jacques, Bayero Diallo and Campel Camara. 1994. "Des Vues au pays de Kinkon." Research done under the Centre d'Étude à l'Environnement et au Développement de Guinée. MEPU/FP de Guinée, Coopération française.

Condé, Kéfing, Mohamed Campel Camara, Daouda Koman, Michèle Sonah Koundouno, and Sadio Diallo. 2005. *Dossier de rénovation du programme de licence en sociologie.* Departments of Sociology at the University of Conakry and the University of Kankan.

Copans, Jean. 1971. "Pour une histoire et une sociologie des études africaines." *Cahiers des Études africaines* 11, no. 43: 422–47.

Diallo, Boubacar Bayero. 1990. "Étude de la déperdition scolaire dans un collège de Conakry II. Application Le collège1 de Donka." Thesis for diplôme de fin d'études supérieures, University of Conakry, Guinea.

———. 2004. "Parcours scolaire des filles en Afrique le cas de la Guinée." PhD diss., University of Quebec at Montreal (UQAM).

Diarra, Mamadou Lamine. 2009. "Idées." *Bulletin d'information du ROCARE,* no. 14 (April). ROCARE.

Diarra, Sékou Oumar. 2002. "Bilan de la recherche en éducation au Mali." Paper presented at the colloquium La recherche face aux défis de l'éducation. Ouagadougou, Burkina Faso, 19–22 November.

Diédhiou, Paul. 2010. "La sociologie au Sénégal: journalisme sociologique et sociologie 'portative.'" In *La sociologie francophone en Afrique. État des lieux et enjeux,* ed. Monique Hirschhorn and Moustapha Tamba. Paris: Karthala.

Diop, Amadou Sarr. 2007. "Pluralité et logiques des paradigmes dans le champ des théories africanistes du développement. Etude des questions épistémologiques et idéologiques." PhD diss., University Gaston Berger, Saint Louis, Senegal, U.F.R. Lettres et sciences humaines, section sociologie, et les Facultés universitaires catholiques de Mons.

Diop, Cheikh Anta. 1963. "Sociologie africaine et méthodes de recherche." *Présence Africaine. Revue Culturelle du monde noir,* no. 48: 180–81.

Erny, Pierre. 1972. *L'enfant et son milieu en Afrique noire. Essai sur l'éducation traditionnelle.* Paris: Payot.

Essè, Amouzou. 2008. *La sociologie de ses origines à nos jours.* Paris: L'Harmattan.

Gérard, Étienne. 1992. "L'école déclassée. Une étude anthropologique de la scolarisation des filles au Mali. Cas des sociétés malinkés." PhD diss., Paul Valéry University, Montpellier III.

———. 1998. "Femmes, instruction et développement au Burkina Faso. Incertitudes africaines." In *L'école et les filles en Afrique, une scolarisation sous-conditions,* ed. Marie-France Lange. Paris: Karthala.

Hamadach Ali, Boubacar Bayero Diallo, and Mouctar Balde. 1997. *L'analyse de la situation de l'analphabétisme en Guinée.* Conakry, Guinea: Unicef-Guinée.

Hirschhorn, Monique, and Moustapha Tamba, eds. 2010. *La sociologie francophone en Afrique. État des lieux et enjeux.* Paris, Karthala.

Kaboré, Idrissa, Jean-François Kobiane, Marc Pilon, Fernand Sanou, and Salimata Sanou. 2001. "Le Burkina Faso Politiques éducatives et système éducatif actuel." In *La demande d'éducation en Afrique. État des connaissances et perspectives de recherche,* ed. Marc Pilon and Yaro Yacouba. Dakar: UEPA/UAPS.

Karsenti, Thierry, Kathryn Toure, and Therese M. S. Tchombe. 2008. *Repenser l'éducation à l'aide des TIC.* University of Montreal: CRDI, ROCARE.

Khelfaoui, Hocine. 2009. "Le Processus de Bologne en Afrique. Globalisation ou retour à la 'situation coloniale'?" *Journal of Higher Education in Africa* 7, no. 1–2: 1–20.

Kolle, Samuel Same. 2007. *Naissance et paradoxes du discours anthropologique africain*. Paris: L'Harmattan.

Kourouma, Passy. 1991. *Étude portant sur les aspects socioculturels et socio-économiques de la scolarisation des filles au niveau du primaire Cas de la Guinée*. Conakry, Guinea: Secrétariat d'État à l'Enseignement Pré-Universitaire.

Lacasse, Denis, Boubacar Bayero Diallo, Gilbert Luc, Pierre Joseph Kamano, and James Toliver. 1998. *Analyse de la distribution des manuels scolaires en Guinée*. Conakry, Guinea: A.E.D.

Lange, Marie-France, ed. 1998. *L'école et les filles en Afrique. Scolarisation sous conditions*. Paris, Karthala.

———. 2003. "Vers de nouvelles recherches en éducation." *Cahiers d'études africaines* 1–2, no. 169–70: 7–17.

Maclure, Richard. 1997. *Négligée et sous-estimée, la recherche en éducation en Afrique centrale et Afrique occidentale une synthèse d'études nationales du ROCARE*. Bamako, Mali: ROCARE. (Also published in English as *Overlooked and Undervalued: A Synthesis of* ERNWACA *Reviews on the State of Education Research in West and Central Africa*. Washington, DC: USAID Bureau for Africa/Office of Sustainable Development.)

Malela, Mwabila. 1980. "Pour une relecture de la sociologie à la lumière de la théorie de la dépendance." In *La dépendance de l'Afrique et les moyens pour y remédier*, Acts of the fourth edition of the International Congress of African Studies, Kinshasa, 12–16 December 1978. Paris: ACCT-Berger.

Marcoux, Richard. 1998. "Entre l'école et la calabasse. La sous-scolarisation des filles et mise au travail à Bamako." In *L'école et les filles en Afrique*, ed. Marie-France Lange. Paris: Karthala.

Marone, Oumar. 1969. "Essai sur les fondements de l'éducation sénégalaise à la lumière des métaphores aqueuses de la langue Wolof." *Bulletin de l'IFAN*, no. 3: 787–852.

Martin J.-Y. 1971. " L'école et les sociétés traditionnelles au Cameroun septentrional," *Cahiers Orstom* (Sciences humaines) 8, no. 3: 295–335.

Mbilinyi, M. J. 2000. "Les défis de l'Éducation de Base, Recherche et Partenariat. Basic Education Renewal Research Initiative for Poverty Alleviation." Paper presented at the Conference BERRIPA, 3–5 November, Arusha, Tanzania.

Munanga, Albert Muluma. 2008. *Sociologie générale et africaine: les sciences sociales et les mutations des sociétés africaines*. Paris, L'Harmattan.

NDiaye, Lamine. 2010. "L'anthropologie africaine, entre mimétisme et routine." In *La sociologie francophone en Afrique. État des lieux et enjeux*, ed. Monique Hirschhorn and Moustapha Tamba. Paris: Karthala.

N'Doye, Mamadou. 2001. "L'histoire du développement scolaire vue d'Afrique in CEPEC de Lyon. Vingt ans de formation et d'éducation." *Actes du colloque international 15 et 16 septembre 1997*. Lyon: CEPEC.

Nga Ndongo, Valentine. 2003. *Plaidoyer pour la sociologie africaine*. Yaoundé, Cameroon: Presses Universitaires.

———. 2010. "La sociologie en Afrique central: États des lieux, problèmes et perspectives." In *La sociologie francophone en Afrique. État des lieux et enjeux*, ed. Monique Hirschhorn and Moustapha Tamba. Paris: Karthala.

Nze-Guema, Pierre-Fidèle. 2010. "La construction du champs scientifique sociologique en Afrique." In *La sociologie francophone en Afrique. État des lieux et enjeux*, ed. Monique Hirschhorn and Moustapha Tamba. Paris: Karthala.

Olivier de Sardan, Jean-Pierre. 2005. "De la nouvelle anthropologie du développement à la socio-anthropologie des espaces publics africains." Paper presented at a colloquium of APAD on "Entrepreneurs et entreprises en quête de normes," Yaoundé, Cameroon, 11–13 October.

Pilon, Marc, Étienne Gérard, and Yacouba Yaro. 2001. "Introduction." In *La demande d'éducation en Afrique. État des connaissances et perspectives de recherche*, ed. Marc Pilon and Yaro Yacouba. Dakar, Senegal: UEPA/UAPS.

Pilon, Marc, and Yacouba Yaro, eds. 2001. *La demande d'éducation en Afrique. État des connaissances et perspectives de recherche.* Dakar, Senegal: UEPA/UAPS.

Proteau, Laurence. 1998. "Itinéraires précaires et expériences singulières. La scolarisation féminine en Côte d'Ivoire." In *L'école et les filles en Afrique, une scolarisation sous conditions*, ed. Marie-France Lange. Paris: Karthala.

ROCARE. 2004. *Session de stratégie du ROCARE 2004/ERNWACA2004 Strategy session, septembre 2004*, Segou, Mali.

———. 2005a. *Rapport annuel ROCARE 2003–2004.* Bamako, Mali: ROCARE.

———. 2005b. *Analyse de la contribution de l'éducation non formelle à la prévention du VIH/SIDA.* Rapport Final de Atelier Régional Africain, December 5–9, Kampala, Uganda.

———. 2006. Communiqué ROCARE du 25 octobre 2006. Bamako, Mali: ROCARE.

———. 2008. Rapport annuel. Bamako, Mali: ROCARE.

———. 2009. *Bulletin d'information du ROCARE*, no. 14 (April). Bamako, Mali: ROCARE.

ROCARE and UQAM. 2003. *Participer au changement en éducation. Manuel de recherche-action pour les chercheurs et praticiens en Afrique de l'Ouest et du Centre.* Bamako, Mali: ROCARE.

Samoff, Joel, and Bidemi Carrol. 2004. "Conditions, Coalitions and Influence: The World Bank and Higher Education in Africa." Paper presented at the Comparative and International Education Society, Salt Lake City, 8–12 March.

Santerre, Renaud. 1968. *L'école coranique de la savane camerounaise.* Paris: EPHE.

Sawadogo, Ram Christophe. 2010. "La sociologie au Bourkina Faso: accompagnement du développement, production de connaissances et formation des cadres." In *La sociologie francophone en Afrique. État des lieux et enjeux*, ed. Monique Hirschhorn and Moustapha Tamba. Paris: Karthala.

Soulez, Philippe. 1968. "Sociologie de la population scolaire en Côte d'Ivoire." *Cahiers d'études africaines* 9, no. 36: 527–45.

Sow, Alhassane. 1994. *Enquête sur la scolarisation des filles en milieu rural Rapport de synthèse.* Conakry, Guinea: MEPU-FP.

Tambo, Mercy, Ibrahima Sory Diallo, Djenabou Barry, and Alpha Aliou Barry. 1997. *Genre et fréquentation scolaire au primaire en Guinée.* Brighton, UK: Institute of Development Studies, University of Sussex.

Tiemtoré, Windpouiré Zacharia. 2006. "Les technologies de l'information et de la communication dans l'éducation en Afrique subsaharienne du mythe à la réalité. Le cas des écoles de formation des enseignants au Burkina Faso." PhD diss., University of Rennes II and University of Ouagadougou.

Tounkara, Brehima. 2005. *L'expérience de la collaboration entre les chercheurs du ROCARE et le Ministère de l'Éducation de base pour la reforme éducative au Mali.* Paper given at L'atelier de réflexion et d'échanges sur la synergie entre chercheurs et décideurs dans le monde de l'éducation au Burkina Faso. Ouagadougou, January 27 and 28.

UNESCO. 1995. *Rapport mondial sur l'éducation.* Paris: UNESCO.

UNESCO and ISSC (International Social Science Council). 2010. *World Social Science Report.* Paris: UNESCO Publishing and ISSC.

Valérien, Jean, Jacques Guidon, Jacques Wallet, and Etienne Brunswic. 2001. *Enseignement à distance et apprentissage libre en Afrique subsaharienne. État des lieux dans les pays francophones.* Tunis: ADEA.

Zoungrana, Cécile-Marie, Joël Tokindang, Richard Marcoux, and Mamadou Konaté. 1998. "La trajectoire scolaire des filles à Bamako. Un parcours semé d'embûches." In *L'école et les filles en Afrique,* ed. Marie-France Lange. Paris: Karthala.

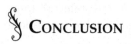 CONCLUSION

ETHNOGRAPHY OF EDUCATION
AROUND THE WORLD
A Thousand Varieties, a Shared Paradigm

Agnès van Zanten

Although there are many things that we can learn through detailed analyses of the development and present state of the art of ethnography of education in a wide array of countries around the world such as the ones included in this rich volume, I have chosen to focus on only two in these concluding comments. The first has to do with the epistemology of this curious scientific object, "ethnography," and how its founding tenets are sustained, extended, questioned, or transformed by its use in very different scientific contexts, and especially by the way it has "traveled" from the countries where it first developed to others, has been appropriated by various disciplines and has become a routine practice in diverse academic institutional contexts. The second has to do with ethnography's embeddedness into different social and political contexts and the way this might modify its main subjects of study and the ethical positions of researchers vis-à-vis social problems, policies, and politics.

In doing so, I am trying to adopt an ethnographer's perspective by constructing ethnography as a global device and ethnographic studies in different countries as local realities in the same way that ethnographers are now becoming interested in how global trends and policies undergo various forms of "creolization" when they are enacted in different contexts, giving way to different local meanings (Anderson-Levitt 2003). I am also trying to provide a "grounded" interpretation of how scientific theories and methods interact with social worlds (Glaser and Strauss 1967), using the narratives provided by each author as a particular kind of empirical material. The analogy with real ethnographic work is nevertheless more metaphorical than real due to two serious shortcomings. The first concerns the limited amount of information that each author could provide for her or his home country or related set of countries and my inability to supplement it with relevant information from other sources. The second is the considerable variation in focus and scope from one narrative to another.

Ethnography of Education as a University Discipline in World Perspective

Although, as we all know, this is also the case in "true" fieldwork, it would therefore be extremely pretentious to use the material of this book to build a theoretical model of ethnography as an academic discipline and, even more, to make generalizations about academic subjects and communities. However, the comparison of detailed presentations of ethnographic work in various countries provides interesting insights into different dimensions relevant to the study of disciplines, such as the analysis of their life cycles and of processes of hybridization across countries and across bodies of knowledge.

A Dual Origin and a Common Migration

The research studies on which the different chapters of this book are built do not enjoy a clear status in the social sciences. Even from a constructivist perspective considering all disciplines as conventions resting on the activities of communities with a limited life cycle (Heilbron 2001), it remains unclear whether we are talking about a subdiscipline, anthropology of education—that is, about a particular form of association between a subject and a technical instrument, or about a method, ethnography, that can either be constructed as encompassing all forms of qualitative inquiry or as a distinctive qualitative approach that might be used by different scientific communities. The comparison of the terms used by the various authors of this volume shows epistemological differences: some refer exclusively to the anthropology of education, others solely to the ethnography of education, while some use both terms to designate the work of the same or different scientific communities in their home country.

Part of the explanation for this lack of consensus on the academic status of the body of knowledge under consideration lies in the dual history of ethnographic studies in education recalled by Delamont in her chapter on anthropology of education in the Anglophone world. The anthropology of education as a subdiscipline is an American invention (Henriot-van Zanten and Anderson-Levitt 1992). It emerged from the work of cultural anthropologists interested in socialization and enculturation in "exotic" societies from the 1930s to the 1950s. It took its modern form when anthropologists came back home in the late 1950s and in the 1960s, "pushed" by decolonization and reduced funding for research abroad and "pulled" by the opening of new positions in the expanding American university system, and started to focus on their own society, on urban communities and on formal schooling. A typical process of academic institutionalization then took place, characterized first by the production of some important case studies, followed by the publication of major readers, such as the different volumes edited by George Spindler, and by the creation of the Council on Anthropology and Education and of a journal, *Anthropology and Education Quarterly.* By the early 1980s, when I myself was studying for a master's degree at Stanford and following the Spindlers' seminars, anthropology of education had become a fully recognized and at the time extremely popular subdiscipline.

However, the methods and techniques associated with ethnography were part of the professional repertoire not only of American anthropologists but also of American sociologists. The scientific movement known as the "Chicago school of sociology," whose key works were produced at the same time as the major studies in cultural anthropology, built its identity, in the same way as anthropology, around naturalistic inquiry in local milieus, in-depth fieldwork, observation, and interviews (Chapoulie 2001). Although this kind of sociological inquiry was initially invented at the University of Chicago where there was not yet a clear dividing line between anthropology and sociology, the two traditions of qualitative research developed separately in the United States. This separation was maintained when the anthropology and the sociology of education emerged as separate subdisciplines within anthropology and sociology and have stayed so since then in spite of the fact that some researchers and some major works have sometimes managed to cross boundaries. Without enjoying a monopoly on qualitative studies in education, anthropology has nevertheless held a preeminent position as regard to sociology in the United States because in sociology, quantitative approaches have been more encouraged in academic circles and enjoyed more social visibility.

This is not the case in the United Kingdom. There, although a few researchers trained in social anthropology did some important ethnographic work on schools in the 1970s, sociologists have conducted most of the ethnographic studies of communities, schools, and classrooms. The sociology of education emerged as a discipline in the United Kingdom in the 1950s thanks to a series of studies carried out in the quantitative tradition of "political arithmetic" developed by the London

School of Economics and imported into education by researchers such as A. H. Halsey. The positivistic stance, the macrolevel of inquiry and the econometric tools of these studies were, however, strongly criticized by the "New Sociology of Education." Researchers that became part of that movement revived the tradition of qualitative studies in the vein of the Chicago school of sociology and took their inspiration from symbolic interactionism, ethnomethodology, phenomenology, and the sociology of knowledge. And although the New Sociology was essentially a label for a heterogeneous set of studies and writings, and one that lasted only a decade (1970–1980) before undergoing in turn strong criticism from other currents, especially neo-Marxism (Forquin 1983), it led to the production of important and original pieces of qualitative research and had a lasting impact on legitimating the use of qualitative approaches in the sociology of education.

This already tortuous historical trajectory of ethnographic studies is rendered more complex in both countries by the migration of many anthropologists of education in the United States and sociologists of education in the United Kingdom from their disciplinary departments to departments in education in the 1970s and 1980s. They were drawn by new opportunities for teaching and research fostered by the development of teacher training designed to cope with mass expansion of secondary education and by the increasing demand for analyses of educational settings and programs from educational decision makers. This migration strongly contributed to the academic development and the social legitimacy of both subdisciplines. However, as pointed out by Delamont for the US anthropology of education—but this is also true to a lesser extent in the case of the UK sociology of education—it has entailed a divorce from the mother disciplines reflected in the lack of reactivity to new trends and controversies in anthropology and sociology and in the development of separate conferences, publications, and audiences.

At the same time, this movement does not seem to have encouraged, as in other cases of "scientific migration" (Ben-David and Collins 1966), the creation of a new autonomous scientific domain based on novel conceptual constructions. This reflects the fact that education is not a discipline—meaning an organization reflecting a long process of professionalization of scholarly knowledge (Fabiani 2006)—but a field of study at the intersection between academic and social interests. The emergence of a coherent body of knowledge is constrained both by the variety and heterogeneity of the disciplines that contribute to the understanding of educational processes and by the fact that, given the social interest in these processes, research studies are frequently driven by the demands of teachers, policy makers, and various stakeholders with a focus on problems, rather than objects of study, and on solutions rather than interpretations (van Zanten 2004a).

Hybridization Worldwide

Given the preeminent position of the United States and the United Kingdom in education research, these two clusters of knowledge, as several authors of chapters in this book point out, have been the major sources of inspiration for the development of ethnographic studies in education in other countries—although in some of them there have been periods when they have been put at a distance as "colonial" by researchers, as in Argentina in the 1960s, or banned as "bourgeois" by political authorities, as in China during the Cultural Revolution. Although both research communities are essentially inwardly oriented, communicate little with each other, and do not have clear expansion strategies, they have become global centers for a worldwide audience. As noted in several chapters of the book, their influence has traveled in various ways.

In the past a major mediating factor has been the work of American anthropologists and British sociologists of education abroad. Although this dimension still continues to play a role, a more crucial factor has always been, and is even more today given the increasing internationalization of students' trajectories in higher education, the circulation of students from their home country to the United States and the United Kingdom, especially of graduate students. These students, after having completed master's degrees or carried out doctoral dissertations, return to their country and play, as described by Gobbo in her chapter on Italy, to varying degrees, the role of "idea brokers" (Smith 1991) not only through their own Anglophone-inspired research work and that of their students but through "scientific entrepreneurship." This includes conferences and seminars involving invited foreign scholars or organized around their work as well as the translation of major works or collections of articles. A third form of mediation is the publication of review essays and "states of the art" bringing different ethnographic studies together. Less common but more powerful are joint programs of research such as the ones mentioned by Ouyang between the United States and China. In all these activities, the local ethnographer has an important role in making sense of foreign research in his or her country.

Of course, in countries where English is the mother tongue or where academic communities are encouraged to read and publish in Anglophone journals, there is less need for brokering and mediation of this kind, leading to a more diffuse but generally more powerful influence

of research in the United States and the United Kingdom on local pro-
ductions. This is the case, for instance, among the countries considered
in this volume, of Israel, where ethnographic research in education—
mostly conducted as in the United States and the United Kingdom in
university education departments and teacher-training colleges—is
produced by researchers strongly influenced by the US anthropology
of education and, to a lesser extent, by European sociological traditions.
Receptiveness to Anglophone research is encouraged by various factors but especially by the lack of research traditions in a young country
where the academic community comprises many researchers born and
trained abroad. A similar but more complex case is that of the Scandinavian countries, where English is also widely spoken; there, at least one
of the three strands of research analyzed in the chapter by Anderson
et al. on school ethnographies seems to have been initially strongly influenced by UK sociological qualitative studies before anthropologists
"stepped in," bringing the influence of American anthropological ethnographic studies.

At the opposite side we find countries such as Germany and France,
which have occupied leading positions in research in the social sciences
at some points in history and developed established traditions different
from the pragmatic philosophical orientation that is behind much of
the anthropological and sociological production of qualitative studies
in the United States and the United Kingdom. This leads researchers in
these countries to show a relative lack of interest in Anglophone ethnographic studies and to passively resist their "colonizing" influence. The
limited national ethnographic production in these two countries is also
due to the way in which research traditions have influenced the organization of university disciplines. For instance, in French universities,
anthropology has traditionally occupied a subordinate position and the
influence of structuralism did not lead to a great interest in socialization.
It was the work of Laurence Wylie, an American anthropologist, who
conducted two famous ethnographic studies in the American tradition
of cultural anthropology in two French villages in the 1950s and 1960s,
that first analyzed educational practices at home and school; however,
with a few exceptions, these studies have been ignored by researchers
interested in education. Sociological qualitative analysis, on the other
hand, appeared only after what Chapoulie (1991) has called "the second
foundation" of French sociology after World War II, which was stimulated, among other factors, by the fact that many of those who became
the French leading sociologists in the 1960s (Raymond Boudon, Pierre
Bourdieu, Michel Crozier, Alain Touraine, among others) had the opportunity to go to American universities and brought back with them

new quantitative and qualitative methods of inquiry. The development of ethnographic studies in the sociology of education was not immediate however, as analyzed in the chapter in this volume by Raveaud and Draelants. Moreover, although review essays acknowledged the "discovery" of US and UK ethnographic studies in education in the 1980s and 1990s, it would be incorrect to assume that a real hybridization between Anglophone and French traditions has taken place, as most of the qualitative studies remain firmly embedded in French theoretical and methodological traditions.

Some countries can be located "in between" in the sense that they seem to have both incorporated Anglophone influences and developed a solid national tradition. The most interesting such case presented in the volume is that of Japan, where there is a long history of ethnographic studies dating back to the 1950s whose development is related to the fact that Japan, more than other countries—probably because of the homogeneous and, from a Western perspective, "exotic" character of its cultural model and linked school system—attracted US anthropologists of education very early. Their influence, but also that of the British "new" sociologists of education—thanks among other things to the translation of the famous reader, *Power and Ideology in Education* (Karabel and Halsey 1977) into Japanese in 1980—seems to be a major factor in the development of ethnographic studies of education. However, the size of the national research communities, their productivity, and the networks—scientific societies, conferences, and publications—they have been able to create both within educational sociology and educational psychology—educational anthropology is not mentioned in the chapter by Minoura—seem to have given birth to a specific national milieu. Unfortunately, this milieu is little known outside Japan because most of the published works have not been translated into English or other languages.

National ethnographic studies in education, whether or not they result from a hybridization between Anglophone and national influences, are embedded in specific scientific and organizational research communities, adding yet more complexity to the more and more blurred distinction in the Anglophone world between anthropological, sociological, and "educationist" ethnographies of education. In many countries, for instance, it is clear that anthropology enjoys a specific, frequently marginal status among higher-education disciplines due to its links with folklore—this being particularly the case in countries under German influence—and with history as a discipline, and to its initial development in museums rather than in university departments. This has had various consequences. In Mexico, Brazil, and Argentina, it seems to have favored a creative incorporation of the historical dimension in ethnographic studies of education concerning both concepts and methods, as for instance the use of archives and oral history. In China, it has contributed, until recently, to the marginalization of anthropologists, seen exclusively as specialists on ethnic minorities established apart from universities in faraway areas, vis-à-vis their colleagues in other social sciences. The position of sociology is frequently more established. However, qualitative sociology is not always recognized as an equal to quantitative sociology. It can be, as in China, criticized overtly for being overinterpretative and lacking "solid scientific evidence" or derided more subtly, as in France, where lay people, editors, and journalists, and even some academics equate qualitative research with philosophical or political essays, based on the presumption that it does not draw on empirical research.

In many countries, too, as in the United States and the United Kingdom, a large proportion of ethnographic studies is produced in departments of education and in many cases by multidisciplinary teams, which bring with them new theories, concepts, and methods from different disciplines, especially sociology, anthropology, social and educational psychology, history, and linguistics. Different combinations arise according to the subjects under study. As pointed out in the chapter by Gomes and Gomes, in Brazil, for instance, studies of youth condition and identity have a strong interface with sociology, while researchers doing studies of childhood engage in dialogue with child and educational psychologists and researchers on black identity with social psychologists. Although, without more information, it is difficult to assess what enrichment has been gained from the interaction of these different disciplines, it is important to distinguish situations where these multidisciplinary teams arise because of common research interests and those where they arise because of organizational constraints. The latter is frequently the case in countries, such as those of Central Europe studied in the chapter by Eröss, or of Francophone West Africa examined in the chapter by Diallo, where research in the social sciences in the area of education is not well anchored in universities for political and financial reasons and is thus strongly driven by international foundations and agencies interested in applied research combining different disciplinary perspectives as well as quantitative and qualitative methods.

Ethnography of Education and Social Realities around the World

The subjects addressed by ethnographers of education and their value systems around the world allow us to see not only differences in disciplinary perspectives but also differences related to the specific features of countries and research communities. While this is true for all social sciences, there is more to be learned from the comparisons of bodies of knowledge that, as ethnographical interpretations, are deliberately strongly contextualized and centered around local meanings.

Nations and Welfare States, Class and Multicultural Societies

The comparative analysis of ethnographic studies conducted in each country clearly shows a link between the subjects chosen for study by researchers and the social and political concerns predominant in each country. For instance, in many national settings, ethnographers of education, following classical studies in cultural anthropology, have conducted work on rites, rituals, and civic ceremonies in schools and other educational contexts. Interest on these aspects of social life appears nevertheless higher in nations such as Germany, where there is a strong focus on the sharing of a common culture as the basis for national social and political integration, than in France, where the focus has been since the French Revolution on individual political citizenship. Interest in civic rituals appears even greater in countries where there are debates about what are the legitimate constituents of national identity—for instance, about the present significance of the heritage from native indigenous groups as in Mexico—or in young countries such as Israel, where politicians as well as teachers feel it is necessary to fabricate a new national identity to prevent the formation of permanent cultural enclaves.

Ethnographers of education have also produced many studies on schools and teachers, but from very different perspectives. The focus on the integrative dimension of schooling and of teachers' work appears stronger in countries concerned about the transmission of what is—rightly or wrongly—conceived as a common and homogenous culture. This is the case in Japan where, according to Minoura, important research studies have been conducted on the comprehensive hold of schools on children through multiple academic and social activities and on the global ascendancy of teachers over students through their various guidance activities. Focus on schools and teachers as agents of change, on the contrary, is more common in countries such as China where the present political regime gives high priority to the transformation of social institutions, including schools, and to the elimination of past legacies that interfere with economic development.

It is also possible to hypothesize from the evidence provided in some chapters that the more the nations in consideration are close to the model of postindustrial societies characterized, among other things, by a plurality of values, the more it is possible to see a displacement of the researchers' interest from schools and teachers towards students and young people. Although this displacement is observable in many countries, because of the development of distinctive youth cultures and movements in and out of schools, it is more marked, among the national spaces considered in this book, in the Scandinavian countries because their welfare regimes value and support youth autonomy more than do others. The emphasis on this dimension seems to have encouraged research to move from analysis of the unidirectional socialization role of schools to that of bidirectional interactions between youngsters and adults in a larger array of institutional settings but also in noninstitutional settings and in families.

Ethnographers of education have traditionally been less interested in the role of schools in social stratification due both to a conventional division of labor between anthropologists and sociologists, where the first have constructed their professional territory around "culture" and the second around "social structure," and to a distribution of roles between quantitative sociologists studying "social stratification" and qualitative sociologists studying class cultures. As many of the ethnographers around the world cited in this volume have been more influenced by US anthropology of education than by UK or other European sociologies of education, especially by recent works on class and education, they clearly have given a priority to the analysis of cultural groups. This is less the case, however, in Francophone Belgium and Switzerland because of the influence of French research. Also, although limited, new efforts to combine creatively culture and social structure, as has been the case in the work of the US anthropologist of education John Ogbu—who has exerted an important influence in many countries including some not mentioned in this book (Gibson 1997)—seem nevertheless promising, as in the case of research in Argentina cited in the chapter by Neufeld that focuses on the loss of status of various non-European poor immigrant groups from Latin America or Asia.

The focus on culture has led researchers in some countries, as in the United States, to devote their attention to "internal colonies," that is to native groups that have traditionally been marginalized. This has logically been the case in countries where there were indigenous peoples previous to colonization processes, as in Mexico or Brazil, but also in countries like China where the Han-dominant group has traditionally given little attention to and has actively excluded diverse minorities and where there is a stark distinction between the social conditions of urban and rural populations, with rural migrants constituting another minority group. This has also been the case in Europe. Gobbo, for instance, talks about ethnography in Italy focusing in the 1960s both on the different languages and cultures that characterized Italy at that time, which were ignored by educational and political authorities pursuing national unification, and on poverty and illiteracy in Southern Italy.

With more and more countries becoming multicultural, many ethnographic studies are devoting attention both to "involuntary minorities," to use Ogbu's term, and to newly arrived immigrant groups. Indeed it is the perceived problems and needs of these groups that has stimulated the funding and development of many ethnographic studies around the world since the 1970s. Nevertheless, because the perspectives of government, funding agencies, educational decision makers, and teachers are able to penetrate and "colonize" educational research to a larger extent than research in other domains, the focus in many studies is more on failures than on success. The most interesting case in this respect in various European countries is that of the Roma families and children. As underlined by Eröss for the Central European countries, in most of the settings, both because of a perception—shared among external agencies, national policy makers, and local actors—of the situation of this group as a "problem" and because of the strong commitment of researchers as well as some of those actors to better the situation, the focus has been on questions such as school segregation and school underachievement. The end result has been reinforcement of the one-sided perspective criticized in the case of US studies by Delamont in her chapter.

However, the influence of anthropological and sociological research on race relations is visible in some countries and is leading away from traditional, and in many cases, simplistic visions of cultural clash in schools and classrooms and of processes of social and cultural exclusion. For instance, in Mexico, research on native groups, partly because it focuses not only on schools but on communities, has been able to show not just submission to mainstream norms and educational failure but resistance and negotiation of access to educational resources.

Ethnography as a Subversive Activity[1]

The chapters of this book also provide some insights into the social and political role of ethnographers in different societies. This role of course differs widely according to the history of political regimes of each country, especially when comparing countries that have undergone periods of dictatorships and undemocratic governments in the recent past with the others. In the former, research in the social sciences has been greatly affected not only academically from having being banned from universities or strictly controlled by political and military groups, but in its relation to society. In some contexts, as in China, the political surveillance of both intellectuals and lay society followed by severe punishment for "deviants" during the Cultural Revolution explains why the first are still very cautious about doing fieldwork and publishing its results. The activity of educational ethnographers, because it offers contextualized insights on social processes, gives voice to grassroots actors, and breaks from established patterns of communication on the public sphere, is easily perceived as challenging existing hierarchies and modes of political control as well as "betraying" local communities in front of strangers. Nevertheless, although it is also difficult to know to what extent the political regime would be willing to tolerate views on Chinese society different from the official rhetoric, the introduction of market mechanisms and of new communication technologies seems to be reinforcing individualization, claims for new rights, and the voicing of personal concerns.

In other countries, as in Argentina, political repression of the social sciences seems on the contrary to have contributed to the endorsement by researchers of a more deliberate political role. In her chapter, Neufeld insists, for instance, on the commitment of the research group she coordinates to study those problems that appear as social priorities, some of which are still the consequence of previous dictatorial political regime. This political stance of ethnographers of education and, more generally, of social scientists, seems well accepted by society despite probable resistance from some elite groups. This is likely the case because in Latin American countries, more forcefully than in other national contexts, the role of researchers in the social sciences, who have continuously been confronted with political and social elites who have practiced usurpation of all types of resources—economic, cultural, political, symbolical—and deliberately closed off opportunities for other groups, has been seen as that of denouncing social injustices. Ethnographers of education have thus been continuously involved in pointing out and criticizing the important gap between official discourse and social and educational realities characterized by high levels of inequality and exclusion. This has implied in the last decade analyzing and denouncing the impoverishment of large fractions of the population linked to national and global liberal policies.

Because in these countries political and social elites have also tried to erase the contribution of some groups—indigenous peoples, blacks—to the construction of the nation-states, ethnographers have used their work as a political tool in the production of a more objective and fair vision of their nation's past heritage and present social dynamics. Clearly in Brazil and, to a greater extent, in Mexico, ethnographic studies of education have been part of a process of integrating indigenous peoples. While some early anthropologists were involved in the assimilation process encouraged by elites through the development of theories insisting on the cultural deficits of indigenous peoples and various minorities, most researchers have adopted the relativistic stance on culture characteristic of anthropologists and have developed a strong commitment to help disadvantaged minority groups. This has encouraged their involvement in developing bilingual and intercultural syllabi, programs, and teaching methods, some of which were conceived as alternatives to official educational policies, as well as in training teachers to do research in their own communities and in multicultural schools.

Another important political stance of researchers in these countries, and in others confronted with marginalized "involuntary minorities," has been to encourage native authoring, which favors the emergence of researchers from indigenous and black groups. These native Indian or black researchers logically show an even stronger commitment to the improvement of the social status of their own and other minority groups. These developments, of course, echo similar well-established practices among US anthropologists and UK sociologists and can be found in lighter versions in countries less multicultural or less organized on the basis of ethnic divisions; they are also visible among researchers conducting ethnographic studies abroad. This is frequently the case for American or European researchers working in Africa. As explained in detail by Diallo in his chapter, in Africa local researchers encounter huge financial obstacles due to the scarcity of economic resources allocated by national governments for research and fieldwork and also to important organizational obstacles, such as limited possibilities for publishing books rather than gray literature.

In most of the countries examined in the book, it is also clear that ethnographers of education are strongly committed to the development of more "democratic" research practices—minimally implying treating the persons they study as "equals," that is, as subjects and not objects of study whose perspectives should be respected, but also developing user-friendly research methods and different forms of collaborative and action research, especially with teachers, who are sometimes conceived of as ethnographers of their own settings. More generally, the work of ethnographers of education in many of the national settings considered in this book has been systematically sympathetic to various social and political movements involving ethnic minorities and undocumented or exploited workers but also youth or women, and their work is frequently directly or indirectly conceived—and perceived—as the provision of symbolic support for their claims and ideals.

In the recent period, parallel to similar, sometimes more precocious developments in the United States and the United Kingdom, a different turn has nevertheless been taken involving a much stronger collaboration between ethnographers of education and policy makers. This is the consequence of two different movements. The first is that ethnographers have become more interested in the impact of policies on localities and schools and have convincingly shown the interest of studying "policy as practice" (Sutton and Levinson 2001), especially in order to understand processes of hybridization of global and national policies in local settings (Anderson-Levitt 2003). As pointed out by Eröss, this could be an interesting breeding ground area for the development of academic ethnographic approaches not exclusively centered on the problems of minority children. However, more relevant and theoretically informed work on educational policies by ethnographers of education will need higher cross-fertilization of concepts and approaches among anthropologists, sociologists, and political scientists.

The second movement concerns the reduction of national budgets for independent research projects initiated by researchers and academic institutions and the increase in funding by governmental and nongovernmental national and international agencies for projects with a reform agenda or for projects on targeted subjects—all of which goes along with an increase in the use of social science knowledge as a policy instrument by policy makers (Hood 1986). This can take place in a very direct manner, as in China where, according to Ouyang, researchers are asked to provide insights for the government on how to gain local acceptance for national reform guidelines. It can also happen more indirectly, as when researchers are asked in other countries to gather and interpret qualitative data in order to evaluate the reception and impact of various policies at the local level with higher levels of autonomy concerning the conduct of their work and their interpretations. In all cases, it is nevertheless clear that ethnographers are seen as possessing useful skills and dispositions both to negotiate and to gain acceptance for reforms from street-level actors and to analyze and legitimate new decentralized, multilevel, and multiagency educational systems (van Zanten 2011).

Conclusion

Readers of the rich chapters included in this volume, whose content is based on in-depth ethnographic studies conducted in many countries around the world, would probably be convinced that there are great differences in the way ethnography is defined and enacted, in the subjects considered appropriate and relevant for ethnographic study, in the political stance of researchers or in the theoretical references that are used and combined to interpret fieldwork data. At a certain level, this is certainly true, and Kathryn Anderson-Levitt, who initiated the process that ended in this publication, was right in looking for differences and on emphasizing variation in her introduction to the book. As a concluding remark, I want nevertheless, on the contrary, to focus on similarities and affirm the existence of a shared ethnographic paradigm.

Is this because Professor Anderson-Levitt is an anthropologist while I am a sociologist, which will lead us back to the dual origin of ethnographic studies pointed out at the beginning of these comments? Perhaps. To me, in any case, the chapters of this book provide abundant evidence of the existence of a shared system of concepts, starting of course with "culture"; a shared mode of perceiving reality with an emphasis on local contexts and local meaning; a shared focus on certain themes, such as cultural integration, and on certain subjects, notably the analysis of ethnic minorities and excluded groups; and a shared normative system centered on values such as cultural relativism, social equality, and democratic interaction with informants (van Zanten 1999) and shared professional *habituses* such as, as pointed out by Eröss in his chapter, modesty as concerns generalization. It thus seems to me that *Anthropologies of Education* provides a guide less to travel in unknown territories than to rediscovery of the core structure of the ethnographic ideal and practice.

Notes

1. This is of course a veiled reference to the famous book by Neil Postman and Charles Weingartner, *Teaching as a Subversive Activity* (New York: Delacorte Press, 1969).

Bibliography

Anderson-Levitt, Kathryn M., ed. 2003. *Local Meanings, Global Schooling: Anthropology and World Culture Theory.* New York: Palgrave Macmillan.

Ben-David, Joseph, and Randall Collins. 1966. "Social Factors in the Origins of a New Science: The Case of Psychology." *American Sociological Review,* 31, no. 4: 451–65.

Chapoulie, Jean-Michel. 1991. "La seconde fondation de la sociologie française, les Etats-Unis et la classe ouvrière." *Revue française de sociologie* 32, no. 3: 321–64.

———. 2001. *La tradition sociologique de Chicago*. Paris: Seuil.

Fabiani, Jean-Louis. 2006. "A quoi sert la notion de discipline?" In *Qu'est-ce qu'une discipline?* ed. Jean Boutier, Jean-Claude Passeron, and Jacques Revel. Paris: Éditions de l'EHESS.

Forquin, Jean-Claude. 1983. "La "nouvelle sociologie de l'éducation" en Grande Bretagne: orientations, apports théoriques, évolution." *Revue française de pédagogie* 63: 61–79.

Gibson, Margaret A., ed. 1997. Complicating the Immigrant/Involuntary Minority Typology (theme issue). *Anthropology and Education Quarterly* 28, no. 3.

Glaser, Barney G., and Anselm L. Strauss. 1967. *The Discovery of Grounded Theory: Strategies for Qualitative Research*. Chicago: Aldine Publishing Company.

Heilbron, Johan. 2001. "A Regime of Disciplines: Towards a Historical Sociology of Disciplinary Knowledge." In *The Dialogical Turn: Roles for Sociology in the Post Disciplinary Age*, ed. Charles Camic and Hans Joas. Lanham, MD: Rowman and Littlefield, 23–42.

Henriot-van Zanten, Agnès, and Kathryn M. Anderson-Levitt. 1992. "L'anthropologie de l'éducation aux Etats-Unis: méthodes, théories et applications d'une discipline en évolution." *Revue française de pédagogie* 101: 79–104.

Hood, Christopher C. 1986. *The Tools of Government*. Chatham, UK: Chatham House.

Karabel, Jerome, and A. H. Halsey, eds. 1977. *Power and Ideology in Education*. Oxford: Oxford University Press.

Smith, James Allen. 1991. *The Idea Brokers: Think Tanks and the Rise of the New Policy Elite*. New York: Free Press & Maxwell Macmillan International.

Sutton, Margaret, and Bradley A. Levinson, eds. 2001. *Policy as Practice: Towards a Comparative Sociocultural Analysis of Educational Policy*. Westport, CT: Ablex Publishing.

van Zanten, Agnès. 1999. "Le savant et le politique dans les années quatre-vingt dix. Quelques problèmes éthiques de la recherche ethnographique en éducation." In *Recherches ethnographiques en Europe et en Amérique du Nord*, ed. I. Martinez and A. Vasquez, 171–91. Paris: Anthropos.

———. 2004a. "Les sociologues de l'éducation et leurs publics." In *Unité et pluralité des sciences de l'éducation. Sondages au cœur de la recherche*, ed. G. Chatelanat, C. Moro, and M. Saada-Robert, 187–203. Berne: Peter Lang.

———. 2011. *Les politiques d'éducation*, 2nd edition. Paris: Presses Universitaires de France, coll. "Que sais-je."

Notes on Contributors

Bracha Alpert is a senior lecturer at Beit Berl College in Israel and serves as head of the research and evaluation unit at the college. Her areas of research and teaching include curriculum, instruction, and qualitative research methodology. She has published articles in *Anthropology and Education Quarterly, Teaching and Teacher Education,* and *Curriculum Inquiry.* She has also coauthored a book in Hebrew entitled *Ways of Writing Qualitative Research: From Deconstructing Reality to its Construction as a Text.*

Sally Anderson is associate professor at the Department of Education, University of Aarhus, Denmark. She is the author of *I en klasse for sig* (In a Class of Their Own) (Gyldendal, 2000), an ethnography of Danish public school, focusing on how children and teachers produce social intimacy and distance through the endosociality of permanent classes; and *Civil Sociality: Children, Sport and Cultural Policy in Denmark* (Information Age, 2008), an ethnography of the cultural organization, morality, and sociality of association sports for children. She is presently conducting comparative research on the relation between children and religion in Danish faith-based private schools.

Kathryn M. Anderson-Levitt is a professor of anthropology (retired) at the University of Michigan–Dearborn and a former editor of *Anthropology and Education Quarterly.* She is the author of *Teaching Cultures: Knowledge for Teaching First Grade in France and the United States* (Hampton, 2002) and the editor of *Local Meanings, Global Schooling: Anthropology and World Culture Theory* (Palgrave Macmillan, 2003). She now teaches at UCLA.

Sara Delamont is Reader in Sociology at Cardiff University, Wales, UK. She was the first woman to be president of BERA, the British Educational Research Association, is the author of *Contours of Culture* (Alta Mira Press 2008) with Atkinson and Housley, and is currently doing an ethnography of diasporic *capoeira* and *savate.*

Boubacar Bayero Diallo is a consulting researcher on international projects, and was a researcher and coordinator of qualitative research for the Transitions Project of the Centre interuniversitaire de recherche sur la science et la technologie (CIRST) of the University of Quebec at Montreal. His research concerns basic education and academic careers through secondary education in Africa and Canada. Before joining CIRST, he was an instructor-researcher in the Department of Sociology at the University of Conakry, Guinea, and a consultant for various development agencies. Publications include "La formation des adultes entre 1997 et 2002" with Mireille Levesque and Pierre Doray in *Développer les compétences au travail*, Bouteiller and Morin, eds. (HEC, 2009), and "Teaching by the book in Guinea" with Kathryn Anderson-Levitt in *Local Meanings, Global Schooling*, Anderson-Levitt, ed. (Palgrave Macmillan, 2003)

Hugues Draelants is FRS-FNRS Postdoctoral Researcher at the University of Leuven in Louvain-la-Neuve, Belgium. His research interests include the sociology of elite education, education policies, and the study of socialization and identification processes in schools and on the internet. He is author of *Bavardages dans les salons du net* (Talking in Net Chatrooms) (Labor, 2004) and *Réforme pédagogique et légitimation* (Pedagogical Reform and Legitimating) (De Boeck, 2009). He has also coauthored three chapters of the book *La formation des élites* (The Education of Elites), edited by Agnès van Zanten (Presses Universitaires de France, 2010).

Gábor Eröss is affiliated with the Institute of Sociology, Hungarian Academy of Sciences. He conducts research in educational sociology and anthropology, ethnic studies, the sociology of culture and of public policies, and is a team leader within the "Knowledge and Policy" project (http://www.knowandpol.eu).

Francesca Gobbo is Professor of Intercultural Education at the University of Turin (Italy), where she also teaches anthropology of education and coordinates the PhD program in educational sciences within the Doctoral School in Human Sciences of the University of Turin. Her research on contemporary educational issues (immigrant and minority pupils' schooling) is comparative and interdisciplinary. She is a member of the International Association for Intercultural Education, the European Education Research Association, and the Società Italiana di Pedagogia, and is on the editorial boards of international journals. She edited *Social Justice and Intercultural Education* with G. Bhatti, C. Gaine, and Y. Leeman (Trentham Books, 2007); *The Legacy of John U. Ogbu*, special issue of *Intercultural Education* 18 (5) (with K. Foster); *Ethnography of*

Education in a European Educational Researcher Perspective, in *EERJ* 3, no. 3 (2004) (with D. Beach, B. Jeffrey, G. Smith, G. Troman).

Ana Maria Rabelo Gomes is associate professor at Federal University of Minas Gerais (UFMG), Belo Horizonte, Brazil, with research interests in schooling processes, indigenous education, learning and cultural practices, and ethnography. Among her publications are "Vegna che ta fagu scriver: Etnografia della scolarizzazione in una comunità di Sinti" (Gypsies' Children in Public Italian Schools), "El processo de escolarización de los Xakriabá: historia local y rumbos de la propuesta de educación escolar diferenciada" (Indigenous Education in Minas Gerais, Brazil); and a special issue "Indigenous Education in Latin America" in *Anthropology & Education Quarterly* (edited with Elsie Rockwell).

Nilma Lino Gomes is professor at Federal University of Minas Gerais (UFMG), Belo Horizonte, Brazil, and coordinator general of the Affirmative Action Program at UFMG. Her research interests include black movements and education; race, gender, and education; and the politics of diversity and education. Her publications include *A mulher negra que vi de perto: o processo de construção da identidade racial de professoras negras* (Mazza Edições, 1995) and *Sem perder a raiz: corpo e cabelo como símbolos da identidade negra* (Autêntica, 2006).

Erika González Apodaca is a researcher in ethnic studies and educational anthropology at Centro de Investigaciones y Estudios Superiores en Antropología Social (CIESAS, Mexico). Among her publications are *Los profesionistas mixes en la educación intercultural: etnicidad, educación y escuela en territorio mixe* (UAMI, Juan Pablos 2008), "Etnicidad y escuela" (with M. Bertely ed., COMIE 2003), and *Significados escolares en un bachillerato mixe* (SEP 2004).

Eva Gulløv is associate professor at the Department of Education, University of Aarhus, Denmark. She is the author and editor of numerous publications on children, childcare institutions, and methodology in ethnographic child research, including the coedited book *Children's Places: Cross Cultural Perspectives* (Routledge, 2003).

Yasuko Minoura is a professor emerita at Ochanomizu University, Tokyo. Her main interest is in bridging psychological and anthropological approaches in the field of human development and education. She did fieldwork in the United States, Bangladesh, Thailand, and Vietnam, focusing upon child socialization, schooling, and maternal health. She is the author of *Intercultural Experience during Childhood* (Shisakusha, 1984), *Cultural Perspectives on Child Development* (University of Tokyo Press, 1990), and "Culture and Self-concept among Adolescents with Bi-cultural Parentage" (in *Child Development within Culturally Structured Environments*, vol.3, Ablex, 1995).

María Rosa Neufeld is a social anthropologist and director of the Departamento de Ciencias Antropológicas, Facultad de Filosofía y Letras, University of Buenos Aires. Her research interests are anthropology and education and political anthropology. Among her publications is *"De eso no se habla": los usos de la diversidad sociocultural en la escuela*, edited by Neufeld and Thisted (Editorial Eudeba, 2000).

Huhua Ouyang is professor of English and director of the English Education Research Center, Guangdong University of Foreign Studies, Guangzhou, China. He is the author of "One Way Ticket: A Story of an Innovative Teacher in Mainland China," *Anthropology and Education Quarterly* 31 (4), and the book *Remaking of Face and Community of Practices: An Ethnography of Local and Expatriate English Teachers' Reform Stories in Today's China* 单位与公民社会的碰撞: 教改者的真实故事," (Beijing University Press, 2004).

Maroussia Raveaud is a research fellow and lecturer at the University of Maine, Le Mans, France, and visiting fellow at the University of Bristol, UK. Her main research field is the study of classroom practice in an international comparative context, with a particular focus on pupil socialization at primary school. She authored *De l'enfant au citoyen: la construction de la citoyenneté à l'école* (From the Child to the Citizen: Shaping Citizenship at School) (Presses Universitaires de France, 2006). She is on the editorial board of an international journal.

Elsie Rockwell, who is Mexican by birth, is full professor and researcher in educational research at the Center for Research and Advanced Studies of the National Polytechnic Institute, Mexico City. Recent publications include *Hacer escuela, hacer estado* (El Colegio de Michoacán, 2007), *La experiencia etnográfica* (Paidós, 2009), and a special issue of *Anthropology and Education Quarterly* edited with Ana Gomes (40, no. 2 [2009]).

Naama Sabar Ben-Yehoshua is an emerita faculty member of Tel Aviv University who is presently heading a program on "Culture of Israeli people and its teaching" for a master of education program at Achva

Teacher College. She was the initiator and the leader of the special interest group on qualitative research methods for teacher educators in teachers' colleges. Her research areas include ethics in qualitative methods and qualitative methodology. Among her publications are *Kibbutzniks in the Diaspora* (SUNY, 2000), *Genres and Traditions in Qualitative Research* (2001, in Hebrew) and *"Who Am I to Decide" — Ethical Dilemmas of Teachers* (2007, in Hebrew).

Simha Shlasky taught in Tel Aviv University and in teachers' colleges in Israel. His main areas of interest are qualitative research methods, gender in education, and residential education. His recent publications in Hebrew are: *Sexuality and Gender in Education,* which he edited; *Communities of Youth: Studies on Israeli Boarding Schools,* which he coedited; and *Ways of Writing Qualitative Research: From Deconstructing Reality to Its Construction as a Text,* which he coauthored.

Karen Valentin has a doctorate in anthropology and is associate professor at the Department of Education, University of Aarhus, Denmark. Her research interests are childhood and youth, schooling and education, planned development, and urbanity and migration, much of it based on fieldwork in South and Southeast Asia since 1994. She is the author of *Schooled for the Future? Educational Policy and Everyday Life among Urban Squatters in Nepal* (Information Age, 2005) and has contributed two chapters to *Youth and the City in the Global South,* edited by Karen Tranberg Hansen (Indiana University Press, 2008).

Agnès van Zanten is a senior research professor at the Observatoire Sociologique du Changement (Sciences Po/CNRS). Her main research areas are the reproduction and transformation of social advantage in education, elite education, the organizational and professional dynamics of schools, and local public action in education. She is also interested in qualitative research methods and international comparisons. Her most recent publications include *Dictionnaire de l'éducation* (Presses Universitaires de France, 2008) and *Choisir son école. Stratégies familiales et médiations locales* (Presses Universitaires de France, 2009).

Christoph Wulf is professor for anthropology and philosophy of education, Interdisciplinary Centre for Historical Anthropology, Collaborative Research Centre (SFB) "Cultures of Performance," Cluster of Excellence "Languages of Emotion," Graduate School *Interarts* at Freie Universität Berlin. He conducts research on historical and cultural anthropology, educational anthropology, mimesis, aesthetic and intercultural education, rituals, and emotions. His publications include the edited volume *Vom Menschen. Handbuch Historische Anthropologie* (Weinheim, 1997); *Anthropologie. Geschichte, Kultur, Philosophie* (Reinbek, 2004); *Zur Genese des Sozialen* (Bielefeld, 2005); *Anthropologie kultureller* (Vielfalt, Bielefeld, 2006); with co-authors: *Das Soziale als Ritual* (2001), *Bildung im Ritual* (2004), *Lernkulturen im Umbruch* (2007); with Gebauer: *Mimesis. Culture, Art, Society* (University of California Press, 1995); coedited with Kamper: *Logik und Leidenschaft* (Berlin, 2002); coedited with Huppauf: *Dynamics and Performativity of Imagination* (Routledge, 2009).

꧁ NAME INDEX

Abé, Claude, 281, 283
Ablewicz, Krystyna, 168
Abramo, Helena Wendel, 120
Abuhav, Orit, 257, 258
Abu-Rabia-Queder, Sarab, 260, 267, 269
Achilli, Elena L., 96, 100, 101, 103
Adler, Chaim, 261
Adler-Lomnitz, Larisa, 75
Afifi-Agbaria, Dima, 267
Ai, Qiong, 246
Akinsanya, Sherrie K., 51
Alaniz, Marcela, 96
Alexander, R. J., 4, 9
Al-Haj, Majid, 267
Alimasi, Ntal-I'Mbirwa, 21, 291
Allwright, Dick, 248
Alvarez Roldán, Arturo, 2
Álvarez, Amelia, 10
Åm, Eli, 200
Amâncio, Íris, 119
Amaro, Liliana, 81
Anderson, Gary L., 11
Anteby-Yemini, Lisa, 264, 268
Antequera, Nelson, 80
Araújo, Carla, 120
Arieli, Mordecai, 262, 263, 267, 268
Ariès, Philippe, 33
Asai, Akiko, 217
Asakura, Kageki, 228
Ashkenazi, Michael, 259
Atkinson, Paul A., 9, 52, 53, 57, 61
Au, Kathryn H., 56
Ávalos Romero, Job, 79
Ávila Meléndez, Luis Arturo, 75, 83
Aviram, Ovadia, 268
Ayalon, Hanna, 261

Ba, Zhanlong, 241
Baarts, Charlotte, 198
Bailey, Paul, 245

Bajomi, Iván, 181
Balandier, Georges, 281
Baldé, Mercedes, 288
Balde, Mouctar, 294
Ball, Stephen, 9, 259
Banks, James, 242
Barcelos, Luiz Cláudio, 119
Baronnet, Bruno, 81
Barrère, Anne, 137
Barrio Maestre, José María, 10
Barry, Alpha Amadou Bano, 288, 293
Bar-Shalom, Yehuda, 263
Barth, Fredrik, 2, 194
Bastid, Marianne, 245
Bastide, Roger, 124n3
Batallán, Graciela, 19, 94, 95, 96, 97, 101
Bauer, Mette, 196
Bautier, Elisabeth, 136
Beach, Dennis, 23n13, 280, 296
Beaud, Stéphane, 139
Bechar, Shlomit, 262
Beck, Robert H., 264
Behar, Ruth, 62
Bekerman, Zvi, 263, 265
Bell, Catherine, 40
Belle-Isle, Lucie, 288
Ben-Amos, Avner, 264
Ben-Ari, Eyal, 258
Benavides, Gloria, 80
Benavot, Aaron, 4
Ben-David, Joseph, 306
Ben-Peretz, Miriam, 263
Bento, Maria Aparecida Silva, 118, 119
Berentzen, Sigurd, 200
Bergamaschi, Maria Aparecida, 122
Bermúdez, Flor, 75
Berner, B. Boel, 196
Bernstein, Basil, 197
Bernstein, Frida, 267

Berry, John, 242
Bertely, María, 73, 80, 81, 82, 84, 85n1
Berthier, Patrick, 133
Bet-El, Ilana, 264
Bettelheim, Bruno, 265
Bilu, Yoram, 266, 269
Bird-David, Nurit, 258
Bjerrum Nielsen, Harriet, 197
Bloch, Marianne, 288, 294
Blum-Kulka, Shoshana, 262
Bodó, Julianna, 174
Boehm, Christopher, 52
Boesen, Inger, 203
Boëtsch, Gilles, 44
Bohnsack, Ralf, 39
Bollnow, Otto Friedrich, 7, 168
Bonhomme, Julien, 281, 282
Bordegaray, Graciela, 103
Boreczky, Ágnes, 172
Borevskaya, Nina, 245
Borg, Karin, 196
Borgnakke, Karen, 197
Bosco, Joseph, 2
Boškovic, Aleksandar, 2
Bouche, Denise, 287
Boudon, Raymond, 308
Boudreau, Françoise, 145
Boumard, Patrick, 12, 141
Bourdieu, Pierre, 21, 60, 97, 120, 132, 142, 147n2, 198, 308
Bouvet, Rose-Marie, 12, 141
Boyadjieva, Pepka, 176
Brameld, Theodore, 52
Brandão, Carlos Rodrigues, 115
Braudel, Fernand, 33
Breidenstein, Georg, 7
Brembeck, Helene, 200
Broch, Harald Beyer, 200
Brown, Karen M., 62
Bullivant, Brian M., 59
Bundgaard, Helle, 200
Burke, Peter, 33
Burnett, Jacquetta Hill, 52, 54, 55
Butler, Judith, 42

Cai, Yuan-Pei, 235
Caille, Jean-Paul, 139

Calderón, Marco Antonio, 83
Callari Galli, Matilde, 151–53, 155, 162n6
Callewaert, Staf, 196
Calvo, Beatriz, 71, 74
Camacho, Luiza Mitiko Yshiguro, 121
Camara, Mohamed Campel, 294
Candela, Antonia, 3, 10, 76
Cândido, Antônio, 124n3
Cao, J. Q., 247
Card, Brigham Y., 142, 143
Cardoso, Rafael, 73
Caria, Telmo H., 11
Caronia, Letizia, 157
Carrano, Paulo Cesar Rodrigues, 120
Carrasco Pons, Sílvia, 11
Carrol, Bidemi, 289
Carvalho, Marília Pinto de, 119
Cavalcanti, Maria Laura, 124n4
Cavalleiro, Eliane, 119
Cave, Peter, 218
Cerletti, Laura, 103, 104
Chapoulie, Jean-Michel, 305, 308
Charlot, Bernard, 136
Chen, Peizhao, 237
Chen, Xiangming, 237, 251
Chen, Z. Y., 247
Chen, Zhenzhong, 239
Cheng, Kai Ming, 245
Chilcott, John H., 51
Christina, Rachel, 14
Clark, Alison, 201
Clarke, Prema, 14
Clifford, James, 61, 62
Clignet, Rémi, 287
Cochin, Jacques, 294
Coffey, Amanda, 61
Cohn, Clarice, 122
Coll, César, 3, 10
Collier, John, Jr., 56
Collins, Harry M., 51
Collins, Randall, 306
Condé, Kéfing, 283, 288
Connell, R. W., 10
Connerton, Paul, 57
Conrad, Joan, 202
Consorte, Josildeth G., 113

Conté, Ibrahima Moriah, 293
Copans, Jean, 281
Corbin, Juliet, 39
Corenstein, Marta, 85n1
Costa, Cecilia, 157
Coulon, Alain, 133
Crossley, Michael, 16
Crozier, Michel, 308
Cruz, Alfonso, 82
Csanádi, Gábor, 177
Csongor, Anna, 171
Cummings, William K., 213
Czachesz, Erzsébet, 172
Czarny, Gabriela, 85n1

D'Angelis, Wilmar da Rocha, 122
Dahlberg, Gunilla, 199
Dallavalle, Chiara, 157
Damasceno, Maria Nobre, 120
Darmanin, Mary, 50
Daun, Holger, 202
Dauster, Tânia, 116, 117
Davidson, Dana H., 213
Dayrell, Juarez T., 115, 120, 121
de Azevedo, Fernando, 124n3
de Garay, Adrian, 79
de la Peña, Guillermo, 80, 82
de la Riva, María, 76
de León Pasquel, Lourdes, 77, 78
Debert, Guita Grin, 120
del Río, Pablo, 10
Delalande, Julie, 136, 146
Delbos, Geneviève, 12
Delgado, Gabriela, 71
Delvaux, Bernard, 168, 169
deMarrais, Kathleen Bennett, 54, 61
Deng, Xiaoping, 236
Denzin, Norman K., 53
Derouet, Jean-Louis, 3, 8, 133, 135,
  137
Deshen, Shlomo, 258
Deyhle, Donna, 56
Diamond, Stanley, 51
Diarra, Mamadou Lamine, 292
Diarra, Sékou Oumar, 284, 285, 292
Díaz de Rada, Ángel, 10
Díaz Pontones, Mónica, 74

Díaz Tepepa, María Guadalupe, 74
Dieckmann, Bernhard, 43
Diédhiou, Paul, 281
Dietz, Gunther, 80, 81, 84
Diez, Cecilia, 104, 105n4
Diez, María Laura, 104
Dimitriadis, Greg, 58
Dimitrov, Georgi, 176
Ding, Gang, 238, 239, 245, 251, 251n5
Dinzelbacher, Peter, 33
Diop, Amadou Sarr, 281
Diop, Cheikh Anta, 281
Dolby, Nadine, 10, 58
Domingues, Petrônio, 118
Domokos, Veronika, 177
Don-Yehiya, Eliezer, 264
Doray, Pierre, 144
Douglas, Mary, 60
Draklé, Dorle, 2
Dubet, François, 137
Duby, Georges, 33
Dumont, R. V., 56
Durkheim, Emile, 132, 137
Duru-Bellat, Marie, 12, 132, 133, 135,
  138
Dzau, Y. F., 250

Eades, J. S., 2
Ebuchi, Kazuhiro, 20, 213, 225
Edgar, Iain R., 2
Egbo, Benedicta, 15
Ehn, Billy, 200
Eigen, Manfred, 31
Einarsdóttir, Johanna, 199, 200
Eisenhart, Margaret A., 56
Eisenstadt, Shmuel N., 268
Eisikovits, Rivka A., 264, 268, 269
Eisner, Elliot, 54
Eldering, Lotty, 13
El-Or, Tamar, 260, 268, 269
Elvir, Ana Patricia,
Erickson, Donald, 56
Erickson, Frederick, 56
Eriksen, Thomas Hylland, 193
Erny, Pierre, 287
Escalante, M. Angel, 82
Escalante, Paloma, 78

Escobar, Arturo, 2
Espinosa, Epifanio, 75
Essè, Amouzou, 281
Estrada, Pedro, 75
Evans-Pritchard, Edward Evan, 34
Ezpeleta, Justa, 74, 102, 117

Fabiani, Jean-Louis, 306
Fabietti, Ugo, 151, 156
Fairclough, Norman, 248, 250
Falconi, Octavio, 74
Falteri, Paola, 154, 155, 159
Farnen, Russell F., 264
Fazzi, Rita de Cássia, 119
Fei, Xiaotong, 236, 240
Feischmidt, Margit, 178
Feldman, Jackie, 264
Feng, Zengjun, 237, 238, 239, 240
Fernandes, Florestan, 112, 113, 124n3, 124n4
Ferreira, Mariana Kawall Leal, 116, 117, 121, 124n6
Fierro Evans, Cecilia, 74
Filiod, Jean-Paul, 16, 121, 146
Finders, Margaret, 55
Fine, Gary Alan, 61, 56
Fine, Michelle, 5, 59
Fischer, Joseph, 51
Fischer, Rosa Maria Bueno, 121
Fisher, A. D., 8
Fisherkeller, Joellen, 55
Fleck, Gabor, 175
Flick, Uwe, 39
Flores Farfán, José Antonio, 77
Flores, Ivette, 82
Foley, Douglas E., 51, 52, 57
Fonseca, Claudia, 117
Fonseca, Marcus Vinícius, 119
Fordham, Signithia, 54
Forquin, Jean-Claude, 133, 306
Forsey, Martin G., 10, 51
Fosztó, László, 175
Foucault, Michel, 198
Franchetto, Bruna, 122
Franzé Mudanó, Adela, 10
Freire, Gilberto, 124n3
Freire, Gilberto, 124n3

Freitas, Marcos Cezar, 112
Fujita, Hidenori, 215
Furman, Mirta, 262, 264, 269

Galeana Cisneros, Rosaura, 77
Gallois, Dominique Tilkin, 122
Galloni, Francesca, 157, 158
Galván, Luz Elena, 82
Gao, Ge, 249
Gao, Jinling, 239
Garb, Yoni, 266, 269
García Castaño, F. Javier, 10
García Rivera, Fernando, 77
García, Fernando, 73
García, Javier, 104, 105n4
García, Stella Maris, 96
Garcion-Vautour, Laurence, 12
Garfinkel, Harold, 137
Gearing, Frederick O., 51
Gebauer, Gunter, 44
Geertz, Clifford, 34, 60, 100, 118, 161n1
Gehlen, Arnold, 32
Geissler, P. Wenzel, 55, 203
Generett, Gretchen Givens, 61
Geng, Juanjuan, 246
Gennep, Arnold van, 40
Gérard, Étienne, 279, 288
Gérin-Lajoie, Diane, 145
Gerő, Zsuzsa, 177
Gibbons, Michael, 169
Gibson, Margaret A., 3, 59, 312
Gillborn, David, 10
Gilliam, Laura, 198, 200, 201, 206n7
Ginzburg, Carlo, 33
Gitz-Johansen, Thomas, 200
Glaser, Barney G., 39, 303
Goffman, Erving, 40, 268, 284
Golden, Debora, 262, 268
Goldstein, Bernice Z., 52
Gomes, Josildeth, 124n3
Gómez, Claudia, 81
Gonçalves e Silva, Petronilha Beatriz, 12, 119
Gonçalves, Luiz Alberto Oliveira, 12, 119
González, Jaime, 80
González, Jerny, 80

González, Lélia, 119
González, Norma, 16
Goodman, Roger, 8, 9, 213, 226
Goodman, Yehuda C., 261
Gordon, David, 266
Gordon, Deborah A., 62
Gordon, Tuula, 8, 9, 52
Grandino, Patrícia Junqueira, 121
Grassi, Estela, 95
Greenberg, Joseph, 4
Greenberg, Norman C., 51
Grekova, Maya, 176
Grimes, Ronald, 40
Grobsmith, Elizabeth S., 56
Grossi, Miriam Pillar, 117
Gruber, Frederick C., 51
Grupioni, Luiz Donizete B., 117, 124n8
Grupper, Emanuel, 268
Gu, Mingyuan, 245
Guberman, Steven R., 55
Gudykunst, William B., 249
Guerra Ramírez, Irene, 79
Guerrero Salinas, Elsa, 79
Guerrero, Alicia, 76, 81
Guerrero, Irán, 77
Guilhot, Nicolas, 2, 4, 22
Guimarães, Antonio Sérgio A., 118
Gusmão, Neusa M. M., 116, 117, 121
Gutiérrez Narváez, Raúl, 81
Gutiérrez, Edgar, 74
Guzmán, Carlota, 79
Haan, Mariette de, 77
Halldén, Gunilla, 200
Halper, Jeff, 258, 261
Hamadach, Ali, 294
Hamel, Enrique, 76
Hammersley, Martyn, 9, 53
Handelman, Don, 262, 264
Hannerz, Ulf, 2, 21, 131
Hannum, Emily, 242
Hargreaves, David H., 9, 139, 259
Harrell, Stevan, 236, 237, 240
Harris, Marvin, 34, 124n3, 161n1
Harrison, Gualtiero, 151, 152, 162n6
Harrison, Jo-Ann, 265
Hasenbalg, Carlos A., 118, 119

Hasse, Cathrine, 198
Hastrup, Kirsten, 193
Hatano, Keiko, 219
Havas, Gábor, 177
Hayhoe, Ruth, 239, 245
He, Bo, 242
He, Xiaoxing, 253
He, Xuan, 242
Heath, Shirley Brice, 53, 56, 131
Hechter, Michael, 54
Heilbron, Johan L., 2, 4, 22, 304
Hendry, Joy, 219
Henriot-van Zanten, Agnès, 3, 8, 9, 133, 134, 135, 304
Henze, Juergen, 245
Hernández González, Joaquín, 79
Herrera, Linda, 14
Hertzog, Esther, 258
Herzfeld, Michael, 57, 60
Hess, G. Alfred, Jr., 55
Hirschhorn, Monique, 281, 282, 296
Hirt, Tomáš, 173
Højlund, Susanne, 198
Holland, Dorothy C., 51, 52, 53, 56, 58, 202, 204
Holland, Janet, 8, 9, 52
Holmes, Brian, 51
Holst, Jesper, 202
Hood, Christopher C., 316
Horowitz, Dan, 257
Horowitz, Tamar, 263, 266
Hostetler, John A., 59
Howell, Signe, 200, 206n7
Hrdlička, Aleš, 168
Huang Aifeng, 248
Huang, Xiangyang, 246
Hünersdorf, Bettina, 7
Hultqvist, Kenneth, 199
Hunt, Christine, 10
Huntingdon, Gertrude Enders, 59
Húšová, Mária, 174
Hvistendahl, Mara, 236, 238

Ianni, Francis A. J., 51
Ichikawa, Shogo, 215
Ihle, Anette Haaber, 203
Ikeda, Hiroshi, 213, 218

Jackson, Philip W., 196, 259
Jacob, Evelyn, 51, 53
Jacobs-Huey, Lanita, 55
Jacquin, Marianne, 9
Jakoubek, Marek, 173
James, Allison, 200
Janky, Béla, 171
Jarvis, Hugh W., 14
Jeanpierre, Laurent, 2, 4, 22
Jenks, Chris, 200
Jiménez Lozano, Luz, 75
Jiménez Naranjo, Yolanda, 80
Jociles, María Isabel, 10
Johansson, Barbro, 200
Jordan, Cathie, 51, 56
Jorge, Miriam, 119
Jorion, Paul, 12
Jovino, Ione S., 119
Julian, Juan, 73

Kaboré, Idrissa, 291
Kacen, Lea, 259
Kainan, Anat, 263
Kaji, Itaru, 221
Kalman, Judith, 77
Kamens, David, 4
Kampmann, Jan, 200
Kapitány, Ágnes, 180
Kapitány, Gábor, 180
Karabel, Jerome, 213, 309
Kardorff, Ernst von, 39
Karnieli, Mira, 264, 268
Karsenti, Thierry, 289, 267
Kashti, Yitzhak, 261, 262
Katahoire, Anne, 203
Kataoka, Yuko, 226
Katriel, Tamar, 262, 268
Kaufman, Carolina, 102
Kawakami, Ikuo, 223
Keenan, Barry, 245
Kemény, István, 171, 176, 177
Kende, Anna, 177
Kézdi Nagy, Géza, 187
Khaldi, M., 15
Khelfaoui, Hocine, 284
Kidokoro, Akiko, 227
King, A. Richard, 56

Kinoshita, Yasuhito, 214
Kipnis, Andrew, 10
Kishida, Yumi, 224, 225
Kjørholt, Anne-Trine, 200, 201
Kjuchukov, Hristo, 176
Klein, Esther, 262, 269
Kleinfeld, J. S., 56
Klette, Kirsti, 197
Kneller, George F., 31
Kobayashi, Tetsuya, 225
Kocourek, Jiří, 178
Kojima, Akira, 222
Kolle, Samuel Same, 281
Kovács, Éva, 180
Kovai, Cecília, 176, 177
Krumer-Nevo, Michal, 259
Kryger, Niels, 197
Kučera, Miloš, 172
Kunda, Gideon, 258
Kuraishi, Ichiro, 218
Kuwayama, Takami, 215

LaBelle, Thomas J., 52
Labov, William, 56
Lacasse, Denis, 294
Lacey, Colin, 139
Ladányi, János, 177, 182
Lahelma, Elina, 8, 9, 52
Lahire, Bernard, 122
Lan, Ye, 245
Lange, Marie-France, 279
Langeveld, Martinus J., 168
Lanternari, Vittorio, 156
Lapassade, Georges, 133, 141
Lareau, Annette, 53, 61
Larsen, Birgitte Romme, 200
Larsson, Staffan, 2, 13, 22
Lave, Jean, 55, 206n6, 247
Lazzarin, M. Giovanna, 154
Leão, Geraldo Magela Pereira, 121
Leibing, Annette, 61
Lengyel, Gabriella, 171
Lerma, Enriqueta, 80
LeRoy Ladurie, Emmanuel, 33
Levinson, Bradley A. U., 11, 19, 51, 52, 53, 58, 202, 204, 206n6, 316

Lévi-Strauss, Claude, 34, 60, 115, 161n1
Lewin, Kurt, 141
Lewin, Pedro, 76
Lewin-Epstein, Noah, 257
Lewis, Arnold, 258, 261
Lewis, Catherine, 219
Lewis, J. Lowell, 56
Li, David, 246
Li, Shanze, 243
Li, Xiaobo, 248
Li, Xiaomin, 242
Li, Xu, 247
Lidén, Hilde, 200
Liebman, Charles S., 264
Liep, John, 194
Lijphart, Arend, 147n6
Lin, Yaohua, 236
Lincoln, Yvonna S., 53
Lindblad, Sverker, 196, 197
Lindquist, Harry M., 51
Liskó, Ilona, 177
Lissak, Moshe, 257
Littlewood, Roland, 57
Liu, Lianghua, 244, 246, 251n6
Liu, Xuan, 246
Liu, Yongcan, 247
Liu, Yunshan, 246
Lo, Nai Kwai, 245
Lomawaima, K. Tsianina, 56
Lomsky-Feder, Edna, 265, 269
Lopes da Silva Macedo, Ana Vera, 117, 122
López Espinoza, Susana, 74
López, Norma Angélica, 81
López, Oresta, 76, 83
Loss, Sándor, 177
Lundberg, Pia, 198
Lunneblad, Johannes, 23n13
Luo, Huiyan, 238
Lutz, Catherine A., 58

Ma, Rong, 242
Ma, Tianyu, 246
Maclure, Richard, 15, 280, 284, 285, 287, 288, 289
Madsen, Ulla Ambrosius, 198, 202

Maeder, Christoph, 7
Magyari-Vincze, Enikő, 175
Maldonado, Benjamín, 80
Malela, Mwabila, 283
Malinowski, Bronislaw, 34, 102, 105n2, 169
Malkmo, Yaakov, 268
Mangez, Eric, 144, 147n6, 168, 169
Manzano, Virginia, 103
Marcus, George E., 61, 62
Mari, Sami, 267
Markström, Ann-Marie, 200
Marone, Oumar, 287
Maroy, Christian, 144
Martin J.-Y, 287
Martínez Buenabad, Elizabeth, 80, 83
Martínez Casas, Regina, 82
Martínez, Janeth, 78
Marx, Emanuel, 275, 258
Masemann, Vandra, 52
Mauss, Marcel, 132
Mayer, Phillip, 9
Mazawi, Andre, 267
Mbilinyi, M. J., 279
McAndrew, Marie, 145
McCarty, Teresa L., 56
McConnell, David L., 217
McDonald, Maryon, 60
McLean, Athena, 61
Mead, Margaret, 8, 34, 112
Medick, Hans, 33
Medina Melgarejo, Patricia, 75, 80
Meinert, Lotte, 200, 203, 206n7
Meirav, Nurit, 266
Meleg, Csilla, 180
Mena, Patricia, 76
Menéndez, Eduardo, 101, 105n5
Menezes, Ana Luísa Teixeira, 122
Meng, Fanli, 242
Menk, Debra W., 55
Mercado, Ruth, 75
Mészáros, György, 180
Meyer, John W., 4, 18
Middleton, John, 9, 51
Milenkova, Valentinas, 176
Mills, David, 50
Mizrachi, Nissim, 261

Moffatt, Michael, 56
Mohatt, Gerald, 56
Monserrat, Ruth Maria Fonini, 122
Monte, Nietta Lindenberg, 122
Montero, Paul, 115
Montero-Sieburth, Martha, 11
Montesinos, María Paula, 97, 98, 103, 104, 105n4
Morey, Eugenia, 95
Morin, Edgar, 30
Moss, Peter, 201
Motani, Yoko, 224
Mott, Luiz, 121
Moura, Clóvis, 119
Müller, Burkhard, 7
Muller, Maria Lúcia Rodrigues, 119
Munanga, Albert Muluma,
Munanga, Kabengele, 118
Muñoz, Héctor, 76

N'Doye, Mamadou, 279
Nahalka, István, 172
Nakajima, Tomoko, 225
Nakamura, Hiroko, 227
Nakamura, Mutsuo, 80
Nakhlen, Khalil, 14, 16
Naranjo, Gabriela, 76
Nascimento, Abdias do, 119
Nava, Refugio, 73, 77
NDiaye, Lamine, 283
Neely, Sharlotte, 52
Neményi, Mária, 177
Németh, Szilvia, 177
Nesher, Perla, 262
Neumann, Eszter, 177, 180, 181
Nga Ndongo, Valentine, 282, 283
Nielsen, Greg M., 145
Nilsson, Bengt A., 196
Nogueira, Oracy, 119
Nørgaard, Katrine, 198
Norman, Karin, 200
Novaes, Regina, 120
Novaro, Gabriela, 97, 103, 104, 105n4
Nowotny, Helga, 169
Noyama, Horoshi, 229
Nudelman, Anita, 268
Nunes, Ângela, 117, 122, 124n6

Nunev, J., 176
Núñez Patiño, Kathia, 81
Nyíri, Pál, 178
Nze-Guema, Pierre-Fidèle, 283

Oblath, Márton, 177
Ochiai, Mikiko, 216
Okano, Kaori, 10
Olesen, Jesper, 200
Oliveira, Gilvan Muller, 122
Oliveira, Iolanda, 118
Olivier de Sardan, Jean-Pierre, 283
Oliviera Gonçalves, Luis Alberto, 12
Olshtein, Elite, 266
Olwig, Karen Fog, 194, 201
Onyango-Ouma, Washington, 203
Oppenheim, Abraham N., 264
Örkény, Antal, 170
Ornelas Tavares, Gloria, 74
Ortega, Florencia, 74
Ortiz, Gladys, 78
Ortner, Sherry B., 59
Osanai, Toru, 222
Osborne, A. Barry, 8, 10
Otsuka, Yutaka, 245
Ovesen, Jan, 193

Padawer, Ana, 97, 104, 105n4
Pagano, Ana, 103
Paine, Lynn Webster, 245
Paladino, Mariana, 117, 122
Palečková, Jana, 171
Pallma, Sara, 97, 98
Palludan, Charlotte, 198, 200
Panayotova, Donka, 176
Paoletta, Horacio, 104
Paoli, Maria Célia, 114
Papp Z., Attila, 179
Paradise, Ruth, 77, 78
Passeron, Jean-Claude, 142
Pastrana, Leonor, 81
Payet, Jean-Paul, 138, 139
Pechincha, Monica, 121
Pechová, Eva, 178
Penso, Anat, 266
Peralva, Angelina, 120
Perazzi, Pablo, 95

Pérez, Leonel, 74
Pérez, Teresita, 75
Pérez Campos, Gilberto, 74
Pérez Pérez, Elías, 80
Pérez Ruiz, Maya Lorena, 79
Pérez S., Sergio, 80
Pérez V., Rosalba, 80
Perrenoud, Philippe, 142, 143
Peshkin, Alan, 54, 57, 60, 61
Pessate-Schubert, Anat, 267, 269
Petruccelli, José Luiz, 124n5
Philips, Susan U., 56
Phitiaka, Helen, 50
Pilon, Marc, 279, 280, 284, 285
Piña, Juan Manuel, 79
Pinto, Regina Pahim, 119
Plessner, Helmuth, 32
Podestá, Rossana, 76, 78, 81, 85n1
Poledňová, Ivana, 173
Pollack, Mica, 51
Pontón, Beatriz, 79
Pontrandolfo, Stefania, 158
Ponzetta, Mila Tommaseo, 156
Popkewitz, Thomas S., 53
Portal, María Ana, 81
Postiglione, Gerard, 242
Poveda, David, 11,
Prince, Ruth, 55, 203
Proteau, Laurence, 288
Prout, Alan, 200
Pugach, Marlene C., 54
Pugsley, Lesley, 52, 57

Qi, Xuehong, 245
Quiróz, Rafael, 74
Qvarsell, Birgitta, 7, 16
Qvortrup, Jens, 200

Rabo, Annika, 206n7
Rahm, Irene, 55
Ram, Uri, 269
Ramírez, Lucas, 73
Ramos Ramírez, José Luis, 78, 80
Ramos, Alberto Guerreiro, 119
Rapoport, Tamar, 266, 269
Rawls, John, 137
Rayou, Patrick, 136

Rebolledo, Nicanor, 82
Rebolledo, Valeria, 75
Reed-Danahay, Deborah, 60
Reguillo, Rossana, 78
Remedi, Eduardo, 75
Remotti, Francesco, 151, 156
Ren, Yunchang, 246
Rial, Carmen Sílvia Moraes, 117
Ribeiro, Darcy, 124n3
Ribeiro, Gustavo Lins, 2
Roberts, Joan I., 51
Robles, Adriana, 78, 82, 85n1
Rocha, Gilmar, 118
Rochex, Jean-Yves, 136, 172
Rogoff, Barbara, 13, 77, 206n6
Rohlen, Thomas P., 213
Rojas, Angélica, 81, 82
Rojas Drummond, Sylvia, 76
Rose, Mike, 55
Rosemberg, Fulvia, 119
Rosen, Stanley, 245
Rosentiel, Annette, 52
Ross, Heidi, 245
Roth Seneff, Andrew, 83
Rueda, Mario, 71, 75, 85n1
Rughinis, Cosima, 175
Ruiz, Arturo, 76
Rydstrøm, Helle, 206n7
Rysst, Mari, 200

Sader, Eder, 114
Sadownik, Alicja, 168
Sagástegui, Diana, 78
Sahlins, Marshall, 34, 115
Sahlström, Fritjof, 197
Sakai, Akira, 217, 227
Sakamoto, Ikko, 213
Salanova, Andrés, 122
Saletti Salza, Carlotta, 159
Samoff, Joel, 289
Sanchis, Pierre, 115
Sandoval, Etelvina, 74
Sangrea, Lucinda, 51
Sanjek, Roger, 61
Santerre, Renaud, 287
Santillán, Laura, 103, 105n4
Sarangapani, Padma, 14

Sárkány, Mihály, 167, 169, 184n2
Sartorello, Stefano, 80
Šatava, Leoš, 179
Sato, Chise, 220
Sato, Gunei, 226
Sato, Ikuya, 214
Sato, Manabu, 217
Saucedo, Claudia Lucy, 74, 79
Saviani, Dermeval, 113
Sawadogo, Ram Christophe, 282, 283
Schaden, Egon, 114, 124n3
Schechner, Richard, 40
Scheler, Max, 20, 29, 32
Schippers, Thomas K., 2
Schnack, Karsten, 202
Schonmann, Shifra, 263
Schoo, Susana, 104
Schutz, Alfred, 141
Schwartz, Henrietta, 56
Scollon, Ron, 246
Scollon, Suzanne, 249
Scott, Peter, 169
Semyonov, Moshe, 257
Seto, Ruka, 216
Shabtay, Malka, 264, 268
Shamai, Shalom, 268
Shamgar-Handelman, Lea, 262, 264
Shapira, Rina, 268
Sharpe, Keith, 9
Shavit, Yossi, 261
Shepel, Elina N. Lempert, 13
Shepher, Israel, 265
Shibayama, Makoto, 219, 220
Shibuya, Maki, 226
Shimahara, Nobuo, 217
Shimizu, Kokichi, 213, 214, 215, 216, 218, 229
Shimizu, Mutsumi, 224
Shkedi, Asher, 259
Shlasky, Sharona, 268, 269
Shmueli, Avshlom, 258
Shokeid, Moshe, 258, 260, 261
Shultz, Jeffrey, 53, 61
Shumar, Wes, 56
Shunk, William R., 52
Sidoti, Simona, 159
Silberbrandt, Henning, 196

Silva, Ana Célia da, 2004 2005
Silva, Aracy Lopes da, 116, 117, 121, 122, 124n6
Silva, Natalino Neves da, 121
Silva, Nelson do Valle Silva, 118
Silva, Paulo Vinícius Baptista da, 118
Silva Machado, Ana Vera Lopes da, 124n6
Silvério, Valter Roberto, 118, 119
Simonicca, Alessandro, 152, 159
Sinclair, Simon, 50, 56
Sindell, Peter S., 52
Singleton, John C., 55, 59, 213, 228
Sinisi, Liliana, 97, 98, 104, 105n4
Sirota, Régine, 3, 8, 133, 135
Smékal, Vladimír, 173
Smith, James Allen, 307
Smith, Linda T., 53
Soares, Luiz Eduardo, 120
Soker, Zeev, 262
Solberg, Anne, 200
Sørensen, Birgitte Refslund, 203
Sosa Lázaro, Manuel, 83
Soulez, Philippe, 287
Soumaré, Aminata Maiga, 288, 294
Souza Lima, Elvira, 3, 12, 13
Sow, Alhassane, 288, 294
Spencer, Jonathan, 6
Spiegel, Ehud, 266
Spindler, George D., 8, 50, 51, 53, 54, 60, 305
Spindler, Louise, 8, 51, 54, 305
Spiro, Melford E., 265
Sposito, Marília Pontes, 120
Stambach, Amy, 204
Štech, Stanislav, 172
Steiner-Khamsi, Gita, 21
Stenhouse, Lawrence, 141
Storey, Edward, 51
Strauss, Anselm L., 39, 303
Street, Brian, 50, 53
Street, Susan, 75, 76
Strong, Pauline Turner, 52, 54
Sullivan, Edward B., 52
Sultana, Ronald, 50
Sun, Jieyuan, 239
Sutton, Margaret, 316

Svec, Stefan, 172
Szalai, Júlia, 173
Szasz, Margaret C., 56
Székelyi, Mária, 170
Szelényi, Iván, 182

Tabachnick, B. Robert, 53
Taboada, Eva, 74
Tabuchi, Isoo, 225
Tamba, Moustapha, 281, 282, 296
Tambiah, Stanley, 40
Tambo, Mercy, 288
Taniguchi, Akiko, 228
Tassinari, Antonella Maria
    Imperatriz, 117, 122
Taukane, Darlene Yaminalo, 122
Tchombe, Therese M. S., 289
Teinke, Ines, 39
Telles, Edward, 118
Teng, Xing, 241, 242
Thapan, Meenakshi, 114
Thin, Daniel, 122
Thisted, Jens Ariel, 96, 97, 98, 99
Thogersen, Stig, 245
Thompson, E. P., 102
Tiemtoré, Windpouiré Zacharia, 291
Timmerman, Christiane, 13
Ting-Toomey, Stella, 249
Tobin, Joseph J., 213, 219
Tokuda, Kozou, 213, 214, 216
Toma, Stefania, 175, 176
Tomatová, Jana, 174
Torday, Emil, 168
Torgyik, Judit, 172
Torney, Judith V., 264
Torres, Carlos Alberto, 14
Tosta, Sandra F. Pereira, 118
Tounkara, Brehima, 284
Touraine, Alain, 137, 308
Toure, Kathryn, 289
Townsend, James R., 249
Trevisan, Paola, 159
Trix, Frances, 56
Troman, Geoff, 5, 10
Trueba, Enrique T., 51, 54
Turai, Tünde, 179, 180
Turner, Victor, 40, 161n1

Ulrich, Catalina, 169
Urteaga, Maritza, 78

Valérien, Jean, 284
Valle, Imuris, 79
Vallet, Louis-André, 139
Van Haecht, Anne, 143
Van Teeffelen, Toine, 258
Váradi, Mónika, 177
Varda, Adam, 264
Vardi-Rat, Esther, 262
Varela, Cecilia, 95
Varenne, Hervé, 55
Vargas, María Eugenia, 80
Veiga, Juracilda, 122
Velasco Maillo, Honorio M., 10
Verhoeven, Marie, 145, 146
Vermuelen, Hans F., 2
Vienne, Philippe, 15
Vierra, Andrea, 52
Vilhena, Luis Rodolfo, 124n4
Villanueva, Nancy, 78
Vincent, Guy, 122
Vinitzky-Seroussi, Vered, 265
Virág, Tünde, 177
Vistrain, Alicia, 74
Viveiros de Castro, Eduardo, 124n7
Vulliamy, Graham, 16

Wagner, Judith T., 199, 200
Wahbeh, Nader, 14, 15
Walford, Geoffrey, 58
Walker, James C., 10
Wallace, Santiago, 95
Wang, Jian, 242
Wang, Mingming, 236, 242
Watanabe, Masako Ema, 217, 218
Wax, Murray, 8, 51, 54, 55, 56
Wax, Rosalie, 8, 54, 55, 56
Weaver, Thomas, 51
Weigel, Valéria Augusta Cerqueira de
    Medeiros, 122
Weil, Shalva, 263
Weiner-Levy, Naomi, 260, 267, 269
Weingrod, Alex, 258, 261
Weis, Lois, 59
Weiss, Eduardo, 74, 79

Weiss, Meira, 264
Wenger, Etienne, 55, 247
Whyte, W. F., 141
Wilcox, Kathleen, 52
Willis, David B., 227
Willis, Paul, 5, 54, 58, 97, 139, 197, 259
Wilson, Herbert B., 51
Wimmer, Michael, 43
Winkin, Yves, 147
Winkler-Oswatitsch, Ruthild, 31
Winther, Ida Wenzel, 200
Wolcott, Harry F., 5, 54, 55, 56, 61
Womack, Brantley, 249
Woods, Marcela, 103
Wright, Susan, 50, 199
Wu, Kangning, 244
Wu, Wenzao, 235, 240
Wu, Xiaorong, 243
Wu, Zongjie, 247

Xie, Dengbin, 239
Xu, Yueting, 247

Yamanouchi, Yuko, 222

Yamashita, Shinji, 2
Yang, Canjun, 245
Yang, Shengmin, 242
Yaro, Yacouba, 279, 280, 284, 285
Yates, Paul, 53
Ying, Danjun, 248
Yon, Daniel A., 52, 53
Yoshida, Miho, 216
Yosifon, Margalith, 261, 262
Yuan, Tongkai, 238
Yue, Tianming, 239
Yuuki, Megumi, 219

Zhang, Shiya, 244
Zhang, Xueqiang, 242
Zhang, Yuan, 245
Zhong, Qiquan, 245
Zhu, Dongliang, 236, 237
Zhuang, Kongshao, 237
Zirfas, Jörg, 40, 41, 182
Zobačová, Jarmila, 173
Zolnay, János, 177
Zou, Yali, 51, 54
Zoungrana, Cécile-Marie, 288

꧁ SUBJECT INDEX

1920s academic, intellectual, and research developments; in Brazil, 112; in Japan, 235; in West Africa, 287

1930s developments, 23n4, 305; in Brazil, 112–13; in China, 235–36; in Mexico, 71

1950s developments, 1, 11, 16, 305, 308–09; in Brazil, 112–13; in China, 236; in Israel, 268; in Italy, 161n3; in Japan, 213; in West Africa, 281, 287

1960s developments, 1, 13, 305, 308, 313; in Argentina, 94; in Brazil, 114; in France, 132, 134, 137, 140–45; in Israel, 257, 269; in Italy, 155, 161n1; in Scandinavia, 194; in West Africa, 281, 283, 287, 296

1970s developments, 1, 9, 17, 22, 305, 306, 313; in Argentina, 100; in Brazil, 114, 118; in Central Europe, 168, 176; in France, 132, 135–36, 142, 144; in Israel, 258–59, 263; in Italy, 155, 161n1, 162n6; in Japan, 224–25; in Mexico, 71; in Scandinavia, 196–97; in West Africa, 279, 281

1980s developments, 9, 12, 305–06, 309; in Argentina, 101; in Brazil, 114–18; in China, 237, 258; in France, 131–36, 140, 142, 144–45; in Israel, 259, 267; in Italy, 158, 161n1; in Japan, 213, 221, 224–25; in Mexico, 71, 72; in Scandinavia, 197, 200, 202; in West Africa, 279, 284, 287

1990s developments, 309; in Argentina, 97, 98–101; in Brazil, 115–18, 125n; in Central Europe, 173, 179; in China, 236–37; in France, 133, 135, 136–37, 140, 144; in Israel, 266, 268; in Italy, 154, 158,

160, 161n1; in Japan, 213, 215, 225; in Mexico, 71; in Scandinavia, 196, 198, 200, 202; in West Africa, 279, 282, 284, 287–89, 291, 293, 296

2000s developments; in Brazil, 121; in Israel, 268; in Japan, 214; in West Africa, 283

ABA (Brazilian Anthropological Association), 111, 117, 124n1

academic disciplines, 19–20, 94 111, 304

Academic Institute for Arab Teachers of Beit Berl College in Israel, 15

acquisition of culture, 12, 36, 220 , 239

action research, 13, 14, 15, 16, 140–41,170, 217, 246, 282, 289, 297, 315

activity theory. See sociocultural theory

actor network theory, 76

actor, turn to the, 4, 76, 83–84, 99, 120, 133, 135–36, 142, 157, 197, 200, 222, 295.

ADEA (Association pour le développement de l'éducation en Afrique/Association for the Development of Education in Africa), 279, 280, 292, 297n1

administrators and non-teaching staff as a research theme, 56, 73

AERA (American Educational Research Association), 53

Africa, sub-Saharan, 3, 7, 15, 202–03, 315. See also Benin, Burkina Faso, Cameroon, Central African Republic, Chad, Democratic Republic of the Congo (Congo-Kinshasa), Ethiopia, Gambia, Ghana, Guinea, Madagascar, Mauritania, Mali, Niger, Nigeria, Republic of the Congo (Congo-Brazzaville), Senegal, Sierra Leone,

South Africa, Togo, Uganda, West and Central Africa, Zambia
African Americans and African Canadians, 54, 56. See also black populations
African Anthropologist (journal), 282
African Brazilians, 113, 118, 119. See also black populations
African Caribbeans, 55. See also black populations
African researchers in diaspora, 15
African Sociological Association, 282
African Sociological Review (journal), 282
Afrique et Développement (journal), 286
agency. See actor, turn to the
AIDS (Acquired Immune Deficiency Syndrome), 95, 289, 290, 292
AISLF (Association internationale des sociologues de langue française), 12, 142
American Anthropological Association, 51
Amerindian thought. See indigenous populations
Amish, 59
Amnesty International, 168, 172, 185
analytical psychology. See psychology and psychologists
Anglophone world, see English-language zone
Anglo-Saxon world. See English-language zone
Annales School, 30, 31–33
Annual Review of Anthropology (journal), 53
ANPED (National Association for Educational Research, Brazil), 111, 124n1
ANPOCS (National Association for Social Sciences Research, Brazil), 111, 124n1
anthropology and anthropologists, 2, 5–6, 10, 11, 12, 13, 14, 15, 29, 30, 49, 50, 51, 57–58, 60–61, 99; in Argentina, 94–96; in Central Europe, 168, 169, 170; in China,

235–37; in France, 136, 308; in Israel, 257–58; in Italy, 160, 161n1; in Japan, 213; in Mexico, 71; in Scandinavia, 194–95; 202; in the United Kingdom, 9, 50–51, 132; in the United States, 5, 50ff 134, 161n1; in West and Central, 281–84; relationship to sociology, 284; status as a discipline, 95, 235, 309–10. See also cultural anthropology, historical anthropology, historical cultural anthropology, philosophical anthropology, social anthropology
anthropology and education (as opposed to anthropology of education), 124n2. See also anthropology of education in Argentina and in Brazil
Anthropology and Education Quarterly (journal), 1, 9, 51, 169, 306
anthropology of children, 17, 193, 201, 205. See also children and childhood as a research theme, childhood studies
anthropology of education, 1ff, 9, 11–12, 49ff, 304; in Argentina, 93ff; in Brazil, 112; in Canada, 50ff; in Central Europe, 167, 168–69, 179; in China, 235ff; in France, 141; 146; in Germany, 7, 30; in Italy, 151ff; in Japan, 213; 309; in Poland, 168; in Scandinavia, 193ff; in Slovakia, 172; in the Czech Republic, 172; in the United States, 1, 8–9, 50ff, 156, 304, 306, 315; in West Africa, 287ff, 304; influence of, 18, 21, 308, 312; relationship to anthropology, 50–51, 57–58, 96, 71, 152, 169, 184, 195, 306; relationship to field of education, 195, 161n1. See also cultural historical anthropology of education, ethnosociology of education, pedagogical anthropology, philosophical anthropology of education, political anthropology of education

anthropology of learning, 6, 8, 13, 17, 181

anthropology of schooling, 6, 8, 9, 10, 12, 17, 73–75, 136. *See also* ethnography of schooling

antiracism, 52

applied research, 14, 15, 18, 160, 168, 281, 310

apprenticeship, 56–57

appropriation, 74, 77, 84, 100, 104

Arab students and schools in Israel, 14, 258, 260, 263, 266–67

Arabic-speaking zone, 14

archival research, 73, 294

Argentina, 4, 11, 16, 17, 19, 85n2, 93ff; 307, 309, 312 314. *See also* anthropology and anthropologists, anthropology of education, social anthropology

Asia, 6, 13–14. *See also* China, India, Japan, Malaysia, Mongolia, Nepal, Pakistan, Philippines, Sri Lanka, Vietnam

assimilation, 132, 152, 159, 222, 225, 258, 264, 315. *See also* cultural differences.

Association of Research Students in Anthropology at the University of Yaoundé I, 15

Augustine, Saint, 29

Australia, 8, 10, 16, 50–51, 59, 223–24

Austria, 7

autonomy of schools, regions, or localities. *See* decentralization

autonomy, personal, as a research theme, 77, 198, 216, 312; of those being studied, 137

Baltic states, 13, 168

Beas speakers, 171

Beijing Normal University, 245

Belgium, 4, 19, 147n6, 312; French-speaking, 12, 132, 141–46; Flemish-speaking, 13

Benin, 280, 286, 297n1

Berlin Study on Rituals, 35–45

bilingualism as a research theme, 76–77, 121, 162n6, 242

Birmingham School (Centre for Contemporary Cultural Studies), 198

black identity as a research theme, 111, 118–19, 123, 310

black Israelis, 264

black populations, 113, 314. *See also* African Americans and African Canadians, African Caribbeans, African Brazilians, black Israelis, ethnicity, race and racism

black researchers, 119, 315. *See also* African researchers in diaspora

bodies, 36, 41, 262; as a research theme, 41, 245, 262

Bolivia, immigrants from, 98, 99, 101, 105n3

borrowing, selective, 21

brain, development of, 31

Brazil, 2, 4, 10, 11–12, 13, 17, 20, 21, 85n2, 111ff, 309, 310, 312, 315; immigrants from, 221–223; influence of, 21. *See also* anthropology of education, ethnography of education, ethnology, sociology, sociology of education

Brazilian Centre for Educational Research, 124, n3

Brazilian-Japanese, 220, 221–23

Bulgaria, 167, 168, 170, 171, 176, 184n4

Burkina Faso, 280, 282, 283, 284, 286, 288, 291, 297n1

CAE (Council on Anthropology and Education of the American Anthropological Association), 14, 50, 51, 305

Cambridge University, 247

Cameroon, 15, 280, 282, 283, 286, 297n1

CAMES (African and Malagasy Council for Higher Education), 282

Camminanti, 158

Canada, 19, 20; as inward-looking, 52–54; English-speaking, 8–9, 50, 54; French-speaking, 4, 12, 141–46; influence of, 11, 15, 281, 289, 292.

See also anthropology of education, North America

case studies, 118, 119, 134, 144, 169, 175, 247, 305

Central African Republic, 282, 297n1

Central Europe, 13, 17, 20, 167ff, 308, 313. *See also* anthropology and anthropologists, anthropology of education, Bulgaria, Czech Republic, Hungary, Poland, Romania, Slovakia

Central University of Nationalities (CUN), China, 237, 240–42

cerebralization. *See* brain

Chad, 282, 283

Chicago school of sociology, 18, 133, 284, 305, 306

childhood studies, 199–201

childhood, prolonged, 31

children and childhood as a research theme, 13, 16, 17, 111, 121, 136, 193, 199–202, 205, 310

Chile, 11, 19

China, 1, 6, 14, 16, 17, 235ff, 307, 310, 311, 312, 314, 316; immigrants from, 98, 177–78, 219, 220–2; influence of, 21. *See also* anthropology and anthropologists, anthropology of education, narrative inquiry, qualitative sociology, sociology, sociology of education

China's Educational Anthropology Review (journal), 239

China's Educational Anthropology Society, 239

Chinese as an academic language, 17

Chinese Sociology and Anthropology (journal), 236

Chinese University of Hong Kong, 238

Chinese-Japanese, 220–21

Choles, 80

CISINAH/CIESAS (Centro de Investigaciones Superiores del Instituto Nacional de Antropología e Historia/Centro de Investigaciones y Estudios Superiores en Antropología Social), 72

citizenship, education for, as a research theme, 176, 202, 203, 205, 264, 291

City University of Hong Kong, 246

civic ceremonies. *See* rituals

classroom ethnography. *See* classroom interaction

classroom interaction, 56; as a research theme, 9, 11, 76, 134, 157, 197, 262

classroom talk. *See* classroom interaction

CODESRIA (Council for Social Science Research Development in Africa), 279, 282, 286

collaborative research, 73, 78, 315. *See also* teachers as researchers.

Colombia, 85n2

colonialism, 16, 58, 62, 95, 281, 282, 287, 307

commonalities across countries, 15–16, 317

community studies, 113, 170, 175, 180

comparative education, 9, 144

comparative research, 2, 3–4, 122, 156, 201, 202, 204–05, 213, 217, 295, 304

Congo. *See* Democratic Republic of the Congo (Congo-Kinshasa), Republic of the Congo (Congo-Brazzaville)

Contemporary Education and Culture (journal), China, 243

Council on Anthropology and Education. *See* CAE

CREA (Consortium pour la recherche économique en Afrique, or the Consortium for Economic Research in Africa), 280, 297n1

creolization, 21, 131, 303. *See also* hybridization, 221, 304, 307–10, 316

critical anthropology or critical sociology, 94, 116, 131, 140, 153, 155, 196, 201, 204, 222, 229, 258, 259, 269, 287

Cultura y Educación (journal), 10
cultural anthropology, 5–6, 8, 18, 30,
    33–34, 57, 77–78, 94–95, 133, 146,
    147n1, 151–56, 158, 160, 161n1,
    167, 184n2, 237, 241, 304–05, 308,
    311; and cultural diversity, 158–59.
    See also anthropology, ethnology,
    historical cultural anthropology,
    social anthropology
cultural deficit theory, 72, 172, 315,
cultural differences, 16, 43, 58–59 97,
    99, 146; as a research theme, 10, 17,
    56–57, 158, 176, 223, 263, 269; as
    deficit, 100–01. *See also* diversity
cultural distance. *See* cultural
    difference
cultural diversity. *See* diversity,
    cultural or linguistic
cultural historical activitity theory
    (CHAT). *See* sociocultural theory
cultural production, 74, 120
cultural relativism, 161n1, 315, 317
Cultural Revolution, 137, 146, 236
cultural studies, 10, 116, 170, 197, 198
cultural transmission, 8, 9, 100, 144,
    147n2, 153, 242, 262, 287, 311
culture clash. *See* cultural difference
culture, 5, 9–10, 16, 31, 34, 71, 73, 75,
    77, 83–84, 100–01, 115–17, 118, 146,
    155, 158, 171, 213, 220, 239, 312, 317
Current Anthropology (journal), 60
curriculum studies, 6, 75
Cyprus, 50
Czech Republic, 167, 170, 171, 172–73,
    178. *See also* anthropology of
    education

daycare as a research theme, 195,
    199
deaf education as a research theme,
    245
decentralization, 137, 143, 170, 181,
    250, 263, 316
deficit hypothesis. *See* cultural deficit
Democratic Republic of the Congo
    (Congo-Kinshasa), 283, 297n1
demography, 280, 295

Denmark, 55, 193ff, 206n4. *See also*
    Scandinavia
departments of anthropology, 194,
    195–96, 206n4, 280, 282, 306
departments of education. *See*
    faculties of education
development (of countries) as a
    research theme, 193, 195, 202–04,
    205; 288, 289; role for sociology, 282
developmental psychology. *See*
    psychology and psychologists
DIE/Cinvestav (Departamento de
    Investigaciones Educativas/Centro
    de Investigación y de Estudios
    Avanzados del Instituto Politécnico
    Nacional), 11, 71, 96
digital literacy as a research theme,
    77, 78
disciplinary context, 5–6, 17, 18,
    20, 71, 81n5, 94, 111, 116–17, 131,
    133–34, 136, 140, 143, 151, 156, 160,
    167, 169, 174–75, 194, 196, 206, 235,
    236–37, 239, 283–84, 295, 304–10.
    See also anthropology, childhood
    studies, curriculum studies,
    demography, discourse analysis,
    economics, educational studies,
    ethnology, folklore studies, history,
    humanities, linguistics, pedagogy,
    policy studies, psychology, Roma
    studies, sociocultural theory,
    sociolinguistics, sociology,
    symbolic interactionism
discourse analysis, 11, 73, 76, 118,
    248, 263. *See also* classroom
    interaction, sociolinguistics
discrimination, 98, 100, 101, 119,
    138–39, 173, 221, 224–25. *See also*
    inequity, race and racism
diversity, cultural or linguistic, 12,
    32, 33, 72, 98–101, 112–119, 123,
    138, 144, 152, 154–61, 158–59,
    161n1, 162n5, 162n6, 175, 178, 179,
    225, 239, 313; as a research theme,
    11, 12, 84, 111, 114, 117, 145, 154,
    156, 158–59, 220–25, 269. *See also*
    cultural differences, ethnicity

domination as a research theme. *See* power

donors. *See* funding

DSUS. *See* University of Sonfonia, Department of Sociology

Dutch-language zone, 3, 13. *See also* Netherlands, Belgium

East China Normal University, 238, 245

economic context of research, 19, 20, 72, 236, 260, 284–86, 289, 292, 296, 305, 315. *See also* funding, internet access, publishing

economics (as a discipline), 296

Educação, Sociedade e Culturas (journal), 11

education as a concept, 73, 201

Education Institute of Hong Kong, 238

education sciences. See educational studies

Educational Anthropology Research Newsletter (EARN), China, 241

educational anthropology. See anthropology and education, anthropology of education

educational ethnography. See ethnography of education

educational psychology. *See* psychology and psychologists

Educational Researcher (journal), 8, 53

educational sciences. *See* educational studies

educational sociology. *See* sociology of education

educational studies (as a field of research), 2, 6, 71, 94, 97, 147n4, 169, 176, 194, 195, 205

Egypt, 14

enculturation, 55, 151, 155, 159, 200, 202. *See also* learning, socialization

English as an academic language, 1–2, 4, 10, 13, 14, 17, 21, 132, 172, 174, 236, 246, 259, 282, 286, 293, 306

English-language zone, 7–10, 19, 33, 49ff, 94, 105n1, 133–35, 145, 146, 160, 172, 175, 285, 304, 307–09;

relationship to French-language zone, 285

ERNWACA (Educational Research Network for West and Central Africa)/ ROCARE (Réseau Ouest et Centre Africain de Recherche en Éducation), 279, 280, 287–89, 292, 296–97, 297n1

Ethiopia, immigrants from, 264

Ethnic Education Study (journal), China, 241

ethnicity, 43, 54–55, 59–60, 71, 83, 84, 98–, 99, 118, 147n3, 155, 169, 170, 173, 182, 224, 224–25, 235ff, 310, 317; as a concept, 182; as a research theme, 8, 9, 11, 12, 13, 14, 38, 58, 78, 79–82, 113–14, 135, 138–139, 145, 162n6, 168, 200, 238–39, 240–44, 259–61, 264, 269, 287, 317; data collection on prohibited, 139, 147n3, 177. *See also* cultural differences, diversity, national minorities, Roma studies

ethnoecology of school. *See* anthropology of education in Slovakia, in the Czech Republic

Ethnography and Education (journal), 5, 8, 10

ethnography and ethnographers, 15, 17, 30, 36, 97, 116, 117, 134, 239, 244, 303, 317; and qualitative research, 75, 260, 296; as a discipline akin to folklore studies, 6, 13, 167; defined, 5, 73, 101–02, 134, 141, 259, 206n1, 280; ethnographic turn, 197; seen as threatening, 19, 95, 249, 313–14

ethnography of education, 1, 5, 17, 49–51, 131, 304; as opposed to ethnography *in* education, 131, 147n1; in Brazil, 20, 117; in France, 20, 134–35, 309; in Italy, 20; in the Netherlands, 20; in the United Kingdom, 1, 17, 50, 139;

ethnography of schooling, 9, 17, 196–99, 204, 214ff

Ethnologie française (journal), 12

ethnology, 6,17, 33; in Brazil,114, 116, 124n4; in China; 235–36 in France, 132–133, 140, 146; in Scandinavia, 206n4; in the United States, 5; in West Africa, 287, 295. *See also* cultural anthropology, folklore studies

ethnomethodology, 133, 140, 147n2, 245, 247, 306

ethnosociology of education, 181

Eurocentrism, 7, 35

Europe, 1, 3, 4, 6, 12, 12–13, 19, 34, 156, 206n4, 281, 313; colonization by, 95; European researchers outside Europe, 85n2, 289, 315; immigrants from, 100, 102, 258; indigenous populations of, 53; influence of, 15, 94, 238, 289, 293, 308, 312. *See also* Austria, Baltic States, Belgium, Bulgaria, Central Europe, Cyprus, Czech Republic, Denmark, European Union, Finland, France, Germany, Greece, Hungary, Italy, Lithuania, Luxembourg, Malta, Netherlands, Norway, Poland, Portugal, Romania, Russia, Scandinavia, Slovakia, Spain, Sweden, Switzerland, Turkey, Ukraine, United Kingdom, Yugoslavia (former)

European Roma Rights Centre, 173

European Society of Ethnographers of Education, 12, 141

European Union, 168, 175, 293, 167

evaluation, 104, 169

exclusion. *See* inequity

faculties of education, 18, 114. 140, 143, 161n1, 195–96, 202, 236, 240, 259, 306, 308, 310

faculties of social sciences, 143

familiarity and unfamiliarity, or "making the familiar strange," 6, 19, 57, 59, 62, 113, 141, 157, 244, 246, 260

families and communities, 103, 239;

as a research theme, 35, 36–37, 56, 75, 77, 78, 81, 83, 84, 97, 118, 157, 173, 200, 227, 312

FASAF (Famille et scolarisation en Afrique, or Families and Schooling in Africa), 279, 280, 292, 297n1

FAWE (Forum for African Women Educationalists), 280, 297n1

feminist theory, 6, 9, 60, 259

fieldwork, 16, 99, 134, 136, 239, 243, 244

Finland, 53, 55

First Nations. *See* indigenous populations

Flemish-language zone. *See* Dutch-language zone

focus groups, 180, 294. *See also* group discussions

folklore studies, 6, 12, 13, 124n4, 167, 169, 309

foreign-language education scholars, 235, 246–49, 250

France, 4, 9, 12, 16, 17, 18, 19, 55, 60, 85n2, 131ff; influence of, 11, 13, 2130, 94, 132, 161n1, 194, 281, 293, 308, 310, 311, 312. *See also* anthropology and anthropologists, anthropology of education, ethnography of education, ethnology, sociology, sociology of education

French as an academic language, 17, 259, 282, 293

French-language zone, 4, 12, 131ff, 279ff; relationship to English-language zone, 19, 285. *See also* sociology of education

functionalism, 105n2, 132, 236, 258, 263, 267, 268

funding, 11, 20, 143, 168, 175, 184n6, 194–95, 204, 289–97, 313, 316. *See also* economic context of research, international aid

Gambia, 297n1

gender, 261; as a research theme, 9, 10, 20, 38, 42, 58–59, 76, 78, 79, 95,

114, 119, 135, 197, 200, 218, 262, 266, 269, 287, 288, 290
George Washington University, 242, 243
German as an academic language, 17, 19, 259
German Educational Research Association (Deutsche Gesellschaft für Erziehungswissenschaft, DGfE), 7, 35
German-language zone, 7
Germans, ethnic, 179, 183
Germany, 1, 7, 16, 17, 18, 29ff, 54, 55, 60, 179, 308, 311; immigrants from, 113; influence of, 4, 13, 94, 168, 194, 236, 293, 309. *See also* anthropology of education
Ghana, 203, 280, 286, 297n1
global flow of ideas, 18–21. *See also*, under names of countries, "influence of"
global flow of scholars, 4, 18, 213. *See also* African researchers in diaspora, 15
global flow of students, 4, 18, 161n5, 305
globalization, 1, 36, 72, 225, 242, 283. *See also* creolization, hybridization
gray literature, 285, 315
Greece, 13
grounded theory, 39, 303
group discussions (as research method), 36, 39. *See also* focus groups
group interviews, 137. *See also* group discussions, focus groups
Guangdong University of Foreign Studies, 246, 247
Guangxi Normal University, 238
Guatemala, 85n2; refugees from, 78
Guinea, 15, 17, 283, 288, 293, 294, 297n1

Han majority (China), 235, 239, 244
Harvard University, 237
Hebrew as an academic language, 14, 259

hermeneutic sociology, 13, 79
hidden curriculum, 180, 196
higher education as a research theme, 9, 56, 75, 80, 122, 198, 199, 229, 247, 267, 269, 289, 290
historical anthropology, 30, 32–33, 35, 101–02, 237
historical context of research, 20, 95, 98, 100, 123, 142, 145, 154, 168, 193–94, 250, 281, 313
historical cultural anthropology, 30, 34–35
historical cultural anthropology of education, 7, 29ff, 35
history (as a discipline), 6, 11, 17, 34, 58, 59, 75, 76, 82–83, 85, 102, 111, 116–117, 119, 122, 147n4, 154, 159, 162n5, 181, 237, 241, 287, 295, 296, 309, 310. *See also* archival research, oral history
history of mentalities, 32–33
HIV/AIDS. *See* AIDS
hominization, *See* human evolution
Hong Kong University, 242, 248
Hong Kong, influence of, 236, 236
hospitals as a research site, 193, 198, 228
human evolution, 30–31
Human Organization (journal), 51
humanities, 34
Hungarian as an academic language, 174
Hungarians, ethnic, 174, 179
Hungary, 17, 167, 168, 170, 176–77, 180, 181; immigrants in, 178; Roma in, 171–72. *See also* cultural anthropology
hybridization, 221, 304, 307–10, 316

IAUES (International Union of Anthropological and Ethnological Sciences), 23n4
identity, 39, 73, 83–84, 118, 139, 154–55, 158, 226; as a research theme, 9, 78, 79, 81, 84, 111, 136, 145, 159, 162n5, 162n6, 183, 200–01, 203, 221, 222, 246–47, 248, 260–61, 264, 266,

268, 269, 270, 310; teachers' identity, 75, 140, 246. *See also* black identity, ethnicity, national identity

illiteracy, 13, 15, 151–153, 313. *See also* literacy and literacy practices

immigrants, 20, 98, 100, 145, 155–56, 194, 257; as a research theme, 8, 11, 12, 14, 20, 54–55, 85n2, 113, 132, 158, 162n5, 177–179, 200, 258, 260, 263–64, 268, 270, 312, 313; in Scandinavia, 194; in West Africa, 283, 287, 296

India, 1, 3, 8, 14, 53. *See also* sociology of education

indigenous education as a research theme, 8, 20, 77–78, 79–81, 82, 83, 85n1, 112, 117, 121–22

indigenous (native) peoples and cultures, 71, 72, 145, 312, 314–15; as a research theme, 11, 54–55, 60–61, 75, 76, 77, 78, 80, 82, 83, 95, 97, 100, 103, 111, 103, 114, 116–117, 124n4, 311, 313; Mixe, 77, 80, 81; Mixtec, 77, 80; Mayo, 80; Mazahuas, 80; Nahuas, 80, 81; Navajo, 56; Otomí, 80, 82; Pasifika, 53; P'urhépechas, 80; Quechua, 77; Tarasco/P'urhépecha, 80; Triqui, 77; Tzotzil, 78, 80; Yaqui, 80; Zapotec, 80; Zinacantec, 78

indigenous researchers, 53, 73, 285, 297, 315. *See also* black researchers

indigenous rights, 73, 84, 81, 121

Indochinese, 223. *See also* Vietnam

inequity, 72, 95, 100, 101, 123, 313, 314; as a research theme, 95, 151, 153, 175, 196, 203, 284, 288

infancy, 31, 41; as a research theme, 77–78

informal education, 239. *See also* nonformal education

institutional analysis, 75, 140

institutional context of research, 18, 305

Inter-American Symposium on Ethnographic Research in Education (Simposio Interamericano de Investigación Etnográfica en Educación), 11, 71, 98

Intercultural Education Society of Japan, 213, 229

intercultural education, 6, 17, 36, 72, 77, 80, 81, 98, 121–22, 151, 155–58, 159, 172, 176, 225, 226, 245, 315

interdisciplinary or multidisciplinary work, 34, 78, 147n4, 155, 170, 194, 195, 280,292, 296. *See also* multidisciplinary research teams

internal colonies, 54, 312

international aid, 16, 195, 202, 204, 288, 292, 296; influence of, 282, 284, 288, 289–294, 296. *See also* funding

International Step by Step Association (ISSA), 168

internet access, 78, 250, 280, 284, 298

interviews, 15, 36, 39, 59, 73, 134–35, 136, 138, 171, 182, 217, 218, 223, 226, 227, 243, 245, 248, 259, 260, 267, 288, 294, 305

involuntary minorities, 162, 313, 315

Israel, 1, 14–15, 16, 17, 257ff, 308, 311. *See also* anthropology and anthropologists

Italy, 13, 17, 20, 151ff, 178, 307, 313; immigrants from, 97, 101, 113; influence of, 94. *See also* anthropology and anthropologists, anthropology of education

Ivory Coast, 283, 284, 287, 288, 297n1

Japan, 1, 2, 6, 10, 13–14, 16, 17, 18, 55, 59, 213ff, 238, 248–49, 258, 309, 311; immigrants from, 113; influence of, 248; *See also* anthropology and anthropologists, anthropology of education, psychology, sociology, sociology of education

Japan Exchange and Teaching program, 217

Japanese as an academic language, 14, 17, 19

Japanese overseas, 226

Japanese Society of Educational Psychology, 214

Japanese Society of Educational Sociology, 214
Japanese, ethnic; returnees from Brazil, 221–23, returnees from China, 220–21
joint research programs, 18, 184n6, 236, 307
Journal of Contemporary Ethnography, 8
Journal of the Royal Anthropological Institute, 60

Kenya, 203, 286
kindergarten. *See* preschools
Koreans: ethnic minority in Japan, 10, 220–26; immigrants from Korea, 98
Kyushu University, 213

Lancaster University, 248
language as a research theme, 9, 76–77, 81, 136, 241
language barriers, 4, 19
language loss and language revitalization, 77, 121–22, 145
language of instruction, 227
language of publication, 3, 17, 167, 285, 309. *See also* Chinese as an academic language, English as an academic language, French as an academic language, German as an academic language, Hebrew as an academic language, Hungarian as an academic language, Japanese as an academic language, Portuguese as an academic language, Romanian as an academic language, Slovakian as an academic language, Spanish as an academic language
language zones, 4
language, 71, 75. *See also* diversity, cultural or linguistic
languages, African, 285, 289, 291
LASDEL (Laboratoire d'Études et de Recherches sur les Dynamiques Sociales et le Développement Local/Laboratory of Research and Investigations on Social Dynamics and Local Development), Niger, 283–84
Latin America, 1, 11–12, 19, 53, 72, 98, 285, 314. *See also* Argentina, Bolivia, Brazil, Chile, Colombia, Guatemala, Mexico, Paraguay, Peru
learning, 5, 7, 75, 160, 205; as a research theme, 16, 35–45, 55, 77–78, 81, 122, 158, 168, 198, 203, 220, 228, 247. *See also* anthropology of learning, enculturation, socialization
linguistic diversity. *See* diversity, cultural or linguistic
Linguistics and Education (journal), 8
linguistics, 8, 77, 117, 197, 310. *See also* sociolinguistics
literacy and literacy practices as a research theme, 15, 74–77, 151–53. *See also* illiteracy
Lithuania, 13
London School of Economics, 305–06
Lovari speakers, 171
Lubavitcher (Chassidic) Jews, 59
Luxemburg, 7

Madagascar, 283
Malaysia, 14
Mali, 280, 284–85, 286, 288
Malta, 50
Maori, 53
Marien Ngouabi University, Brazzaville, 283
Marsaryk University, Brno, 173
Marxist theory, 60, 94, 115, 132, 161, 180, 196, 197, 281, 306
masculinities, 57. *See also* gender
mass schooling. *See* schooling, expansion of
mathematical knowledge as a research theme, 82, 117
Mauritania, 297n1
media as a research theme, 35, 38, 121
memory, 43, 57

Mexico, 4, 11, 17, 20, 21, 71ff, 309, 311, 312, 313, 315; immigrants from, 54; influence of, 11, 96. *See also* anthropology and anthropologists
Miao (China), 238, 243
microethnography, 37, 60, 196, 214
microsociology, 132, 133–35, 138, 147n2
Middle East and North Africa, 7, 14–15; immigrants from, 258. *See also* Egypt, Israel, Palestinian scholars, Yemen
mimesis, 17; as a research theme, 36–45
Mizrahim, 14, 258, 261, 266
Mongolia, 202
Moso (China), 243
multiculturalism, 43, 98, 144–45, 151, 154–58, 172, 175, 179, 224–25, 242–43, 257, 312–13. *See also* diversity, intercultural
multidisciplinary research teams, 280–81, 310
multidisciplinary work. *See* interdisciplinary or multidisciplinary work
multilingualism. *See* diversity, cultural and linguistic
museums and museum studies, 6, 94, 194, 309
mutual intelligibility, 10, 13, 206n3

Nahuatl, 77
Nanjing Normal University, 238, 244
Nankai University, 238
narrative inquiry, 16, 77, 79, 227; in China, 235, 238, 245–48; in Israel, 260, 267, 269
national culture, 124n4, 152. influence on anthropologies or ethnographies of education, 4, 22. *See also* national identity
national identity, 17, 112, 176, 179, 242, 260, 264, 309, 311. *See also* ethnicity, identity

National Institute of Anthropology and History, Mexico, 85n5
national minorities, 179
National School of Anthropology and History, Mexico, 85n5
Native Americans. *See* indigenous education, indigenous populations
neo-Marxism. *See* Marxist theory
Nepal, 202, 203
Netherlands, 3, 13, 17, 20, 21, 55, 147n6; influence of, 290, 292. *See also* ethnography of education
New Sociology of Education, 133, 213, 306
New Zealand, 8, 50, 55
Niger, 283, 297n1
Nigeria, 15, 60, 286, 297n1
nonformal education as a research theme, 74, 288, 291, 292
Nordic language zone (Danish, Norwegian, Swedish), 13
North America, 8, 21, 50ff, 94, 131, 134, 139, 213, 289, 293; influence of, 238. *See also* anthropology and anthropologists, Canada, United States
Northwest Normal University (NNU), China, 238, 240, 242–43
Norway, 206n4. *See also* Scandinavia
nursery schools. *See* preschools

Open Society Institute, 173
oral history, 73, 83, 241, 246, 310

Pakistan, 14
Palestinian scholars, 14, 15, 16
Palestinian schools. *See* Arab students and schools in Israel
Pan African Anthropological Association (PAAA), 282
Paraguay, immigrants from, 99, 101, 105n3
participant observation, 15, 16, 36, 118, 120, 134, 145, 157, 170, 182, 244, 247, 260. *See also* ethnography, fieldwork

pedagogical agendas and practices as a research theme. *See* teachers and teaching

pedagogical anthropology, 1, 29, 195, 205–06

pedagogy, 29, 143, 172, 195

Peking University, 235, 236, 242

performativity, 35–36, 39–45, 182–83

Peru, 85; immigrants from, 98, 220

Pestalozzi, 29

phenomenology, 13, 140, 245, 306

Philippines, 14, 55

philosophical anthropology, 5, 7, 13, 18, 30, 31–32

philosophical anthropology of education, 5, 7, 10, 13, 17, 168

philosophical methods, 30

pluralism, 52, 144. *See also* diversity, multiculturalism

Poland, 13, 17, 168, 170; immigrants from, 97. *See also* anthropology of education

policy and politics, 16, 21, 72, 104, 105n6, 132, 169–70, 204, 236–37, 240, 137, 143, 146, 150; as a research theme, 80, 144, 181, 183, 215, 261, 316. *See also* policy as practice, policy studies, political anthropology of education, political context of research

policy as practice, 74, 316

policy studies, 73, 147n4

political anthropology of education, 13, 181–83

political context of research, 11, 19, 72, 95, 115, 131, 133, 137, 139, 168, 175, 176, 178, 184, 199, 251, 261, 263, 281, 284, 291, 296, 307, 313, 316, 318. *See also* economic context, policy and politics, social context

political science, 316

Portugal, 11

Portuguese as an academic language, 17

Portuguese-speaking countries, 10–12

postmodernism, 60, 259, 269

poststructuralism, 60, 259

power, 34, 37, 40, 41–43, 45, 71, 73, 83, 84, 115, 132, 144, 169, 197, 198, 249; as a research theme, 95, 242, 262. *See also* policy and politics

practitioner research. *See* teacher as researcher

Prague Group of School Ethnography (Prazska skupina skolni etnografie), 172

preschools, 37; as a research theme, 172–73, 181, 193, 198, 200, 219–20, 258, 262, 264. *See also* day care

private schools and colleges as a research theme, 14, 75, 83, 219

private schools and colleges, 138

psychology and psychologists, 6, 11, 14, 50, 94, 97, 111, 115, 117, 136, 143, 147n4, 157, 173, 177, 214, 229, 282, 310; analytical psychology, 75; developmental psychology, 78; in China, 21; in Czech Republic, 173; in Japan, 214, 229; psychology of education, 17, 309; social psychology, 75, 118, 119, 169, 310

psychology of education. *See* psychology and psychologists

publishing, 1, 21, 167, 238, 241, 244, 250, 251, 279, 283, 285, 296, 315. *See also* gray literature, language of publication, textbooks in anthropology of education, translation

Punjabi in California, 59

Qualitative Inquiry (journal), 62

qualitative research, 13, 51, 53, 73, 147n1, 237, 248, 259, 269, 304, 305, 310. *See also* action research, archival research, case studies, community studies, comparative research, discourse analysis, ethnography, ethnomethodology, evaluation, fieldwork , focus groups, grounded theory, group discussions, group interviews, institutional analysis, interviews, microethnography, microsociology, narrative inquiry, oral history, phenomenology, philosophical methods, policy studies, qualitative sociology, research methods, teachers as researchers, video-based observation, visual anthropology

qualitative sociology, 10, 176, 259, 310, 312

Qualitative Studies in Education, International Journal of, 62

quantitative research, 12, 120,177, 251, 259, 261, 263, 265, 305, 309, 310, 312; combined with qualitative research, 15, 16, 137, 280, 294, 296

Quebec. *See* Canada, French-speaking

Queen's University, 242

Quranic schooling as a research theme, 287, 291

race and racism, 20, 23n13, 139, 157, 313; as a research theme, 8, 10, 12, 114, 116, 118–19, 123. *See also* antiracism, ethnicity

racial democracy, myth of, 12, 114, 118

reflexivity, 34

reform, 45; as a research theme, 15, 57, 75, 82–83, 103, 112, 144, 245, 246, 287. *See also* policy and politics

refugees as a research theme, 78, 178, 194, 200, 223–24. *See also* immigrants

religion and religious education as a research theme, 266–67, 288

religious diversity, 114, 144, 147n3, 155–57, 162n5, 162n6, 260

religious schools, 14, 261

remedial education. *See* special education

reproduction, social, 72, 74, 131, 132, 135, 138, 169, 196, 295

Republic of the Congo (Congo-Brazzaville), 282, 283

research abroad, 9, 10, 16, 85n2, 132, 161n1, 202, 213, 258, 307, 315

research at home, 9, 16, 18, 195, 198, 305

Research Institute for Comparative Education and Culture, Kyushu University, 213

research methods, 19, 38–39, 61, 62, 73. *See also* qualitative research

research reports, unpublished. *See* gray literature

research themes. *See* administrators, autonomy (personal), bilingualism, black identity, bodies, children and childhood, citizenship education, classroom interaction, cultural differences, day care, deaf education, development (of countries), digital literacy, diversity, ethnicity, families and communities, gender, higher education, identity, immigrants, indigenous education, indigenous peoples, inequity, infancy, language, learning, literacy and literacy practices, mathematical knowledge, media, mimesis, nonformal education, policy and politics, power, preschools, private schools and colleges, Quranic schooling, race and racism, reform, refugees, religion and religious diversity, resistance, rituals, Roma, rural and urban compared, rural contexts, school failure, science education, social class, socialization, space, (the) state, street children, students or pupils, symbols, teacher education, teacher unions, teachers and teaching, time, urban contexts, vocational education, youth

resistance as a research theme, 58, 72, 80, 95, 139, 153, 158, 197, 222, 313

reviews of the literature, 3, 8, 11, 52, 53, 75, 76, 85n1, 133, 237, 289, 307

Revue Africaine de la Recherche en Éducation (journal), Africa, 289

Revue Africaine de Sociologie (journal), 286

Revue de l'Enseignement Supérieur Africain (journal), 286
rhetorical turn, 60, 61–62
rituals, 17, 181, 183; as a research theme, 35ff, 74, 119 244, 262, 264–65, 266, 311
ROCARE. *See* ERNWACA
Roma Education Fund, 168
Roma studies, 13, 17, 161n1, 169–70, 182
Roma, 162n5, 170–72, 177; as a research theme, 13, 158–59, 168, 172–77, 313
Romani language instruction, 175
Romania, 167, 168, 169, 170, 171, 174–76, 179
Romanian as an academic language, 174
Romanians, ethnic, 179
Royal Anthropological Institute, 50
rural and urban compared or rural-urban migration as a research theme, 59, 60, 72, 114, 237, 245, 312
rural contexts as a research theme, 11, 54, 74, 76, 78, 103, 242
Russia, 3, 13; immigrants from, 264, 268; influence of, 13, 18, 21, 236

saberes docentes (teaching knowledges). *See* teachers and teaching
Scandinavia, 13, 16, 17, 23n13, 60, 147n6, 193ff, 308, 312. *See also* anthropology and anthropologists, anthropology of education, ethnography of education, ethnology
school and classroom culture. *See* classroom interaction, schools and school culture
school ethnography. *See* ethnography of schooling
school failure as a research theme, 8–9, 14, 17, 57–60, 62, 97, 152–53, 180, 313
School Review (journal), 56
schooling, expansion of, 18, 133, 203, 279, 306

schooling, focus on, 8, 9, 12, 18. *See also* anthropology of schooling, ethnography of schooling, sociology of schooling
schools and school culture as a research theme, 73–5 13, 14, 73–75, 262, 263, 270
schools of education. *See* faculties of education
science education as a research theme, 76, 290
semiotics, 60, 82
Senegal, 202, 290, 297n1
Sephardic Jews, see Mizrahim
sexual diversity, 121, 147n3
Shenzhen University, 248
Sierra Leone, 280, 286, 297n1
Simposio Interamericano de Investigación Etnográfica en Educación. *See* Inter-American Symposium on Ethnographic Research in Education
Sinti, 158
Slovak Governance Institute, 173
Slovakia, 167, 170, 172, 173–74, 176, 179; minority from, 178. *See also* anthropology of education
Slovakian as an academic language, 172
social anthropology, 6, 9, 17, 33, 57, 94–96, 132, 167, 197, 305
social class, 9, 58, 114, 138, 152–53, 171, 173, 288; as a research theme, 9, 10, 12, 58, 120, 145, 269, 312
social context of research, 17, 20, 84, 98, 201, 314. *See also* economic context, political context of research
social justice, 154, 155, 160, 314
social movements, 72, 75, 83, 95, 114, 115, 118, 120, 315
social psychology. *See* psychology and psychologists
socialization, 132, 136, 137, 194, 312; as a research theme, 7, 35–36, 42–43, 77–78, 81, 112, 120–21, 122, 136, 197, 202, 204–05, 215, 243, 268,

304–05, 308. *See also* enculturation, learning

sociocultural anthropology. *See* cultural anthropology, social anthropology

sociocultural psychology. *See* sociocultural theory

sociocultural theory (neo-Vygotskian cultural historical activitity theory), 6, 10, 12, 13, 17, 18, 21, 75, 76, 77, 79, 81, 198, 248

sociolinguistics, 11, 21, 76, 78, 82, 133, 136, 171, 197

sociology and sociologists, 6, 8, 9, 11, 17, 50, 61, 75, 79, 94, 97, 135, 169, 177, 196, 213, 214, 258, 269, 305, 310, 312, 313, 316; in Brazil, 111, 112, 114, 118, 119, 120, 124n3, 124n4; in China, 235, 236, 240, 244; in France, 12, 13, 132–142, 146, 147n4, 308; in Japan, 214; in the United States, 305; in West Africa, 281–284, 293, 295; status as a discipline, 310. *See also* hermeneutic sociology, microsociology, qualitative sociology, sociology of education

Sociology of Education (journal), 8

sociology of education, 61, 183, 259–60, 263, 267, 281–82, 306, 309; in Brazil, 115, 117; in China, 238, 244–45; in France, 131; in French-speaking world, 12, 142, 146, 147n1, 309; in India, 14; in Israel, 259; in Japan, 214, 223, 229, 309; in the United Kingdom, 305–06; in West and Central Africa, 279–80, 287–89, 296; relationship to sociology, 306. *See also* sociology

sociology of knowledge, 306

sociology of schooling, 55, 59, 131

sociology of science, 51

sociology of social science, 2, 29

Soros Foundation, 168

South Africa, 10, 286

South China Normal University, 246

Southwest University (SU), China, 240, 243–44

Soviet Bloc, former, 167

Soviet Union. *See* Russia

space as a research theme, 42, 180

Spain, 3, 10–11, 13, 17, 85n2, 178; immigrants from, 97

Spanish- and Portuguese-language zone, 10–12

Spanish as an academic language, 17, 105

special (remedial) education, 103, 172–174, 177

Sri Lanka, 203

state, the, as a research theme, 72, 80

street children as a research theme, 77

structuralism, 60, 196, 308

students or pupils as a research theme, 56, 73, 116, 136, 157, 227, 263, 269, 312

Sweden, 206n4. *See also* Scandinavia

Switzerland, 9, 19, 142; French-speaking, 4, 12, 132, 141–46, 147n6, 312; German-speaking, 7; influence of, 292

symbolic interactionism, 9, 133, 141, 245, 306

symbols, 42, 84, 115–16, 169, 181; as a research theme, 79, 80, 122, 180, 262

teacher education, 6, 57, 114, 117, 140, 143, 202, 225, 245, 246, 259, 306; as a research theme, 75, 121, 247. *See also* faculties of education

teacher unions as a research theme, 75, 83, 147n3

teachers and teaching, 8, 16, 95, 151, 311; as a research theme, 9, 56, 73, 75–76, 106, 100, 105n5, 116, 198, 213–215, 215–23, 229, 245, 246, 247, 263, 269, 288, 311

teachers as researchers and collaborators, 15, 141, 157, 214, 246, 315

Teachers College Record (journal), 51

Teaching and Teacher Education
   (journal), 51
Tel-Aviv University, 259
textbooks in anthropology of
   education or ethnography of
   education, 51, 53, 213–14, 237, 243,
   259
time as a research theme, 43, 180
Togo, 280, 286, 297n1
trabajo docente, the work of teaching.
   See teachers and teaching
translation, 2, 19, 195–96, 235, 307;
   into Chinese, 237, 241; into English
   from Chinese, 236; into French,
   133; into Italian, 156, 161n1; into
   Japanese, 213, 309; into Spanish, 10,
   94, 96
Turkey, 13
Tuyao (China), 238

Uganda, 203
Ukraine, immigrants from, 178
UNESCO and UNESCO Institute for
   Education, 292
UNICEF, 168, 291, 293
United Kingdom, 1, 8, 9–10, 16, 21,
   53, 55, 305–06, 307, 310, 315, 316;
   as inward-looking, 307; influence
   of, 10, 18, 19, 21, 131, 133, 155, 194,
   213, 236, 248, 257, 259, 307–08, 309;
   resistance to influence of, 236, 307,
   308. *See also* anthropology and
   anthropologists, ethnography of
   education, sociology of education
United Nations Development
   Program, 168
United States, 1, 13, 16, 20, 50ff,
   85n2, 113, 218, 226, 310, 312, 316;
   as inward-looking, 52–54, 307;
   immigrants from, 220; influence
   of, 10, 11, 15, 18, 19, 21, 30, 112,
   131, 133, 155, 194, 198, 202, 213,
   236, 238, 259, 289, 307, 309, 312;
   resistance to influence of, 146, 236,
   307. *See also* anthropology and
   anthropologists, anthropology
   of education, ethnology, North
   America, sociology

University of Buenos Aires, 11, 93, 94,
   95–98
University of Chicago, 305. *See also*
   Chicago school of sociology
University of Conakry, 280, 282, 293
University of Córdoba (Universidad
   Nacional de Córdoba, Argentina),
   98
University of Dakar, 281
University of Kankan, 293
University of La Plata (Universidad
   Nacional de La Plata), 95, 96
University of London, 236, 243
University of Manchester, 9, 243, 257
University of Mar del Plata, 95
University of Montreal, 292
University of Ottawa, 289, 292
University of Oumar-Bongo, Gabon,
   282
University of Padua, 156
University of Paris-8, 141
University of Pennsylvania, 242
University of Quebec at Montreal,
   293
University of Rosario (Universidad
   Nacional de Rosario), 95, 96, 98
University of Salta, 95
University of São Paulo, 124n6
University of Sonfonia (Conakry)
   Department of Sociology (DSUS),
   380, 285, 293, 296
University of Tokyo, 214
University of Toronto, 243, 292
University of Yaoundé I, 15, 282
unpublished research. *See* gray
   literature
urban contexts as a research theme,
   74, 77, 81, 82, 84, 104, 116, 151, 159,
   258, 305
USAID, 292, 293

variations across countries, 16–17, 317
video-based observation, 36, 39, 141
Vietnam, 14, 203; immigrants from,
   54, 178–79, 223–24
violence as a research theme, 78, 120,
   123, 145, 262, 290
visual anthropology, 180

vocational education as a research theme, 168, 180. *See also* apprenticeship

welfare states, 17, 193ff, 312
West and Central Africa, 4, 6, 16, 20, 279ff, 310. *See also* Africa, anthropology and anthropologists, anthropology of education, Benin, Burkina Faso, Cameroon, Chad, Democratic Republic of the Congo (Congo-Kinshasa), ethnology, Gambia, Ghana, Guinea, Mauritania, Mali, Niger, Nigeria, Republic of the Congo (Congo-Brazzaville) Senegal, Sierra Leone, sociology, sociology of education, Togo
World Bank, 95, 291, 293
World Council of Anthropological Associations, 2
World Educational Research Association, 2

Worldwide Email Directory of Anthropologists, 14
writing conventions, 19

Xiamen University, 236
Xinjiang Normal University, 244

Yemen, 258
Yi (China), 241
youth as a research theme, 13, 16, 17, 35, 38, 78–79, 103, 111, 116, 119–121,193, 199–202, 204, 268, 310, 312
Yugoslavia, former, 168
Yunan Normal University, 239

Zambia, 203
Zapatista communities, 72, 81
Zhejiang Normal University, 248
Zhejiang University, 248
Zhongshan University (Guangzhou), 236, 244
Zhuang (China), 238

Lightning Source UK Ltd.
Milton Keynes UK
UKOW05f2150170117
292266UK00009B/350/P